Despite warnings, you have dared to enter the realm of the daemon legion who have cast misfortune upon mankind and orchestrated his suffering since the fall from grace. Beware, for this is the legion that cast out the messiah of egypt, taunted the savior of the christians, and corrupted the religion of the prophet of islam. The legion tears at the soul of humanity without mercy or conscience. Once you have entered their domain, there is no way of escape.

There is but a single key, couched in a magic word, which offers a ray of hope. Only this word can reach the daemon, quell its restless heart and subdue the rage it has inflicted upon humanity. Only this will exorcise the tormenters from the tormented.

Learn well this magic word and study all of its implications for full comprehension of it uncorks a seal within each seeker that unfurls an ever-lasting light and compassion that can reach all creatures and spirits. Only this word can tame the beast and make him purr, but more importantly to you, it is the only way of surviving the ordeal within the bottle of brass.

It is still not too late to turn back, but if you do, knowing what you now know, you will be relegated to a life of chaos and the accompanying madness which ensues. Tread lightly man, for this is a perilous journey and the most important one you will ever make. Study the word. For those who turn their back, I commend you to your future nightmares, for this was a spell cast long ago and it cannot be undone.

MASTER OF THE GREEN JINN OF SABIA

TRANSLATED FROM THE TABLETS OF KOR

SYNCHRONICITY & THE SEVENTH SEAL

BY PETER MOON

SkyBooks

NEW YORK

Synchronicity & the 7th Seal
Copyright © 2004 by Peter Moon
First printing, March 2004

Cover art and illustration by Denny Unger
Typography by Creative Circle Inc.
Published by: Sky Books
           Box 769
           Westbury, New York 11590
           email: skybooks@yahoo.com
           website: www.skybooksusa.com

DISCLAIMER This book is based upon personal experiences which are sometimes told in a context of "parallel universes" that are not necessarily deemed to have any particular origin nor complete substantiation in reality on the Earth plane. They should therefore be understood in the context of a parody, not only of life on Earth, but of the entire Cosmos itself.

Library of Congress Cataloging-in-Publication Data

Moon, Peter
      Synchronicity and the Seventh Seal
by Peter Moon
      464 pages
        ISBN 0-9678162-7-0
1. Occult 2. Time Travel 3. Religion
Library of Congress Control Number 2003115883

To Mary Ann

Other titles from Sky Books

by Preston Nichols and Peter Moon

The Montauk Project: Experiments in Time
Montauk Revisited: Adventures in Synchronicity
Pyramids of Montauk: Explorations in Consciousness
Encounter in the Pleiades: An Inside Look at UFOs
The Music of Time

by Peter Moon

The Black Sun: Montauk's Nazi-Tibetan Connection

by Stewart Swerdlow

Montauk: The Alien Connection
The Healer's Handbook: A Journey Into Hyperspace

by Alexandra Bruce

The Philadelphia Experiment Murder:
Parallel Universes and the Physics of Insanity

by Wade Gordon

The Brookhaven Connection

by Joseph Matheny with Peter Moon

Ong's Hat: The Beginning

FINAL WARNING

If you have continued this far, you are either interested, curious or skeptical. For those who are skeptical, there is one last loophole that will enable you to get off the hook. You can turn back now with relative impunity in that your world will stay more or less the same. This loophole applies as well to reporters, media personnel, followers of fascist religious organizations, and all members of secret societies. For the aforementioned, this book is designed to undermine the authority structure on which you depend for general guidance, instruction, prestige or whatever it is that attracts you to your masters. In the post Civil War era, many freed slaves suffered in the chaotic times of Reconstruction and sometimes longed for "the good old days" when survival was harsh but far more predictable. Turn back now.

If you think these are idle words or a silly game, heed once again the curse referred to by the Master of the Green Jinn. Further, recall or study the horrible fate of the man who unsealed King Tut's tomb and the actual occult forces surrounding him at the time of his death. If you remain flippant in your attitude, cease to read, for if you continue, your fate is out of my hands. You have been warned.

For the rest of you, turn the page and carry on. There is no turning back. I have done my best to make your adventure a successful one.

ACKNOWLEDGEMENTS

Rosemary Collins
George and Madalyn Frey
Joseph Matheny
Moya McNulty
Denny Unger

To all of the intriguing and incredible characters that have walked their way into my life and have served as literary icons from which I will never be able to easily separate myself, including but not limited to: Preston Nichols, Duncan Cameron, Al Bielek, Marjorie Wilson Cameron Parsons, Amado Crowley, Jack Parsons, L. Ron Hubbard, and David Anderson.

And, most important of all, I would like to acknowledge each and every one of you readers. Without your interest and desire to learn the truth behind the mysteries of the universe, I would never have manifested.

CONTENTS

GUIDE TO THE READER

The dramatic wording surrounding this text might make you inclined to think that I, as an author, have set a high bar for myself in terms of expectations to be fulfilled. It is true that the bar has been set very high, but it is not there for me to jump over. It is for you. The admonitions, as well as the book cover design itself, are laced in occult principles which were invoked not only to safeguard the precise transmission of the information herein, but to protect all concerned, including yourself.

The ominous warnings do not reflect any intention on my part to either entice you or to solicit your awe and admiration. That would be pretentious. It is also inaccurate to believe that I am in any way trying to frighten you in the manner of a horror writer. Two of the most popular and successful writers of our time indulge in frightening people out of their wits, and they have endured much personal suffering as a result of the demons they have unleashed upon their readers. While I cannot say how much it has affected their readers, I can say that it has backed up on them like a sewage cesspool. They lead "successful" but broken lives, and I certainly would not wish such a thing upon myself.

If the words thus far conveyed have at all excited your interest, perhaps you have already received a gift because interest is the first ingredient required in any great adventure. Interest in your own life and the circumstances around you is also your first tool of protection. Besides interest, a great adventure also requires considerable risk. If there is nothing to overcome or no adversary, there is no point. In the event that you have mastered life and can content yourself to a perpetual existence in a pastoral setting where you enjoy lemonade and cookies, I commend you. This book is not for you, and I certainly would not begrudge anyone their own personal nirvana. You are a lucky soul indeed.

This book is purported to be something more than an ordinary adventure as it embraces the ultimate adversary. Although Satan is probably the most popular term for such, others have cited the Divine Father to be the ultimate adversary. Personally, I have seen Christian clerics as well as ordinary Christians react with a complete psychological horror when the name of Babalon or Babylon is mentioned. Sometimes known as the Whore of Babylon, one has to wonder if the words "horror" and "whore" are linked in the subconscious as they sound so similar. While there are different versions of the primary adversary in the collective unconscious, you have your own idea, somewhat unique to yourself, of who or what is your personal adversary.

Countless mythologies have repeated the same themes over and over throughout history. Actual historical records will tell you that many saviors and adversaries have come and gone. The human condition still faces the same predicament. If you voraciously study the sages of centuries past, you can really be certain of only one thing. These great characters of history are no longer here. You are the only identity that remains. Think about that for a minute. The very best that humankind has had to offer has been consumed by the physical plane through the various procedures of death. You, as a thinking being, are still here. Perhaps that is the greatest blessing in the universe. As a citizen of Earth, you have inherited a whole world with a considerable amount of information and knowledge. But, no author can assure you of absolutely anything. Only you yourself can be sure of what is true or not true. In addition to interest, this would be your second gift: you are a conscious survivor. You have made it this far. You can also make your own decisions — writers and historians can only point you in different directions.

When you think about the above proposition, death might seem to be a more apt description of an adversary than some of the other archetypes presented by religious leaders. But, in this day and age, death is not as mysterious as it used to be. Throughout history, religions exploited the idea that one lives beyond the grave. They claimed to know more about the after-death-state than their parishioners. This is not working so well in today's culture. Many people not only believe in life after death, they think they can see beyond the veil. Although death is still a worthy adversary for any of us who have to face the gallows or our own personal demise, it is no longer considered to be the ultimate threat.

If you carefully study the subject of death and your own adversary, it soon becomes obvious that your greatest opponent has to do with the forces in the universe that abrogate consciousness. Abrogate means to nullify, invalidate or rescind. Archetypal entities like Satan, the Devil, or even a demonized Christian pantheon can serve your own mythological reference frame very well. Although it can be very helpful and less intimidating to keep everything in a mythological sphere, there comes a time in everyone's life when they have to face an absolute truth.

In actual fact, when you seriously study the processes of the unconscious and what it is that makes it the "unconscious" as opposed to the conscious, you run up directly against the phenomena that mythological archetypes are meant to represent. Sometimes, these "phenoms" of consciousness are not very much different from the mythological archetypes you have read about.

Suggesting that you truly face your adversary is not unlike examining your horoscope to find out the time period in which you will face your own death. But, if you can gaze past the fear or "horror" factor, you can look it as a positive charge facing a negative charge. In electricity, a positive and negative create energy. Thus, looking at your own adversary can have some very energetic positive effects if you do not get lost in the polarity of either side. You will become a source point of energy.

If any of what I have written thus far sounds too grim, I should add that there is another loophole which will allow you to get out of reading this book. There is a psychological affliction that mental health practitioners have diagnosed as "apeirophobia." Meaning "fear of infinity," this affliction would also undermine anyone from grasping the principles of quantum physics and all the endless possibilities which that branch of science has to offer us. If you suffer from aperiophobia, you should not read this book but instead seek out a competent professional. For the most part, the daemon legion has suppressed or down-played apeirophobia as being an affliction at all. Many of our institutions and mental health practitioners suffer from it themselves.

If you are still interested in pursuing your adversary and possibly surviving the ordeal of the Bottle of Brass, you are almost ready to move on. Interest in any subject, when it is directed and intensified, projects into enthusiasm. When you have accessed enthusiasm (meaning "in deios" or "with God"), you have been put in touch with the creative spark that lives within each one of us. As was said earlier, interest is an essential ingredient for setting out on a great adventure. Enthusiasm is an even bigger asset. Your own interest in life and your enthusiasm is your greatest protection. Do not let it be blunted. There can, however, be problems with enthusiasm.

Most of you have seen people who become wildly enthusiastic about something and then fly off the handle and never do anything. Manic-depressives are well known for this type of behavior. When dealing with the occult, your enthusiasm should be guarded and tempered at times. This cannot be overemphasized. Too much unbridled enthusiasm, if not properly directed, can lead to excessive chaos and an emotional breakdown.

As this book is intimately involved with occult matters, I would like to give you a reference frame for how this subject should be approached. Occult simply refers to that which is occluded or hidden; however, there are various adversaries in the stream of life which work very hard to keep things hidden. This creates a wave of energy which can be very hard to penetrate let alone navigate. We are basically dealing with waves of energy that either propel one on a course or keep one away from a desired path. The best analogy I can think of is in the sport of surfing. It will serve one well.

The romance and adventure of surfing long ago captured the imagination of popular culture, but to serious practitioners, surfing is a religion. One faces an ocean of chaos on a small platform and navigates through various degrees of fluctuation which are sometimes extreme. The wildest rollercoaster can be far more predictable. Intuition, agility, and instant reaction time are crucial. At any time, due to negligence, lack of agility, or the sheer force and unpredictably of chaos, one can wipe out. Occultism, not unlike surfing, tests our boundaries as we navigate a sometimes perilous ocean of data which lies hidden below the surface where King Neptune orchestrates both illusion as well as life giving support.

Surfing is also an excellent example because it is symbolic of a frequency wave. Consciousness, in many respects, could be considered to be a manifestation, bombardment, or recognition of different frequency waves. Some of these are easy and enjoyable to surf while others are more foreboding. Choose your waves wisely and do not taken on any that are unsafe or too big for your level of expertise.

There is yet another truth about surfing. Most people on our planet will never even have a good opportunity to surf. Most people live too far away from the ocean and many who live nearby are not up for the exhausting physical challenge. Additionally, many of the people who do surf will not challenge the bigger waves. In the 1950's, when confronted with the monster waves of Hawaii that the locals would not touch, California surfers spent many years studying the waves before they rode them. Only then could they be successful. This is no different from studying the different frequency waves of consciousness. If you look at them and investigate them long enough, they will be less intimidating and considerably more navigable.

The book you are about to read is meant to be challenging. Although I have made considerable efforts to be clear, the various chapters and information are precisely put together in an intended format that is designed to wake up unconscious aspects within yourself. It is not intended to be a typical book or a novel. You can go elsewhere for that. It is a unique way of looking at the world that is expected to give you viewpoints and ideas that might not have otherwise come to you.

There is also another very important point. This book is intended to be read at least twice. Although it should make sense the first time, it will reveal more the second time through.

You are about to begin on your journey. As you do, you will be summoning the legions of darkness and light and creating an admixture of white and black which will serve as a separate Rorschach blot for each individual reader. Will you see Christ at the crest of the wave and Aleister Crowley in the trough — or the reverse? And, never forget that a surfboard is a surfer's best friend when he is in the water. It cannot only act as a life preserver but can carry one on an exciting ride. It is what takes one out into the ocean but also what brings one back. You are about to paddle out into the ocean and face the oncoming waves. This book is meant to serve as your surfboard by which you can approach the Apocalyptic tsunami wave that has come into view on Earth's horizon. The wave can now be ridden, but the question remains. Will you wipe out? Good luck and never forget the underlying reason why people surf: it is a challenge and tremendously fun!

PREFACE

For those of you who are not familiar with myself, I have authored or coauthored six other books that have been considered more than very controversial by different parties. In fact, they have been so controversial that through 2003 there has been a virtual ban on Preston Nichols or myself from appearing on major media outlets. Media figures have also been reported to torpedo any mention of my work or the characters involved in it. One extremely popular and wealthy radio host has also been known to stay up late and call other media people in order to slander me. In some respects, this is very flattering, and it certainly makes most people wonder what the fuss is <u>really</u> all about; however, many people have been upset by such negative reactions, and I have been asked to give a response. As the exact nature of the media ban and the slander invites considerable complexity, I will be as succinct as possible and stick to the facts.

In 1992, Preston Nichols and I were catapulted to international notoriety upon the release of our first book, *The Montauk Project: Experiments in Time*. For those of you who are new to the subject, it is important that I give you a brief summation of that topic. Additionally, it is necessary that I state exactly the general context in which the subject should be approached and understood.

It is absolutely crucial to realize that the Montauk Project itself, as originally recounted, is a blend of incredible legend and archetypal (cabalistic, if you will) mythology mixed with certain irrefutable facts. Although he is by no means the only person to have been involved in this chaotic mixture of documentation and myth, Preston Nichols is the primary source of this legend. Aside from his reputation as one of the leading experts in electromagnetic phenomena in the world, Preston Nichols has also served as compiler, composer, and story teller of the Montauk mythos.

The genesis of the Montauk Project revolves around the idea that the Navy conducted invisibility experiments aboard a ship in 1943 by utilizing degaussing coils which canceled the magnetic field around the ship and caused bizarre disturbances in the space-time continuum. The primary casualties were the sailors. Some suffered spontaneous combustion and some became amalgamated with the bulkheads of the vessel. Others experienced extreme horror and psychic trauma.

The study of this phenomena excited the minds of scientists as never before as it not only embraced the hard core aspects of all the physical sciences, including quantum mechanics, but encompassed the full nature of the consciousness of human beings, with particular significance placed on the scientific measurement of human thought processes. Research was carried on in secret at Brookhaven National Laboratory where scientists, headed by Dr. John von Neumann (whose primary titular auspices was associated with Sperry-Rand), painstakingly recorded empirical observations of how human beings react to all aspects of the electromagnetic spectrum. A particular emphasis was placed on amplification of radio frequency microwaves and how they interrelated with the psychic nature of the mind. Eventually, the exact nature of microwaves, particularly those wavelengths which contribute to or are aligned with what we term "psychic energy," were harnessed in such a manner as to access the Unified Field of creation and thereby access the quantum potential of the universe and literally manipulate time. The successful construction of a time chamber at Brookhaven led to more exotic experiments at Montauk Point, New York where a portal was allegedly opened up between August 12, 1943 and August 12, 1983. From this time tunnel, countless side tunnels were opened up which involved multiple experiments of time travel. That, in essence, is a very quick summary of the Montauk Project. As the project evolved and began to operate at full tilt, things became very chaotic and various negative agendas began to appear. It was then sabotaged by various factions from within.

When the above information was released in the original book, it caused quite a stir because it not only gave people a new paradigm by which they could view the Government and the universe, it also gave a wide-open overview with regard to the quantum potentials of existence. Additionally, it told or insinuated a plausible history of how those quantum potentials had been hidden or obscured from us. A very large amount of people thought it made a lot of sense and wanted to know more.

One might think that this alone should have been enough to secure a permanent place in the heart and mind of the collective body known as Mankind; but, to anyone who has studied the history of new ideas, particularly when such concern the religious and political arenas, one finds that this is not necessarily the case. These new ideas were resisted in many quarters, such resistance being directly proportional to the status quo mentality of those who resisted. Nevertheless, a quantum ripple did explode on alternative communication lines which eventually made the Montauk Project a permanent fixture in the mythos of our culture. This was only the result of ordinary human beings who were simply interested in the phenomena being reported upon.

The Montauk Project legend rests on a firm bedrock of irregular and sometimes outrageous behavior by certain government authorities with regard to the defunct Air Force Station at Montauk Point. There are other anomalies associated with the area that include excessive kilowatts being pumped into the defunct base and ostensible traces of a massive underground facility. The more sensational aspects of time travel are legend for the most part, but traceable phenomena exists in that area, too.

Thousands of people have come forward claiming to have been involved in such a project. Some of them are latching onto the phenomena to solve a personal identity crisis, but many have tangible stories and are sincere. Others claim they are afraid to reveal their secrets.

The investigation of the Montauk Project and its accompanying phenomena is a bold attempt to understand the subject of time and how it relates to human consciousness. In our limited human construct, the study of this subject can be likened to trying to understand a beast when you can only see its tail emerging through the bushes. One knows the rest of the beast is there even though one cannot see it. One grabs the tail only with great caution in order to avoid the possibility of being torn to shreds. Most people are unaware of the presence of the tail and too many that are made aware of it find it easier to deny there is any such beast present that might be influencing their life or consciousness. Others yet have a vested ignorance in maintaining the beast as it is and do not want any more discovery to take place. Certain people of a Christian persuasion just might identify those who want us to remain in ignorance of such a beast to be the Beast of Revelation himself. In such a context, one finds that the opposition to the truth being discovered is disproportionate to most people's desire to find out the truth or even to contribute to such an endeavor. Only a very small handful are genuinely interested in peeling back the layers of opposition. In such an environment of suppressed communication, one is encouraged to take an alternative approach.

My original intent was to publish the legends of Preston Nichols; however, there was a legitimate question in our own minds as to whether or not it should be categorized as fiction or nonfiction. Government documentation for such a project was not exactly in abundance. I, however, before the subject became popular, had met too many people who knew about the project in order for it to be completely made up. The problem at that juncture was that Preston was virtually the only one (besides Al Bielek and Duncan Cameron) who was willing to come forward and give his version of what had happened. Therefore, Preston and I decided that we should offer his personal account of the project and let the audience determine for themselves whether it was fiction or nonfiction. Additionally, we would see if, by releasing the book, others would come forward with substantiating data. Since that time, many people have come forward claiming to have been involved in the Montauk Project. Some are credible while others are seeking a means by which they can identify their own personal problems. Some are simply seeking notoriety. Detractors and media detractors have falsely claimed that there is no documentation. In this, they are quite wrong. If one actually reads the books and newsletters on Montauk, one will find that it is an incontrovertible documented fact that a considerable amount of energy has gone into obscuring what operations have gone on at Montauk. The local authorities even went so far as to try Preston Nichols and Duncan Cameron in civic court for allegedly having trespassed on the Camp Hero property (where the time travel experiments were said to have occurred) which is in fact legally authorized to be a state park. Why would someone be so disproportionately upset over time travel investigators simply walking into an area that is technically designated as a state park? Not only did Preston and Duncan win the case, they embarrassed the officials involved. These are facts and are legally verifiable. It is also a fact that the case was deliberately delayed until all the other cases were cleared out of the court room for that particular day. Then, the one remaining spectator in the court room, a friend of mine by the name of Mike Nichols (no relation to Preston), was ordered to leave. He refused to be intimidated and watched the trial as it was his right as a citizen to be there. This proves funny business.

Additionally, illegal transmissions have been identified as emanating from the "defunct base" as well as megawatts of power being funneled into it. These are all identifiable facts which prove there has been secret and clandestine activity at the base. There are countless other facts and documents if one does their homework. The more sensational aspects of the Montauk Project legend are corroborated from time to time, but they are not provable by their very nature. Some of the time travel experiences are part guess work as well, but this has never been denied.

The important point in the Montauk investigation, and one that all critics overlook, is that the anomalous and bizarre experiences of Preston Nichols, Al Bielek, and Duncan Cameron have given rise to the fact that a very secretive and mysterious enterprise was conducted at the Montauk Air Force Station that still exists in some form to this very day. Before the wild stories, there was no broad public awareness of any secret project. Had there not been any wild stories, no investigation would have been done or chronicled. This alone says a lot. Therefore, we should not exercise contempt or dismiss the stories even if we cannot accept them fully for purposes of a linear investigation that deals with ordinary facts and circumstances.

Some people, which I find very amusing, get very upset over the fact that we cannot demonstrate time travel for them personally and that the Montauk investigation and research is therefore tainted or invalid. For those who were around and remember, it is an incontrovertible fact that when the Montauk Project was published and released to the world, there was a very definite impact and reaction. The ideas, theories, and descriptions about time were completely unique and more than unprecedented in the field of university physics. We received letters from many scientists and others who were moved and impressed by what had been offered. Many of them believed that the truth about physics was deliberately obscured by academe.

We hoped that people would get on board and help uncover further truths about the Montauk Air Force Station and what had occurred there. Instead, there was a rather extreme counter-reaction. Instead of people helping or assisting, I observed various typical human reactions. Some people were jealous that they had not come up with certain ideas first. Others felt shown-up by the data or tangible tie-ins that Preston Nichols offered. On the other hand, there were lots of supporters. Radio Moscow announced that the Russians knew about some aspects of the project and said that the "authors were very brave" to release the information. While "very brave" is an overstatement, others have shown complete cowardice on the subject. The acknowledgment on Radio Moscow was appreciated. The Japanese were also early advocates as they picked up the translation rights and filmed a documentary for Japanese TV. Thousands of people found their way to our PO Box. For a short while, it seemed as if the entire world was ready to listen to anything Preston Nichols and Peter Moon had to say about Long Island. In retrospect, we had introduced a quantum ripple into the status quo consciousness that pervades ordinary everyday reality; however, the information we were circulating was too wild and could not be easily accounted for in the ordinary reality structure of society. It was obvious to us that if our reputation was allowed to grow, the entire world would be coming to us to find out what was going on. These were very exciting times, and it could be said that the importance of Preston Nichols and myself (along with Duncan Cameron and Al Bielek) expanded to arguably exaggerated proportions due to the fact that very few people, if any, were communicating similar information.

It became obvious that various authorities had something to lose if we were allowed to go unchecked. Preston Nichols and I became blacklisted from appearing on any major media. Shows were cancelled at the last minute. We were not stopped from appearing on small market radio stations or small time television shows, but when you see how feeble these shows are in reaching America, you soon discover why there are such huge advertising dollars at stake in major media. At the same time, Hollywood stepped in and got very creative with many fragments of the Montauk Project and produced several spin-offs on the various themes and ideas. All of a sudden, the name "Duncan," (Duncan Cameron was the primary psychic involved in the Montauk Project) was featured prominently in many shows. In what was Hollywood's greatest (and perhaps strangest) coup on these subject matters, an unemployed surfer was taken off the beach to produce one of the most successful shows of the 1990's: *The X Files*. This show served as great damage control for those trying to quiet down the chaos created by the release of the Montauk Project. After watching a few shows of *The X Files*, people hearing about the Montauk Project often say, "Oh! That sounds like the *X Files.*" People who watch such shows then have a reference in their mind when hearing about secret government projects. It takes the edge off, and people do not take the data so seriously. Unfortunately, people identify very strongly with television. As a result, many of them either identify us as a spin-off of a TV show or as someone who is ripping off the idea from TV. *The X-Files* was only directed at entertaining and entraining people. It never pretended to be a disseminator of truth or legitimate information.

One of the most auspicious attempts to censor mention of *The Montauk Project* occurred just prior to the year 2000. Local newspapers, cable TV, and even New York City TV stations covered Preston Nichols and pictured him in a school bus equipped with surveillance radios and stated he was an example of someone who was prepared for any disastrous occurrences that might ensue as a result of a Y2K computer glitch. Although Preston is locally and internationally famous for being an author of *The Montauk Project*, there was a deliberate attempt not to mention the book. One of the media personnel personally told Preston that the subject was banned. If the stories are so ludicrous, then why does the media take them so seriously? Perhaps it is because the information, if disseminated and digested by millions of people, would not be laughed off by the public. There would be a genuine demand to know more about the secret aspects of our government.

Since the National Security Act was passed after the so-called Roswell Crash in 1947, the United States Government has operated under a blanket of security. Senators have even stated that a policy of secrecy makes it difficult, if not impossible, for the public to trust the Government. When the Government breaks the public's trust in fiascoes such as Ruby Ridge, the Waco Massacre, and the like, the trust factor is compromised even further. When the public hears about the Montauk Project, they become even more suspicious.

The Kennedy Assassination is a prime example of how far a body politic will go to cover up facts and vast operations of which the ordinary citizen has no idea about. One can expose blatant disregard for an honest investigation in the Warren Report, but there is no genuine or meaningful response by the authorities. In the 1960's, when nothing but news about the Kennedy assassination was broadcast for three straight days, the entire nation was in an uproar about the assassination. Almost a half century later, the public remains fascinated about all the secrecy and manipulation that occurred after November 22, 1963. The public is not in an uproar about the Montauk Project, but if all of the information concerning it were broadcast for three days straight, you can be sure that they would be.

After writing and exposing various facts about the Montauk Project for over a decade, I can say quite humbly, at this time at least, that my efforts have not been sufficient in terms of completely tipping the scale of consciousness towards a complete recognition of what happened there. With unmarked cars and megawatts of power, the real life Montauk Project operates with impunity in an atmosphere of secrecy. Blankets of secrecy in the media make the task even more difficult, if not impossible. It is all about secrecy. Therefore, it is time to rejuvenate our approach towards the subject of secrecy itself.

What is secrecy? It is hiding things. It means that certain information is privileged, confidential, and not for your personal view. Of course, we understand that people have a certain right to have their personal lives remain somewhat secret, but that is not what we are talking about. People in power hide the truth because they can gain and exploit others by it. One sees this readily with insider trading in the stock market. Political blackmail is one of the oldest professions in the world and is still quite common in our modern world although it often takes form as "shades of gray" in what could be more accurately termed "graymail." While the world of politics struggles to hide and the public seeks to find out more, it is time to back up and look deeper at the nature of secrecy.

The analogy of the Beast serves very well when we consider the secret and mysterious nature of the physical universe. Our carbon-based material universe is based upon the analogy of "666" whereby the carbon atom contains six electrons, six protons and six neutrons. This principle underlies the religious mythology that 666 equates to the Beast. In essence, this suggests that "slaying" the Beast equates to understanding and coming to terms with the aspects of our existence that consume us. The more you study the universe, you will understand that the universe itself is a mysterious encryption system. Not only is matter encrypted, but so are the faculties of creation that erected it. The Montauk Project itself is no different. The very nature of it, along with those who participated and authorized it, are wrapped up in encryption.

This puts us in the same proposition as the astronauts in the original *Planet of the Apes* movie where the Forbidden Zone contains the secret history of the planet. Every major authority acts as a stooge for secrecy who will exact a serious toll on anyone who seeks forbidden knowledge.

This book penetrates the Forbidden Zone. Those who are thoroughly indoctrinated to not question certain aspects of existence will either not be able to understand it or will reject it utterly. It is totally understandable that people will reject something they do not understand. No one who does not understand a foreign language will accept a book in that language as acceptable entertainment. However, most people with a foreign language barrier seldom attack that language or a book in that language simply because they do not understand it. Thus, when certain people in or out of the media go out of their way to stop the dissemination of books or the communication of authors, it is obvious that something has triggered them into their behavior. Most likely, the author's writing has triggered a behavior pattern that is so ingrown and deep that it is almost part of the organism itself. However, such a behavior pattern is completely irrational and no self-reflecting organism would tolerate such it its own system. Therefore, it is time to take yet another look at what is actually going on with people whom are "triggered" and experience silent or vocal emotional tantrums when the either the Montauk Project or the names of the authors are brought up. After a certain point, it becomes naive to believe that completely irrational reactions on the part of people is due to something whimsical or innocuous. One is not only dealing with an adversary, but someone or something that does not want certain things mentioned or held up for further examination. As was said earlier, adversaries that abrogate consciousness represent phenomena that is parallel or analogous to mythological representations such as a daemon legion. Therefore, it behooves everyone reading this book to understand that severe emotional or hypercritical feelings one might experience with regard to the information presented in this book, including feelings toward the author and his colleagues, just might have something to do with what is going on inside your own head. If you want to use the word "demon," it might well serve, but we are definitely talking about a phenomenon that is similar to that archetype. Statistically, only one out of five of you will experience some sort of severe reaction, but most of those can more properly be traced to psychological pressure exerted upon you by an adversary in your own environment.

As was said earlier, this book is not an ordinary journey. It is an adventure which facilitates an exorcism on the collective unconscious. When the demons fly away, they are replaced by knowledge, certainty, and enlightenment. Please accept the following information as an invitation to look beyond the system that delivered you to your current state of consciousness. There is always a better way.

INTRODUCTION

Many years ago, a magician by the name of Kenneth Grant predicted the unveiling of the "space-time projects." Before you ask who Kenneth Grant is, you might want to consider what exactly he meant by a "space-time project." Space-time actually refers to space and time, but physicists prefer space-time as these two elements are deemed to be inextricably connected to each other. The concept of a space-time project, which is entirely "outside the box" of common human thinking, implies a contraption or organized method that controls time and space and/or our perception of it. Although there have been unparalleled advances in quantum physics over the last hundred years, the idea that the very mechanics of space-time might be controlled or engineered seems to have escaped academe entirely. At least no one has considered this idea too seriously. Hollywood has given us the *Matrix* movies, but these films are more directed at sensationalism and special effects than in getting you to look at the oppressors of consciousness in your own environment. Even conspiracy theorists in the UFO field seldom concentrate on the intricate aspects of space-time. Usually, they are preoccupied with forcible subjugation of unwitting victims or with aliens carrying out various agendas in a space opera drama.

Unleashing university scientists to study the universe and not guiding them to first consider the political science of space-time is like taking a group of alien scientists (who know nothing about the United States), placing them in the Los Angeles Coliseum and telling them to figure it out and how it got there. Additionally, you make certain rules. You do not tell them about the Olympic Games of 1932 and how it was built by human beings under the direction of an Olympic Committee. Further, you do not allow them to talk to Earthlings or to go outside of the stadium. In fact, you do not even suggest that Earthlings might exist. The poor scientists would be struggling with cement, locker rooms, grass, various vending apparatus, lavatories, press boxes, and other artifacts. Eventually, they would probably come up with some representation of human beings. But, suppose the masters of the scientists did not allow the theory of human beings to be considered at all? This would be a very restrictive environment which is somewhat similar to what human beings suffer from when they try and crack the codes of existence. When one contemplates the origin of the universe as a young child, one is generally directed to a religion which is more obsessed with a hierarchal structure of control and patronage than it is with teaching individuals enlightened truth. One is again forced to observe the science of politics which, in this instance, is in the context of religion.

If we look at the universe as our own environment, we are not too much different than a gladiator pitted in a colosseum of old. We may succeed or we may fail, but we are very much steered into battle with whatever forces await us on the planet. Most important of all, we are not encouraged or allowed to question the society that put us in the arena, let alone the Emperor himself.

In order to understand myself or my own work, one must accept the proposition that time and space are constructs of a controlled system of consciousness that propagates itself according to its own terms and conditions. One can call this system "god," "the devil" or anything one wants, but we are basically dealing with a creative principle that manifests creation in a prescribed format with some liberal allowance for chaos and mutations that do not run according to the norm. The most difficult aspect of this control system is that, up to this point in recent history, it has sought to remain obscure and free from detection or change.

If we want to approach this theologically, we might say that God created the Heaven and the Earth. Therefore, we are seeking to know or reach God. The conspiracy could be determined to be with God or surrounding God, depending on your point of view. In any case, it is the subject of God or creation which remains mysterious. It is no wonder that so many wars have been theologically based with each side trying to assert its own control system on the other. For the most part, whichever control system wins does not resolve the true mysteries of creation and consciousness.

They only seek to propagate the original control system with its myriad variations.

When Kenneth Grant obliquely referred to space-time projects in his work, he did not say too much about it, but he did say that there was a considerable amount of machinery involved in space-time projects. Perhaps this reference point is a good beginning to explain how I became involved in exposing such space-time projects with particular regard to "The Montauk Project," an experiment that was originally recounted by Preston Nichols, a Long Island scientist who discovered his own role in secret projects which sought to control consciousness and featured exotic attempts to manipulate space-time. Books I have written with him are mentioned elsewhere in this publication. Although reading them might increase your comprehension of this material, it is not at all necessary to read them prior to this text. In this work, I will introduce a general groundwork from which to investigate space-time and proceed from there.

When one thinks about space-time, Einstein's Theory of Relativity and the Unified Field Theory pop into the mind for most Westerners. There is also the realm of quantum physics. These are the relatively codified forms of scientific thought which describe the universe. As brilliant as these theories and the scientists who developed them may be, they have not quenched man's thirst for further knowledge about the universe(s) and his role in it. One of the primary problems with these theories is that they do not completely or adequately embrace what is commonly known as human experience. There are remarkable theories in quantum physics, which we will touch upon later, that actually open the door to unlimited possibilities in terms of human experience but, for the most part, they have been not been vigorously pursued and have even been obscured as to their true value. It is intended that this book will serve as a catalyst of understanding to scientists and people everywhere so that they may embrace and activate the full quantum potential of their own existence. Keep in mind that full potential means that you will have plenty of opportunity for choice and that you can also reverse past choices.

My own entrance to the entire subject at hand was through the principle of synchronicity. As I began to work with Preston Nichols and investigate his stories about space-time, I soon encountered remarkable synchronicities that were extraordinary in terms of their meaningful significance. Although this resulted in a writing career for myself, I had never paid too much attention to codifying the full theoretical and philosophical principles by which I had worked. I knew how to investigate, but it was clear that I was not investigating ordinary data or experiences. Most professional journalists are forbidden from investigating certain areas unless they want to risk their life or profession. This inhibits true investigation. When you are investigating, you look for things that do not make sense or do not add up. You pursue the various leads and, if you are on a hot trail, you find more things that do not add up. In the case of the Montauk Project, I found many smoking guns and certain evidence that projects of a clandestine nature had taken place there. Additionally, it was clear beyond any shadow of a reasonable doubt that certain authorities were trying to hide this fact. These are dutifully recorded in previous books and newsletters, but the most sensational and specific documentation of the space-time aspects, at least in terms of an official paper trail, has been stonewalled. As an adjunct to the regular real-world investigation, there was something else that did not add up as I looked into the Montauk Project. I began to notice the principle of synchronicity. What started off as rather small and somewhat significant experiences of synchronicity began to snowball into phenomena that was so extraordinary that I was experiencing synchronicity at a level that was certainly unprecedented in terms of the ordinary experience of human beings as they existed at the turn of the Second Millennium. These experiences have compelled me to write and publish.

It is now an entire decade since I began to experience and write down my adventures in synchronicity. The purpose of this work is not only to categorize and summate the experiences I have had, but to offer an increased awareness of this process to the reader as well as the collective consciousness of mankind and the morphogenetic grid, that ever changing function of life which evolves in concert with the environment.

1

SYNCHRONICITY & THE UNIFIED FIELD

When we begin to study space-time, it is the component of time that has always served as the great mystery. When Einstein achieved public acclaim for his theories, he was struck by the fact that although there were probably only ten people in the world who could understand his theories, everyone treated him as if they appreciated his work. He knew he was being admired by people who were not only ignorant of his work but had no personal experiences by which to comprehend his theories. They were all "believers." This clearly demonstrates how a priestly caste could form around such a seemingly complex subject as physics. To this day, I have only met or heard of only one scientist who understood Einstein's theories to the point where he could actually apply them (specifically to time) on a real-world basis. That is David Anderson, the former President and proprietor of the Time Travel Research Center on Long Island who was pressured to reenter the military industrial complex after September 11, 2001. Before he was forced to leave Long Island, David was planning to write a text book on the subject of time travel. Having routinely demonstrated his theories to skeptical professors and university audiences, he wanted to write a simple academic text that would put the subject to rest so that he would not have to continually explain the subject.

The Government was well aware of David's brilliance. They employed the Time Travel Research Center to correct the drift of satellites in space. Satellites do not maintain perfect orbits for transmission purposes and generally move several meters each year. You can imagine the havoc this could create on the Global Positioning System if not corrected. David, who is an expert mathematician, realized that the most effective way to accomplish a correction in satellite displacement was through time warp theory. In other words, the space-time fields of the satellites were actually being manipulated. Further advances were also being made in time travel. Investors in the medical sector had financed research whereby a self-contained field, about the size of a soccer ball, could slow down or speed up time. This was projected to be very useful for maintaining vital organs for transplanting purposes. The problem with the self-contained field was that it required a lot of power to amplify the size of the field. He needed an expert in instrumentation to help him with this problem. I saw this as a perfect opportunity to connect David with Preston Nichols, who he already knew, as Preston is an expert in the field of instrumentation. Although I was eager to connect the two of them, this was the last working meeting I had with David Anderson. The Government took over his operation. The website for the Time Travel Research Center, which used to host Sky Books and was the leading vanguard of information on the scientific pursuit of time travel, is now defunct. Space-time research is the most exciting research imaginable, but it has been taken away and is under cover. This not only corroborates my theory on the idea of space-time being manipulated, it demonstrates it beyond any shadow of a reasonable doubt.

David noted that while much of academe was incredibly arrogant, there was a major trend in modern physics to understand the spiritual nature of mankind. It seemed that physics had finally arrived at the point of including creatures. He realized that if he was going to understand the universe in its entirety, then he was going to have to seek out knowledge of the human spirit. This is one of the reasons why he sought me out and also listened to lectures by Preston Nichols. Defensive of the work that Preston and I had done, he suggests that his colleagues should look into the whole picture before they criticize it. In fact, we had just begun planning a major physics event for the east coast which was going to feature a presentation on the Montauk Project, but as was alluded to earlier, this was not meant to be.

Besides his interest in the spiritual aspects, David had experienced remarkable synchronicity in his own life, and he found my experiences in that regard to be of value. As one of the most accomplished scientists of our time, David Anderson is a very humble person who does not claim to have all the answers. Therefore, it would behoove those scientists who are not capable of actually applying Einstein's Theory of Relativity to pay a little more attention to the phenomena surrounding space-time rather than to maintain a narrow view that only includes classical physics and little else.

It is with this view in mind that I would like to introduce or reintroduce you to the world of synchronicity. As a word, *synchronicity* does not appear in most dictionaries, yet it is used by people on a daily basis. It was coined by Dr. Carl Jung, a famous Swiss psychologist who was a colleague of Sigmund Freud. The first apparent historical record of the word is when Jung lectures at the Tavistock Clinic: "Tao can be anything, I use another word to designate it, but it is poor enough. I call it synchronicity."

The Tao is an ancient Chinese word for the mysterious principle underlying creation, yet it cannot be confined to that definition because it is, by definition, without definition. In other words, "the Tao that can be defined is not the true Tao." In this respect, it is no different from the Judaic concept of God as "the name which cannot be named." In the above quotation, Jung is describing synchronicity as a "poor man's Tao." More constructively, it could be defined as the phenomena that one expects to encounter when one reaches the Tao.

Science is continually discovering or rediscovering either what ancient philosophers knew or what texts such as the Vedic Hymns taught. One of these principles is that the entire universe is made up of consciousness. Carl Jung was penetrating various aspects of consciousness in his patients as he worked with them on an individual basis. Observing that synchronicity came into play with the mind and experiences of his patients, he took serious note of the subject and became quite adamant about its importance in the overall scheme of things.

One of Jung's more noteworthy patients was Wolfgang Pauli, a contemporary of Einstein who was famous for codifying the principles of quantum physics in the first half of this century. A great admirer of synchronicity in his own life, Pauli was so well-known for his encounters with it that his fellow physicists referred to the remarkable coincidences in his own life as the "Pauli Effect." It was said that his presence alone was enough to cause scientific equipment to misfire.

Pauli had a brilliant and critical scientific mind. His contributions to science are legendary, but his personal life was a mess. Pauli's critical mind became too critical and his sarcasm became unbalanced. Perhaps his forays into quantum mechanics generated chaos in his personal life, but whatever the truth of that is, his life was in serious turmoil when he consulted Carl Jung for help. For a brief time, the mind of a brilliant scientist became intertwined with an occult psychologist who was a trained and patient observer. The two men became friends and collaborated on various observations about the universe. Anyone interested in synchronicity will be well served to study the historical antics of these two men, but the point here is that synchronicity was respected by superior scientists.

The most aggressive attempt to categorize synchronicity and what it all meant was an Austrian biologist by the name of Paul Kammerer. In 1919, he wrote a book entitled, *Gesetz der Serie* or the "Law of Seriality." Although this work does not exist as an English translation, you can read a summary of it in the appendix of Arthur Koestler's *The Case of the Midwife Toad* which is a biography of Kammerer.

Kammerer kept a logbook of coincidences for a period of twenty years. In this, he classified coincidences into "Series of the First Order" and "Series of the Second Order." The Series of the First Order might be continuous repetition or encounters with a specific number or name. The Second Order might be the same type of coincidence, but with a different number. He further categorized synchronicities by the following four terms: Typology, Morphology, Power, and Parameters. Typology refers to the type of situation, number, names, etc. Morphology refers to the number of successive coincidences. It also implies by its name a changing condition. Power refers to the number of parallel coincidences. Parameters refers to the number of shared attributes. Additionally, Kammerer spent hours sitting in public places and noting observations of random facts for tabulating coincidences.

Ultimately, Kammerer observed that certain synchronicities clustered together, not unlike a lucky streak in gambling. These defied ordinary probability factors. He concluded that there is an "a-causal" principle in the universe that tends towards unity. It is based upon affinity and acts on form and function to bring similar configurations together in space and time. Known as the "Law of Affinity," Pauli, Kammerer, and the scientists of the day commented that it is outside of the known laws of ordinary physics. The Law of Affinity brings like things together. Kammerer further stated that "Seriality" (he is talking about synchronicity here) is, "the umbilical cord that connects thought, feeling, science and art with the womb of the Universe which gave birth to them."

The unity Kammerer was talking about is obviously referring to the "Unified Field." I have always stated that consciousness was the Unified Field and Kammerer would agree, at least if I said "consciousness of synchronicity." Synchronicity itself is the connective glue. In its most unbridled state, it could be considered affinity as in the "Law of Affinity." Even so, synchronicity reaches beyond what is commonly considered to be the Law of Affinity because it not only zones in on the consciousness of time, but it serves as a link to an acausal principle which determines things. But, it is not enough to simply state that the Unified Field equals consciousness. That is only a start. There are many fields, dimensions, and reference points that make up the sum of existence. The creative principles that ignited them in the first place ride on the strings of consciousness. Kammerer was a scientist who reported his observations and sought the mystery behind it all. Although he made considerable progress and studied the subject for twenty years, he befell a most unfortunate fate. As a biologist, Kammerer was what was called a Lamarckian. This meant that he understood that certain acquired characteristics in an organism were the result of inheritance. The orthodox "science" of his day, which was neo-Darwinism, had great problems with this theory. Kammerer was the last of the "Lamarckian Scientists," but he was the only one who had provided specimens which proved his theories. These included reptiles, amphibians and sea-squirts. Unfortunately, his experimental animals disappeared during World War I. Those of you who have read Val Valerian's *Matrix* publications and have studied the agenda of Darwinists may well realize that they would have gone ballistic about Kammerer's theories. After the war, only one of Kammerer's so-called specimens turned up. It was called a "midwife toad." His antagonists pointed out that the specimen had been tampered with so as to fake the evidence. Although it was not tampered with by Kammerer, his reputation was ruined. A few weeks after this information was released, Kammerer was found dead in the Austrian mountains. It was said he shot himself. If you read Arthur Koestler's *The Case of the Midwife Toad*, you might conclude what I did. Kammerer was probably deliberately discredited by his opponents and killed in a manner to make it look like a suicide. In such a manner, the first, or at least the most notable person, to scientifically study and publish work on synchronicity in modern times was snuffed out.

Kammerer was not only investigating some very interesting areas, he was investigating *THE* bridge that "unifies the Universe." In those very words, we see that the Universe is called the Universe because it is all unified by some mysterious principle. Perhaps the most significant thing Kammerer said was that synchronicity or seriality is "the umbilical cord that connects thought, feeling, science and art with the womb of the Universe which gave birth to them." This is the very concept of a matrix, a word which has recently been popularized by a motion picture which is evocative of some of these principles.

If we consider that someone deliberately killed Kammerer in order to discredit his work, the most obvious motive would be to interfere with the discovery and exposition of the principle of synchronicity, the divine tool by which we can not only understand the universe but by which we can participate in its reconstitution.

Who would want to interfere with that?

There are plenty of possible answers to that question, but we need look no further than the concept of a priestly caste of "scientists" to understand that the politics of space-time are not only a factor in our lives but the leading factor when it comes to regulating our existence in terms of consciousness. Throughout history, changing the fundamental way we look at the world has seldom been encouraged. This book is not only an attempt to change your view, but an encouragement to take a deeper look at synchronicity and how it might jump-start your consciousness.

2

INTRODUCTION TO QUANTUM PHYSICS

Before we tackle the principles and experiences in synchronicity that will be featured in this book, it is important to address the scientific state of the universe itself, at least as scientists view it. For the average reader, it is also very important that I make this as simple and non-confrontational as possible. The mere name of Einstein, let alone his ideas and those of his colleagues, can be quite intimidating to many readers. After all, most of us are not expected to have a pedigree of intelligence that is even close to his. The intimidation factor is what the priestly caste uses to inhibit the understanding of individuals from understanding the true nature of the universe. In fact, they thrive on it.

Many of you have heard the words "quantum physics" before. Although many aspects of it can be quite complex, the basic foundation of it is not. To understand space-time from the current perspective in our civilization, the basic principles of quantum physics is an excellent starting point. I will be as simple as possible so as not to confuse the lay reader but also to offer a simple explanation that will describe the basis upon which a universe or system of perception can be constructed.

Before there was ever such a thing as quantum physics, scientists primarily relied on the theories of Sir Isaac Newton whose ideas served well for mundane physical calculations. However, as the atom was discovered and explored, Newton's laws came up short. Scientists discovered they were working with a new and complex set of factors when they examined the nucleus of the atom. Newton's models worked well for those who lived within the "prison" of the universe, but it did not serve at all for those who wanted to step closer to the Grand Architect of Creation.

Before 1900, most scientists assumed that energy was a continuous stream of force that was not particularly discernible. In other words, electromagnetic waves were assumed to be constant. Max Planck countered this assumption when he discovered that when radiation emanates from a glowing body, it changes color as the temperature rises. It changes color in conformity with what we now commonly know as the spectrum. This demonstrated that energy exists in individual units (like matter) and that it was quantifiable. Of course, "quanta" in Latin means "number" or "unit" and its root can be observed in the English word *quantity*. The idea that energy can be quantified was originally touted as "Quantum Theory" and became the theoretical basis for modern physics. It has developed considerably since 1900, and we will touch on just a few of the important developments.

In 1924, Louis de Broglie observed that there was no fundamental difference between the way energy and matter behaved. This applied to the atomic and subatomic level where scientists contemplated the age old proposition of whether the wave or particle is a more fundamental manifestation. Broglie's theory became known as the principle of wave-particle duality. It did not really answer the question of which was more fundamental, but it stated plainly that both energy and matter, depending on particular circumstances, manifest as either particle or waves.

In 1927, Werner Heisenberg theorized and demonstrated that it was virtually impossible to measure a wave of energy and a particle in tandem. In other words, the more precisely you measure a particle, the more flawed will be your measurement of a wave and vice versa.

While certain areas of science and technology were able to develop by reason of these accomplishments, it only obscured the most fundamental questions of what was at the root of energy and matter. Was it a wave or a particle? This proposition became known as *quantum uncertainty*.

Heisenberg was strongly influenced by Wolfgang Pauli, a colleague who was present when Niels Bohr came forward with what became known as the Copenhagen Interpretation of quantum physics. This theory asserted that a particle or wave is whatever it is measured to be; however, it cannot be assumed to have specific properties (such as a wave or particle) until it is measured. In fact, it cannot even be assumed to exist until it is measured. This is quite an existential observation by a sound and pragmatic scientist. It further gives rise to the principle that we do not really know what the state of any object is until we measure or look at it. It therefore simultaneously exists in all of its possible "quantum" states until the time it is observed. The observer is actually creating "time" in a sense because he is measuring or observing and is distorting from the "simultaneous" state of "now." This relates to a principle called *superposition* that claims that while we do not know what the state of any object is, it is actually in all possible states simultaneously, as long as we do not look to check.

The most famous and popular illustration of this theory is the analogy of Schrodinger's Cat. If a living cat is placed inside of a thick led box, we know that it is alive. If we then throw in a vial of cyanide and seal the box, we have introduced an uncertainty as to what might happen. Only when we open the box and participate as an observer do we know the answer. According to quantum law, this is called a superposition of states. Either state (the cat being dead or alive) is present until we begin to observe.

Although the Schrodinger's cat paradigm has been a time-honored proposition in physics for the better part of a century, it is the exact point where many people go nuts. One time, I was attending a public physics lecture at Brookhaven Laboratory and listened to an Austrian professor who was recognized by the university system as one of the top physicists in the world. When he was drawing a diagram of Schrodinger's cat, most everyone in the audience (primarily physics students) began to smirk and giggle. The professor promptly steered them away from any contemplation of open-ended reality by strictly saying that we would not deal with that. Ironically, his entire lecture was about how to encrypt information by hiding it within the structure of atoms. His lecture was brilliant, but it was all about how to make things more secret. I am not saying that the speaker was nuts, but his steering of the audience away from a contemplation of infinite reality is only too typical of what happens in the physics field.

As quantum theory developed, a new and highly creative theory evolved that is known as the *Many-Worlds Theory*. This holds that when a potential exists for any particular object to be in any particular state, the universe of that object transmutes into a series of parallel universes equal to the number of possible states in which that the object can exist. Each universe contains a unique single possible state of that object. Further, it is possible for there to be a mechanism or mechanisms for interaction between these universes that somehow permits all states to be accessible and affected. This indeed was a very big step in the evolution of quantum theory, but it has been completely underrated and under emphasized by academics. This theory, which has not really been significantly rejected by any major scientist, is recognized, but it is primarily left to drift in the wind as far as public avocation of it. In fact, this theory literally offers infinity at your fingertips by telling you that any possible reality is a reality. This suggests limitless opportunity as well.

The only problem with the *Many-Worlds Theory* is that just because all of these realities are potentially at your fingertips, it does not mean that you can readily access them. To access them, one is obviously going to have to indulge in an observer based reality. Further, it means creating your own reality. This is another phrase for what I call *quantum self-determinism*, the ability to decide your own fate and orchestrate your own destiny within the vast ocean of chaos. This might seem like a tall order to those who are unempowered, but it is the only choice if one wants to *choose* reality as opposed to being assigned a number and a destiny.

What I have just given you is a very simplified view of key points of quantum theory that is designed for the lay reader. There are plenty of books on the subject for those who want to study the exact propositions. The main point in my narrative is that the construct of space-time works like a conspiracy that does not want to be discovered. At the very least, the explanation of it is coded; however, the entire proposition is exacerbated by those who play along with the attitude "not to look" and "not to contemplate."

Physicists long ago separated into two camps: those who were "determinists" and those who embraced the chaos of a multi-verse that was completely open-ended. The determinists basically believe that every reaction has a cause that can be traced by material means alone and does not allow for what is termed acausality. Acausality includes theories like synchronicity whereby there is no apparent "real" or ordinary cause for a specific occurrence. The problem with the determinists is that they are no different than prison officials voicing the company line to the prisoners. If the prisoners are told they cannot escape and that any efforts are futile, they are not as likely to break out. The prisoners who buy into this have no possibility of escaping whatsoever. Those who do not toe the company line not only have a chance of breaking out, but they can be demonstrably observed to have more vigor for life. Demonstrable advances in chaos theory and quantum theory have left most determinists in the dust. There are not too many left; however, it is important to point out that not even the best quantum scientists dismiss cause and effect totally because it has plenty of relevance in our day-to-day lives. As with life, science is never a closed book. You can imagine if all the prisoners were granted an amnesty and let out of prison. Soon, they would be foraging for food, shelter, and clothing. If this was not provided, along with jobs, they would soon find themselves in a similar or worse situation. By the same token, if all humanity were instantaneously freed from the prison of ordinary body-consciousness, you would see fallout as well. There are plenty of predatory thought forms imbedded into the substructure of consciousness that are waiting to devour the wayward escape artist.

As I alluded to earlier, science routinely discovers what has long been known by the ancients. In the last millennium, there was a very notable character who fully embraced the idea of quantum theory. He lived about a thousand years ago and his name was Hassan Sabbah. He said words which paraphrased certain concepts in quantum theory when he stated that "Everything is permitted." What does this mean? It means that everything you can think of, in some manner or form, exists. This very idea alone sends certain conservative and determinist types around the bend. Hassan Sabbah was the founder and leader of the ancient sect of Assassins. For centuries, this group was believed to program people through the use of hashish and have them carry out any duties their masters called for them to do. Recent scholarship has proposed evidence that neither Hassan Sabbah nor his followers used hashish at all. This suggests that much of what was said about them was propaganda from politico-religious coalitions which did not like them. It should therefore be recognized that, even without Hassan Sabbah, modern scientists in white coats were not the first to contemplate the basic character of quantum theory. The multiverse and its principles have been around for a very very long time. The recent civilization of Earth, including its academic institutions, have not.

Synchronicity has no room in a determinist's view. It is called an acausal phenomena. Of course, neither the universe nor the multiverse can be explained if strictly limited to causal principles. Wolfgang Pauli, who could play determinist science as good as anybody, was besieged with synchronicity in his own life. He, not unlike many of his colleagues and successors, became participants in the stream of consciousness of life. These men, Carl Jung included, contemplated the deepest fundamental laws of existence they could grasp. As they did, synchronicity sprung forth like a fountain. For those who want to wrestle with synchronicity as a valid scientific concept and how it relates to causal reality, I invite you to read *Synchronicity: The Bridge Between Matter and Mind* by E. David Peat. It is a decent book which seeks to demonstrate that synchronicity does have a role in even the most hard-nosed scientific paradigms.

A determinist has no need for synchronicity because it is only a coincidence. If there are an extraordinary number of coincidences, each one is only an extraordinary coincidence. If spiritual forces were then connected to those extraordinary coincidences and were demonstrated in a repeatable pattern, that would only be repeated coincidences. Eventually, the determinist, if he were to have genuine and honest experiences, would have to admit that a concept such as synchronicity was valid. Of course, he would have then become an observer. Synchronicity is only relevant to observers or to those who recognize the observations of others. Ultimately, synchronicity has to do with experience.

As my own encounters with synchronicity have been primarily participatory in nature, I have had to catch up with the general theories on the subject. This book, in part, shares my current theory on the subject. There is always more behind a creative effort than what is "put on the table" in a book, but when it comes to my own experiences in synchronicity, it seems as if the process has taken over my own personal existence to the point where my life would seem to serve as a testimony to such. As people read this book, many will wonder why I have experienced so much synchronicity and how did I precipitate all of this. I have already been asked that question many many times. A great deal of what I know of this is shared in this book, but there are other loose ends and even other foundations that are too unwieldy to be elaborated upon at this point. It is therefore best to start at what could be termed a linear beginning in my own life.

One of the earliest experiences with synchronicity in my own life had to do with what is termed "stream of consciousness." When taking a class in creative writing, I was told to keep a journal of whatever thoughts or inspirations popped into my head. As it turned out, I did more writing in my journal than in any other format. We were not necessarily directed to write in linear prose but to just compose based upon the creative part of the brain. I remember one time having an inspiration where I wrote several words that had no particular grammatical order or coherency. Not too long after finishing that course in creative writing, I picked up the book *Finnegan's Wake* by James Joyce and was shocked to see that the first paragraph of that book was "taken" from my journal. I had never seen the book before. My narrative was not word for word with his, but it was too close to be a mere coincidence. The only reason I picked up *Finnegan's Wake* was that I had been reading another one of Joyce's works for another class. That work was entitled *Portrait of the Artist as a Young Man,* and it was the first exposure I had to James Joyce. Even though I did not particularly consider past lives to have any real significance at that time, this experience was so novel that it caused me to wonder if I had been James Joyce in an earlier life. After thoughtful and careful consideration, and without dismissing the idea of past lives, I rejected the idea resoundingly. I concluded that, while studying and applying the concept of a "stream of consciousness" in creative writing, I had picked up on the stream of consciousness of James Joyce. This should not be too surprising because Joyce wrote strictly from the perspective of consciousness. He was also a master linguist who understood several languages and used puns and multiple word meanings to their fullest extent. Picking up a Joyce book is an adventure in nonlinear thought. His most famous work is *Ulysses* which was banned for its sexual content and became quite the literary rage in the early part of the last century. Most people did not understand it, and that is why they were impressed by it. The best way to understand Joyce is in discussion groups where one reads and gets the feedback of literary aficionados who might have a little more experience in interpreting his work.

I have introduced the technique of James Joyce because it will help you to understand a transmission that is about to come from another universe. If I just let the transmission suddenly appear in my narrative without any explanation, a certain percentage of the audience would become alienated and some would even attack the idea. But, it is important to remember that this is an open-ended universe we live in. It is becoming more open all the time. The only draw back with contemplating parallel universes is when that activity confuses one and makes no sense. This transmission you are about to read is bizarre. It is intended to be so, but it also has a purpose. It links various streams of consciousness, particularly those I have dealt with in the past, with the proposition of unsealing the Seventh Seal. Although the Seventh Seal is the focal point of the Book of Revelation, the concept has it roots in earlier documents as well as other religions. In its most pure and innocent sense, the Seventh Seal is representative of the final or top seal of the seven energy centers of the human being. Each seal uncorks a series of seven energy centers that run up and down the area of the human spine and are collectively known as kundalini by the Hindus. Each energy center represents a more highly evolved effort to survive than the previous one. The first seal, when uncorked, is a wheel (or chakra) of energy which concerns itself with raw survival of the organism. The second seal deals with sex and reproduction of the organism. The third deals with power and the struggle to overcome foes that would inhibit one's survival. The fourth is the seal of the heart which not only deals with human compassion but is also the proper processing station by which the higher and the lower can interface in an integrated and harmonious manner. The fifth is that of speech and expression which is intricately connected to the mind/brain function which is representative of the sixth seal. The Seventh Seal represents the extension of the human being to those realms which are beyond the ordinary world. In other words, we are talking about man's ability to

46

interface and integrate with infinity. This book represents the opening of the Seventh Seal and is designed to put you in touch with the infinite.

The following transmission, as is most of this book, is an opportunity to exercise those portions of your mind that are dormant and not particularly functioning at a high roar. Remember, anything is possible. If we either believe or understand the laws of quantum physics, we also realize that the word *possibility* is an understatement.

3

THE SOUND OF
ONE HAND CLAPPING

THE FOLLOWING TRANSMISSION
IS FROM A PARALLEL UNIVERSE

Zen masters have long recognized that the past and the future are but an illusion. We actually live in one eternal moment known as "now." One technique of Zen masters was to produce an enlightenment of the eternal now in the student by giving them a seemingly nonsensical riddle which was called a koan. The most famous of these riddles is "What is the sound of one hand clapping?" Contemplation on such a question was designed to bring about an enlightenment.

After long and careful research, I can finally announce to the world what exactly is the sound of one hand clapping. My research into the question was prompted by uninformed or non-intelligent comments about my own work. Some of these included comments such as "your work is not documented." I always thought these were extremely farcical remarks as I have documented several points in my own investigations. Of course, the more sensational aspects include legendary accounts of time travel. They are also based upon memories which have not been completely authenticated. Nevertheless, an astounding amount of evidence both proves and corroborates that something of a highly irregular nature took place at Montauk Point. Criticism of my work never bothered me because actual criticism should be constructive. If someone does not like what one does, they should do something better or seek to improve what they do not like. Unfortunately, most critics are arm chair critics who have nothing better to do in life. If they were out doing something, they would not have time to criticize. Although I am not irritated by either constructive or inept criticism, I was forced to take notice that, in my case, it was becoming obsessive and vitriolic. It got to the point where I was encouraged to take notice of it and invited to respond to it. Rather than react to it, I decided to study and look into the nature of such inept but passionate and vitriolic criticism. This experience is what prompted me to look exactly at the Zen riddle: "What is the sound of one hand clapping?"

During the course of my research, I discovered that there was a parallel universe very similar to ours except for one major difference. The people in that world were a blend of human and sea lion DNA. Their scientists had discovered a remnant creature of such whose tissue had been preserved in a very cold spot in the ocean. This turned out to be a very convenient discovery because their entire civilization was preoccupied with an impending flood that was prophesized and scientifically projected to engulf them. In order to prepare for this future flood, the same kind as had befallen their own version of Atlantean civilization, a blend of DNA between the species of sea lions and human was considered desirable. Not only would it give the sea lion better access to the fish markets and more to bark about, the human aspect would be more able to survive a flood by its ability to immerse themselves in water. After different progressions of evolution and lab work, virtually all humans ended up with bodies that were predominantly human save for snout-like noses with whiskers and a flipper for a left hand that could propel one through the water at great speed and keep one afloat with relative ease. The lung capacity was also greatly enhanced so one could stay under water for a good ten minutes. Soccer and water polo were the primary sports. Baseball, best played with two hands, became unpopular and died out.

In their world, they also experienced the Philadelphia Experiment and Montauk Project, but these creatures were a highly skeptical lot. Unless they had been oriented to the information and trained to understand it, they could not comprehend it too well. If something was controversial, it was rejected because they only believed what appeared on "fair and balanced" news coverage at the hours of six and eleven o'clock.

In this world's version of Christianity, Jesus dealt with Pontius Pilate in a much different manner. In an attempt to demonstrate his divinity, He shape-shifted into a six-foot fish, but this was misconstrued by the Roman Court as escaping execution. The fish was then roasted on a spit and served to the multitudes. As Christianity developed, the cross had no special meaning to them, but the fish symbol served as its equivalent. Every time one of these creatures ate a fish, it was considered a Eucharist.

In this universe, a large event was held on August 12, 2013 at Sea World in a large stadium which housed over 100,000 creatures. The main speaker at this event was a famous minister by the name of Oral Swaggart. His prominent snout was extra long and he called himself "The Seventh Seal." After beginning his oration by saying "Jesus loves you," he handed out over 100,000 government documents which proved beyond the shadow of any doubt that the Philadelphia Experiment and Montauk Project actually took place. There was a letter from FDR to Nikola Tesla saying that his help was crucial to the invisibility experiment in Philadelphia. There were also notes in Einstein's personal handwriting stating that he would go to Philadelphia as an observer but that he had an eerie feeling about what might happen. There were even long-detailed government reports about what had happened to the *USS Eldridge* and the effects on the crew. Documents released from the Pentagon revealed that Montauk was the headquarters for the Eastern Shield Defense during the 1950's and that an extensive underground had been built for that purpose. It was searching through the "Eastern Shield Defense System" that produced the actual Montauk documents through the Freedom of Information Act. Documents were also supplied revealing that mind control and time experiments had actually taken place there. These documents were all witnessed, signed and "sealed" by "reliable government witnesses."

Although no one yet had time to read any of the documents, the Seventh Seal known as Oral Swaggart gave a brief synopsis and proudly announced that the Philadelphia Experiment and Montauk Project had now been completely proven. It was a done deal. After all, they could read it for themselves; therefore, it must be true. The creatures began to clap resoundingly. Never had such a clamor of applause and cheering been heard in their history. Finally, and at long last, the ancient riddle had been solved. The sound of one hand clapping, one hand against a flipper, had been heard and was now fully understood. When shown linear "proof" in a linear world, they now BELIEVED other worlds were possible. These trained seal people responded much like a trained seal in an aquatic park. Although that explains the enigmatic and thunderous "sound of one hand clapping," there is considerably more to the story.

When the ovation died down, Oral Swaggart began to prance and pace about the stage. His clothes were imported from Florida for this very special occasion. He wore a lime-green jacket with white shoes. His lemon-yellow slacks were rolled up to his knees in a deliberate fashion statement which symbolized that he was ready for the flood. Holding his finger up to the air, he began to move it in a circular motion that became more rapid until a bubble-like orb appeared and began to spin off the tip of his finger, not unlike a basketball spinning on the finger of a Harlem Globetrotter. As the orb continued to spin, he spoke to the congregation and told them they had responded very well to the truth and would be accordingly rewarded. Telling the audience to take their human hand and imitate the motions he had performed with his hand, they all performed the trick until each one had produced a spinning orb. Instructing them to follow his lead, he took the spinning orb and placed it on his snout as it continued to spin at a very high rate. They all followed suit until every member of the audience had an orb spinning on the end of their nose. At this point, the "Seventh Seal" said they would now get their reward. The orbs suddenly stopped spinning and a sizeable fish appeared in the middle of each globe. The Seventh Seal then relaxed his neck and swallowed the entire fish whole and let it go down his gullet. Again, the audience followed suit. Oral spoke again:

"You have all heard the truth and then swallowed the Word made Flesh. The Seventh Seal has been revealed and now I am going to ascend. He then began to ascend a lucite spiral staircase that had been placed near the stage. As he ascended the stairway, clouds began to appear at his feet. Reaching the top of the staircase, he extended his arm upward as if he were Superman and shot straight into the air, never to be seen or heard from again.

Despite the miraculous nature of the proof thus demonstrated, these seals were still a skeptical lot. After a few weeks went by and they were no longer fed, they no longer believed in the miracle that had been performed and certainly rejected any idea of the Philadelphia Experiment or the Montauk Projects having occurred.

By now, you might have a low opinion of the seal people, but there were creatures on this planet who were far more sophisticated than the crowd at Sea World. One such creature was the President of the Free World who was composed primarily of walrus DNA; however, he thought, talked and acted like a human. He also wore spectacles and was extremely well read. Long ago, ancient scientists determined that the leaders of their culture should be dominant and display prominent teeth. The tooth was considered sacred because it was the first part of the anatomy to take part in the consumption of flesh when engaged in the sacred rite of eating. As any dynamic walrus, the President displayed healthy tusks.

Unlike the attendees at the Seventh Seal event, the President was not dismissive. He was too intelligent for that. Personnel from the Government had been in attendance at the Seventh Seal event and reported and video recorded everything that had taken place. He observed exactly what had happened.

One month after the celebrated event by the Seventh Seal, twelve specially selected seal people were brought to the White House by presidential decree. Once there, they were met by the Great Walrus and he addressed them:

"You have all been brought here for a special project and are going to form a special unit. But first, I must give you a briefing. I am not only your president in this world, I once served the same role in a universe where I was known as Theodore Roosevelt. The name 'Theodore' was given to me because I adore Theos or God. I am going to try to teach you the same, but you look like a rather motley crew."

The seals began to groan in hunger, and he could get no further with them until he had his personal secretary, Elmo Evans, bring in a bucket of fish and give each one of them a fresh mackerel. The walrus, or T.R. as he liked to be called, liked to talk a lot and was quick to realize that the only hope of seriously interesting these twelve elite seal people was if he kept their bellies fed.

"Ever since Oral Swaggart, the Seventh Seal, released himself, all hell has broken loose. Pandora's Box has been opened. Entire cities of women have simultaneously exposed their genitalia in public and have begun to stream a wild form of satanic energy through their bodies. They are no longer following the old ways, and we must do everything within our power to alleviate this situation. Things are in complete chaos.

"Now, perhaps because my name is Theodore and I am 'adored by God,' I have a special ability to communicate with other worlds. In that other reality where I was Theodore Roosevelt, I had taken a trip out to Montauk Point and visited the site where Marconi had tried to perfect the technology of wireless transmission. In that reality, I began to receive strange transmissions from myself as the Great Walrus in the world we are in now. From this world, I sent messages to Theodore Roosevelt of the United States that we needed to consolidate sea power. In order to save our existence, we needed to take their world by sea. As he and I are were both the same person, but on different time lines, he decided to help me. Together, we agreed that the seal would be the totem by which to conquer Earth. Both of our worlds were obsessed with the concept of the flood and Atlantis. Only by conquering underneath the water would we have a chance to make our mark on history and, more importantly, save ourselves. It was this realization that brought me to accept President McKinley's appointment as Assistant Secretary of the Navy.

"In that life, I was Dutch by ancestry and had strange connections to the House of Orange. Through the House of Orange, I was related by blood to Kaiser Wilhelm of Germany as well as the King of England. One reporter even referred to them as 'my cousins,' but I did not think that was very funny. Sea power was crucial to preserve the business interests of these three nations: Germany, England, and the United States. Even though there was great rivalry and factionalism between us, we worked together to consolidate the interests of I.G. Farben, the biggest industrial cartel in the world who had more to say about world business than any of us."

As the seals listened to the Great Walrus, some of them began to snooze. Noticing this, T.R. utilized his flipper to push a button which made a loud and obnoxious buzzing noise. Elmo Evans then entered the room with a cattle prod and prodded the seals in order to ensure they would stay awake. T.R. then continued speaking.

"I consulted with Nikola Tesla in my capacity as Assistant Secretary of the Navy and alarmed J.P. Morgan into thinking that Tesla's Wardencliff Tower was going to be used to give everyone free service. This was really a ploy to take Tesla's technology underground and keep it secret in order to preserve the interests of our current mission. Tesla also worked for Telafunken, the German phone company. They worked with me to build undersea bases and communication systems. I also knew George Sylvester Vierick, the man who was the Kaiser's main U.S. operative during that period and who also served as a conduit between Tesla and Aleister Crowley.

"It was actually the release of the information on the Philadelphia Experiment and Montauk Project which caused all hell to break loose and the Seventh Seal to open. The experiments themselves were, in some respects, the first crack in the seal, but most of humanity experienced the effects of these experiments on an unconscious level. As they slip into the subconsciousness, the effect expands exponentially. I know some people still think it is all bunk and that the story about the Cameron brothers is fanciful. I can tell you that the Camerons were very much involved. In fact, it might interest you to know that Duncan Cameron Sr. used to come over to Sagamore Hill as a little boy. In fact, my role in the Philadelphia and Montauk Projects was crucial and it's all fully documented. People say it's not, but it is! It is, I tell you!"

By this time, some of the seals had started to fall asleep, but T.R. began to pound his flipper on his desk as he asserted himself. He pounded it so hard that he hit the equivalent of the funny bone in his walrus elbow.

"Elmo! My elbow! Elmo! My elbow!" he cried.

At that point, Elmo Evans ran in to see what was the matter. T.R. moved himself to the floor as Elmo went to retrieve an ice pack for the flipper of the Great Walrus. Vice President Ronald Reagan then came into the room to see what all the commotion was about. Reagan was young in this world, and his seal snout was quite becoming on his handsome face.

"What's all the trouble about?" he asked in his patented friendly tone.

"You know, Ron, people don't believe me. They don't believe in secret societies. They don't believe the interdimensional projects. They don't even believe that your fancy with astrology goes far more deeply into occult matters than anyone would care to think about. But, most of all, no one believes that I was involved in the Montauk Project!"

At this point, T.R. the walrus began to pound his other flipper in frustration until he hurt that, too.

"The Gipper! My flipper!" he cried. "The Gipper! My flipper!"

As Reagan sensitively and calmly tried to calm the Great Walrus, T.R. continued to mutter the word "Gipper" until he finally said, "I see the Four Horsemen, too."

T.R. was referring to the Four Horsemen of the Apocalypse. In both universes, Reagan was known for his movie portrayal of George Gipp, the star running back from Notre Dame who was part of a famous football backfield that were affectionately called the Four Horsemen because they were so devastating to the reality of other football teams.

As Reagan listened to the Great Walrus, Elmo returned with the ice. But now, T.R. had gone unconscious. It seemed as if he had suffered a mild stroke. Only at this point did the twelve seals suddenly become animated and very interested in their surroundings. In fact, they were worried that their food source might be taken away from them.

"We believe him!" they shouted. "We believe him! Let's look at those documents on his desk and reassure him."

"Look!" one of the seals said. "Here is a letter from his friend, Henry Adams to Mrs. Don Cameron written on January 12, 1902."

The seal began to read aloud from the letter.

"As usual, Theodore absorbed the conversation. If it tried me ten years ago, it crushes me now...Really, Theodore is exasperating, even to me and always was...what annoys me is his childlike and infantile superficiality, with his boyish dogmatism of assertion. He lectures me on history as though he was a high school pedagogue...I heard only the repetition of 'I, I, I.' "

Another seal picked up another letter from Henry Adams. This one was to his brother Brook in February 1912. The seal read aloud from the letter which said that T.R.'s "mind has gone to pieces and has disintegrated like the mind of society until it has become quite incoherent and spasmodic."

"He is, as Taft justly said, a neurotic, and his neurosis may end like LaFollette's, in nervous collapse or a stroke or acute mania."

After another seal looked at the documents for himself, he said that it did not matter that the Cameron referred to in the letter was not actually Duncan Cameron Sr.

"Listen, we have to stick together and convince him that he is right. We are getting hungry and need more fish. Try and stay awake when he gets up and pay attention to everything he says."

As if the sudden willingness of the seals to listen had brought him out of a deep sleep, T.R. began to come alive. After digging his tusks into a big mackerel that Elmo had brought him, the Great Walrus was ready to speak again. As he prepared to address the seals, they spoke up.

"We believe you! We believe you!" they cried. "We already know the Philadelphia Experiment and Montauk Projects were real. We saw the documents from the Seventh Seal, Oral Swaggart."

The great walrus, looking pleased, motioned for Elmo Evans to bring in more fish which the seals rapidly ate up. It was now time for T.R. to speak.

"Of course, you realize that twelve is an incomplete number. It is now time to bring in your leader, the thirteenth seal. It is the "Great Seal of the United States of America." Bringing in the Great Seal, T.R. explained its significance to them.

"You see the olive branches in the eagle's talons? Pay attention to them because they are very important. But for now, look at that eye at the top of the pyramid. It is the All-Seeing Eye. Remember, seal means "see all" and that is exactly what the All-Seeing Eye can do. It can track you down anywhere you go, so don't try and buck it. The eye also represents the Dog Star Sirius. That's another reason you seals were chosen. You are known for your canine qualities. I couldn't be more Sirius about this. The pineal gland in the seal also has very unique properties.

"Now, the All-Seeing Eye did come into view at Montauk. During the Montauk Project, they ran the greatest remote viewing program in history known as the Seeing Eye whereby the psychic in the Montauk Chair would leave his body and see anywhere he was directed. Of course, this was a harmonic mimicry of the true

All-Seeing Eye and acted as sympathetic magick to the Godhead itself. As the Seventh Seal itself is undone, it starts on a small and unconscious scale and this project at Montauk was the tip of the iceberg although it is still submerged beneath the water in most creature's minds.

"Of course, people will tell you that the All-Seeing Eye represents a conspiracy known as the 'Illuminati.' What you really have in this conspiracy scenario is the fact that all consciousness is one and part of the same Godhead. God is God, and we are it, but we suffer from fragmentation, not unlike a hard drive in a computer that is divided into sectors and fragments. There is a split across the continuum. In fact, a crack in the Cosmic Egg, but there are many cracks. When you go into the separate fissures which represent the descent into the embryo or Seat of Mankind, you will see that the separate fissures all come from the same place. But, perhaps I've said too much. I am only a fragmented piece of consciousness myself as well as being the grand image of a patriarch. Additionally, I am aggressive and assertive and preoccupied with my own self-image. Never has any president so embodied God the Father as myself. I am also an old windbag.

"You see, complete chaos out of Pandora's Box was opened here when the Philadelphia Experiment and Montauk Project were proven beyond the shadow of a doubt. They moved into everyone's consciousness. The feminine energy was released: shakti, Kali, kundalini. I find this completely chaotic. Sometimes I even see shape-shifting reptoids around every corner when I feel that the continuity of consciousness is being destroyed.

"But , we're not hopeless. There are still plenty of threads of our old consciousness. We need a secure base in another world. Therefore, you seals must go to this other universe and maintain the patriarchal information and control zones so that we may continue our own continuity of consciousness."

At this point, one of the seals spoke up and said, "And most importantly, be fed!"

"That's right," said the Great Walrus. "Be fed."

Another seal looked up in a bewildered fashion.

"Why us seals? I mean, why are we chosen?"

"That's an excellent point," replied T.R. "There is a very specific reason the totem of a seal was chosen for this mission. The seal is one of the most potent animal totems ever derived. Some etymologists think that the word *seal* derives from Old High German *seleah* which in turn came from the Indo-European base *selk* which means to pull or draw (this is in reference to the seal's labored movements on land.) In a sense, this could represent the pull to another universe where things are not so static and still. This is true, but there is even deeper meaning in the word seal. Phonetically, the word is pronounced "sea el" which means "God of the sea" and is observed in the term *sea lion* which is the true name for the seal. The lion represents the gate keeper of Babylon and is the most powerful sign of the zodiac. Christ was even known as the Lion of Judea. Myself, I was known as the Lion of Ong Island which is better known as L-ong Island.

"But, in its most pure etymological sense, we have yet an even deeper meaning for s*eal*. It derives from the word "sigil" which was a wafer of molten wax pressed into a distinctive seal to confirm or DOCUMENT authenticity. You want proof? I'll show you proof, damn it!

"Now, the sigil is very important because it symbolizes or works as a code interface with the angels. *Angel* is another one of those magical words. Just like *seal*, it means different things. Angel was originally just another expression of the word *angle* which signifies a bend, a corner, a turn or a twist from an original position or viewpoint. The original angels were angles of creation or God. This is why God is called the Grand Geometer because he equates to the sum measurement of all the angles when we look at things geometrically. Angle also means perspective, position, slant or viewpoint. In this regard, angels are different viewpoints or angles of God or from which to view the Godhead.

"But, the word *angel* does not stop there. There once was a mysterious man who not only studied these things; he brought them into our world. John Dee was the court magician of Queen Elizabeth I who worked with Edward Talbot Kelly to interpret and codify an angelic language into different sigils. Each sigil was an encapsulation or code frequency of a certain generic stream of consciousness. Dr. Dee was a mighty conjurer, too. It was not just his fate to codify and interpret this language but to utilize the consciousness thereof to manipulate matter, energy, space and time. Of course, if you know anything about conjurors, there is also a dark side and other forces or entities begin to have a profound influence on matters.

"There is much more I could say, but I have to tell you the truth. I am more than a little frightened. I'm afraid that if I explore this, it will pull out the props from underneath my flippers. I won't know who I am anymore as I will completely lose my identity and my own continuity of consciousness. I won't be able to think in the manner that I'm used to and that scares the hell out of me! I want to hold on to my patriarchal reality where I'm important and can walk softly and carry a big stick. Therefore, I have concluded that if John Dee's work is undermined, I will be, too. But it's not an easy dilemma. I have to open some portals by using this language so that I can preserve what little integrity I have left.

"Now, the English language which is the ruling language of the Earth has very strange properties for it is a conjuration in its own right. Within English is one of the key sigils that relates to, but is not defined by, this entire proposition. It is a modern-day sigil and is not too much like the original glyphs that John Dee used. It takes me back to my days in the White House when I called together a rules committee on the game of football. It is a game which I highly approved of, but there were far too many injuries. It became a brutal proposition, so I called together key people of the time period and held a rules committee. The purpose was to create a game that could be enjoyed with minimal injuries. Out of these meetings, the game we know today as football was created. Of course, there was Knute Rockne, the Gipper, and the rest is history. But, if you look at the logical progression of this game, you will find an interdimensional means of communication and transference. First of all, the footballs of my day were pudgy and roughly sewn together straps of pigskin. Interdimensional research showed that interdimensional transfer occurs when two self-contained fields in the shape of a sphere (known as orbs by magicians) begin to cross-reference or impinge upon each other's fields. When these two spheres intersect, they make the fish symbol which we know as the vesica pisces or that which represents the Christ Consciousness, at least in Christianity. The vesica pisces is a two-dimensional symbol that really represents a three dimensional interface which looks just like a modern NFL football. So, you see how the Super Bowl is not only the climax of football culture but that it has been conjured into our existence as an interface for transferring mental and subliminal images to a stupefied population. The Super Bowl is the biggest advertising bonanza in history.

"Now, if you look carefully at a close-up of a modern-day football during the Super Bowl, you will see six letters emblazoned upon it which is a modern-day sigil of significance. These letters spell the word "WILSON." This is the sigil I was talking about. It is a catch word by which all of these interdimensional angles work. When you see the word WILSON, it often means you have come into the field or sphere of another realm. But, alas, I do not have time to tell you all of the different meanings. These are just a few key signposts to help you along the way."

At this point in his narrative, St. Elmo's fire began to crackle around the windows of the Oval Office. T.R. became agitated and quickly looked around the room in a paranoid fashion. Suddenly, the Great Walrus began to hyperventilate before passing into an unconscious state.

As if on cue with the St. Elmo's fire, Elmo Evans suddenly entered the room to find an unconscious president. Elmo was holding a piece of paper that looked like a telegram.

"Tetragram!" he said.

With T.R. now unconscious, Vice-president Ronald Wilson Reagan, who was still in the room, was now elevated to head of state and would have to answer whatever communication that Elmo was conveying.

"Did you say telegram, Elmo?"

"No sir, I said Tetragram."

As Reagan picked up the piece of paper and began to read it, St. Elmo's fire continued to crackle.

"My God," said Reagan. "This is from Mikael Gorbachev. Since the Seventh Seal has opened, the Russians have built a psychic wall around America. That could be what is making these twelve seals so damn lethargic. Get me the hot line."

As soon as Elmo brought over the hot line, Reagan picked it up and said animatedly, "Mr. Gorbachev, tear down that wall!"

The sheer force of Reagan's passionate voice awakened the Great Walrus from his slumber. Looking around the room, it was obvious that T.R. immediately recognized where he was.

"Nothing like a Wilson (referring to Reagan's middle name) to wake me up and move me on to the next dimension," he said.

"All right, you seals. I've given you enough of a briefing on the overall scene. Your next trip will be to the Pentagon where you will be indoctrinated and conditioned for your mission. Thereafter, you will be taken to Plum Island and Brookhaven Labs to have your seal snouts and flippers converted into human attributes. You will then tele-universe to Earth where you will begin work as Navy Seals, a secret service within the U.S. Navy that is beyond compare. The original orders for the Navy Seals were first formulated by myself when I was Assistant Secretary of the Navy. This was after I had received transmissions from myself in this universe. The orders for the Navy Seals were later confirmed by my relative, Franklin D. Roosevelt, when he worked as Secretary of the Navy. He conferred with Tesla and they recruited the Cameron brothers for their special mission. The Seals were to remain secret and the orders for this specific unit were "sealed" until the time you seals would arrive and activate them. The Navy will take good care of you and feed you although your desire for fish may reduce with the physical changes you are about to undergo. Most of all, never forget the Great Seal of the United States, particularly the olive branch in the right talon of the eagle."

After Elmo Evans escorted the twelve seals out of the Oval Office, the Great Walrus got up and walked around the room. He was quite proud of his dissertation. In fact, he was much more proud of his dissertation than he was confident in the idea that the Navy Seals might succeed. But, he felt good about his understanding of the Great Architect of the Universe and his own role in it. As he looked in the mirror, he began to dance and prance about as he began to sing a melody from the Beatles.

"I am the Walrus... I am the Egg Man.... I am the Egg Man......"

4

THE MASTER KEY

As was said earlier, the transmission from a parallel universe you have just read is loosely based upon the stream of consciousness as popularized by James Joyce. Whether it is as good as Joyce in terms of literature is certainly highly arguable and is certainly not the point, but one thing is very clear: it is intended to be clearer and easier to read than his work. As Joyce's wife once said to him, "Why don't you write something people can understand?"

Joyce was considered a great literary figure, in part, because no one understood him. On the other hand, those that could understand him at all saw a vast richness in his use of etymology, linguistics and how they interplayed and synchronized with the collective unconscious and the unused portion of the human brain. The very fact that he showed a command of the collective unconscious has made him an object of veneration in the literary world. In other words, people respect his work because he communicated values that most of us have lost.

When we talk about opening the Seventh Seal, this subject has everything to do with that portion of the human brain that is not fully utilized by us as conscious human beings. That unused portion is commonly thought to be about ninety percent although some consider that we might use a bit more than ten percent in our normal conscious awareness. Some refer to this area as *terra incognita* or "unknown land" that is yet to be discovered.

Human beings are too easily frightened and triggered by what they do not understand or have familiarity with. It is not unlike the

Munchkins recoiling in fear after the Wicked Witch of the East has been killed by Dorothy. They have to be coaxed out by the Good Witch before they can even begin to assimilate who or what Dorothy might represent. Dorothy, who has a big impact on their world, actually comes from a parallel universe. To the Munchkins, she represents pure magic. On the other hand, Dorothy sees the world of Oz itself as magic, and she has been thrust into the midst of it. Although no one can solve her problem of getting back home, all believe that her solution lies in the hands of the Wizard. In Oz, the belief in magic is much more prevalent than common sense, and it is a very fearful crowd.

If you were to announce to Earthlings that you came from a parallel universe, you would generate some of the fear of the Munchkins but much less sympathy. Even more so, you would be an irritant to the cultural habits and patterns of our society. Beneath that irritation you might even find an unbridled fear that far exceeds that of the Munchkins.

The human brain is studded with booby traps and pitfalls that make a full conscious activation of its neural pathways an apparent impossibility. With very rare exceptions now and then, academic institutions reinforce these pitfalls. However, this was not always the case. Long ago, men of learning recognized that there were not only unused capacities of the brain but that they were actually divisible into different pathways that could be named and identified. If one could open up these various pathways and light up all circuits in the human brain, one would then be functioning at full throttle. This suggests an extremely powerful state of being, particularly when you consider that some of these pathways are relegated to the province of what our culture calls either spiritual phenomena or paranormal phenomena. According to this perspective of the human brain, if you accessed the right pathway, you would or could be in total sympathy or in concert with the phenomena our culture describes as "God." This also represents a conduit to infinity.

According to historical legend, there was a character who actually mastered the various pathways of the human brain. To the Muslims, he was known as Sulyaiman but our culture knows him as Solomon. Each of these pathways could be opened by seventy-two different keys, and these are sometimes known as the Keys of

Solomon. Sometimes these keys are personified as jinn or daemon or with the jinn or daemon as the guardians of the keys.

Solomon was said to have mastered the jinn by placing them in a brass vessel or head. Many of us have heard the tale of the brass bottle, but we do not too often hear about the head. Sufi alchemists have often referred to "making a head of gold" which is their term for denoting the path of the alchemist. In my book *The Black Sun*, a "head of gold" equates to increased superconductivity in the chemistry of the brain by reason of consumption of white gold, sometimes through consuming the body of mummies. When the process was complete, an isotope of gold actually secreted out of the third eye or pineal gland of the initiate.

Now, if you were to visualize being inside the brass bottle and seeing all of the dormant and different pathways that were blocked off, you might feel like one sorry human being. On the other hand, if some are opened, you might see very clearly in some areas or have extraordinary abilities. Although this is a "dead subject" for most of humanity, it is not really a dead proposition. The very legend of seventy-two pathways to the brain is suggestive of the current state of humanity. To the degree they are blocked in each and every individual, humanity is blocked.

This subject has been codified and practiced by magicians for centuries and it is known as *goetia* or the goetia. Each separate pathway is known as a different strain of *goetia*. The literal meaning of the word is intrinsically connected to the German word for God which is *gott*, but there are many more aspects to the etymology which will be addressed. The full activation of the human brain would be very suggestive of a Godlike state of being.

The very idea that there is such a subject and method should be stimulating to most minds; but, over the centuries, that path has been laden with pitfalls. It is a taboo subject which has been relegated to the Forbidden Zone. As this region of exploration has been taboo throughout history, these aspects of the brain have been associated with black magic and the like. One of the reasons for this is that the procedures of goetia are intimately concerned with the subject of demons. Demons, of course, either frighten or alert contemporary Christians. There are also those who brighten up and sparkle when the subject of demons is brought up. Personally, I would suggest a more sober countenance when dealing with such a subject. Assuming the role of an umpire or referee will serve one far better.

One who enters the realm of goetia should not study demons because he is frothing at the mouth to unite with them nor because he feels he is doing something saintly and holy. One is simply trying to activate the full panorama of human potential. The word *demon* itself is something of a misnomer. It derives from *daemon* which comes from *deity*. This word puts us at the source point of creation which is often called God in our western culture. A more ancient definition of demon was "divide" which is very representative of the energies of goetia. The word *divide* is very applicable in two respects. First, in this system, the brain has been divided into many different pathways with each separate pathway being said to work in parallel with a specific spirit or goetia which has a particular identity and characteristic. In this scenario, each spirit or demon rules a different aspect of the brain. Second, the word *divide* applies once again because each spirit or demon has both a positive and negative aspect.

Besides being related to "live demons" or, at the very least, brain circuitry which operates like demons for all practical purposes, the strains of goetia are also represented by visual seals or glyphs. These glyphs are designed to be recognized by the brain for the purpose of opening up dormant or clogged areas.

The background of goetia is very rich in lore but much of it is unknown, obscure or possessed by darker forces that oppress its dissemination. The very words *goetia* and *gott* are related to *Gothic*. *Goetic* literature as well as Gothic cathedrals do not appear until centuries after the Gothic peoples have left the pages of history as a potent force. Much of this association comes from the sacking of the Roman treasury by the Visigoths who made off with the remaining artifacts of Solomon's Temple which the Romans had plundered. Some say that the Ark of the Covenant and the Holy Grail itself were in those spoils. If there indeed was such a treasure, or a substantial legend which accompanied the spoils, this explains the word association. Goetia was the name attributed to the Keys of Solomon by which he could control the jinn.

A more common etymology of goetia is that it comes from the French word *argotique* which signifies "language of the birds." Argotique was literally the process by which the secret wisdom of

Solomon is encoded in the Gothic cathedrals. The Church would never have tolerated dissemination of this information to the masses as it was forbidden. The illuminated Freemasons of the time therefore encoded the secret wisdom in the cathedrals so that it would communicate to those initiated to see it. Originally, the secret societies were serving a noble purpose by keeping things secret. They were trying to bypass the oppression of the Church and communicate knowledge. Ironically, the word *argotique*[*] sounds a lot like the word *architect*, a subject which obsessed the Freemasons.

The etymology of the word *goetia* pretty much speaks for itself. It would not be so rich if it were not for the amount of power that has been invested in the word. Although we are not going to go into a treatise on the background of the Goths or even goetia, it is very important for the reader to grasp the basic principle of what goetia is about and to realize there is a very rich heritage that is lost, forgotten, and obscured. This is not a text book on goetia. One has already been written, but I can tell you ahead of time that most of the practitioners are fumbling and stumbling in the dark. The average reader is not likely to do any better.

---

[*] The etymology of the words *goetia* and *argotique* continue to fascinate when we realize that *argotique* is a word in Old French which means slang. English dictionaries do not have an etymology for the word *slang*, but it is based upon two English words: *slander* and language. *Slander*, particular the *sla* part of the word (as if to say "slay") refers to offensive speech. The *lang* part of *slang* can be considered to equate to language or *lingua* (tongue). Slang is certainly considered to be offensive speech, particularly in days gone past. One could even equate it to "offensive language of the angels" where the "ang" in the word *slang* refers to angels. It is important to remember that John Dee coined Enochian, his language of the angels, and explained it in vulgate, the familiar speech of the Angles which was spoken by the commoners of England at that time. The only known etymology of *slang* I have seen is that is was known as the language of thieves and tramps in the 1700's. Although *argotique* refers to slang in Old French, it more commonly refers to "language of the birds." Again, we stumble on tremendous synchronicity. In UFO lore, the Aviary refers to a secret network of CIA personnel who "spill the beans" and offer information on the UFO situation. In gothic masonry, it referred to the passing on of secret information by means of coded symbols. Even today, intelligence networks use this old form of symbolic reference. The word *argotique* itself has more to do with *argos* in its construction than anything else. *Argos* was the name of the ship Jason used in his quest for the Golden Fleece in Greek mythology. *Argos* means ship and it derives from the word *Ark*. The language of the birds also reminds us of the dove approaching Noah with an olive branch.

One of the problems that practitioners of goetia often have is that they address specific goetic spirits for different problems. This often centers around money, sex, or some form of personal empowerment. In this regard, the overall ecosystem of the brain and the universe gets short-circuited. Personally, I have experienced and tried to pay attention to what I refer to as the Master Key. This begins with all aspects of the brain acting with synchronization. In this sense, synchronicity would be considered the Master Key as one is studying or experiencing the interlocking forces of the mind. In *The Book of the Law*, Aleister Crowley referred to the "Key to it All" which can be likened to the Master Key.

Goetia is not the only way to activate the human brain, but it is one of the hallmarks of secret western culture and so much of our Western Civilization is under its spell, both figuratively and realistically. Activation of the Master Key dissipates the need to invoke or activate all of the different goetia. When that is activated, all of the others tend to fall in line.

When we return to the analogy of Solomon mastering the goetia by placing them in a brass vessel or head of gold, there are some very interesting implications when we consider the head, particularly when you consider the theme of white gold being an activation of the full consciousness of the human being. Consider the word *Golgotha* which is commonly defined as "the place of the skull." *Golgotha* can be broken down into the syllables *gol* and *gotha*. *Gol* is very similar to the pre-Indo European word *ghel* which means gold. The root *gotha* takes us back to the Goths again. In this sense *Golgotha* could be construed to mean "gold of god" or "gold god." More properly, *gotha* refers to the goetic pathways of the brain or head and "golden pathways of the head" might serve as a better definition.

The regular dictionary gives further insight. They describe *Golgotha* as a Latin and Greek word deriving from Aramaic. In Hebrew, which is similar to but not identical to Aramaic, it is *gulgoleth*. The root *goleth* is fascinating because it is similar to the English word *gullet* which means "throat" or "swallow." The word *gullible*, which means to swallow a story or information, derives from *gullet*. In this sense, *Golgotha* (where *Gol* represents gullet and gotha refers to God) signifies the place where God was swallowed as it is also a tomb for the burial of Christ.

There is even more subtle meaning to the root *goleth* when we consider that the gullet refers to the throat or speech. In this sense, one is invoking God or a spirit/daemon. Thus, we have Golgotha referring not only to the place of the skull or brain, but to the activation of it through the throat or gullet by invocation. This is exactly what goetia is supposed to be: the full activation of the God force. When the brain is completely activated at full throttle, either by the proper consumption of white gold or by a Master Key, the secrets of resurrection and eternal life are at hand. In this sense, the story of the resurrected Christ is a perfect analogy to what can be accomplished in terms of human brain potential.

Although it is a crude analogy, it will serve to point out what happens when a part of the human brain is damaged. For example, when a person loses the ability to walk, it is common for another part of the brain to take over and to regain that ability. If one addresses synchronicity, particularly through the elements of word meanings, puns, and how they relate to the unconscious, one is reconnecting lost links in the brain and reteaching oneself how to operate on all cylinders.

Aleister Crowley taught that the word *sin* means division. Conversely, the word *yoga* means union. In this sense, division of the brain into relatively irretrievable parts would represent sin whereas complete unification of such would represent yoga. This is why master yogis have supernatural attributes. They have mastered the chemistry of the brain on some level. But, even these master yogis have more unification potential. If they did not, I would not be writing this book because we are talking about an enlightenment of the human race, not just a few wise men in the Orient. The Hundredth Monkey* concept applies in full. The comparison between yogis and monkeys is unfortunate and was not intended; however, it is important to point out that most yogis would not care whether you thought of them as monkeys or not. They are well beyond that sort of reaction.

Western magicians involved in goetic work practice in great secrecy and darkness. Like yogis, they are seeking to activate

---

* The Hundredth Monkey principle refers to studies demonstrating that when a certain number of monkeys (arbitrarily set at the number of 100) learn a particular function, that skill automatically transfers to the entire species through the morphogenetic grid.

potentials of the human brain; however, most of the ones I am aware of would take great exception at being compared to monkeys. It is sometimes very hard not to compare them to the censorship council from the Planet of the Apes. In fact, if you know much about western magicians, you might find them very adverse to the Hundredth Monkey concept. One of the problems with them is that if you approach them or seek out help on the subject, too often you will be repelled. Sometimes it is not by the magician himself but it is his goetic circuitry interlocking with yours. If you are really a good student and potentially sharper than the magician concerned, you might be rejected even harder. There are always exceptions to the rule, but petty jealousies and power plays have made the subject of goetic magick a forbidden zone. Lower primate behavior too often enters the fray.

Goetia is not a particularly easy concept to explain, and it will be an entirely new subject for many people reading this book. One has to describe the word demon and the fact that the word does not really means what people think it means. At the same time, one has to point out that the word *demon* has the potential to mean exactly what you really thought it meant in the first place. By the same token, I find it very difficult to describe western magicians without describing demons, gargoyles, or the like. When you consider what they are working with, it is no wonder. Most magicians are possessed by darkness and secrecy, and although they may have attained what they consider to be "great powers," they are operating on a short circuit if they are not working with the Master Key. Working with the Master Key has its own pitfalls as well. If you use the Master Key to open up the boiler room, you just might find all the backed up sewage from short-circuited magicians. This is a very ample description of the Montauk Project.

The complete union or yoga or synchronization of all the channels of the brain would result in a new prototype of a human being. This is the true value of synchronicity. It is a connective and associative principle. It increases intelligence with regard to relationships. When Jung defined synchronicity with the Tao, he was describing the prime aspect of divinity. Yoga, synchronicity, and the Tao all seek harmony and a unification with the ecosystem of consciousness. In this respect, synchronicity itself can be considered the Master Key of It All.

5

THE LAUGH OF GOD

*THE FOLLOWING TRANSMISSION
IS FROM A PARALLEL UNIVERSE*

After studying goetia and the Keys of Solomon for the first time, I had a most peculiar reaction: I began to laugh uncontrollably. At first, I was not sure why I was laughing because I did not think of goetia as being a funny subject. My reaction did not make any sense, but it did not matter. It was late in the evening, and I was about to go to sleep. That night I had a very strange dream.

I dreamt that Solomon the King had a jester who wore the three pronged jester's cap with bells on the ends. Although his bells were making noises, the jester was bidding me to be silent as he put his hand over his mouth as if to impart some great secret. The jester then pointed to King Solomon who was sitting all alone and on his throne. As he sat on the throne, a full moon began to make itself known by shining a light through an aperture in his palace. As moonlight was cast upon his face, Solomon's head began to solidify into a head of gold which soon became a skull of gold and then projected to a distance three feet in front of the king. Like a magician, the jester then began to pull beautiful silk scarves out of the golden skull. The scarves were seventy-two in number with each being brilliantly colored and containing a separate goetic symbol. As he pulled them from the skull, the scarves began to dance as if each one was alive in itself. It was a beautiful sight, and the ensemble continued until the jester had pulled the last scarf out.

71

It was a brilliant silver. With it, the jester orchestrated all of the other scarves to dance to his tune. Suddenly, the gold skull began to spin until it lost its shape and then became a vessel of brass. The jester then waved the silver scarf as all of the beautiful scarves jumped into the brass bottle. When they had all entered, the jester stuffed in the silver scarf and sealed the top of the bottle so nothing could escape. At this point, Solomon the King, who had been stone-faced but apparently watching the whole procedure, began to laugh uncontrollably. His spirit could then be seen as an astral form that had been freed from the confines of his body or, more specifically, his head.

As I awoke from my dream, it was the middle of the evening, and I began laughing once again. Perhaps the laugh of Solomon was infectious. I was still not sure, but I could not stop until a stray thought entered my head. It occurred to me that goetic materials are covetously guarded over and the knowledge thereof is often paraded in front of aspiring magicians as if they might be barking seals. I soon found this thought to be very amusing as well and began laughing uncontrollably once again. I was not laughing at the idea of magical students barking, but as I would regain fleeting moments of what could be termed "regular thought processes," I was soon overcome with an incredibly strong and intuitive impression that none of the details of goetia might be all that important to me. This realization, if it can be called that, caused rushes of laughter to cascade in me, not unlike a series of waterfalls. Maybe all of the different symbols I had seen in the texts and dream had ignited the proper reaction in my brain. I do not really know. But, when the thought entered my head that each separate invocation of the goetia was a trap door, I began to laugh even louder. Tears of laughter began to flow.

After a period of release and calming, I realized that my views would meet with great disapproval by the magick crowd. This brought on a whole new wave of laughter as I knew that if they had mastered any significant degree of goetia, they would be laughing, too. Then, the thought occurred to me that I did not have to tell anyone at all and that made me laugh even harder. Each thought of success gave me the laugh of success. Each thought of derision that could be directed at me made me laugh even harder. I was laughing so hard I began to feel like a popcorn machine of laughter.

It was then that I had the sensation of feeling like I had completely left my body. It was very similar to what I had witnessed in my dream of King Solomon.

I know well that the psychological state of mind that is termed an "out-of-body experience" can be frightening to some and it is certainly disorienting to one's normal mode, but when I experienced the perception of looking down on myself, the laughter started up again. Whatever truth or key I had discovered from reading the Keys of Solomon was visceral and made the out-of-body state just as funny as everything else. There was no spiritual disorientation or fear. Realizing others of lesser persuasion might become all the angrier at me for achieving this, I lost myself in laughter again.

LAUGH, LAUGH, LAUGH. NO MORE IMPRISONMENT IN THE BODY. LAUGH, LAUGH, LAUGH.

After laughing myself back to sleep, I began to dream once again. This time, Solomon's Jester was standing on the assembly line of a factory. He was cramming those same colorful scarves into skull after skull, but this time, the skulls were made of bone. After being crammed with goetic scarves, the skulls were placed on the heads of bodies and became fully realized human heads. The human bodies were walking out of the factory to take their place in ordinary society. The impression of the dream was clear. Goetic "programs" had been placed into everyone's head and all were walking around in ignorance of them. Solomon, who had the good fortune, apparently courtesy of the jester, to have his scarves placed in a sealed brass bottle, was free from the spell. He laughed and laughed and laughed. Solomon appeared and said the various stories about him were not all that true. He was free and would always remain so. Unfortunately, at least in the dream, this did not apply to all other human beings. But, I was not even aware of that aspect at that particular time. I was only aware of the laughter of this so-called version of King Solomon. The laughter was infectious and I woke up laughing uncontrollably again. The simplest of thoughts continued to propagate extreme laughter.

I knew that I was experiencing extreme euphoria, and it occurred to me that mental clinicians and psychologists expect euphoria to be followed by depression, sometimes extreme. Then it occurred to me that they said this, in part, due to the fact that they themselves were depressed, if only by the human condition itself and the so-called "scarves within their own head." After all, we live amidst a trance of sorrows according to Buddhism. To my state of mind at the time, laughing at the ideas or "known wisdom" of these clinicians was like laughing at a very obnoxious person who had just been humiliated. The laughter did not quit for several days. Even then, it calmed down, but I still continued to giggle. A profound state of well being took over and continued.

This state of laughter continued for the better part of two weeks. Sometimes the laughter was intense and sometimes it was just comfortable and light. My normal life went along quite smoothly as I did not have serious tasks to perform or deadlines to meet. Everything was just fine until I turned on the television set one evening before going to bed. I had left the TV off for weeks, and, in retrospect, I wonder if that is what started things going so well in the first place. It does not matter in any case because I turned it on and the rest is history. When the television came on, a PBS channel was on and there was a documentary on Negro League baseball. I remember an interesting and entertaining speaker named Buck O'Neill, but I soon fell asleep.

The next thing I knew, my laughter had completely exploded and there was no sensation whatsoever of being confined to a body. I began to laugh so loudly that it felt as if I was penetrating deep space. Suddenly, I became conscious and looked around. There was no bed, no television, and nothing but deep blue space. It was exceedingly peaceful. I thought or felt that I could do anything or go anywhere I felt like. Whether it was a dream or another type of experience, I still do not know to this day. Finally, I saw a mist of white vapor in the distance that came spiraling toward me until it surrounded me. What had been vapor had now materialized into a council of nine angels that sat around me. They were old, serious, ponderous, and judgmental in their demeanor. All in all, these angels did not look like they enjoyed my laughter. I had to wonder if they were actually demons disguised as angels. I still do not know exactly what they were, but they seemed hell bent on monitoring or inhibiting my laughter which seemed to be resonating across the whole damned universe.

As I sat there in deep space, the angels looked at me. With their glances, they did not have to say anything. I began to pick up their intentions telepathically. They felt that they were in council to take care of me or account for me in some manner. It suddenly dawned on me that I had reached a state of freedom so profound that it had reverberated to the far reaches of creation. This was some sort of counter-reaction to my laughter and freedom. Maybe, if I could have curbed my own laughter, I would have escaped detection and could have kept roaming the universe at will. I began to size them up and just stare.

Before any of them could say or do anything, I knew it was in my best interest to start saying or doing something. In fact, I thought it best to throw up a smoke screen. As they were angels and purporting to play the role of do-gooders, I began to rail against the injustice of the Negro Leagues as it was fresh on my mind and I thought it might win me some points with them. Although I knew absolutely no details about the subject, I began to rave and rant about how good the Negro League players were and how they exceeded the skill of many major league ball players. I even cited statistics which I completely made up. There were actually only two Negro League players I had ever heard of. One was named Josh Gibson and the other was Satchel Paige. I made up the names of the rest.

Apparently, the smoke-screen worked. The angels seemed completely befuddled by me. Whatever they thought they were here for was now in question. I had inserted a dagger into their game. They did not know what I was talking about, and with the lack of certainty in their eyes, I was able to pounce on them.

In a sudden and penetrating voice, I said, "You don't even look like angels. If you want me to respond, then bring me some beings that look and act like angels. How about something feminine with some curves and some nurturing qualities? Now, get the hell out of here!"

When I finished speaking, the angels departed as if a spell had been broken.

I was now quite self aware and was very conscious of the idea that my feelings of euphoria or extreme freedom had offended somebody or something in some part of the universe. I also knew that it is not good to laugh at the expense of someone else. This is why I brought up the Negro Leagues. These people had suffered extreme hardships that symbolized the whole plight of racial injustice in America. It was my intention to balance some energy here and fling it back on the angels who I felt were a tribunal of some sort. Apparently, I had successfully rejected their judgment.

As I sat there in deep space and contemplated my mysterious fate, I eventually saw the same misty vapor that I had witnessed before. The vapor manifested into angels once again, but this time they were soft, feminine, and nurturing, just like I had asked for. While these creatures were much more acceptable and certainly less confrontational, I realized that there were still issues to be dealt with. As these angels telegraphed their intentions, they tended to express sympathy with their eyes and other features. This was touching until I realized that they were there to get across the same issues as the original crew. It was now a softer and sweeter approach.

Without going into all the gyrations and nuances, these softer versions of angels were telling me that it is wonderful that I had achieved such a wonderfully free state. In fact, they were very happy for me, but no one can escape the suffering and deterministic fate that has been inflicted upon humanity. I would have to reenter human kind and take on a role and do my part in relieving suffering that had been inflicted upon others. As I looked into the eyes of one angel, I could see overtones of sympathy that allegedly cried out for suffering souls everywhere. I saw this as a karmic trap, and I was suspicious. It is fine to relieve suffering souls, but it is perhaps more appropriate to have those who inflicted the suffering take responsibility for it. Apparently, these angels had a big job to do and were trying to recruit me. My understanding of karma was that people create their own fate, and I could only assume this angel was atoning for her own karma. I wanted no part of the karmic stimulus-response button she was offering, and I wanted no part of her in general.

Another angel approached me and put on an even kinder front as if she really understood me.

"Perhaps you would like to play in the Negro Leagues?" she said.

At that suggestion, I was astonished. This angel was trying to use tact and understanding, but she did not understand anything at all. The Negro Leagues were not a desirable place to be. Further, they did not exist anymore as far as my time line was concerned.

These angels had power, but they certainly did not understand too many details. This made me trust them even less.

I now felt as if I was surrounded by a band of cretins that wanted me to do something offbeat and irregular. They continued to offer me alternative paths I could take or identities I could choose. Basically, it seemed they had to give me some sort of an assignment, any old assignment, as if they were placement counselors and could not rest until I had a valid job in their eyes. To me, it appeared as if they were low order bureaucrats in a heavenly hierarchy who were actually hell bent on me experiencing some sort of reduced freedom that was really enslavement. Perhaps, if I went unchecked in my current state, it would have a ripple effect on the rest of the universe. That might be considered dangerous by creatures of their ilk.

Finally, after being needled and cajoled by these beings beyond a normal breaking point, I suddenly and automatically remembered something that an old friend told me to try if I ever found myself in a spiritual predicament that was particularly rough. I then addressed the angels in a loud and penetrating voice.

"I AM THAT I AM!" I exclaimed.

This worked like a charm. The unwanted "angels" split as if an atom bomb had gone off. They never did return either. Although the words came out of me primarily as a visceral reaction to unwanted attention, it was as if my "gray matter" knew what to say on its own. In the Bible, the words "I am that I am" were spoken by both God and Christ. Upon reflection, I realized that these words have just as much to do with the expression of an artist or creative person. Artists are all about individual expression and they work on a completely creative frequency.

The angels I had to deal with represented a hierarchal structure that demands conformity. Society also has a tendency to demand conformity and rub out individualism. The words "I AM THAT I AM" completely champion the individual nature of who one is. Artists and creative people are often considered "bad boys," but when they create according to their own true inner expression, they are certainly more in conformity with the Creative Spirit than those who would seek to limit this expression by hierarchal institutions.

I had also personally witnessed that the phrase I used was a powerful talisman. It not only got rid of the unwanted angels, but it also told me that whoever used that phrase, whether it be Christ or God, was not going to be too popular with angels or anyone else who seeks conformity in human beings.

I felt free again and stated the words "I AM THAT I AM" once more. It was as if I was writing with a liquid white crayon against a hue of deep blue sky. Then, I turned the letters in the phrase around backwards, just to see what they would say. It came out as "MAITAHTMAI." It sounded very similar to MAHATMA.

I began laughing once again.

6

CHOOSING REALITIES

It is obvious to me that when people read the various transmissions from parallel universes that I have transcribed that they are going to wonder if I indeed have experienced some of these things. It is therefore important to address this topic so that there is no misunderstanding.

In the sea of infinity, all of us have experienced these things and more. Everything that is comprehensible, no matter how bizarre, can be experienced. In my ordinary three-dimensional reality, I have absolutely not had such experiences. It is true, however, that some of these experiences might parallel or be in sympathy with real events in my own life. In some cases, these "quantum events" are inextricably related to experiences of my own that are rather deep and profound.

According to Dr. David Anderson, one of the key issues that continues to come up in international physics symposiums is the quantum spirituality of Mankind. By this standard, our current juncture in human history depends upon the average man's ability to interface with quantum reality. This includes the infinite sea of time. One only needs to look at the advances in biology and technology alone to realize that we are on a collision course with what can best be termed "reality streaming." By reality streaming, I am referring to all the possibilities that can or will evolve in the technology sector as well as every other sector.

There is no question that we live in very interesting times, but some people take reality streaming too far. There are many who think that when the Mayan calendar ends after 2012 that we will have reached the end of time. This is only true in a sense, and while the general idea should not be dismissed, it should not be taken too literally either.

A system of synchronicity, such as astrology, will tell you that Pluto will enter Capricorn around the general time period of 2012. Capricorn is ruled by the planet Saturn and both of these rule time as well as structure. Saturn is also known as Father Time. In its astrological function, the planet Pluto purges, transforms and transmutes whatever it moves into. Therefore, Pluto moving into Capricorn will not only transform time and our perception of it but will restructure everything. As Pluto is the "plodding planet," it will be a long and slow overhaul, but it will be very profound as well. Just as our ancestors looked at life quite differently than ourselves, so will our progeny.

The key point is that as the veils that encumber Mankind's perception are lifted, the universe appears to be more and more wide open. Quantum reality and quantum probability dictate that all possible realities must be taken into account. Each individual has to face different quantum probabilities according to their own nature and experiences. My concern, based upon my observations from the various letters I receive and comments that I hear, is that many people are not easily digesting the aggregate experiences of what is taking place on the Earth.

Mankind's own inability to deal with quantum reality is superbly demonstrated with the aftermath of the 1947 flying saucer phenomena. The human behavior that ensues is absolutely ridiculous, both on the part of the Government as well as that of the contactees. One not only observes charlatans and others seeking attention but also a very sinister operation that operates beyond the scrutiny of the public and most government authorities. When you take away all the "space brother" nonsense and the abduction phenomena, the general public is left holding an empty bag. One is left to conclude the following.

We are not alone. There are beings with a superior technology who are unwilling to reveal themselves by any means that could be considered "normal." Normal political and communication channels do not work for the purposes of getting to the bottom of this phenomena or having an exchange with these beings. If the beings with the superior technology are not aliens, then there is a faction within the Government which is carrying out the same role. Again, the main point is that there is nothing one can do about it by normal means. The only communication with such beings occurs through grueling abduction experiences or, in some cases, "enlightened contact." The key point or question becomes, "Why are our normal senses or communication channels deemed insufficient?"

The implication is clear. If there is going to be an integration of two such divergent viewpoints, either we have to develop our paranormal sensibilities to communicate better, or these creatures will have to become more in line with speaking regular Earth languages. That, of course, presupposes that there is going to be an integration of separate cultures which is not necessarily the case. Potential integration of species is not really the crucial point. The fact that the information behind the UFO and related phenomena has remained hidden classifies it as "occult" simply because it is hidden from view.

If Man is going to evolve, he has to account for quantum realities and all possibilities that are before him. But, it is not enough to just consider all possibilities at once. That can jam one's mind with too much information and will cause an overload that cannot be processed. Insane asylums are filled with beings that cannot process and integrate information. Sometimes those creatures have the right information, but they cannot relate it properly to their current environment. Others refuse to integrate with ordinary reality. All of this has to do with what I earlier described as the "digestion process." As Mankind makes its quantum leap, or is forced to cope with the times ahead, he will be dealing with all possibilities and probabilities. At the very least, this means opening the door a little bit to chaos.

People who embrace flying saucer or occult phenomena with too much relish often become very confused and undermine their own interface with ordinary reality. This is basically taking on too much chaos. There has to be a healthy ratio between chaos and order. If there is too much order in one's life, one needs some chaos to create interest. If not, one will be very bored. If there is too much chaos, one needs to increase the amount of order. Otherwise, one will be very confused and possibly be at the mercy of very chaotic forces. Harnessing an optimum ratio between chaos and order is the key to surfing occult phenomena, surviving the Apocalypse, or just plain living. This is a stable reference point by which one can willingly increase or decrease the amount of order or chaos in one's life. It is an excellent tool.

If one is going to face the prospect of parallel realities and universes, one had best be prepared. You already live juxtaposed against a sea of quantum realities. The primary difference between now and the past is that these realities were hidden from view and did not have to be dealt with. Times have changed. It is therefore advisable to pick your realities wisely. You have plenty of choice in the matter. Some realities will serve you and others will be more difficult. The amount of fun you might have with the various realities you choose should also be taken into consideration.

7

BEHOLD A PALE HORSE

THE FOLLOWING TRANSMISSION IS FROM A PARALLEL UNIVERSE

When I first studied goetia, I could have chosen any reality. I could have studied with a magical order and become very caught up in ceremony, pomp, and bric-a-brac. Instead, I experienced a reality of laughter. Perhaps I was just lucky, but maybe I should also admit that this was not the only thing going on in my life at the time. Actually, I was involved with another very peculiar study and that has to do with the subject of white noise, a term that signifies the sum of all possible frequencies across the spectrum. In some respects, one could consider white noise to be the sum total of all inevitabilities or realities because white noise has no limits.

Normally, the term "white noise" is used in conjunction with the discordant hisses and chaotic sounds you hear on a radio when it is not adjusted to a specific station that plays music or whatever. To sit and listen to white noise can be a bit much, but one of my friends pointed out that it could also be accessed by looking at the "snow" on a television. When you turn your television to a channel where there is no transmission received, you will usually see "snow" or a visual representation of white noise. If one begins to focus and concentrate on the actual picture, one can see that there is a lot more going on than just a bunch of dots shaking. One can see certain patterns repeat. Additionally, the brain is synchronizing with patterns and frequencies that it is not used to seeing. If one is trained or disciplined, or just plain lucky, one can get a glimpse of other realities.*

As I said earlier, I had been laughing my head off and having a grand old time. I noticed that food began to taste really good, but I am quick to point out, however, that this was not the "Marijuana munchies." Each meal could be an experience, but my increase in taste was also complemented by an increase in feeling, hearing, sight, and other perceptions. One morning, after having a hot bath and a late breakfast, I sat in front of my television and watched the television snow. I was deeply involved in a state of focused concentration when I heard the phone ring. It was the first time I had heard the phone ring in some time. Instead of being annoyed at being dragged away from my "meditation," I welcomed it as part of the experience.

A mysterious but calm voice spoke into the phone, "Hi, this is Phil. It's great to have a good laugh, isn't it?"

It was decidedly odd that someone would know that I had been laughing so much. While I did not question his apparent telepathy or the synchronicity of his statement, I had no idea who "Phil" was. I scanned my mind to see if there was some Phil that I knew and had forgotten about.

"There's nothing better than laughter," I said, playing along to the tune of this stranger who had mysteriously engaged me. "Did you hear the one about the Irish donkey?" I asked him.

"Yeah, I showed him myself," he laughed, repeating the punch line of an old Gaelic joke.

I then began laughing and he followed suit, but I still had no idea who this person really was. All I knew was that we were laughing in sympathy. In the background, the white noise blared on the screen.

"Why did you call, Phil?" I asked. "I mean, I haven't heard from you in a very long time."

---

* This activity is not advised for epileptics, people prone to seizures, or anyone with physical, emotional, or mental dysfunctions. While certain mind-altering drugs would certainly enhance the perceptions concerning white noise, these are not advised. It should also be mentioned that most people might not experience anything by looking at a television with snow. Being surrounded by a video wall which includes the ceiling and floor would, however, give a much better opportunity of experiencing something, but such a set-up is financially prohibitive for most. It is not necessary either.

I was pretty sure by now that I did not really know this person, but I assumed there was some odd force at work. Maybe he even had the wrong phone number. In any case, my words had been designed to throw him off guard by pretending I knew who he was in order to gauge his response.

"Well, you might think you've done pretty well for yourself by laughing your way into nirvana, but there's some work to be done. You have studied time travel, but you're not really time traveling. Well, perhaps I should say that you haven't done enough. Let me put it this way. The Seventh Seal, or your crown chakra, has got to open up completely."

To make a rather long and involved story short, our conversation ended when the phone line began to sound like static or white noise. My state of utter euphoria had also subsided by this time, but when it did, it was replaced by a warm feeling of well being and the best countenance I had ever known. The patterns I saw via the white noise were only of the pleasant variety. Phil never did identify himself on the phone, but that may have had to do with the fact that I never asked him to. In any event, I was very happy and was experiencing the deepest peace I could imagine.

As nothing remains the same forever, I was eventually interrupted from my peaceful state. One night, I fell asleep in front of a television full of snow. When I woke up in my arm chair, I remember witnessing St. Elmo's fire crackling around my house. Well, it might not have gone around the entire house, but I certainly saw it go by my window a couple of times. It was the middle of the night, and no one in the neighborhood could account for such a disturbance. The only thing I knew was that I now had a very specific set of memories that may have come from a dream or from somewhere else. The memories, however, were quite detailed and much better ingrained than my normal memories. I will repeat it as best I can.

Somehow, I had suddenly and inexplicably found myself in a city of ruins, and there, staring me in the face was the golden horse from the Montauk Project that was said to be resting on a pedestal at 6037 A.D. in the future. For those of you who are not already familiar with the Montauk Project story, this golden horse was a key but enigmatic feature of the legend. According to various accounts, time travellers from the Montauk Project were sent to this locale in 6037 A.D. where they witnessed this statue of a golden horse amidst a ruined city. About the only thing known about it was that it was a marker in time. The horse that I saw was exactly similar to the accounts I had heard about it except that it was not exactly gold. It was a very pale gold if gold at all. I was not even sure if it was the same horse from the Montauk Project, but it sure looked like it. There was only problem. There was a man sitting on the horse. He was wearing a T-shirt that had the words "Horselover FAT" printed on it. All of a sudden, everything began to make a little bit more sense.

Horselover Fat is an alternative name (not a pen name) for a well known science-fiction author by the name of Phillip K. Dick. His credits include the story for *Total Recall* and *Blade Runner*, two movies which were suggestive of experiences similar to the Montauk Project. The name Horselover Fat is featured in Dick's novel *VALIS,* an autobiographical work of fiction which was written in both the first and third person at the same time. This was a unique literary trick in which he referred to himself as "Horselover Fat," a name he chose after studying the etymology of his own name. *Phillip* is Greek for "horselover" and *dick* is an old Germanic word for "fat."

Seeing "Horselover Fat" on the Golden Horse from the Montauk Project, I now realized that the "Phil" I had heard from on the phone was none other than some representation of the author himself, if not the actual spirit of Phil. There was one minor discrepancy though. The man on the horse had his "last name" spelled with all capital letters. I thought this was a good place to break the ice.

"How come your last name is spelled all in capital letters?"

"Well, you guessed pretty good. My name is really Phil, but I used the name Horselover because I love the golden horse from the Montauk Project. It gets me around. The reason it is so pale, by the way, has to due with some literary insight on my part. If you're going to write about the Seventh Seal, you've got to throw in a Pale Horse, otherwise certain people might feel cheated or suffer extreme disorientation if they read your book.

"You know," he continued, "you used this horse for the cover of *The Montauk Project*, but did you ever consider why you used pink aethyr for the cover of this book?"

"It was suggested to me by an artist," I replied.

"Yes, but I referred to a pink light in my book *VALIS*. When I used to get contacted by that strange force which could only be equivalent to the creative force called God, I used to have perceptions that were not in the range of the spectrum. The only way I could even describe it was as a sort of pink light."

"If you look at the cover closely," I said, "you will see that the pink light is going around the spine of the cover and submerging into a black hole where it then reemerges through the seal. That is the idea of Denny, the illustrator."

"Well, it certainly fits right in. But, you wanted to know about the capital letters in FAT. That stands for the Free Archives of Time."

"That's very clever," I said. "I see that you really do love horses, too, don't you?"

"Yes, that is the synchronicity of how I acquired the name 'Horselover.' It has to do with the fact that I also adore the synchronicity of time. Your ordinary dictionary has a question mark when they contemplate the derivation of the word *horse*. It is really quite obvious if you look at it. *Hor* means "time" and you see that in words like *horology*, the study of time. *Hor* is also suggestive of *whore* which suggests the attributes ascribed to the Goddess Babalon which is a manifestation of Kali, the goddess of time. From Kali, we get words like *calender* which derives from *kala*, a cycle of time in the Vedas. Taking *hor* further, you will find that in a French word like *hor d'oeuvre* (which means 'outside the main course') *hor* means outside. It can also refer to a boundary. So, perhaps you understand why I love horses. So, *hor* is not only "time," but it is a whore which suggests love. Time and love are all wrapped together and that shows up in the name Horselover. But, I think you have heard enough from me. I have introduced you to the concept of the horse as representing the boundary of time, but perhaps you should talk to the horse yourself."

As I mulled over my admiration for Phil's insight into the horse, St. Elmo's fire began to crackle around the pale horse and Horselover Fat disappeared. The horse began to fade out, transform, and fade back in. It was still a pale horse, but it seemed familiar. I was sure I had seen it before, but I was not sure. My focus on the horse increased to the point where I could see its lips moving. It then spoke to me. I then realized that my mind had mocked up the only talking horse it could muster from the depths of my subconscious. It was from a television show I saw as a child and the horse's name was Mr. Ed.

"Hello, I'm Mr. Ed. Where's Wilbur?"

Even though I understood what was happening, I was irritated as I hated the TV show that was called *Mr. Ed*, a campy television show from the 1960's which featured a man named Wilbur who owned a talking horse. Although I detested Mr. Ed showing up at all, I soon realized that I should treat this experience as a dream and analyze it as such.

Here I was at the furthest stretch of consciousness imaginable to me. I was an author of the Montauk Project books which feature a horse in 6037 A.D., an extreme marker in the construct of time itself. In fact, I was really tired of hearing people ask me about the horse. Even to Preston and Duncan, the two who had originally accounted for its existence, the golden horse was pretty much a mystery. Now, I took stock of myself and realized that maybe this was my consciousness trying to tell me something. At least, it was some form of consciousness trying to tell me something. Overcoming my destestation for the TV show known as *Mr. Ed*, I decided that I did not hate the horse itself. I decided I would communicate with it.

"There is no Wilbur," I finally said. "How do you justify your existence?"

"Well, why not? You know, you've been writing and talking about the fully activated human brain. That provides for all possibilities, including the possibilities generated by dreams. There are NO limits to the imagination and the cross references that ensue when something like the Pale Horse is invoked. After all, don't you remember the Hall of Infinite Realities?"

Suddenly, I recalled the Hall of Infinite Realities. Many years ago, an artist came to a lecture I was giving. He had a beautiful pencil sketch that he wanted to share with me. The artist explained that, one evening, he dreamt of going out to Montauk Point, long before there was any book on the subject, and accessed an underground structure that was identified as the Hall of Infinite Realities. It was beautifully studded with orbs, planets, and about every piece of architecture you could associate with a galaxy or solar system. This artist titled his work "The Hall of Inifinite Realities." Not until "Mr. Ed" reminded me of it did I recall it.

"Look it," the horse spoke up again, "if you and others really want to know the truth, you had all better get up to snuff on the fact that EVERY POSSIBLE REALITY has validity. Further, it is already being played out on some plane of existence. It is no longer possible, relevant, or shrewd to deny such. "

"Why?" I asked.

"Because you are at the END OF TIME. I am Hor — the goddess of time. They derived the name for the Egyptian god Horus from me. The Pale Horse is really a reference to a horse of white gold which has all of its cranial and cosmic circuits activated. That is why the horse is a marker in time as described in the Montauk Project. We are at the border of realities and that includes timelines."

The horse known as Mr. Ed next began to morphogenetically transform into different horses. I was in a dreamlike state that featured state-of-the-art holographic representation. I saw the horses of my youth that I knew from television. There was Fury, Flicka, Silver, Trigger, and many others. Finally, after several more manifestations of different horses, "Mr. Ed" came back.

"I hope you see that I am not just a stupid talking horse from television."

"Well, I hope you don't think that I'm just a stupid spirit-person from the so-called real world."

"That brings me to why you are here and have accessed VALIS: the Vast Active Living Intelligence System."

For those of you who are not familiar with Dick's work, VALIS is a concept conceived and/or encountered by Phil Dick wherein the universe includes a Vast Active Living Intelligence System which is messianic in nature as it is a good force which is trying to correct or redeem the original mistakes that took place after the Fall. The book should be consulted for further details, but VALIS is essentially a network of consciousness dedicated toward redeeming spiritual beings.

"Goetia is not the only system that activates the human brain," the horse continued, "but western civilization sure hangs in the balance over the precepts and conjurations that have been carried out in the name of it."

"I am also aware," I said to the horse, "that Phil Dick believed the Christian fish symbol, which is really just an expression of the vesica pisces, was meant to symbolize another 'original' dimension or home universe that we could all revert to if only we could remember it or the codes which make it memorable."

"That's one way to put it," he said. "The original disciples of the Christic energy really did access this home universe and that's why they were never afraid to die. Being relieved of their earthly misery was a small price to pay for seeing all of their loved ones in the other world. But, things took a different turn on Earth when Saul fell off his horse. I mean, why do you think the horse bucked him off?"

"Wasn't it a bolt of light or something?"

"Same difference, as you will soon see. In any case, what happened with that religion happens with all positive movements on Earth that seek to let in the light of truth. There is an insidious virus which Horselover Fat explained so well in *VALIS*. In other words, the saving grace factor of humanity or civilization is transmuted into the enemy. This happened in the case of the early Jews. Their body politic evolved into something that would kill a messianic force. Eventually, the so-called messianic force assumes the presiding office of the enemy which was housed in Rome. Rome used to "Romanize its enemies." That meant making them Roman citizens so that they had a vested stake in the Empire. The Christic energy literally ate away at the foundations of an Empire that had just reached its peak. Romanizing the Christians and the Jews did not work. Instead, they acquired the talismans or holy relics of both religions as they sacked the temple in Jerusalem. Then, over time, they dawned the costumes of Christianity and continued the Roman administrative bureaucracy and reaffirmed that 'all roads lead to Rome.' As Phil Dick said, 'the Empire never ended.' In your world, you would be surprised at how many power lines still lead to Rome. The same thing happened with the Muslims, too. A religious leader comes to correct the mistakes of the past, but once the correction is done, the old guard infiltrates the new guard and the Empire continues.

"And, remember one thing. The *Book of Revelation* is based on earlier sources. It was a work of political and religious expediency that was tailored to the times of the Roman Empire. If you read the original sources, you will understand. Latter day Christians came to be in league with the Empire and used the *Book of Revelation* as an enemy doctrine to browbeat, scold and intimidate people."

At that point, the talking horse I knew as Mr. Ed was surrounded by St. Elmo's fire, a "special effect" which was becoming quite familiar and losing any possible intimidation factor. Mr. Ed disappeared. Now, here I was on an extreme orbit of consciousness that reached far beyond the bounds of ordinary and mundane awareness. Feeling as if I was occupying space at the outermost border of the phenomena known as "time," I looked upon the empty pedestal which had just housed Mr. Ed. When everything was quiet and the pedestal was completely empty, a new round of St. Elmo's fire began to crackle and surround the structure. Something new was about to manifest. Although the fireworks no longer impressed me, the horse which replaced Mr. Ed most certainly did. It was the most beautiful steed I had ever witnessed or conceived of, pure white with resplendent wings. I thought to myself that if the archetype of the horse represents time, I was viewing the most splendid example imaginable.

8

BEYOND BAROQUE

THE FOLLOWING TRANSMISSION IS FROM A PARALLEL UNIVERSE

When the brain opens up to all channels, it can be intriguing how one concept leads to another. In this case, I had been looking through my mind's eye at a horse explaining time which, in turn, brought to the consciousness the most sacred horse of ancient Palestine. More aptly, this sacred horse not only symbolizes the ascent to heaven but also holds the key to understanding the ancient ruins and underground beneath what was once Solomon's Temple. When I looked at the resplendent white winged horse, I realized it must be Al Buraq (sometimes 'Al Barak,' 'El Burak' or 'Al Borak'), better known as the horse by which the Prophet of Islam journeyed from Mecca to Jerusalem.

"I do not often talk," said the beautiful stallion, "but your mind has stumbled into an area which is numb to history. There is very little said about me in the Koran or in modern chronicles, but my heritage and pedigree go back well before the Biblical accounts of Enoch. My history is in the very rocks and soil of Mount Moriah, the land upon which the Temple was built. The secrets of this area have remained hidden and mysterious for so many millennia that even the custodians of the secrets have forgotten or lost them. You can, however, crack the code to any mystery through the instrument of etymology. If you will permit me, I will explain how the etymology of my name demonstrates this fact.

"My own namesake has different meanings. One of them is that it means 'lightning' in Arabic. Just as my cousin Pegasus carried the thunderbolts of Zeus, I am the means by which Allah expresses the light and electricity of divinity.

"I flew Muhammad to what is now the Dome of the Rock but which at that time was the ruins of Solomon's Temple. You might refer to what happened there as a space-time project, but this locale has always been known as the crossroads of the continuum. It is where heaven meets Earth and where Solomon built his temple, but this location was well known long before that was constructed. This is the exact rock upon which Abraham began to sacrifice his son. This rock was also slept upon by Jacob (who wrestled with an angel — from which the name Israel was said to be derived) when Jacob's Ladder manifested before him. This was the same ladder upon which the Prophet himself was said to have ascended to heaven. There are countless earlier stories, but I have only mentioned the ones you will readily recognize from history.

"My name is further related to this area when you consider that it signifies "rock." The Arabic word *baraq* is the plural of *burqah* which means 'pebbly ground,' a misnomer for *rock*. You will even find the phoneme *"roc"* in the last syllable of my name. This rock has always served as the philosopher's stone. The word *stone* itself means a concentration of light or spectral light. That is why I was recognized as taking the Prophet to heaven from the rock of Jacob and Abraham. I am the bridge between realities or the reference between time lines.

"This sacred rock sits on the promontory that is known as Mount Moriah, a name whose true etymology has been lost to scholars. I have witnessed many adventures and absurdities in this region throughout history, all of which have been chronicled by the patriarchy. Most of these accounts have the area first being settled by the seventh son of Adam who is known by the Semitic name of Enoch which means 'initiated' or 'dedicated.' In Greek, it refers to the 'inner eye.' Inspired by a dream, Enoch built an underground temple with his son Methuselah. This consisted of nine vaults, each of which represents a sephiroth from the tree of life. The deepest vault was the keystone which holds up all the other vaults, and above them, the two pillars of the Temple itself. Within the deepest vault, was a porphyry (which means purple) stone upon which Enoch inscribed the greatest secret in the world and which is deemed to hold up the entire structure of the universe. Upon two golden deltas (triangles) did Enoch write the language of the angels who communicated with him. The two pillars, eventually named Joachim and Boaz, themselves were metaphorically indestructible but only to the degree they were sustained by the great secret. Upon these pillars did Enoch inscribe the art of building and the sciences in order that they not be lost by the coming flood which he foresaw.

"All of these stories are an analogy for the architecture of this universe, but it was an architecture that was to be sought after as if it were powerful real estate. The patriarchy borrowed and created a name called Melchizedek who was said to have come after the flood whereupon he became King of Salem. Melchizedek means "king of the pillars." The area is ripe with other legends which include it being the burial place of Adam and the actual location where Christ was crucified. The underground waterways were used by King David to overcome the Philistines.

"If you notice these stories, all of them concern men; and there is no mention of any women of any significance, except perhaps in the name Moriah which is a women's name. As I said, the etymology of this word has been lost to scholars, but it can be seen in the name itself. Moriah stems from *Mor-Io* which can be better understood as *Mor-Iao*. This is only a clue to the true keepers of the knowledge which was lost: the Moors or Mers. A testimony to this fact can be witnessed by virtue of the *Moor's Gate* which is one of the four entrances to the Dome of the Rock. Despite this entrance being named the *Moor's Gate*, there is no common history involving Moors at the Temple Mount.

"The Moors or Mers were the mariners of the sea, and their etymology can be traced back to Meru or Mu. The Moors inspired legends of the original Mer-men, ancient men of the sea who settled civilization. Consider them to be like the pilot and tug boat crew who ushered Noah and the Ark into the harbor. The Maori natives of New Zealand are just one example of the Moorish namesake and influence. In that sense, *Maori* means "people of another land." The Moors traveled to many lands. They facilitated and oversaw the emergence of the Egyptian civilization from Atlantis and fostered the development of the Arabian peninsula and helped bring Vedic culture to that locale. To this day, one *moors* a ship to the dock or one is *marooned* at sea.

"There are many secrets beneath the Dome of the Rock, but the Moor's Gate is the key. It sits there in simple remembrance, but do not forget it as it is your entry point to understanding the mysteries of this locale.

"In Biblical history, the area of Mount Moriah was owned by Arvana the Jebusite. King David paid him for the property as the authors wanted no dispute about the property and its rightful ownership. In common practice, this is a legendary justification for occupation of the land.

"Arvana the Jebusite's name is interesting. Jebel means mountain in Arabic and *Arvana* is a Sanskrit root which refers to the origin or birth of horses. This places Mount Moriah as the mountain of horses where *mor* is similar to *mare*, a female horse. It also suggests that Moriah is the birthplace of horses."

"Well," I said, "the Stables of Solomon were famous for housing horses underneath Mount Moriah. The Templars themselves used those stables."

"Those stables could house vast armies and did so," said Al-Buraq. "Before that, however, there was a deeper mystery in my identity as a horse. When we mention horses, we are talking about the boundaries of time, and there is a land which time has forgot of which modern day Jerusalem is only a small part. That is the land of horses: Arabia.

"Arabia was originally known as Arabistan. If you look in the dictionary, they will tell you that 'arab' means 'desert wanderer' or some such; but, if you look at the actual history, you'll find that it was known as Arabistan. This derived from the Sanskrit term *Arvasthan* which means 'Land of the Horses.' The Vedic culture used to breed prize horses in this region. It had such a splendid reputation that the land became known as *Arva-Sthan* where *arva* means horse and *sthan* means place.

"Vedic worship in Arabia centered around the Sabian or Sabean region and its most holy shrine, the *Kaaba*. The Queen of Sheba or Sabia is the most famous character from this region. It was her union with Solomon which symbolized the unification of the Patriarchal Light of David with the Feminine Ray of the Crescent Moon. Although it is mostly obscured and under-emphasized in common discussions, the Temple of Solomon was a tribute to male and female polarity. It was loaded with healthy feminine attributes and pagan worship. In actuality, this land and shrine once belonged to Sheba, and it was her wisdom alone that perpetrated the agent legends. When the authors of the Bible came along, they could not deny her influence. The story was changed so that Solomon appeared to be the wise man.

"Further, it was upon horses that the trade routes were established and the wisdom of Sabia was transmitted. The Moors were the best horsemen in the world and they made all this possible."

"Wait," I said. "I didn't know the Moors were such great horsemen. I knew they were the most skilled sailors of antiquity. I mean, they were using astronomy for celestial navigation long before Prince Henry the Navigator ever came along," I said.

"Where do you think he learned it from?" the horse replied. "Sometimes, people do not make the obvious connections. The Moors were indeed some of the best horsemen of history, but they were much more than sailors and equestrians. Did you ever consider why they were so adept with horses and ships? These were the instruments by which they carried the lightning or light of wisdom and preserved the sacred torch which was symbolically lit over the Library of Pharos at Alexandria. The Moors were not initially Muslims, but they adapted that religion and circulated their wisdom throughout the Iberian Peninsula. After the Spanish Inquisition, they were forced to transfer their seat of wisdom to Italy, but they did this through my very namesake. You will find that, in Florence, the Catholic Counter-Reformation was expressed through both the artistic and musical periods known as Baroque. This artistic style was known not only for its ornamented style but for its metaphysical attributes. It was followed by Rococo which was suggestive of the fairy tale. People do not realize it, but the word *baroque* is derived precisely from my name, Al Buraq."

"I thought you said your name means 'lightning' and 'pebbly ground,'" I said.

"Yes, it does," the beautiful horse replied, "but, like Hebrew letters, my name has a multitude of meanings. I have laughed at etymologists who have directly denied my influence on the word *baroque*. There is plenty of historical evidence that is sitting right in front of their face. In English, *baroque* signifies elaborate and even grotesque ornamentation. Whether in good or bad taste, something described as baroque always causes the viewer to stretch their boundaries. The etymology has always been controversial, but you can trust me for I am the very reason for the word's existence. The French borrowed it from the Portuguese who borrowed it from the Moors.

"I am not always thought of as a horse, you know," said the great white steed. "In some versions, I have been painted with a horse's torso, sometimes thought of as a mule's torso, but with the head of a woman and the tail of a peacock. This bizarre rendition is what caused the Portuguese and the French to refer to anything fantastically absurd or grotesque as 'baroque.' You see, my name is associated with anything that is considered bizarre or surrealistic and where components of one matrix have been mixed with that of another."

"I find what you say fascinating," I said, "and I hope it explains to people why I have chosen to write such a baroque book myself, but I have to ask you something about the name Moriah, the land of which you seem to be the patron myth."

"What is it?" the horse asked me.

"I could not help but notice the primary phoneme in Moriah is *mor* which is very similar to the words *morte or muerte* which signify "death."

"With that," said the great steed, "you have stumbled upon an even greater mystery, and that is the very mystery of my namesake. The most mysterious and obscured locale beneath the Dome of the Rock on Mount Moriah houses the souls of the dead. It is called the 'Well of Souls.' It was even recognized during the days of Solomon's Temple, but the history was always kept hidden. It is my greatest secret. You see, I have been depicted with various component parts from different matrixes because I represent the potential of a realignment or reconstruction of such parts. I symbolize a new reality, including a new reality beyond death. This is why, since time immemorial, I have been chosen as the archetypal patron of Mount Moriah."

"Tell me more of the Well of Souls," I said. "The name itself suggests that we can draw from it as if it were a resource. I would like to know more of the Well of Souls."

"That," he said, "is another story."

9

THE WELL OF SOULS

Although it is not recognized as such, the most popular and celebrated depiction of the Well of Souls in our modern culture can be seen in the movie *Raiders of the Lost Ark*. Although this film serves as an excellent graphic example for certain aspects of archetypal phenomena, it contains a very false and misleading reference to the Well of Souls. In *Raiders*, they refer to the Well of Souls as being at Tanis, Egypt, where the Ark is held. In actuality, there are no known historical or mythological references to the Ark ever being at Tanis. However, the Well of Souls is a very ancient concept that has crept its way into various cultures. The most well known of these locales is the Dome of the Rock which is erected on the site of what was once Solomon's Temple in Jerusalem. Beneath this very rock is a chamber that is known as the Well of the Souls. Although the area is filled in with dirt, it is known to hide a much deeper conduit or cavity. It is known that the area beneath the Dome of the Rock is loaded with tunnels and caverns which include waterways.

According to very ancient legend, the Well of Souls represents all the dead ancestral souls who are to be summoned at the Day of Judgement. In the movie *Raiders*, the screenplay depicted the Well of Souls as manifesting out of the Ark of the Covenant itself. Although this unleashing of souls might better have originated from the Well of Souls, there is an esoteric tie-in this depiction to the Ark. As was explained in *The Black Sun*, the substance inside the Ark, as depicted in the movie, was manna. This is known as the food of the gods as it was ingested in ancient times to fully awaken the brain and hopefully create a state of spiritual continuity after physical death. Its physical properties not withstanding, manna is an archetypal representation of the conduit between man and the Creative Force.

In most languages, *manna* or *mana* originally referred to magical properties, and this was used in conjunction with the Goddess. The *Old Norse* language designated the word *man* to refer to the female of the species. This is related to *men* or *moon* and is where we get the word *menses*. As patriarchal culture vanquished the matriarchal culture, the word for female was appropriated and *man* was designated to signify a male. Hence, *manna* was originally thought of as feminine magic.*

Palestine was not the only site to house a well of souls. Prior to Rome and during its heyday, a well of souls could be found beneath the "lapis manalis" in the Forum. Lapis means stone and manalis was named after the goddess Mana and her male consort Mantua. Together, they presided over the ancestral well of souls which included the entire panorama of dead spirits. Ghosts came under the domain of Mana. Once a year, people would pay homage to the Goddess Mana or Mania and these celebrations gave rise to the adjective *manic* which derives from the wanton behavior that is associated with so many Roman holidays.

Today, *mania* refers to a state of relative madness or excitement. Originally, these features were more socially acceptable in society and conduits were made for manic expression. Manic behavior was also revered as being divinely inspired. Although there were many representations of this principle, the god Dionysos was a major patron of this energy.

In *Raiders*, the Nazis are consumed because they cannot reconcile the chaotic forces which represent not only the ancestral spirits of the past but the angelic hierarchy itself. The hero, Indiana Jones, employs a discriminator by closing his eyes and survives the ordeal. In other words, he did not take on too much chaos. The idea of souls escaping through an orifice or a device like the Ark

---

* Additionally, the word "mass" originally meant discharge of the menses with rituals of old utilizing the menstrual blood as a source of life, inspiration, and magic. The Catholic Mass is a very distorted version of what was once the original Mass.

is no different than the idea of Pandemonium which combines both the names *Mania* and *Pan*. In Roman mythology, the satyr-god Pan was the male counterpart of this excited energy. As Christianity developed, Pandemonium became defined as the "House of All Demons." Besides being the name for a deity, *pan* means "bread" (similar to mana or to that which in consumed in the Eucharist) in Latin, but it also means "all" as in the term Pan-American.

It is clear that the Christians cultivated a state of mind where one was completely terrorized when one thought of Pandemonium or a "house of demons." Much of this misunderstanding is that the word *daemon* was never properly understood. *Mana* also meant the "Mother of All" which is the Mother of Pan.

The Well of Souls, as a symbol of the female organ, is not really much different than the vesica pisces as both are positioned as the conduit to All. Any free spirit can potentially incarnate through the vagina. The fact that there is a Well of Souls beneath the Dome of the Rock is an amazing example of how archetypal phenomena weaves its way into human drama. The legends of that locale, as said earlier, are rooted far deeper into history than the Bible suggests.

The Well of Souls is completely open-ended. It not only represents all the souls and potential souls whoever existed, it represents the infinite quantum stream(s) of consciousness. The Temple itself was a structure of containment and is based upon the concept of orderliness. The Temple has traditionally been aligned with the solar deity. The first syllable of the name *Solomon* is *sol* and is suggestive of the sun. The last syllable is *mon* which is akin to terms such as *menta*, *amenta* or *moon*, all suggestive of the lunar energy which represents the Well of Souls. Traditionally, Solomon united with many pagan wives and his success was dependent upon his intercourse with many different people and nations.

The most important thing about the Well of Souls is what it will mean to you personally as well as to the collective consciousness. The truth of quantum consciousness and the Well of Souls work hand-in-hand. Both not only imply but dictate the theme that I continue to repeat: all possible potentialities exist. Anything that could or possibly might occur will occur. It is this very idea which the Catholic Church and many other Christian institutions fought so hard to overcome. There is only one way and it is their way. All other souls, viewpoints, or potentials must be bottled up like a genie. The problem with bottling something up is that it will eventually be released.

Western Civilization has been conditioned to live in a rather bottled up way. Of course, opening up to every spirit or reality in the book is not a very fun way to live either. It might broaden one's horizons and even make one "quantum chic" in some circles, but there are plenty of realities out there that none of us particularly want to contemplate or live out. One does not want to be a slave to quantum thinking. This means employing a discriminator which allows the creative forces to flow in while at the same time not having it overwhelm your life or well being. This is the same as maintaining a healthy ratio between order and disorder in one's life. Again, it encourages one to choose one's reality wisely. Again, it is surfing the wave between order and chaos.

When we consider the collective consciousness, however, there are other issues at stake. The Masons have built their entire lore over the concept of what actually held up the Temple. As the Temple is in ruins, this suggests that the secret itself is lost or not in its proper place in the continuum. If we consider once again that the Temple is a structure of containment and the Wells of Souls a complete stream of infinity, this implies that there is or should be a bridge or conduit between the physical temple itself and the Well of Souls. As the real life Well of Souls is either obscured or filled in with dirt, this hints at other problems. When the quantum stream of consciousness, as represented by the Well of Souls, is completely cut off, one does not even need a temple as it serves no purpose. Therefore, it stands to reason that man's ability to recognize, rectify, and interface with the Well of Souls would be of primary importance. Located at the crossroads of space-time and representing the bridge to infinite consciousness, the Well of Souls serves as a real life location for Man's greatest mystery.

10

QUANTUM ATTACK

Serving as the quantum bridge between the aethyric world and the physical plane, the Well of Souls has gone largely unnoticed or has been under-emphasized in recorded history. It is, nevertheless, representative of the key paradigm when it comes to understanding how spirit and matter interact. Although I have never really discussed it too much, my own experiences in synchronicity spring from a sphere which is commensurate with the phenomena surrounding the Well of Souls, particularly where spirit and matter interact. This last statement, if not qualified, might sound too vague and abstract. It is therefore advisable that I address some new ground which will put this in a more understandable format for most readers. This has to do with the subject of remote viewing.

Remote viewing, which has been a popular but very misunderstood and exploited subject, is just one offshoot of this quantum bridge between the physical plane and the so-called aethyric realm. Ever since *The Montauk Project* was written, I have received overtures and letters of enthusiasm from various people who wanted to get me involved and/or interested in remote viewing. These letters were extremely naive and were written by people who had been caught up in the moment of the glamour and potential of remote viewing. Having seen many people go astray on this path, perhaps it is time I comment on why I have never budged in this direction.

First and foremost, the area is ripe with hucksters who are either trying to enrich themselves by offering courses that do not help the aspirant, or there are genuinely talented people who are either mind controlled or carrying out an agenda that is not in the interest of anyone in particular. Remote viewing, however, is a very serious subject.

One of the most talented and scientifically validated remote viewers in history is a gentleman by the name of Ingo Swann. Hailed as the "Father of the Remote Viewers," Ingo has been featured in many large conferences of remote viewers. He is esteemed beyond belief in these circles. Ingo is the author of many books, including free internet editions of his history in remote viewing. There is, however, some interesting history about this gentleman that is largely unknown which also reveals a deeper aspect to some of the mysteries concerning my own work.

Ingo Swann caught the attention of the U.S. Government in a very big way when he demonstrably affected, through mental or psychic processes alone, a supercooled magnetometer that was encased in solid concrete five feet beneath the foundation of the Varian Hall of Physics at Stanford University. This was solidly witnessed by Dr. Arthur Hebbard, Dr. Marshal Lee, and six "doctoral candidates" who were allegedly students of Hebbard. In other tests, Ingo demonstrated an uncanny accuracy when dealing with psi ability.*

This experiment, which took place under the auspices of the Stanford Research Institute, caught the Government's interest for at least two primary reasons. First, they knew they were well behind Russia when it came to psychic spying and psychic warfare technology. Second, anyone who could influence the magnetic field of a nuclear weapon was potentially very dangerous (the guidance systems on nuclear weaponry are based upon a magnetic field). Obviously, this was something neither the intelligence agencies nor the military could let slide by.

Most, if not all, of the original development of Remote Viewing in the Government has been attributed to Ingo Swann. While this is not completely correct, his influence was very large. Others have even sought to rip-off or run with their own versions and have even obscured his contributions to this field. What is

---

* For further information see the article: "The Department of Dirty Tricks;" by Thomas Powers; *Atlantic Monthly*, August 1979; Volume 244, No. 2; pages 33-64.

even more obscured is that Ingo only demonstrated these abilities on a large scale after he had reached the highest levels of Scientology in the late 1960's. In fact, his legendary work was accomplished with two other high level Scientologists known as Hal Puthoff and Pat Price. What is particularly noteworthy about this aspect of the Scientology connection is that when a Congressional committee issued their final report uncovering past scandals of CIA mind-control experiments, including MK-ULTRA, BLUEBIRD, and ARTICHOKE, there was no mention whatsoever of the remote viewing projects. Even more notably absent were the names of the key personnel and the fact that they were full level Scientologists who had intelligence agency backgrounds and were using the Scientology techniques in their research.

I can say without any hint of exaggeration that the entire subject of remote viewing is a shard or offshoot of a phenomena which L. Ron Hubbard and Scientology describe as *exteriorization*. Exteriorization refers to independent perception without reference to the normal perceptic channels of the human body. In other words, you can see, feel, hear, touch, and perceive everything the body can perceive completely independently and irrespective of the body. You never, never, never hear the word exteriorization in New Age, psychotronics or mainstream versions of the subject. Instead, the term "out-of-body experience" is used and is often abbreviated as OBE. The term OBE slowly began inculcating its way into the culture after Ingo's initial experiments and has picked up considerable momentum over the last decade. Similarly, the words *dysfunction* or *dysfunctional* have become prevalently used instead of Hubbard's word which was *aberration*. If people were to call dysfunctional behavior aberration, it would either give too much credence or shine too much light on Hubbard's early work and techniques.

Pat Price, mentioned above as one of Ingo's colleagues, was actually said to have been the most accurate of the remote viewers. According to Ingo's writings, Price complained of someone slipping something into his coffee before he died of a sudden and unexpected heart attack in 1975. Besides this mysterious episode, a so-called "friend" of Price's showed up at the emergency room with "a briefcase full of his medical records" which apparently convinced the emergency room physician to wave an autopsy.

Hal Putoff was the other member of the Scientology trio, and perhaps he was the most powerful of them all. Puthoff worked for the National Security Agency prior to joining Scientology and moving up to a high Scientology level designated as OT III (in Scientology "OT" is an abbreviation for "Operating Thetan" where the word "thetan" is an equivalent to the word spirit). Immediately thereafter, he joined the CIA created remote viewing program at the Stanford Research Institute.

In those early days of OT III, one was not allowed to be a bonafide completion on this level until one fully exteriorized from the body with full perception. Later on, Hubbard modified the expectations on this level and created the level of OT VI where one was expected to be fully and stably exterior from the body. In today's Scientology, the level that was once known as OT VI has been abrogated and is no longer available as a level from Scientology. Substitute levels have replaced it so that the OT VI of yesteryear is no longer what it was nor do they even purport it to be.

In the aftermath of the work at the Stanford Research Institute, Scientology doggedly pursued the Government, including the National Security Agency, using the Freedom of Information Act in an attempt to clean up false reports that the Government had written about it or L. Ron Hubbard. In response, the NSA used very clever wording in responding to the Church's request under the FOIA. On February 14, 1975 they said the following:

"The NATIONAL SECURITY AGENCY (NSA) replies to FCDC's (Founding Church of Scientology of the District of Columbia) FOIA action that it has not established any file pertaining either to FCDC or L. Ron Hubbard, and that it has transmitted no information regarding either to any domestic agencies or foreign governments."

As Scientology pursued their course of investigation, proceedings against the Department of State and the CIA revealed that the NATIONAL SECURITY AGENCY (NSA) had at least sixteen documents concerning Scientology and related organizations. This embarrassed the NSA who had been lying by saying they had no such documents. All of a sudden, when confronted and backed into a corner with the truth, the NSA located all but one document and then took legal action to prevent the release of the

materials on grounds of national security.* This is a rather astonishing fact in itself. What on Earth could a church that was
allegedly a fraudulent setup have to do with national security?

When one realizes that the key remote viewing experiments at
the Stanford Research Institute were done by Scientology OTs
who could exteriorize from their bodies, it is clear that Scientology
would have been deemed a security risk at the highest level of
government. Not only could Scientology OTs exteriorize and
potentially spy on government secret projects, they could conceiv-
ably influence the magnetic factors crucial to the proper instrumentation of nuclear weapons. This includes military secrets and
logistical movements as well. It was only a potential threat, but a
very real one.

There are some vagaries as to the relationship between the
Government and Ingo Swann, Pat Price, and Hal Puthoff. Some
accounts have them as government spooks who infiltrated
Scientology in order to learn these techniques for their own use.
While this is not necessarily the case, no one can argue that their
connection to the Government make them suspicious on that
count. In the end, they were all up to their waist in Government
connections.

There is an amazing date-coincidence with the time-line of
their work and the subsequent development of the Montauk
Project in the 1970's. Some of the Scientology theorists believe
that the Government's infiltration and attack of Scientology was as
a direct response to the onset of Scientology and the promulgation
of the OT Levels. The Government was definitely researching the
paranormal long before Scientology even existed. Nevertheless,
Scientology was a potent movement that enabled one to operate in
a fashion that was rather unprecedented for normal human beings.
There are countless theories. The facts give cause for ample
speculation. Unfortunately, most of the theories proposed, particularly those by former Scientologists, are lacking in complete-
ness and objectivity although many bring up interesting and
relevant points. It would require too much study at this point for

---

* For further info, see "The FOUNDING CHURCH OF SCIENTOLOGY OF
WASHINGTON, D.C., INC. Appellant, v. NATIONAL SECURITY
AGENCY et al. No. 77-1975. United States Court of Appeals, District of
Columbia Circuit."

me to even try and take on exactly what happened and all of the subsequent ramifications.

To the point of my topic, I will revisit Ingo Swann, the Father of Remote Viewing. If he truly is the Father of Remote Viewing, and no one has really begrudged him this appellation, then that would make L. Ron Hubbard the "Holy Ghost of Remote Viewing." Ingo sought to distance himself from Scientology in the past, and he also mentioned being persecuted "in the minds of some" as being a Scientologist. Instead, he makes a distinction as always being "a student of Mr. Hubbard's ideas and techniques." After all, it was Hubbard who not only devised original techniques for exteriorizing from the body but who studied out-of-body experiences intensely since the early 1950's.

People sometimes think that former Scientologists would be buddies or the like. This is not only decidedly untrue, but Ingo, by all appearances, wants to keep at a distance from me. There is an interesting story behind this. One time I went to a conference in Greenwich Village to meet up with a friend. She was standing off of a balcony and was watching me engage in conversation with a UFO advocate who was grilling me about Montauk. While I spoke, I noticed this strange little man circling me and behaving oddly. He would stop for a while, move to a different location and stop. It was very irregular. When I joined my friend, she looked surprised and said, "I can't believe you didn't connect with Ingo!"

When I asked her what she was talking about, she had noticed that Ingo and I were practically circling each other but did not make verbal contact. She thought it was quite odd that we did not communicate. I was in the middle of a communication with a person who was asking me very intentful questions about Montauk and wanted serious and responsible answers. It was taking up all of my attention. I never did talk to Ingo nor did I see him again on that day. I heard he left shortly thereafter or perhaps he just made himself inaccessible. Years later, my friend told me that Ingo was adamant about going to a picnic where some of her friends were going to be. She heard that he expressed a strong interest in monitoring her psi fields. Apparently, he had been monitoring mine as well. After returning home, I eventually asked Preston Nichols if he had ever encountered Ingo Swann. The answer was yes. Many years ago, when he was first investigating the Montauk

Project, Ingo had come to him under a different name and told him to stay away from it. In other words, Ingo was apparently a representative of the Government or Psi Ops Corps and was telling Preston not to look into the Montauk Project.

In subsequent years, I have tried to have people contact Ingo on my behalf. I have been told that he does not want to talk about his government connections and that he seems to go blank or just not respond when Montauk is mentioned. There also have been reports that he has blanked out utterly during certain periods of his life. I cannot personally vouch for this last statement, but I can certainly say that he seems to blank out on the subject of Montauk.

There is no question that Ingo has demonstrated some paranormal abilities. He has also done some valid research and come up with some interesting information. His work should be studied before any sort of judgment or conclusion should be placed upon him, and judgments are very suspect anyway. My point in bringing him into the fray is for two reasons. First, he is a rather hallowed and recognized figure on the paranormal circuit who utilized high level Scientology techniques in order to demonstrably link spirit or mind with matter. The second reason is to show how incestuous and subversive the remote viewing community is. After the release of *The Montauk Project: Experiments in Time*, wherein Preston gave a description of remote viewing which was unique and new for its time, a whole remote viewing community and cottage industry began to emerge. Much of it seemed designed to steal whatever thunder Preston had created and tended to act as a counter-wave to the Montauk information. After all, here were "government psychics" telling you "the truth."

I am familiar with the techniques Ingo Swann utilized from his Scientology days. Additionally, I am also trained in how to spot when these techniques have been incorrectly used or have led people astray. There is a good reason why I have resisted people's desire to have me become involved in the remote viewing phenomena. When you put somebody in an exterior state from the body, they are in a vulnerable state and are predisposed to the reactive part of their unconscious mind kicking in on them, sometimes in a very hard manner. Sometimes this factor is minimal and sometimes it is null, but there are also more subtle factors that come into play. When one operates on this level, negative or painful indoctrinations in one's past lives or quantum lives can incline one toward conditioned or programmed behavior. This is why Hubbard left these levels to be pursued only after a state of "Clear" had been attained. That is a state of being where one has literally cleared all of one's negativity or conditioned predispositions from the past.

In the case of Ingo Swann, there is another factor at work. Many websites have him listed as being gay. This is no revelation to many of the people I have spoken to who either knew him or are familiar with him. In his own writings, he does mention having an affair with a women from the United Nations who led him into Scientology. This would indicate bisexuality at the least. I bring this up not to malign him in anyway because we now live a culture where everyone has human rights, and it certainly should be that way. My point here is to bring up a factor with his Scientology forays as well as his endorsements of Hubbard's teachings. Many people have stated that Hubbard was anti-gay or the like. This was not true. In fact, he did not discriminate against them within the organization. But, his research, which was not based upon opinion but observation, was that gay people are self-destructive and covertly hostile to their environment and/or the people in it. This is due to painful indoctrinations they have suffered either in their current life or in past lives (which would also embrace quantum lives). This was usually very deeply buried.[*]

One can also argue that some men like men because they want to like men. This is true, but one can also ask the rhetorical question of why such a person chose to be in a male body instead of a female body where one would experience a more balanced condition. Of course, most people are not aware of "choosing" any body. This is where the painful indoctrination comes in. Most people are not aware of any states of consciousness outside the realm of normal homo sapiens. If one awakens in their current life only to discover that they have acquired a body of the wrong sex, this person is obviously in a predicament where he is wrestling with his own past. One has to come to terms with one's own "self-

---

[*] It should be noted that this is only an abbreviated summary of Hubbard's information. While many of my own personal observations coincide with his, this is not my conclusion or full statement on the matter. Gays are a complicated subject.

destructive" decisions of the past. In the end, it all comes down to a matter of choice and that state of mind which I have labelled quantum self-determinism.

Another aspect of the gay factor is that the Montauk Project thrived on programming individuals through homosexual techniques. If the gay attributes ascribed to Ingo are true, and I have no reason to believe they are not, he would be a prime candidate for tampering. Based upon his resistance to discussing Montauk, this would seem a decided probability.

Besides the above, there is another factor which makes Ingo suspect with respect to serious investigation of either the Philadelphia Experiment or Montauk Project. At one time, he was seriously involved in his remote viewing research with Jacques Vallee. In the book *The Philadelphia Experiment Murder*, it was demonstrated that Vallee had deliberately written disinformation about the Philadelphia Experiment in an article in *The Journal of Scientific Exploration* entitled *The Anatomy of a Hoax*.

Although Ingo is a brilliant man and a successfully proven psychic, his actions have led me to conclude that he either worked for the Government from day one or that he was tampered with. His talk about his heterosexual experience was prior to Scientology. It is entirely possible that, after achieving a potent state of consciousness, he was taken in and conditioned to respond in certain ways on different subjects. In his writings, Ingo claims to have joined the intelligence community when he realized that all military failures are basically intelligence failures. He sought to help the Government ward off the Soviet menace. This is a very suspect view for someone who indulged in Scientology or the teachings of Hubbard. Hubbard himself believed that all wars were created by cartels who would profit from them, either by money or control. In any case, Ingo Swann was viewing the Cold War as a real event and "patriotically" chose sides. He ended up working for the same people who would conduct an unprecedented raid on the Church of Scientology and end up convicting some of its higher officers.

What was all that fuss really all about? Were Scientology techniques really all the powerful?

11

MAGICK AND SCIENTOLOGY

Hubbard called the Scientology level of OT III "The Wall of Fire" because it was meant to signify a purification. In alchemical terms, this would be a "trial by fire." It was intended to be a very intense but precise procedure that was designed to be administered to people only after a considerable amount of preparation and initiation. People were warned that death could occur if the materials were shown to an individual prematurely or if the processes was not properly administered. Although pieces of the procedure have been released on the internet and elsewhere, I have not heard of people dying off as a result; however, there is something to be said for that idea. If you ever had occasion to hang around the inner sanctum of Scientology's advanced courses, you would find that it was not uncommon for people to occasionally find themselves in very precarious positions or even relative states of acute psychosis. There was a term Hubbard used for people who went out of control on this level. It was called "freewheeling." This was where people would be agitated to the point where they could not sleep. This sometimes required extensive intervention by various Scientology personnel. If the known procedures were properly administered, these symptoms were not hard to alleviate.

The press and others on the internet have made light of the OT III procedures in many different ways. They never mention, however, that these materials, long before the creation of the internet, were sold on the black market for a pretty penny.

Scientologists, as well as their adversaries and competitors, consider these procedures to be quite potent.

One day, after I had been familiar with the materials for about a year and had completed the OT III level, I was speaking to a friend of mine who had worked as a supervisor for Scientology's advanced courses. I told her that if I had seen these materials early on in my Scientology experience, I was quite sure that it would not have approached anything close to death. Her comment was that I was a relatively stable individual and was not "that type of case." This freewheeling phenomena did not occur in a high percentage of cases, but it did occur and that is why there were warnings.

Over the decades, much fuss has been made over L. Ron Hubbard and Scientology. Most of the fuss is centered at the level of attack where two opponents are going at each other fiercely. Amidst the salvo, the subtler truths are lost. When we recede to the wisdom of what the Chinese call the Tao, one learns to recognize that ferocious anger or passion does not, in the end, overcome much more than itself. One follows the path of water and watches how it patiently seeks the course of least resistance.

Hubbard often stated that he attended the first college class in nuclear physics which was called "Atomic and Molecular Phenomena." His critics like to assail him on the point that his transcripts indicate he failed the class. Unfortunately, they never bring up his side of the story. Hubbard was a brilliant individual who did not conform to the norm. Even at an early age, he was highly aware of quantum phenomena, and he resoundingly rejected the fixed propositions being chanted at him. According to him, he argued with the professor and was going to be failed no matter what. Further, he incorporated the "Law of Affinity" into an entire philosophy which was dedicated to probing the quantum realms. Neither those who assail him nor those who praise him ever positioned him as a quantum explorer, but that is primarily what he was, for better or for worse. Had he toed the line, become a "good student" and completed his matriculation in nuclear physics, he would have ended up spitting out chalk as a professor somewhere and would have become a noble, worthy, and hallowed alumnus. The world would never have known the controversy, high drama and interest surrounding his adventures into magick, the occult, and the region he called *terra incognita*.

Although Hubbard seldom used the term synchronicity to my recall, he took very serious notice of it, particularly when it concerned statistics. For example, he noted that the gross income of Scientology International was directly proportional to the amount of square inches of rust scraped off the *Apollo*. On a ship exposed to the open seas, one has to constantly battle rust or the structure of the ship will literally waste away. When he saw the international stats reported, he noticed that these two factors were in affinity. Although he had no explanation, he said this was very important and to take note of it. To him, the implication was obvious, if you take care of your immediate environment, the exterior environment will act in kind. To this end, he encouraged us to pay attention to the environment and notice what things are in sympathy with each other. It helps one manage life even if it defies apparent logic or programmed thinking patterns.

Scientology was actually far more concerned with rehabilitating the will or intention of the individual. In other words, a person who has gone through life taking it on the chin is someone who is not getting his intention across or getting his way. Scientology procedures were designed to rehabilitate the individual to the point where one is able to place proper values on their own desires. Higher levels of Scientology, and often the lower ones, would or could induce great periods of synchronicity where one suddenly has everything going one's way.

The reason Scientology never created a perfect world is that the ocean of quantum chaos has its own function. When you have mastered one wave of the ocean and ride it to applause on the beach, a bigger wave can come and knock you over. Life and the ocean are both unpredictable propositions.

King Solomon did not build a perfect world either, but his story offers the hope of a unified world where the crossroads of the world meet and a full-fledged conduit to the Creative Force is constructed. How ironic is it that his temple was built over the Well of Souls, a quantum sea of individual spirits who offer an infinite and unpredictable array of potentialities?

Although King Solomon and L. Ron Hubbard both delved deeply into magick, there are great differences in what they did and what they were trying to accomplish. There are, however, some very interesting and sympathetic parallels.

Solomon is the only character in popularized history or legend to have mastered the elemental forces of the jinn. He amassed a fortune unparalleled on Earth and was known not only for his wealth but for a cultural exchange that was unprecedented. Solomon married pagan wives of every persuasion and built temples to their deities. Despite its accomplishments, Solomon's civilization was not a totally free one. The empire was built by slaves and was sustained by excessive taxation. Nevertheless, Solomon commanded the jinn, and the jinn brought about his will. That included slaves to fulfill it. While his empire left a considerable amount to be desired, Solomon's will was supreme. If he willed something, it was done.

People sometimes think of Scientology as a slave empire, too, but that is really not correct. Scientologists are not supposed to be slaves, but none of them would argue against the fact that they are carrying out Hubbard's will. My point here is not for you to think that Scientologists are slaves (in actual fact, some have slave attitudes and others do not), but that Hubbard had harnessed a power that was similar to Solomon's when it came to having his will accomplished. But, as I said, Solomon and Hubbard were not really doing the same thing.

Hubbard was working with individuals in such a way as to give what could be called personal freedom. This means getting rid of your baggage, realizing your own personal power, and then accruing the natural psychic potential that comes naturally as a result. In some cases, such as the crew Ingo Swann worked with, these powers could be quite remarkably demonstrated. There is no record of Solomon working with individuals like this. Instead, he was unifying the world under one banner and building a temple to the Creator. More appropriately, the story of his life serves as a symbolic reference to the conditions of creation. In legend, Solomon was the most powerful king the world has ever known.

There is no question that L. Ron Hubbard also demonstrated an uncanny power that most men will never know. In terms of force and magnitude, the power of a president, which lasts only four years, is somewhat laughable in comparison. It is not the power of a president is funny — it is not. My point is that a president is only a temporal power and spends more time answering to the calls and needs of the people, Congress, lobbyists, and other pressures (including hidden agendas) than he does administering to anything that could be considered his own will. Hubbard, when I lived with him, had a ship full of people (over 400 at one point) who were completely dedicated to carrying out HIS will. Additionally, there were thousands of additional staff across four continents who backed this up. On top of that were regular Scientology staff members and public who also worked towards carrying out his will.

If you accept what I have said thus far at face value, it can be readily realized that Hubbard's personal power and charisma only rose to great levels once he had put together and organized a philosophical practice that administered to the quantum dynamic of the individual. It was only individual people, impressed with his research techniques, which could give him the loyalty and effort required to amass such a huge movement. When you consider that he was, in a sense, lifting his head above the clouds and observing the so-called contents of the quantum universe (including spiritual phenomena) and how it worked, you have a man who was reaching beyond the ordinary bounds of consciousness. To him, this was exploration. He had established a beach head in the quantum universe and was attracting the elements of earth which brought money and power. His motive, however, was not just to attract wealth. That was primarily a war chest for continuing his work which was definitely in a spiritual or quantum reference frame.

The fights and power struggles concerning Scientology are not only symptomatic of typical primate behavior, it obscures the fact that there might be anything of real value involved in the movement at all. The lawsuits, infiltrations and general bad karma have now become the stuff of legend. For many Scientologists and their opponents, baiting the enemy has become a full time preoccupation. The legal and intelligence warfare, on either side, is a far cry from the luxurious state of being exterior outside the body and viewing environments from a distance. One can also adeptly argue that if Scientology can actually enable one to remote view, they should be able to shut down their opponent. But, as I told you, Scientology no longer offers this level to either public or staff. This will cause many to believe that infiltration succeeded. There are many other factors involved and doing a good job of explaining it all might require more than a single book. All I hope to get across at this point is that force breeds counter-force. Subtler ways have their own virtue. I watched these two opposing forces clash in my Scientology days and knew better than to get deeply involved in this drama. I saw infiltration on both sides. The whole point of opposition and stirring things up is to distract one from the truth.

If there are truly peaceful and luxurious states to be experienced via the procedures of Scientology, one has to look in splendorous wonder at the amount of fighting and contentiousness that has gone on surrounding its name. What is really going on here? Is this just typical primate behavior or is it symbolic of something else? Could it be a host of jackals waiting to consume the karmic heart of anyone who fails the test of Ma'at?*

If you study the actual history of Hubbard, in his own words, you will find that he was admittedly fascinated with the mystery cults of the Middle Ages and with Aleister Crowley (the two never did meet face to face) to the point where he referred to him as "his friend." Two of the primary cults of the Middle Ages, and certainly the most famous, were the Knights Templar and the Assassins. Both based their doctrines, to some degree, upon the legends, facts, and circumstance of Solomon's Temple.

In the early years of Dianetics, many people would experience what Hubbard called "going up the pole." This was indeed the same as what people now familiarly recognize as a kundalini experience. It was a state of consciousness where one was exceeding the normal boundaries of perception. It was a form of exteriorization although it was not necessarily pleasant for the individual. Too many times these sort of experiences gated in past experiences in different lives where the individual had been thwarted when in such a free state. Complete spiritual freedom in this universe has never been considered to be an easy task. Rising above the predisposed forces of the universe brings about a counter-reaction. The physical universe is very much a universe of force. When we "fool" or break those lines of force, the "policeman" or security guards come out to check on you and reel

---

* The test of Ma'at refers to the Egyptian myth where the heart of the recently deceased was placed upon a set of scales (which belonged to Ma'at, the female consort of Thoth — Ma'at was sometimes known as Lady Justice) and balanced with a feather. If the heart was heavier than the feather, the candidate (most particularly, his soul and heart) were consumed by jackals who were waiting below in hope that there would be failure.

you in. In the analogy of Solomon, this security force was called the jinn.

In *The Black Sun*, I demonstrated how L. Ron Hubbard's genetic line was intrinsically related to the ancient heritage of Charlemagne and the descendants of the Holy Grail. His brilliant red hair was just one of the symptoms. Besides the grail lineage, this book also revealed a genetic connection to the Prophet of Islam via the secret Celtic clan name of Ahmroun (from which the name Cameron was derived). Ahmroun is spelled Amrin in the popular English editions of the Koran where it not only signifies the family name of Muhamet but of the Virgin Mary. Historically, Muhamet's family were also known as the "Sons of Sheba." Everything comes full circle when we realize that, in the Bible, Christ was from the House of David. Solomon was the child of David and Bathsheba, thus signifying a unification of the bloodlines of Christ and Muhamet. Solomon then marries the Queen of Sheba in what is a historical or legendary reiteration of the two bloodlines.

All of these Biblical and Koranic characters revolve around the myth or history of a union between the patriarchal bloodlines of David mixing with the matriarchal bloodline of Sheba with the Well of Souls serving as the ancestral cornucopia of spirits. At the very least, if only symbolically, this site serves as the link between the quantum world and the physical Newtonian world.

Although my past research indicates Hubbard's bloodline is a part of the Solomonic heritage, that aspect is really not so important. What is important is that Hubbard, Solomon, and even Ingo Swann pierced the veil of the quantum universe in an extraordinary manner. I bring up Ingo again because, in his writings, he refers to a psychic monitor which comes into action in an adversarial role when one reaches beyond the range of ordinary perception. In the case of Solomon and Hubbard, we have rather grandiose examples of the veil of the quantum universe not only being pierced but of its forces being mustered and impinged upon the temporal world in a big way. When one rises above the veil of ordinary perception, whether in a "good" or "bad" role, one is going to attract considerable attention from the so-called security guards or Watchers.

The Watchers represent the forces of the Hebrew name of God as it appears in the Old Testament. This is known as Tetragrammaton which means four letters or "four letters put together." In Hebrew, these four letters are *Yod He Vau He* where each signify the elements of Fire, Water, Air and Earth. These creative elements of matter are considered to be an extension of the Creative Force. God himself, if one chooses to personify him, is said to be the Grand Weaver of the Grand Design. In other words, we consider that, from the top of creation, he can look down and weave us out of trouble or manifest as he wishes. One can also potently argue that the Ruling Authority which concocted this universe the way it is is certainly not a "good" force. This is not really the point. We are talking about a ruling force of creation. Like the daemon, it can turn on a dime, depending on the circumstances.

In the historical and legendary accounts of Solomon, he pretty much retained power until his death. After that, his son was a poor ruler and the tribes of Israel divided. In the case of Hubbard, he never attained the unified geopolitical empire that Solomon did, but the fact that he accomplished what he did practically by himself makes him a comparable achiever. By himself, I meant that he did not have the political backing of all the various kingdoms that Solomon did. Solomon, if we believe the legends, also had the backing of the "Almighty." Again, I am not trying to make a case that one was better than the other, but that both had harnessed the powers of the elementals in a big way. I have woven their paths together for a reason.

Hubbard's death, and the circumstances surrounding it, is somewhat similar to Solomon's in that his departure from the organization saw hordes of Scientologists splintering off and going their own way. Many ex-Scientologists, including those who were close to the situation, have insisted that Hubbard was murdered or at least neglected and left to die on purpose. They claim that Hubbard's will was forged. It was apparently signed only a few days before he died. Additionally, a request for no autopsy was signed by Hubbard just before he passed away. This was allegedly a forgery, too. The Coroner's Report has pictures of needle marks on his buttocks and reports traces of psychiatric drugs in his blood. Hubbard did not believe in psychiatrists. None of these are my claims but are what is available on the internet. It is a vast subject of conspiracy, some of it true and some gone too far. To present the other side, the Scientologists claim that Hubbard deliberately "dropped his body" as the physical body became an impediment to his further research of the state of OT (operating thetan).

Whether there was foul play or not, my observation is that, whatever the circumstances, it was Ron's time to go. Death is a natural process, but the conditioning and programming of our society predisposes one to be afraid of it. But, death is more than just a natural process. It is also an expression of the life force we carry. How we die is also a statement about ourselves and the circumstances of our life. Hubbard's death will be studied for hundreds of years as will the situation and people surrounding it. It is a teacher and has its own legacy of lessons.

It is understandable that anyone reading about the alleged gifts and accomplishments of various individuals such as Hubbard, Solomon, or Christ might regret that none of them were able to roll up the whole universe in a little ball, hand it to us, and welcome us into a realm of heavenly wonder. That would be nice, but we have to do the work ourselves. We can, however, learn a lot by studying the accomplishments and histories of others. So, in retrospect, you need to put these characters into your own personal Well of Souls. Whatever their relative value, they are there, lurking, along with everyone else.

12

HIRAM ABIFF

I have included the Scientology theme, somewhat reluctantly, but it is absolutely necessary in order to convey the synchronicities I have experienced as well as the writing career that has been generated as a result thereof. Part of my reluctance has to do with the fact that it would take an encyclopedic volume in order to make various aspects of the Scientology experience completely understood. The legacy of Solomon is much easier to encapsulate. Solomon, of course, was known to possess the keys to the kingdom. Hubbard was said by some to possess or have sought after the "Key of It All" as was alluded to in Aleister Crowley's *The Book of the Law*. When you consider that the physical embodiment of these two men eventually became skeletons, you can consider that neither held the key to physical immortality, but that is not the game here. We are talking about a spiritual continuity or consistency that reaches beyond the boundaries of the physical body.

Another interesting parallel with Hubbard that has been suggested to me is that he is more akin to Hiram Abiff than that of King Solomon. Hiram Abiff was the Master Mason assigned to build Solomon's Temple but was murdered in the process and prior to its completion. In esoteric traditions, it is not uncommon for someone to build a temple or similar structure with themselves ending up as the "holy sacrifice."

Whether we consider the "Key of It All" or the Master Word of the Master Mason, Hiram Abiff was depicted in Masonic lore as the only man who possessed this key. There are many different legends about Hiram Abiff and who he actually was, but perhaps the most esoteric one is that he was a member of the Dionysiac Architects whereby he was contracted by King Solomon to build his temple. Upon completion of the Temple, and only then, was Hiram Abiff going to share the secret word. This would have been fine for everyone but, primate behavior being what it is, twelve of his disciples conspired with three thugs to wrest the secret from Hiram prematurely. If Hiram did not comply, he would suffer death. At the last minute, his twelve Fellow Craftsmen (disciples) could not go through with the diabolical plan, but the thugs could not be stopped. They were only workers or Entered Apprentices in the Masonic tradition. During lunch, at "low noon," the workers milled outside the temple while Hiram went inside the Holy of Holies and planned out the work for the rest of the day. Upon emerging from one gate, he was accosted successively by each of the ruffians until the third killed him with a maul by striking him on the forehead. Hiram's body was then taken to a locale on Mount Moriah and was buried with an Acacia branch marking the spot. When Hiram turned up missing and the disciples confessed to the evil plot, Solomon sent them in parties of three to find the three thugs. Eventually, a ship captain who refused the thugs passage indicated their probable whereabouts. They were captured and executed but not before revealing the location of the grave. When the body was identified, Solomon ordered an Entered Apprentice to make Hiram rise from the dead by utilizing the grip of his rank. When this failed, Solomon ordered that a Fellow Craftsmen raise him from the dead with the grip of his rank. This cause the flesh to be separated from the bone and was not successful either. Only Solomon, by using the grip of a Master Mason known as "The Lion's Paw," was able to resurrect Hiram from the dead in order that he could complete the temple.

This story upsets bibliophiles because it is apparently at odds with the Bible. If you stick with this book and read to the end, you will discover that the story of Hiram is a useful analogy that pretty much explains the whole purport of the Bible or what a Bible should be in the best of circumstances. It is not, however, a Bible story. There is a tremendous amount of symbolism in the story, but most Masons are not necessarily apprised of the living truth. Most of them just go through the motions of tradition with the inner meanings long since lost to all but the most astute. As can be expected, this hidden truth has been very twisted by various secret societies but also by some of our most established institutions. Hiram Abiff's word was known to be the ineffable name of God which has been identified since time immemorial as YHVH or *Yod He Vau He*. This was not to be spoken or said aloud and the name Adonai was substituted by Rabbis and various others. But, YHVH is not the secret word of Hiram. In esoteric tradition, Hiram Abiff's true name was also Adonai. In other words, in both Masonic and esoteric tradition, Hiram Abiff, as the Master Builder, symbolized the mystery of mysteries: the power we know as God. In particular, he was possessed of the ability to effect resurrection. In Masonic ritual, a substitute word is used for the lost magic word and it is *Ma-Ha-Bone* which means "What — the builder?" This is not, however, the magic word referred to on the very front page of this book. *Ma-Ha-Bone* is a substitute.

More interesting than the traditional story of Hiram Abiff are the anecdotes and legends that are not so well known. According to many of them, Hiram did not receive the "Key to It All" until he was probing beneath the site where the temple was to be constructed. This was the area known as Solomon's Stables which had once been a threshing floor and was where the Knights Templar eventually kept their horses. It was there, while stumbling upon a hidden chamber, where Hiram discovered the supreme secret. Only when he acquires this treasure does he become the fully empowered Hiram Abiff. The story of his subsequent murder is only an allegory with regard to what has happened to the ultimate Creative Force in this universe.

As was said earlier, it was Enoch who settled in the area of Mount Moriah. Known as the "Old Man of the Mountain" and the father of Methuselah, Enoch was a master builder who represented the zenith of all existing knowledge. The word *enough* is actually derived from Enoch and symbolizes the fact that he was the epitome of full attainment. We use the word *enough* in a sense that is a bit different, but it still translates. Of the two pillars Enoch constructed in the underground, one was made of marble in order to be fireproof. The other was made of brick in order that it could not sink. In this manner, the knowledge carved upon these pillars could be preserved forever.

Another historical legend has Hiram Abiff finding *The Book of Enoch* in this domain and that it was this text which served as the so-called treasure from which he derived his knowledge. According to this version, Solomon derived his knowledge from Hiram who had first discovered the secret. *The Book of Enoch* had scholars confused for years because no one could ever find any written transcripts or even fragments of it. There were only allusions to it. It was a work which repeatedly reached and influenced consciousness yet apparently had no tangible reality. In this respect, it was similar to both the Philadelphia Experiment and the Montauk Project. But, one day in the 1700's, a version of *The Book of Enoch* was discovered in Ethiopia. It has since been printed. *The Book of Enoch* is a bit obtuse and dry at times, and arguably not even well written, but it gets across some pretty key concepts which are not only the basis of Masonry but also Christianity and Wicca. In this respect, I am talking about the Watchers. These were referred to earlier as the jinn or guardians at the gateway. They represent the four watchtowers of Tetragrammaton. It is interesting to note that the word *watch* derives from *wacca* or *wakka* which actually means "watcher." It may seem ironic to many that Wiccans honor the four watchtowers which are quite plainly represented in the Bible. The letters of Tetragrammaton have even been academically interpreted as "Eve" where YHVH is pronounced as "Yve" or "Yeev." Another traditional spelling of the name Eve was always preceded with a "y" and was "Yves."

Perhaps the most interesting clue to all that I discovered in perusing various literature on this subject was that the names of the twelve disciples of Hiram, who conspired to murder him but lost heart, were inscribed upon the pillars of the various watchtowers. This suggests to us that those disciples equate to or are representative of the jinn themselves. They would be the elemental "Fellow Craftsmen" who are designed to carry out the intentions of the Master Mason or Master Magician. The fact that the twelve disciples were part of the conspiracy to obtain the secret tells us that the jinn themselves do not have the Master Key. They can do just about anything in terms of carrying out instructions in this universe, but as far as anything that we might roughly call their "personal needs," they are lost in a relative state of limbo. In the parable of Hiram's Murder, the jinn themselves were conspiring to find the secret. That they lost faith in the assassination attempt only shows that they understood that to kill off the source of creation might offer them a worse fate and no existence at all.

On the other hand, the three thugs or ruffians who assaulted Hiram present a different outlook. Their names were Jubelo, Jubela, and Jubelem* and together were known as the Juwes. Jubelem was the character who actually finished off the murder of Hiram by utilizing a maul. The best etymology I could find for Juwes was that the word derives from the namesake of an area in medieval churches which is right behind the "rood screen." A rood screen was a part of the church with a crucifix where a parishioner would kneel while doing penance and would either say their prayers or, in some cases, suffer lashings. Together, the three Juwes represented ignorance, fear and superstition. Impatience, which I could not help but notice was the greatest flaw of all the conspirators, is not mentioned.

In summary, what we have in the mysterious legend of Hiram Abiff is a demonstrable representation of the predicament of the universe wherein the Creative Force, although not fully inoperable, has been rendered relatively impotent by virtue of ignorance, fear and superstition. The magic word is the keystone which is supposed to make everything function in harmony, but it seems to apply more to an individual than the collective in the analogy of Hiram. Each disciple and thug wanted to possess the secret word for himself so that he could be a Master Mason and carry out his own work. Amidst this macrocosmic view, we are also allowed to

---

* Jubelem, the murderer, has an interesting etymology behind his name. One must remember that "j" is pronounced with a "y" in Hebrew and Aramaic. The etymology of *jubelem* shows that it is a Latin word *jubilum* which originally came from Ecclesiastical Greek as *iobelaios* which was derived from the Hebrew *yobel*. In *iobelaios*, "io" suggests the dual nature of God (in various theological respects) in the same way we relate it to *diabolos*. In Hebrew, *yobel* signified the spiral horn of a ram which is still used today to signify the beginning of the Jewish new year. In Latin, *jubilare* means "to shout for joy," while *jubilum* is a "wild shout" and is related to "yowl." Based upon this etymology, we see that the murder of Hiram by Jubelem symbolizes a howling or wild shout of the beast as the lower energies apparently overcome or subdue the higher or regenerating Source. A wild shout can be for positive or negative reasons, but in either case, it is highlighting great excitement. It is very appropriate when we consider the murder of Hiram and the dual nature of the deity that is at play.

peer within the Watchtowers and see that these mysterious elemental forces that we sometimes refer to as the jinn are not unlike utility companies which provide heat, water, gas, and sanitation. They get the job done. Their personal lives are a non-factor, and they answer to a Governing Authority.

In the legend of Solomon, we are left with an analogy that tells us there is a grand pattern that can once again be attained. In the case of L. Ron Hubbard, he not only peered into the Watchtowers and began a program of enabling himself and others, he started creating his own utility companies. This caught the attention of someone's version of the Ultimate Power Authority and caused some problems.

All that matters to you is that you find your way through life with relative happiness and accomplish any goals your have set for yourself. Fortunately or unfortunately, your deepest goals or the wherewithal to complete them generally lie wrapped up within the mysteries thus far expounded. In this regard, you have to overcome ignorance, fear and superstition. If one is patient enough to learn and fully understand the secret word, particularly as it applies to one's true self and destiny, then one can become the master of their own fate. In both a historical and esoteric sense, there has always been something which stands between this key secret and the ordinary aspirant. It is a phenomena which abounds with ignorance, fear and superstition and is represented, once again, in the Well of Souls.

13

THE WALL OF FIRE

When I worked close to L. Ron Hubbard in Scientology, I noticed that he had a great grasp of mystery. He understood very well how people's minds could be captured and intrigued by mystery. Although he did not view mystery as a high state of consciousness, he observed that people loved what he called a "mystery sandwich." In other words, everyone enjoys a good thriller at the box office or in a novel. The reason for this is that both the subconscious and the collective unconscious are wrapped up in blankets of mysteries.

In the evolution of consciousness, or life organisms for that matter, there are a series of progressions (which can also be broken down into pure numerology) that repeat in harmonic patterns, but as they do, they mutate and change according to the new landscape. There are continual repetitions and numerical synchronicities, but one of the most basic and repeatable phenomena, particularly that which is conducive to life organisms, is the spiral or serpentine form. The very essence of the word reptile is analogous to the word and etymology of "repeat." The ancient Vedas had words for these which would roughly translate to the "Great Repetitions" which signified the ruling principles of life. In connection with the spiral or serpentine form was the number seven. In other words, the number seven was often found to be associated with the serpentine form and this culminates in the kundalini system with its seven wheels or chakras whereby one's consciousness follows this serpentine pattern en route to enlightenment. As the various patterns and repetitions get very sophisticated, you have full blown human drama, the basics of which are represented in the mystery plays and initiations of the ancient world. The mystery schools, when they were played and acted out to their full potential, represented the full panorama of consciousness as it was then known to man.

When L. Ron Hubbard came along, he did not make a big deal about the study of mystery schools. Instead, he observed that people were wrapped up in their own mysteries that they themselves had created over a quantum existence that invariably involved many lives. The task he took on and taught was the discovering of those personal mysteries for the individual. By addressing what people were very interested in dealing with, his philosophy and counselling techniques made him extremely popular with different people. How well he and his disciples did this is not going to be judged by myself. But, if one studied and applied his techniques as I knew them, you might find that you have all created your own version of the mystery schools deep in your unconscious mind and that, in some capacity, you are living out these mysteries, for better or for worse.

As Hubbard researched, he noticed that different people shared common experiences in their past lives. I noticed this myself as well. If you counselled different people with Scientology techniques (or even other techniques for that matter), you might find that there were many who were at the crucifixion of Christ. In fact, you would find more were there than could be housed in Yankee Stadium. Those who are too ready to judge this sort of phenomena will believe that these people are all crazy. This is not necessarily the case. Instead, they were confronting quantum representations of different experiences that occurred on some plane of existence, even if only in their mind. Personally, I noticed that some of my own recalled experiences from past lives seemed to be uncannily on the money as far as the so-called history of the real world is concerned. Others were extremely suspect. As a result, I took the various experiences with a grain of salt. But, it should also be pointed out that one was not traversing these experiences to "prove" anything. One only consulted past or quantum existences in Scientology in order to resolve a problem or situation that was impinging upon one's current existence. For example, if one is being excessively laughed at in life and under-goes past life therapy and realizes he was once a clown and is still dramatizing the mannerisms of such, it does not matter whether the experience was actually true. It only matters that the person realized he was acting like a clown and that this was what was causing the laughter they were uncomfortable with. That really was the core of Scientology therapy. One was not trying to objectify anything in terms of "provable phenomena" but only trying to improve or enhance one's personal ability to interface with the environment.

These techniques, which I have barely described at all, were quite successful if the practitioner knew what he or she was doing. It made Hubbard an unparalleled success in the field of self-improvement. I am also well aware that to people in the conspiracy crowd, Scientology has often been accused of being a mind control cult. Originally, Scientology was one of the first movements ever to expose what could be called mind control. Hubbard commented that any activity which seeks to resolve the negative dramatiza-tions of society could easily end up dramatizing those negative dramatizations itself. When I was involved in the movement, it was routine for negative dramatizations to be exposed within the group. After all, you are dealing with human beings, and primates are primates. It should also be noted that, in the early days of Dianetics and Scientology, Hubbard predicted that the movement would be taken over.

I have been told that I inspire a great deal of fear or apprehen-sion with different people because I was involved with L. Ron Hubbard. All I can answer is that these people are reacting out of ignorance, fear, or superstition. As with the lessons of Hiram Abiff, these are inhibitors to true understanding.

In an earlier chapter I spoke about the Scientology level that was entitled OT III. Again, this means "Operating Thetan Level Three" which was called the "Wall of Fire." I found the phenom-ena that I encountered on this level to be a very apt analogy to what was described earlier with regard to the Well of Souls. Once one got through the so-called Wall of Fire, one was supposed to have attained "total freedom" and to be completely self-determined. This might sound wonderful, but I can tell you one thing that is very certain. When you exhibit any significant degree of freedom and self-determinism in a group of primates that are not self-determined, they will ape their own enslaved condition and demonstrate either a predisposition or a frenzied passion to not only reduce your freedom but, more importantly, the means and methods by which you attained freedom. People are slaves primarily as a result of their own ideas. When you start changing their ideas, that in turn starts upsetting the mental mechanisms (which can be quite complex) of their enslaved condition.

When I referred to Scientology's "Wall of Fire" as a "purification by fire," I was using alchemical terms. This would be a "trial by fire" whereby you busted through the Well of Souls and demonic gate-keepers to the point where you accessed your own personal version of Enoch's or Solomon's secret and could command the elementals in accordance with your own higher will. Of course, this connotes tremendous power, but I will be quick to point out that this is an internal power. In a sarcastic light, there were many people I witnessed in Scientology who had visions of becoming fire-breathing dragons or superheroes. This sort of aggrandized ridiculousness is only the result of an aspirant missing an important step to the point where he not only fails to pass through the portal of initiation but ends up becoming an imitation of one of the guardians of the gate. When you see this type of person in action, it discourages one from wanting to learn or have anything to do with the truths that Scientology or any similar subject might hold. In such a scenario, the gate-keeper has done a remarkable job and is to be congratulated.

There have long been many mocking derisions of the level of Scientology known as OT III. Most of it is by the press or disaffected people who feel that "Scientology got the better of them." Shrewder souls will realize that the so-called ridiculing demons that appear at the portals of various gateways often transmute their way into real life souls and situations. In any typical religious tradition, you have to pass by the Watchers which are often popularly portrayed as gargoyles or the like.

In Scientology, one could only properly approach this phenomena and the upper levels after undergoing a tremendous amount of preparation. When I actually passed through what Scientology termed the Wall of Fire, I could not help but notice that I was far better trained and prepared than most of my contemporaries (but certainly not all) who did this level. The experience is different for each and every individual. To me, part of the procedure included the creation of what could be termed a virtual reality of hell and all that might mean to you on a personal level. Then, you had to experience and pass through it, but only for the purpose of vanquishing it from you psyche. This was an intense procedure but not horrific. In fact, it was exciting and adventurous if properly done. This is a gross oversimplification, but I should also add that it was not uncommon for people to "pass through" this level without actual doing it. Some people do things with ignorance and sometimes with status as their primary motivation. No matter what philosophy, religion or discipline you are involved in, you are always dealing with human nature and that includes reactive primate behavior. Therefore, when dealing with so-called heavenly progress or spiritual states of freedom, you will not only find beautiful and aesthetic renditions but also all of the degenerate mockeries that livingness and the imagination can manifest. It is a quantum universe.

The upshot of passing through the so-called Wall of Fire was that, after I confronted what could be termed my own "personal demons," the "demons" or negative thought forms projected by other individuals had little to no impact upon me. You would be surprised at how busy and active people are with entities they cannot even see. Life became a hundred times easier. It also gave me the ability to interact with my own "Well of Souls." The benefit of this is that it gives you a great deal of choice with what spirits or souls you are dealing with. In other words, you do not have to experience the quantum well of souls all at once. You can pick and choose and turn down those negative experiences you do not desire. Hubbard called this self-determinism. No matter what it is called, it is the only sensible way to deal with quantum phenomena. I have therefore used the appellation "quantum self-determinism."

While considering my own experiences, it is important to remember the central thesis of this book. All possible and potential realities have some degree of validity. There are universes where Scientology and the techniques herein work to utter perfection. There are also universes where they do not work at all.

I cannot include everything for brevity's sake, but much of the central core of applied Scientology has to do with something called the "postulate," a word which is rooted in the study of magick. Authors with limited understanding or with personal agendas to serve have stated that Scientology is based upon the theories and practices of magick. While there are some similarities and even sometimes identical attributes, I would be misleading you if I told you they were one and the same. An in-depth study or analysis of Scientology and its techniques are not the subject of this book, so I will spare you any potentially intriguing details, but one of the most basic and important maxims to learn in Scientology and magick is something called a postulate. In normal English, a postulate refers to a hypothesis. That means a supposition or idea that is put forth, usually for the purpose of establishing a theory about observed phenomena. While there is an intuition that a postulate is true or is desired to be true, it is not something that is, by definition, considered to be true. In Scientology, a postulate is defined as a cognition, decision or resolution. It is something that is decided. It can go a long way towards positive thinking, too.

After years of studying and practicing various techniques and experiences, including the Wall of Fire, I attained the peak of my Scientology experience. I found myself in the realm of postulates. Certain aspects of my life became kind of miraculous.

Of course, if you study home sapiens very closely, you will find that there are always a certain percentage who will seek to modify, minimize, or completely nullify anything that could be considered miraculous or above the realm of cold hard statistical analysis. As a Scientology auditor (counselor), you were trained to expect miracles. If they did not happen within certain contexts, either the wrong procedure was being done or you were misapplying the materials. While there is no limit to what a miracle might include, it is based upon the word *mira* which means "look." A miracle is simply something noteworthy because it is beyond the bounds of what is commonly considered to be normal experience. This is not altogether different to what Aleister Crowley referred to as "phenomena," the main difference being that "phenomena" is not necessarily considered to be an upbeat proposition.

Another thing to learn about miracles is that they are not necessarily produced upon demand. If you follow the best player in a particular sport, you might have to wait long intervals before you see him hit a home run, score a touchdown, or accomplish a particularly amazing feat. But, if you watch him play every day, you will see what he can and cannot do. The player himself also has to show up every day and play by the rules, laws and knowledge he has acquired about his sport. "Miracles" or "look-sees" in sports only have an impact on the people who perceive and follow the activity. The pygmies of New Guinea or the aborigines of Australia are not moved or affected by what occurs in stadiums across America; however, you might someday see one of their offspring wearing an NFL T-shirt so that aspect cannot be completely discounted either. In summary, miracles should neither be understated nor overstated. Context is very important.

In my personal case, I was getting better and better at making my own postulates happen. I will not risk boring the reader with personal details of my own life, but I began to feel that I could manifest anything that I wanted. After experiencing that I could manifest with more impetus than I had ever known before, I suppose I could have asked for money, fame, or the most beautiful girl in the world, but my attention was not on any of these things. Instead, people and circumstances in my own life (which are too complicated to explain now) caused me to not only consider my own personal fate but that of all living things. You could say that my attention was extremely extroverted and projected itself out into the far distant future on this time line. For some reason, whether right or wrong, I decided that all would be best served if all hurtful mechanical conditions of existence could be abated or modified. In other words, if you get in an automobile crash, there is sometimes not too much you can do about a broken body. I was seeking a world that was more like the holodeck on *Star Trek* where you could "uncreate" a bad situation.

Although I was not making a prayer in a religious fashion, my postulate was much like a prayer. It was a solemn moment but was soon forgotten. A short while later, I saw a huge explosion in the sky which looked like fireworks, but it was gone in an instant. It happened so fast that my only reaction was to not go into denial that I had seen something of a very irregular nature. The explosion made no sense and there was no audio connected to it. A Chinese girl walked by, and I told her what I had seen. To my surprise, she indicated she had seen strange things in that area before. In the span of one year from that time, I found the girl I wanted to marry and the spiritual forces of quantum self-determinism led me away from the pack of Scientology. It was made very clear to me that if I wanted to stay, I would have to become one of the "sheeple." My departure was laced with synchronicity. When I signed my official "departure papers" leaving the Sea Organization, I could not help but notice that it was exactly eleven years from the day I had officially entered the organization. When I moved to Long Island shortly thereafter, it was only a few weeks before August 12th, 1983, a day which was said to be the climax of the Montauk Project. At that time, I did not even know there was a locale known as Montauk Point. At the time, my only comment on moving to Long Island was that it was filled with psychic interference. I incorrectly attributed this to the abundant materialism that Long Island is famous for. As *The Montauk Project* demonstrated, it had more to do with a transmitter that ran at 435 megahertz, the window frequency to the human consciousness.

Postulates are like prayers. They do not always occur exactly when you expect. When you make a pure postulate of thought, you are in a pristine state and are moving it into the Earth plane which is not so perfect. Therefore, sequences and events sometimes come out in a clumsy manner. For example, you might wish for a pot of gold and end up having someone give you a golden colored flower pot instead of receiving a pot full of gold coins.

There is also a zone where postulates move in accordance with the exact desire of the individual. This has been studied in sports to a limited extent where athletes refer to this experience as "the zone." Numerous professional athletes have described a state of mind where they literally cannot do anything wrong. They shoot the ball at the basket, and it goes in, even if it hits the rim and bounces around a lot. It occurs not only in all sports but with other people in real life as well. Gamblers also experience "the zone" when they hit lucky streaks. The game of baseball is particularly loaded with momentum and "lucky streaks." There is a fine line between being in "the zone" and having your postulates come true in a more haphazard and unpredictable way. A lot of it has to do with the size of the arena you are playing in. Manipulating a poker game is a lot easier than manipulating the entire New York Stock Exchange. Just as in sports, your competition and your attitude will have an impact on your ability to stay in "the zone."

In my personal case, I had entered a "zone," but there was a time release factor at work. Things did not happen instantaneously for me. I went through a few necessary schools of learning before I could come up with all the required requisites necessary to launch Sky Books. It took ten years after my initial sighting of "fireworks" in the sky over Clearwater, Florida before I could get a good grasp of what actually happened. One day, while having a reunion football game in Clearwater with some of my old friends, I pointed to the general area of where I had witnessed the fireworks explosion and asked one of my friends if we could explore the area. It was located near a rather large antenna station at the G.T.E. building on Cleveland Street. When we approached the exact area over which the explosion must have occurred, there was a rather sizable vacant lot at the time. My friend, who is not a UFO buff, commented that he had once seen a UFO over that exact area.

In the book *Encounter in the Pleiades: An Inside Look at UFOs*, I speculated that I may have accessed something called the KOALA Project, a group set up by the "Inner Light Network" which was designed to counterbalance the Montauk Project and other such negative endeavors. This information had been fed to me by various sources and was an incomplete and stopgap answer to phenomena that was unexplainable. Now, after another decade, I have an explanation which, while not really contradicting the idea of a KOALA Project, is closer to home. That is the description of VALIS as mentioned earlier in this book. I had opened up a higher functioning aspect of my brain and was put in touch with Creative Forces that were beyond the ordinary perception of the human state. Incredible synchronicities unfolded in my own life which ended up placing me in the vicinity of Montauk Point right before August 12, 1983. If the legends and archetypal experiences of the Montauk Project are even partially true, it is highly significant that I ended up in this locale, particularly if you consider that Montauk represents the key to reorganizing matter, energy, space and time as we have known it throughout millennia. The Montauk Project tapped the powers of creation, but the ethics of the project left much to be desired. Much of this is still a mystery, but it is a mystery that has been opening up more and more.

My associations and synchronicities with science fiction author Phil Dick began when a manager of a health food store on

Long Island told me he met L. Ron Hubbard in 1973 when at the home of Lou Dick, a dealer in occult books that operated out of his house in Far Rockaway, Queens.* As Lou Dick was deceased at that point, I could not find out anything about him. A cursory search at the library revealed there was a famous "Phil Dick," but the store manager did not know if they were related. I only began to look into Phil Dick's work fourteen years later when Joe Matheny referred me to him on a question I had about early Christianity. It is, however, more than ironic that Dick translated his name to "Horselover Fat" and how well that fits in with the archetypal horse of the Montauk Project. Phillip Dick is also the author of the book upon which the movie *Total Recall* was based. In the *Montauk Project: Experiments in Time*, Preston Nichols indicated that *Total Recall* was based upon experiences from the Montauk Project. Other than what has already been said, the associations between Phil Dick and Montauk leave a lot unsaid. What we do know for a fact at this point is that whatever mysterious circumstances I experienced in conjunction with that "explosion" took me to the boundaries of consciousness which fits in very nicely with the archetypal explanations given elsewhere in this book. The horse is a great metaphor in this regard.

According to my own subjective perception, my experiences in Scientology ended up going far deeper than the ordinary parishioner or even loyal staff member who pursues that path. There are three reasons for this. First, I completely dedicated myself to finding out all I could about the secrets of life which Scientology readily embraced in theory. Second, I worked close enough to L. Ron Hubbard which educated me in a manner which was very different than ordinary Scientologists will ever experience. Third, I never lost sight of my own individuality and never compromised my own integrity. In other words, I did not let other people mess with me. In essence, it was as if my Scientology adventures had built a launching pad by which I could take off from and examine "outer space." However, there were a few things to adjust on the launching pad before the shuttle was ready to take off.

---

* For security reasons, L. Ron Hubbard moved from Tangier, Morocco and lived in Queens, New York from December 1973 until the following summer. The above eye-witness testimony contradicts information in disparaging biographies about LRH which state that he never left his apartment.

14

WITHIN THE WATCHTOWERS

THE FOLLOWING TRANSMISSION IS FROM A PARALLEL UNIVERSE

Going to sleep one night, I dreamt I was on a shuttle craft making its way to the moon. Looking upward, I could no longer see the spacecraft but only full and luminous stars. The next thing I knew, I was floating freely in space. Zooming past the moon, I was travelling through a system of stars that was quite foreign to the Milky Way. I proceeded at a high rate of speed until I came upon a simple but beautiful edifice of alabaster. The next thing I knew, I found myself in front of pillars as I ascended to a stairway to enter the structure. Inside was a clearly a symbolized rendition of the throne room of Solomon the King. On the throne was the skeleton of Solomon which was adorned only with a golden crown studded with gems. The skeleton pointed to another room, and I pursued that direction until I came upon a lush courtyard. At each corner of the courtyard was a tower of beautiful alabaster which reached into a deep blue night. Atop each tower was a beautiful colored flame which corresponded to the Hebrew letters of Tetragrammaton. The flames periodically transformed themselves into aethyric images that flowed as self-contained units of energy. Occasionally, they would take on creature-like forms. It was clear that they represented the images of the jinn. I realized I was before the Watchers in their courtyard, but I was not sure why.

139

Out of a pond in the center of the courtyard, a pedestal arose with a beautiful woman. She could have been Isis or a host of other goddess names. Although she looked more like an Egyptian version of Cleopatra, I heard a voice identify herself as Sheba. She smiled at me and thanked me for answering her summons.

When I asked her, "What summons?" she smiled as her clothes fell from her body.

It was clear that I was witnessing the most beautiful version of a naked woman that I had ever seen. Before I could think a thought, most of the body dissolved until only the breasts remained topped by a pyramid, the base of which rose from the breasts and reached its apex at the throat. This image remained only long enough for me to get the idea that this shape was mimicked within the human body. The breasts and pyramid were now turned upside down so that it looked like a human heart as it turned into the following symbol which was fully colored and radiant.

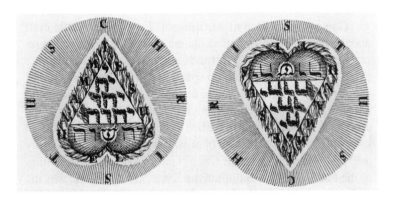

TETRAGRAMMATON OF THE HUMAN HEART

I then heard Sheba's voice. It was soft and tender but mostly instructive.

"You have been summoned to my temple because of your wish to change the universe. You have entered my bosom and you shall never be forgotten. There is a secret to dealing with the jinn. When you activate your higher will through the true desire of your heart, the jinn will obey. The heart is the key and they will obey."

140

As I sat in this beautiful courtyard, I soon found myself reclining on a lounge chair looking up at a beautiful crescent moon. The various watchtowers emitted a beautiful display of electromagnetic energy that could have been engineered by the staff of Disney World. As I reclined, I could see a room next door without even using my eyes. An angel with beautiful brown hair and a character who looked like a genie were discussing my fate. I did not like this but was forced to listen. The genie was speaking.

"It is true this man is a free agent, but I cannot condone sending him to Long Island in the way you have laid out. The woman will give him trouble and her affiliation with the Crowley connection is designed to kill him or at least his physical modality. There has got to be a better way, perhaps through reincarnation. The Aleister Crowley connections are far too messy."

"You are right that the connections are messy," replied the angel, "but he is tough enough to persevere and wrest the wheat from the chaff. I have every faith and confidence and will do my very best to ensure his safe and successful passage."

"The Montauk Project itself is even far messier than all those things I have thus far described," replied the genie. "It even struck the creator of the spiritual methods he found so useful."

"His karma will allow him, and I will boost that," said the angel.

"And, if you fail?" questioned the genie.

"If I should fail," replied the angel, "I would beseech thee to release an army of jinn so magnificent that they would carry forth in my stead."

"What gives you the right and the impetus to make such a request?"

"If the universe has a heart, then this is the heart of the matter."

The angel then whispered the magic word to the genie whereupon he smiled and laughed.

I soon found myself falling deep into sleep and was soon riding a shuttle craft back to the Earth. While I knew I might encounter some turbulence on the earth plane, I knew someday that I could return to the courtyard of the watchtowers. A voice over the shuttle intercom announced that there was time to get a full nights sleep before entering the Earth's atmosphere.

141

15

IN THE WAKE
OF MAGICIANS

I will never forget the day in 1986 when I heard the news that L. Ron Hubbard had passed away. I was living on Long Island but had only the loosest affiliation with Scientology at that time. My only connection was that I was working in New York City with a couple of individuals who I had known in Scientology. My boss took me into a separate room from the rest of the staff and read a telex indicating that L. Ron Hubbard had died. After receiving this somewhat shocking news, I walked out the door and almost ran into the owner of an adjacent company on the same floor. As he walked by, he looked me right in the eye and spoke.

"The shuttle just blew up," he said.

He was talking about the *Challenger* space shuttle which had exploded. This news really hit me, not because I was a fan of the space program but because it was like a one-two punch without any lag in between. Somebody I had known well and worked for had died, the news of which was followed by a completely unexpected disaster which included more death. Noticing the extreme coincidence, I tried to connect the two incidents beyond the obvious but could not. Years later, I realized that Hubbard's old friend and magical partner, Jack Parsons, was responsible for the discoveries that made the solid fuel rocket possible. This technology was used in the shuttle and was a direct result of his research. In this sequence of events, Hubbard and the astronauts were tied together by death and by Jack Parsons.

It was a little over a year later, in 1987, when I began to get the first clue about the relationship between Hubbard's death and the space shuttle. After work one day, I was in the Forbidden Planet bookstore in Manhattan and saw a new book for sale. It was *L. Ron Hubbard: Madman or Messiah?* by Bent Corydon and L. Ron Hubbard Jr. Both of these sources had credibility problems in my mind, but I read the book nevertheless. Although I know some of the information to be suspect, I did find information which discussed Hubbard's connection to Jack Parsons as well as his interest in Aleister Crowley. I was fascinated as I had studied Hubbard for over a decade, and if he was a fan of Aleister Crowley, I wanted to know what was so special. Subsequently, I read everything I could get my hands on that was by Aleister Crowley. As for Parsons, he had been a live disciple of Crowley and was a passionate advocate of his work. Crowley had taken on the mantle of the Antichrist and identified himself as "The Beast — 666." The specifics of my synchronistic encounters with Aleister Crowley and his work are covered in the book *Montauk Revisited: Adventures in Synchronicity.* A short summary will follow.

Although I did not know it at the time, my study of Crowley and connecting the dots with Hubbard would turn into a launching pad for my writing of the Montauk Project and subsequent other books. It all began on November 7, 1990 when I sought out Preston Nichols because I heard he was an incredible inventor. I was interested in one of his machines. Visiting him at a meeting at the Long Island chapter of the United States Psychotronics Association, I noticed something peculiar about him that I have never before divulged because it would have been out of context. Meeting him briefly before the meeting, I noticed that he had the energy field of what was termed an "operating thetan" in Scientology. Without even talking about it, I could see that he was fully aware of himself as a spiritual being and could operate on that level. This was indeed a rarity in my walk-about experiences on Long Island. He told me that I would have to listen to a lecture on "Earth Changes" and catch him at the break.

Most of what was talked about that night was the Philadelphia Experiment and the Montauk Project, two experiments conducted via the military that tapped into the Unified Field and resulted in teleportation and time travel amongst other bizarre concepts. Two of the alleged time travellers from the experiments, Duncan and Edward Cameron (the latter who is better known as Al Bielek), were also present that night. Preston himself was intimately involved in the experiments from the Montauk end of things. To me, this was the most bizarre science fiction story I had ever heard. I also thought it had obvious elements of truth, but these were not so easy to distinguish from the legends and "abduction" accounts that always leave a lot to be desired in terms of linear reality. Asking if there was a book I could read about the Montauk Project, I was told there was none.

None of the above was synchronous in and of itself. What started that course of events to eventually snowball was when Preston talked about the secrecy surrounding the Philadelphia Experiment and how the story of that was leaked with the release of the movie *The Philadelphia Experiment*. Allegedly, a movie was produced by Thorn, E.M.I., a British electronics company which not only told the real story of the Philadelphia Experiment but included a trailer documentary of the real incident. Some have said it actually included footage of the Cameron brothers and included their names. A lawsuit was filed that kept it out of the theaters. A second movie was eventually released which Thorn, E.M.I. distributed as a video.

Preston said he believed that the release of the Philadelphia Experiment video was engineered by the Wilson Brothers. According to Preston, the Wilson Brothers were the first manufacturers of scientific instruments in Great Britain and were friends of Aleister Crowley's father. Together, Mr. Crowley and the Wilsons became business partners in a concern which eventually became known as the Thorn Company. Thorn later merged with E.M.I. before it released the video tape of the movie *The Philadelphia Experiment*.

When Preston Nichols mentioned that the Wilson Brothers were connected to the Crowley family, it immediately caught my interest. He further stated that, in a previous life, he and Duncan Cameron were the Wilson Brothers and were known as Preston and Marcus Wilson respectively. I had never heard of the Wilson Brothers in my reading of Crowley, but I soon began to search his books for any possible reference to them. I did learn that Crowley was initiated into the highest Masonic degree in Mexico City by a Wilson, but there was no reference to the Wilson Brothers.

Besides the Wilson in Mexico City, I noticed some other surprising synchronicities upon consulting Aleister Crowley's autobiography entitled *Confessions*. It stated that Crowley's birth name was not Aleister but was Edward Alexander Crowley. This was ironic because Edward and Alexander were the names of the Cameron Brothers involved in time travel. Duncan Cameron, the other brother, had the full name of Alexander Duncan Cameron. Besides that irony, I became quite surprised when I saw that Crowley also mentioned that he had a friend by the name of Duncan Cameron. All of this was a little too odd. Looking for a reference for the Wilson Brothers, I found a coincidence concerning the Cameron Brothers as well as the name of Duncan Cameron, the primary time traveller of the Montauk Project.

All of the above could have been cut short and considered a dead end had it not been for other experiences I had. As I shared these experiences, I found more synchronicities with the name Cameron. One friend who had experienced missing time when she was out at Montauk said she ran into the name "Cameron" all the time. Additionally, she told me about a psychic friend of hers who had also been picking up the name "Cameron" for some time. This was even more odd. I contacted the psychic who had been perplexed about what she was receiving. She was also puzzled by the fact that the name "Wilson" kept coming up, too. She had no idea why, but was a bit relieved when I explained how it was all fitting together. As we continued to dialogue, she informed me that the name "Shelley" was also connected and that I should look into that. I soon found myself in the biography section of the library looking for books on Percy Shelley, the famous poet and writer whose wife, Mary Shelley, penned *Frankenstein*. I soon found out that Shelley's quintessential biographer was none other than a man named Kenneth Cameron. All I knew at this point was that there was a "psychic wind" pushing me along.

As I shared the information with my friend, Chelsea Flor, she was struck by her own remembrance of her first meeting with Duncan Cameron. There was a bit of confusion with his name because she already knew a Cameron Duncan, a man her sister used to date. Finding this odd, it piqued my curiosity. I asked her what this Cameron Duncan was like. The first thing out of her mouth was that Cameron Duncan had a twin brother. This was another strange coincidence because Preston had made it quite clear that all of the techniques at Montauk were based upon Nazi research conducted on twins. She additionally told me that the twin loved Aleister Crowley's work and that their father worked at Princeton, the locale where the Philadelphia Experiment was said to be hatched with the help of Albert Einstein. All in all, a very odd series of synchronicities that erupted from following a simple trail of the name "Cameron." Asking her what the name of the twin was, she did not remember but said she would check with her sister. When she got back to me, she informed me that the twin of Cameron Duncan was named "Kimberly" Duncan. He was said to be extremely effeminate.

All of these associations were hauntingly familiar, but things came to a head one evening at a psychotronics meeting where a video was being shown about government psychics committing mayhem. Two of the characters were named Cameron and Kimberly. Preston explained that these names often appear in movies about time travel and mind control. This synchronicity caught my eye once again. Afterwards, I spoke to Duncan and asked him if there was anyone in his family named "Kimberly."

"Yes," he said. "My sister."

Although the field was already thick with synchronicity, this was the most dramatic of all the coincidences I had encountered thus far. The more I pursued this line of investigation, the more remarkable were the coincidences found. It all defies the laws of probability. It is what Jung called a meaningful coincidence and indicates there is another acausal factor in the mix. Most remarkably, and perhaps to be expected, an even more dramatic synchronicity awaited me. It turned out to be one of the most riveting experiences of my entire life and also proved to be an appointment with destiny that has shaped my life and writing career ever since.

This next adventure began when I saw an advertisement for a book by Jack Parsons in a catalog. Entitled *Freedom Is A Two-Edged Sword,* the book was a collection of Jack's essays and the ad mentioned that it was edited by his wife "Cameron." There was no first name or last name, only "Cameron." That was not only odd in itself, it fed the synchronicities encountered previously. Here was Aleister Crowley's chief disciple in America, Jack Parsons, having a wife whose name was listed only as "Cameron." Had a first name been appended to "Cameron," it would have been much less auspicious but still of considerable significance. Over a year would pass before I would run across the actual book in a Manhattan book shop. It just sort of popped out at me one day, and I immediately bought it.

The book stated that Cameron was an avant garde artist whose work had aroused considerable controversy, primarily because it was uninhibited about nudity and sex. It was also apparent from her short biography in the book that she must be in her seventies. I very much wanted to contact her, and I knew that there was a relatively short window in terms of her availability. As the book was also coedited by Hymeneaus Beta, the titular name for the Outer Head of the O.T.O. (a magical order with roots back to Germany that claims to adhere to the teachings and principles of Aleister Crowley as well as other universal truths), I realized my best chance of contacting her was through him as his address was in the book. It was a PO Box in New York City with the number "7666," the last three numerals (666) being the self-assigned identification of Aleister Crowley. Another coincidence perhaps?

Things were very busy in my life at that point. *The Montauk Project: Experiments in Time* had just been released, and I was just about to attend the largest book conference in the United States which was to be held at the Anaheim Convention Center in 1992. I was also excited because I had grown up not too far from Anaheim, and I was looking forward to visiting my old neighbors who I had not seen in fifteen years. On a bright sunny morning in New York, I placed a letter to Hymeneaus Beta of the O.T.O. in the mail box and waited for a taxi that would take me to the airport. This turned out to be a rather bizarre ride because the driver, who was rather seedy, talked about voodoo and sex magick. He was Caucasian and looked as if he was of either Italian or Greek descent. He was not from the islands. All in all, it is highly unusual for a typical cab driver to speak of such things. Whether I liked it or not, my path of investigation was taking me through the litter and residue of the subject at hand.

When I made my way to the book convention, I was surprised that the first thing I saw was a selection of Aleister Crowley books. Seeing a man at the booth who looked like a biker, I asked him if he had ever heard of Cameron. I figured he knew who I was talking about, and he did. He referred me to a company called Mystic Fire Video and said that there was a man who worked there who knew Cameron. Although I did not know it at the time, the owners of Mystic Fire had a house at Montauk, and I eventually visited them there years later. They distributed the video *Inauguration of the Pleasure Dome*, an esoteric film produced by Kenneth Anger that Cameron starred in. The man who knew Cameron worked at Mystic Fire as an executive at that time, but he was not the owner. After staking this gentleman out, I got to speak with him and told him the story of the Montauk Project, the Philadelphia Experiment, my synchronicities with the name Cameron, and my interest in meeting Cameron. Giving him a copy of the *Montauk Project,* he told me about Cameron and said that she lived in the L.A. area. After talking to this man off and on for a couple of days at the book fair, it became evident to me that he was in fact the Outer Head of the O.T.O., the very man I had addressed my letter to days earlier. Informing him that I had written him a letter several days prior, I announced that I had arrived before it had! He also told me that the PO Box 7666 to which I had addressed my letter was assigned at random. I thought it had been requested by their organization, but he said this was not the case. When he eventually gave me Cameron's phone number, I could not help but notice that the last four numbers of it were "6606." Although I was surprised and a bit dazed by another remarkable synchronicity, I was very firm of purpose and exactly sure that I was on the right track.

Making my way to her house on Genesee Street in West Hollywood, I discovered that she lived in an area that is predominantly gay and very run down in some sections. Meeting Cameron was a pleasure. Her house was small with no frills and she described it as rustic. Although her natural demeanor is a bit stern or even foreboding to some, she was very polite and friendly. Without me prompting her or asking her any questions, she began to speak about her experiences with Jack Parsons and L. Ron Hubbard. At her memorial service years later, I learned from one of her best friends that reporters and writers had been trying to pry this information out of her for years. They often wanted her to sign an exclusive, but she would never comply. Now, she was sharing her experiences of those enigmatic and legendary years. In retrospect, I wish I had known this as I would have taken better notes at the meeting. I will cover most of what I remember in the next chapter.

After I patiently listened to Cameron's stories, it was my turn to tell her about the Philadelphia Experiment and Montauk Project. She was not familiar with the information but listened intently. She was not stupid and would never discount a quantum possibility. Finally, I told her all about the synchronicities that had led me to her and how the name Cameron had been a highly charged lead. At the end, I explained how I would have travelled a long ways to meet her but was most lucky that I could fit it into this trip without any extra expense. Still, I told her I really had no answer as to why I was here or how she fit into all of this. I was looking to her for an answer.

When I was done, she was silent and intentful. It was clear that she had digested everything I had said and was willing to serve me in this dialogue. She then dropped a bomb on me.

"My name is not really Cameron. It's Wilson. And so was Ron's (meaning L. Ron Hubbard). He was a Wilson, too."

I was completely shocked at this revelation and could not begin to understand the full implications of it all. All I knew was that I had struck pay dirt.

Cameron explained that her father's original name was Hill Lesley Wilson, but he became known as Hill Lesley Cameron because he was adopted by an uncle named Alexander Cameron. Here was the name "Alexander" coming up again. As for Hubbard, she said that she had read in a book that he was also a Wilson. Checking up on this, I discovered that Ron's father, Harry Ross Hubbard, was born a Wilson but was adopted by the Hubbards. Besides the red hair they shared in common, both Cameron and Hubbard looked genetically similar. Both Harry Ross Hubbard and Marjorie Cameron were from Iowa. Further synchronicities and associations of the Wilsons and Camerons are in *Montauk Revisited: Adventures of Synchronicity*, but in this book, I will concentrate on continued developments that took place in the wake of that investigation.

Originally, I was seeking to verify the existence of the Wilson Brothers, two scientists who were believed to be time travellers and had supposedly worked as an unseen influence in a company that would eventually release a movie about the Philadelphia Experiment. While I did not exactly find the Wilson Brothers, I did find myself on an investigative trail which led me to the focal point of an experiment that was intended to bring about the end of time. It was authored by Cameron's husband, Jack Parsons, and was called the Babalon Working. Cameron herself was the focal point of this working, and as a result, she was besieged ever afterwards with the dubious appellation of "Whore of Babylon."*

---

* In this text, I will use either Babalon or Babylon, two different spellings for the same word. Babylon is the commonly accepted English usage spelling which also appears in the Bible. I will use this spelling when I am referring either to the Biblical or common historical interpretations of the geographical region or feminine archetype. Babalon is generally recognized as the correct spelling in magical circles and was used by Jack Parsons and Aleister Crowley. I will use that spelling when I am referring to magical applications. In a similar sense, I will use the word *magick* when I am referring to applications of ritual magic with reference to Aleister Crowley (he coined this particular spelling), his antecedents, his successors, or to those who utilize similarly inclined rituals or applications. I will use the word *magic* when utilized in a more general sense. In either case, these different spellings are a rather trivial matter, but some readers might be confused if I were to write otherwise or not make a distinction.

16

THE BABALON WORKING

The Babalon Working was a series of invocations and rituals that were designed to serve as a catalyst towards manifesting the end of linear time, a circumstance which has also been identified as the Apocalypse. The Apocalypse itself is one of the most misunderstood terms I have ever encountered. When people read the Book of Revelation, they do not realize it was based upon earlier sources and, as said earlier, that it was copied and contoured to fit the social times of the Roman Empire. It is not an original work at all in its own right but is an interpretation and manipulation of earlier works.

The word *apocalypse* is thought to mean catastrophe or destruction, particularly at the end times. While there is going to be a certain amount of fallout if linear time ends, this is only one shortsighted aspect of the phenomena. In Greek, the word *apocalypse* breaks down into *apo* and *calypse. Apo* means "away from" or "to take the cover off," or "to uncover." *Calypse* is another way of saying or spelling *Calypso*, the nymph goddess who was queen of the island of Ogygos in the Atlantic and kept Odysseus sequestered on that island for seven symbolic years of sexual initiation. Only then could he go back to his faithful wife Penelope and overcome those who had sought to dethrone him. In Greek, the word *Calypso* further breaks down to "Kali" and "ipso" which means "by way of Kali" or "by fact of Kali." Kali, of course, is the Hindu goddess of time and has many manifestations, one of which is destruction. Thus, the Apocalypse really means a revelation or uncovering of the Goddess. The trite Christian analogy of the Apocalypse is an understandable attempt to protect oneself from a tidal of wave of destruction and evil that could, will, or might ensue during the upheaval of our consciousness as it relates to the potential end of linear time. At their best, these renditions can only mimic or imitate any higher truth that might be involved.

The Babalon Working, as stated by its progenitor, was intended to counterbalance the aspects of power, violence, and energy that are not only characteristic of the god Mars but of the abusive hierarchal structure of the Catholic Church which has championed those characteristics over the years. Mars is also a key focus of Aleister Crowley's *The Book of the Law*, the text of which served as a basis for the rituals concocted for the Babalon Working.* There is, however, a missing component in the *Book of the Law* and that is the full female aspect. Parsons was trying to fix that. In this regard, Jack Parsons believed that the Babalon Working was the completion of Crowley's work.

The Book of the Law is a complex and coded document. I liken it best to a roulette wheel. It rotates from exquisite and splendid descriptions of the Goddess to the most heinous and disgusting aspects of existence. It is based upon the purest warrior aspects of Horus which is known as Menthu, Monthu, Heru or Hero.** This warrior aspect of Monthu is highlighted in *The Book of the Law* when the extraterrestrial author talks about the '40's and '80's.*** Camp Hero was constructed in 1942 and the Philadelphia Experiment happens in 1943. The Montauk Project, which is a prime

---

* The connection between Mars and the Babalon Working was first brought to my attention when a friend happened to stumble across a book written by an author named Cameron. This friend called me up and read to me that the city of Cairo, which is properly pronounced Al-Kahira, means Mars. Mars was also said to be incarnated in the Egyptian god Horus.

** Menthu or Monthu both correspond to Montauk. The Montauk Air Force Station was ironically named after Captain Andrew Hero, Jr. Although little is known about his background at this time, his father, Andrew Hero, Sr. was a 33rd degree Mason who had served in the Confederate Army under Robert E. Lee and Stonewall Jackson. He became a famous attorney in New Orleans after the Civil War but continued his military affiliations.

*** From *The Book of the Law*: "I am the warrior Lord of the Forties: the Eighties cower before me, and are abased. I will bring you to victory and joy: I will be at your arms in battle and ye shall delight to slay. Success is your proof; courage is your armour; go on, in my strength; and ye shall turn not back for any!"

example of a warrior god defrocked of its female component, experiences its peak performance in 1983.

The missing feminine component is also quite prevalent in the legends of Freemasonry, but there is an interesting comparison between Menthu and Hiram Abiff. Menthu or Horus were both known as the son of the widow Isis. Masons have always specifically referred to Hiram Abiff as the Widow's Son. There is a key difference between Hiram and the others however. Menthu and Horus are most always depicted as fierce warrior gods. Hiram was a builder, which is a masculine profession; however, we do not really learn of any feminine aspect in him until we hear the story of his death. There is a complete lack of any male element when he does not fight back against his aggressors. In fact, he seems to exaggerate the principle of being yin or passive. This mimics the story of Christ who also behaves in a very passive manner. Both are exhibiting secretive and female characteristics, but both hold the true power of the universe according to their prospective legends. Freemasonry, however, is traditionally composed only of males. The only observable traces we see in the Masons of the female element is in the tradition of the Templars and certain mythological interpretations of the Goddess. An obvious glance would see that the "Lost Word" might have something to do with the feminine.

Crowley was a Master Mason himself, but when he joined the lodge he could not help but notice that it was "dead." They used rituals that had lost their meaning and no one was really too sharp on what the subject was really all about. Using his colorful and lively knowledge of mythology, secret doctrine and the occult, he subsequently put some life into their rituals. Although Crowley is often thought of as a petty and selfish individual, it should be realized that Crowley, in certain respects, surrendered his will to the universe and the collective unconscious. In this manner, he was also a classic exercise in yin. As a medium or portal, one never knew what was going to come out of his mouth. This is one reason he terrified people, and today, the mere mention of his name can stir up hornets. This characteristic should be recognized as an attribute of magicians (both male and female) as well as the subject of magick itself. His energy field was so open (or yin) that he would completely and often unconsciously accept the energy of those he encountered. As magicians are highly reflective in terms of being a mirror image, these energies could bounce back on the individual and, in some cases, this was said to be quite horrific. The reason for this is that magicians study a high level of truth and a truth that is rather intense. The dual nature of the deity, at its most extreme nature, can be likened to a rapidly removing door where the doors are alternately painted black and white. You are either going to be in synch with the guardian at the gate and allowed passage or be bounced back on your ass. It is not that Crowley was really a "good" person or that his own personal desires did not enter into some of these equations, but he was an apex of different entities and consciousness. Crowley was not, however, fully conscious of all the phenomena that was mustered through him.

Crowley's most famous foray into the unconscious began on August 12th, 1903 when he had sex in the King's Chamber of the Great Pyramid with his new bride, Rose Kelly. He believed this experience acted as a catalyst for his wife receiving a transmission that told him how to invoke Horus, the Widow's Son. Rose was not an occultist per se, and he was completely surprised when she directed him to the Boulak Museum in Cairo and showed him an image of Horus on the Stele of Menthu (which Crowley later called the Stele of Revealing). Most of all, he was struck by the fact that the exhibit was numbered 666. Subsequently, he cited these experiences as the inspiration which led to him transcribing *The Book of the Law* on April 8, 9, and 10 of the following year.

The Book of the Law claimed that someone would come after Crowley and find the "Key to It All." This key has been hotly debated and studied in occult circles, but I have never particularly noticed it being associated with the lost word of Freemasonry. Crowley had his own word for the key, but he often stated that he was confused and perplexed by his own involvement with it. Sometimes he stated that his whole life was an attempt to understand *The Book of the Law*. The unconscious was a major factor in his life, and he certainly was not privy to all of the meanings behind the various manifestations he was involved in.

It is easy to get lost in and complicate such matters. Anyone who has studied oriental philosophy to some extent can relate to the idea that the Tao itself is the greatest secret. The Tao that can be named is not the true Tao. When you find yourself inside of the

Brass Bottle within the Well of Souls, it is up to you to find your own key and maneuver accordingly. I only know that when I studied these matters, it served as a key to success and wonder which has continued to this day. I also expect this "key" to continue beyond the grave and into infinity. Your challenge, if you should choose to accept it, is to find your own key that works for you. Just as there are quantum realities and a plurality of truths, so there are different quantum interpretations of this key.

In the case of Jack Parsons, he was not just working for a personal key but to a key that would reverberate across the continuum(s). Much of his attention was focused on reversing the patriarchal enslavement of consciousness. The Babalon Working was his personal work of magick designed to accomplish this. My own analysis or interpretation of the Babalon Working is based upon live experience with the phenomena, no small part of which was my interaction and conversations with Cameron. You can find more detailed information on the Babalon Working in the *Book of Babalon* by Jack Parsons which is available on the internet.

A few writers have described various aspects of the Babalon Working, but none of them seem to have caught the inner meaning of it or grasped what really happened. Cameron was quite adamant on this point. The book *Sex and Rockets* gives a lot of good biographical information on Jacks Parsons, but it fails to understand the Babalon Working. Many magicians are patriarchal in the extreme and would not recognize the Goddess if you placed her right in front of them (which, by the way, is often done in the Gnostic Mass). This is one reason Cameron and I got along so well. I simply extended her the courtesy of recognizing who she was on a personal level but also on an archetypal and quantum level.

The genesis of the Babalon Working really begins with the appearance and association of L. Ron Hubbard. Jack was quite surprised and happy when he met Ron and found a kindred soul who was interested in magick. It was only after he met Ron that he set out on the adventure that was to become known as the Babalon Working. At the inception of the work, Jack realized that he lacked a proper "familiar." When a magician engages in a magical act, it is common for them to utilize a "familiar" which is often a cat or other life form imbibed with the magical will of the magician in the hopes that this creature will facilitate the master will of the magician. In his notes on the Babalon Working, Parsons states that he did not have a typical familiar so he decided to use Ron instead! While this last statement might rub certain adherents the wrong way, Parsons actually wrote such in his notes. Of course, this gives us a rather different slant on what actually happened, but first let us examine the Babalon Working itself.

In January of 1946, Parsons decided he would find an elemental mate to help him in his endeavor to invoke Babalon. He decided to use the Enochian Tablets that were utilized by Dr. John Dee and Edward Talbot Kelly from their necromancy sessions four hundred years earlier. Primarily, Jack would invoke and receive occult transmissions from what was considered to be the Goddess Babalon. Ron served as the scribe, but their roles did reverse per his notes. After six days, Jack stirred up some "phenomena" when he heard nine strong rapid knocks. A table lamp at the opposite corner of the room was thrown violently to the floor and broken. Five days after that, the lights of the house failed. Ron, who was carrying a candle across the kitchen, was struck strongly on the right shoulder and the candle was knocked out of his hand. He called Jack and the two observed a brownish-yellow light which Jack banished with a magical sword. The next day, Ron developed "some sort of astral vision" and described in detail an old enemy of Jack's of whom Ron had never heard. Later that night, Jack heard the raps again with a voice crying "let me go free." A feeling of tension ensued for four days until, on January 18th in the Mojave Desert, it suddenly ceased. Jack looked at Ron and simply said, "It is done." He was absolutely certain that his elemental mate had been found.

Soon after returning to Pasadena, Marjorie Cameron suddenly appeared at Jack's door. Although I have heard different versions of what occurred, Cameron had been involved in a minor traffic accident nearby and was led to the door of Jack's house. Although she had no idea of what was going on, she was ready and eager to work with him.

From January 19th to February 27, 1946, Jack, Marjorie and Ron worked together to invoke the Goddess Babalon. This included ritual masturbation on Jack's part in order to create a moonchild as per the eighth degree of the OTO. Then, the Ninth Degree ritual of sexual intercourse occurred between Jack and

Marjorie that was designed to incarnate the moonchild that had been created or made to manifest during the Eighth Degree working. Ron was present during the workings.[*]

On February 27th, Ron went back east to New York and Jack returned to the Mojave to invoke Babalon whereupon he was commanded to write *Liber 49*, a manuscript of seventy-seven verses dictated from the Goddess Babalon. It is during this dictation that Babalon commands him to take the Black Pilgrimage. This will be touched on later, but it was the ultimate in self-sacrifice. In other words, his invocations and magical actions were to lead to his personal demise.

When Ron returned about a week later, Jack kept his recent invocations of Babalon secret from Ron, but they continued their work. Now, Ron acted as the dictator and Jack acted as the scribe. Ron was transmitting Babalon and instructions were given to construct a black box. It is not completely clear, but it appears that this black box was utilized to hold the sacrament which would have most likely been the genital excretions of Jack and Marjorie.

Ron's instructions are followed and the eventual outcome was that Jack was completely sure that Babalon had been incarnated on the Earth. At the time of the working, Marjorie Cameron had no idea of all the esoteric significance nor did she have any idea that she was or might be Babalon.

The Babalon Working itself has a multitude of variables and is consequently challenging to examine. It is an original admixture of various disciplines compounded by the very live energy of three magically imbibed people. One noteworthy find is that all three participants were related. At the Pasadena Library, I found a book on the Wilson clan which indicated that they could trace their lineage back to the wife of Henry the VIII, Catherine Parr. A search into the genealogy of the Parsons clan indicated that the name Parsons derived from Catherine Parr as well.

When I first met Cameron, I was not at all aware of anything other than the most general implications of the Babalon Working. I had not even read the *Book of Babalon* at that time but had only read distorted accounts from the various publications that lumped

---

[*] A moonchild is the stirring up, recruiting or the "creation" of the spirit that is to be incarnated. That is the purpose of the Eighth Degree while the Ninth Degree concerns the physical manifestation or incarnation of the moonchild.

it as "Black Magic" in an attempt to discredit Scientology. All I knew was that the Wilson name had come up strong when I had pursued the various synchronicities associated with the name of Cameron. I was hot on the trail of something, but I had no idea what I was going to find.

17

THE BLACK PILGRIMAGE

At the time I met Cameron, I was not particularly interested in the details of the Babalon Working but was merely trying to reconcile how the name "Cameron" fit in with so many synchronicities previously encountered. It eventually became clear, however, that elemental forces and coincidences that were clearly beyond the realm of ordinary experiences were empowering my life and work. These not only enabled me to become intimately involved with Cameron but with the energies of the Babalon Working itself. This, in and of itself, was never particularly my desire.

Having had many long and intimate conversations with Cameron, it is hard to begin describing her. When I first met Cameron, she did all of the talking. She talked about the old days at their home in Pasadena which was known as "the Parsonage." Although it was full of bohemians, it was also frequented by top scientists and sometimes military personnel.

Cameron talked quite a bit about Robert Heinlein, a man she was not too fond of and referred to as a "cad" who was full of himself. Heinlein was very interested in Jack and hung around him a lot. He definitely borrowed Jack's ideas and philosophy for his most popular book which was entitled *Stranger in a Strange Land*. She did not see Heinlein as a participant in magick although there is certainly a case to be made for that. Heinlein was quite famous himself at that point and was completely fascinated with magick. He was already on very friendly terms with L. Ron Hubbard. A series of articles written in *Green Egg* magazine demonstrated that Heinlein was not only interested in magick but was also an avid practitioner of it. His surviving wife ruthlessly denied these charges, but she also reportedly denied that her husband had anything more than a passing meeting with Jack Parsons. As this is decidedly untrue, she would seem to suffer a rather severe credibility problem when it comes to her husband's role in magick.

Besides the natural human interest in Robert Heinlein, I mention him because he was a real wild card in Earth history. He definitely appreciated sexual magick, and his book, *Stranger in a Strange Land* became the Bible for the free love generation. Based upon *The Book of the Law,* it was published in 1960 and was broadly recognized as a forerunner and major influence of the so-called "hippie phenomena." As a result, many people in the San Francisco Bay Area to this day are avid followers of Aleister Crowley and some even treat Crowley as if he was their personal savior. They are serious about this to the point of not being much different than a devout Catholic in terms of their faith. Heinlein, however, would routinely disappoint his hippie following when he would show up for a Santa Cruz lecture in a business suit and espouse a right wing conservative philosophy. Heinlein lived in a compound in Big Sur and was highly protective of his privacy due to the extreme amount of onlookers and worshippers that were attracted to him as a result of *Stranger*. Many hippies and others viewed him as a prophet. Heinlein, who was also an old navy officer, never fully let go of his military connections.

In addition to her stories about Heinlein, Cameron also told me about the interesting observations of an astrologer when she had a chart done on her deceased husband. The astrologer, who had an excellent reputation, had said that Jack had the perfect chart for being in charge of the CIA. Although she accepted the death of her husband, she never dismissed for a minute that he might still be active in some capacity.

It was in the late 1940's when Heinlein would visit and frequent "the Parsonage." Every Sunday evening, all sorts of offbeat and unique creatures would gather at the Parsons' house for a potluck event. There were many stimulating creative and esoteric discussions. It was an opportunity for all sorts of networking. It was into this environment which L. Ron Hubbard came, but he arrived before the advent of Cameron. Cameron liked Ron very much and indicated that he and Jack were like brothers. She said that as a Pisces, he was spiritual and very deep. She believed that Ron had been a Wilson in a past life as well as having Wilson lineage in this one. She did not particularly agree with the scathing articles and publications which have portrayed Hubbard as a scoundrel for absconding with Jack's money. This is in reference to an incident in 1946 when Jack, Ron, and Sarah Hubbard formed a partnership known as Allied Enterprises. Allied was set up to buy yachts on the east coast and sell them for a profit on the west coast. Jack put up most of the money, and when Ron and Sarah arrived in Florida, they purchased a yacht and seemed to be indulging themselves in a pleasure cruise to the detriment of the partnership. Jack had to employ the law, and he sued them in order to retrieve about one-third of the entire investment. Cameron believed that Ron had every intention of bringing the yacht to California, but she felt that the aftereffects of the Babalon Working were still operating in his psyche. First, she thought the familiarity of the Caribbean waters reminded him of a time in a previous life when he was a pirate, most probably Henry Morgan, who she thought was also of the Wilson lineage. But, more importantly, she felt that when Ron and Jack engaged in the Babalon Working, they were emulating the earlier work of John Dee and Edward Talbot Kelly.

Although Dee and Kelly are pretty well known by most people who study magick, the full significance of their work is not fully appreciated by most magicians and is certainly not a staple to the studies of ordinary history. In fact, John Dee has pretty much been blackballed from academic history. That is another matter that will be addressed later on in this book.

Edward Kelly had a reputation as a scoundrel and even had sex with Dee's wife at one point when Kelly's spiritual sources indicated they should indulge in wife swapping. By reason of the fact that Jack and Ron were so deeply invoking the magical aethyrs that had been translated and scribed by Dee and Kelly, Cameron was not in the least surprised that some aspects of their personalities might have rubbed off on Jack and Ron.

Another thing that Cameron said in defense of Ron was in reference to the many disaffected Scientologists that had come to her over the years. They often complained about all of the money they had spent in Scientology. Although Cameron said that she had never really studied the subject of Scientology, she said that the price of freedom is irrelevant. Whatever it costs to break the chains that bind you, it is worth it. She also understood that anyone pursuing Scientology was interested in personal and spiritual freedom. In fact, she told me that she was ordinarily not fond of visiting with people who had experienced Scientology. What let me in the door, she said, was my response to what Hymeneaus Beta had told me. When I first asked him about Cameron, he had indicated to me that she thought that her magical work in the Babalon Working was related to the onrush of UFOs that followed in the next few years. To my good fortune, he accurately relayed my reply that "there might be something to that." She then recognized that I had an open mind and realized that I not only respected her statement but that I might further appreciate what other phenomena she knew to be real. She also revealed to me that she had witnessed a UFO over the Arroyo Seco, the same area in which Jack had performed his pioneer rocket experiments. Her sighting was accompanied by a feeling of sheer joy.

Amidst all of the information she shared with me on that Spring day in 1992, one of the first things she told me on our first visit was that anyone who became intimately involved with her becomes famous. One such example, she explained, was Dennis Hopper, a film maker she knew quite well before he hit it big with *Easy Rider*. At the time I met Cameron, I had no idea I would achieve any significant notoriety beyond being the ghostwriter for *The Montauk Project*. At that time, I was very content to take a back seat, which is actually my preferred mode of operation, and let Preston Nichols, Duncan Cameron, and Al Bielek be the stars of the Montauk Project. After all, the tales of the Montauk Project and the Philadelphia Experiment were based in part upon their experiences and recollections. These stories, which I found very interesting, although not necessarily completely true in a linear sense, were an extraordinary vehicle for me to fulfill a postulate that I had made when I was fifteen years old: to be a professional writer. For that, I will always be eternally grateful to the Montauk crowd for having the courage to stand up for their convictions and to offer all of us a unique glimpse of quantum reality. They have expanded our horizons and opened a view of limitless possibilities.

I never expected to discover and generate so many synchronicities surrounding the phenomena of the so-called Montauk Project. Although I did not realize it at the time, my meeting with Cameron and the subsequent literature that was to ensue catapulted me into a position of notoriety.

Having worked close to Hubbard, I was not a stranger to fame, but that fame was his, not mine. I learned at an early stage that fame has a definite dark side. One of the first things you were taught in his employ, if you were close to him, was that people within the organization would target you just for being near him. In other words, they knew they could not "hit" him so they would hit at you. Consequently, he could be very protective of his staff. Keep in mind that these "attacks" were from Scientologists who were supposed to be loyal, dedicated and loving beings. This is the primate side of life. People often tried to misuse his authority to enhance their own agendas or projects in a parasitic fashion.

Fame only attracts parasites or attention because there is perceived power in it. More often than not, that perceived power is illusionary. Hubbard obviously possessed considerable personal power. He even worked out a "Power Formula" in order to instruct others to obtain and maintain personal power. Many people in the magical community believe that Hubbard obtained his power from the Babalon Working or his association with Jack Parsons. Based upon my own inside knowledge and my conversations with Cameron, I believe this is at best only partly true.

Cameron told me that Ron was very "shaken" after the Babalon Working. There was a lot of occult force involved, and he was changed forever. There is no question that he was deeply influenced by the occult elemental forces that hovered around the working. But, Hubbard exhibited paranormal characteristics long before his involvement with Jack. In fact, he was quite a character in his own right. There were many other factors at work as well. According to all of my research and investigations, the real key of power with Cameron, Parsons and Hubbard revolves around their Wilson lineage. I had studied the power of Hubbard and Scientology at a very close range. It was never my interest to be "powerful" beyond my own personal needs but studying the subject of power went with the territory. My own personal interest had much more to do with consciousness than achieving personal power. One of the reasons I never returned to the Scientology movement was that I knew from first hand experience that Hubbard's power had been aborted. There is still considerable power in that organization, but it is at least one step removed from the original source. When one frolics in spiritual or quantum phenomena, you had better be very sure where your power is coming from and who is holding what strings. If you do not, you could be abruptly surprised. The source of power is very important. All I knew was that I had witnessed considerable power in my association with Hubbard. I knew the difference between his and my personal power. With Cameron, it was a decade later and I was rummaging through the "power installation" of the Babalon Working. It was sort of like Preston Nichols discovering all this machinery at Camp Hero and then discovering the nature of the Montauk Project. There was a definite residue of power in the Babalon Working. Studying it and reporting on it propelled me in certain directions, most notably, the path of synchronicity. As synchronicity equates to the *Tao* or the unifying force, it is a power within its own right.

On the surface, the Babalon Working was a bold, and some would say insane, attempt to create a moonchild and thereby manifest Babalon in all her glory. Crowley himself was very wary of Jack Parsons' work in this particular regard, but he was also very dissatisfied that Parsons was not sharing the whole operation with him. As per the advice of "Babalon" to Parsons, "the work was to be kept secret."

As far as Crowley was concerned, the Babalon Working was unorthodox. Whatever the case, many magical ingredients, instruments, and props were utilized that were designed to facilitate a manifestation that would reach beyond the boundaries of the ordinary. In my opinion, the most potent force in the entire working was the "love obsessed" passion of Jack Parsons. He was a handsome man who readily attracted the opposite sex, but he ultimately transferred all of his passion into what he considered to be the "Goddess of All." He was a religious fanatic, but a very sincere fanatic. He believed that the patriarchal religious system on Earth was designed to control and subvert, not only conscious thought but the major feminine aspects of existence. He took it upon himself to correct this maladjustment and chose the instruments of a magician to influence the elements of fire, water, air and earth (YHVH). Even more important than his effort to utilize and influence the elements was his use of love. I have never seen rituals of a magician which contained such deep love and passion for the goal that was desired. In fact, I cannot imagine anyone creating and manifesting such passion without getting some form of answer or result.

If you wish, you can now read up on the mumbo-jumbo and particular ritual aspects of the Babalon Working on the internet. I am not so much concerned with the details of that, but I have been a recipient of the energies and have been charged with a certain responsibility for seeing that certain things are communicated. When one employs a washing machine, one is trying to obtain clean clothes. When one drives to Chicago, he is trying to get to Chicago. How one obtains clean clothes or gets to Chicago is not as important as the end result one is trying to achieve. Therefore, please excuse me if I do not frolic in the procedures and format of how things were done. I have seen many magicians drool over the contents of the Babalon Working, and I can only liken this to rubbernecking at a spectacle along the highway.

When one postulates or indulges in magick, the results are not so specifically predictable. Cameron was quite aware of that. One is dealing in sympathies. In one sense, Cameron was the elemental Jack sought to help him incarnate Babalon herself. During the Babalon transmissions, Jack was warned that the elemental could destroy him. Cameron believed, and there is reasonable evidence to suggest this, that her presence eventually led to his demise in human terms. But, besides being the elemental, Cameron believed that she was actually transformed via the Babalon Working into the Goddess Babalon, but this only occurred at a later date. I must be quick to point out, however, in honor of her memory, that she was not on an ego trip and did not believe that she was the only entity in the universe who could lay a claim to this title. It was not even something that she particularly wanted but was a metaphorical transmutation of her beingness. During the time of the rituals, she said that she was not particularly clued in as to what was going on. It took many years and the death of Jack himself for her to realize exactly what had happened.

Cameron was a vibrant and outrageous redhead. Not too many years after Jack died, Cameron was still a young woman, but she began to methodically transform into a different archetype of a woman. Her reddish hair began to whiten, and her face started to become craggy. She started to carry a staff, wear capes, and looked as if she could have been a relative of Gandalf the magician. She said that she was literally transformed by the operation to not only manifest the Goddess herself but a cronish version thereof. This became more and more manifest with her as she advanced in age. As it was, Cameron thus became a living flesh incarnate or representative of the Goddess Babalon.

Jack Parsons death certificate indicates he died on June 17, 1952 in an explosion at their coach house in Pasadena which was apparently caused by mercury fulminate. At that time, the newspapers reported that he was involved in devil worship at the time of his death and painted a very somber and macabre version of the Jet Propulsion Laboratory's most famous rocket scientist. None of the newspaper reporters had the mental fortitude or training to look beyond the obvious and to comprehend that Jack had written a book called *The Black Pilgrimage* in which he foresaw his own death. In addition to this, he had penned *The Manifesto of the Antichrist*. A casual and uninitiated observer will readily conclude that Jack was crazy, was seduced by the devil and sacrificed his own life in the process. In his own mind, he was performing the supreme sacrifice, not unlike the legend of Christ in the Bible. This was during the same general time period that Gandhi had been declared an esteemed mahatma in response to his willingness to allow himself to be beaten and attacked for simply demonstrating civil disobedience against repressive laws in both South Africa and India. Gandhi put his head on the chopping block and was revered throughout the world. Parsons was exercising a different type of civil disobedience, but he was not appealing to politicians. He was taking his appeal to a higher realm which could only be exercised through the archetypal realm of Pluto. This meant death for the physical body. I should be quick to point out in this narrative that I am not an advocate of such rituals nor do I encourage anyone to indulge in this type of behavior, but it is important to explain the exact nature of what was being done. Human beings are a timid lot and tend to cringe at what they do not understand. At the sign of death and blood, most of us become skittish and ill at ease. These pathways of perception are normally closed to common folk, but it is absolutely vital that light be shed on them because it broadens one understanding.

Eventually, I spent a full day of research at the Pasadena Library probing into the death of Jack Parsons. That will be addressed later on, but the most important fact regarding his departure was not in any of those newspapers. What nobody knew as they examined his ruined laboratory and his charred body was that his work, his ritual, and his intention were to have significant ramifications beyond the grave.

18

THE AMADO CONNECTION

On the very first day that I met Cameron, she was quite adamant about one idea that she had learned from Jack. She said that you cannot really begin to properly judge a man until 100-150 years after his death. By this, she was talking about their contributions and relative worth to humanity. It takes at least fifty years, she said, before you can begin to get the first inklings of how things might line up later on. At this writing, Aleister Crowley has been dead for 55 years, Jack Parsons has been dead for 51, and L. Ron Hubbard for 17. The full legacy and impact of these men will not be realized for many years to come.

As I became involved with Cameron and the wake of the Babalon Working, I was still primarily following the Wilson trail. After all, that was what led me to my remarkable meeting with her. About six months after meeting her, I was in a book store and stumbled across a book by Amado Crowley. My first reaction was that this was a cheap trick by a would-be author who was using the Crowley name to promote himself. Any one who has read the typical literature on Aleister Crowley will find no references to Amado Crowley. Nevertheless, I picked up the book and looked inside. When I immediately saw a reference to a British journalist by the name of Snoo Wilson, I decided to take the book a little more seriously and bought it. Had it not been for the Wilson name appearing, I would not have considered the book for a moment.

Reading Amado's books definitely changed my impression. He not only revealed a keen sense of humor and wit, but a deep knowledge of the occult. Opposed to most other authors, he spoke with a familiarity of Crowley which is in stark comparison with those who revere him. I wrote him a letter and told him very briefly of my interest in the Wilson lineage and asked him if he had ever heard of the Wilson Brothers. Although he had not read any of my work at that time, he gave me a polite response informing me that he did indeed remember his father talking about the Wilson brothers. Further, he stated that they were friends of H.G. Wells and might have inspired his tales about time travel. The most interesting and corroborative piece of data he offered that revealed he was a genuine occultist was that he said that, to the best of his recollection, the Wilson brothers were sterile. While he did not state it openly himself, a friend of mine who is an occultist readily recognized that sterility is an indication that these Wilsons were most likely moonchildren, i.e., the product of a virgin birth. *Montauk Revisited* received a lot of serious attention in occult circles because it explained this ancient occult technique whereby the zona pellucida of the female could be "fooled" by a male protein already genetically inherent from her father. In such an instance, the zona pellucida "believes" that the male protein is in fact a sperm and, for all practical purposes, the body treats it as a sperm and gestates a child. The male protein does not appear unless it is triggered by a specific process. The resulting offspring often turns out to be sterile twins. Sometimes, the process is aborted or abbreviated and the twins do not fully manifest. Instead, the "magical child" is born with an extra nipple or set of nipples which are sometimes referred to as "witches tits."

While the above did not prove Amado was Crowley's son, it certainly put him in the ball park. He advised me that the OTO were not very fond of him. In fact, they were just on the verge of having what he termed a "magical war." When I allowed the Outer Head of the OTO to review my manuscript of *Montauk Revisited*, he was helpful with certain editorial corrections that needed to be made, but he was very unhappy that I had included anything about Amado, a man he considered to be a fraud. Besides Hymenaeus Beta, I have found out that the OTO hates Amado with a passion.

I was not pleased to see occultists fighting. Actually, I thought they both had something to bring to the table and both were of assistance in my efforts. I certainly had no axe to grind with the

OTO as Hymenaeus Beta had facilitated my meeting with Cameron. Besides the letter about the Wilson Brothers, Amado thought that I was really on to something with the various synchronicities I had strung together and he offered a considerable amount of help. We subsequently had a long and voluminous correspondence. Amado stirred the pot for my research again when he forwarded me a picture of Men-a-Tol, an ancient stone torus (doughnut shaped) in Cornwall, England where he claimed the following:

> "On the 12th of August, 1943, Aleister Crowley, myself, and five other people were gathered round an ancient stone monument, called Men-an-Tol, near Morvah in Cornwall, England. You will note the remarkable similarity of the name to Montauk. I enclose a photocopy of a postcard. The stone itself is called "a quoit" because it has a large circular hole in it. I was made to lie on a length of board, and this was inserted (me with it) into the hole. It was like the ferrite rod that is put into an electric coil. Aleister performed a ritual which appeared to "cause" a line of "rough water" between this spot in southern England, and Long Island in the USA."

The OTO hotly disputed this claim, but Amado stood his ground. Virtually all the occultists and psychics I spoke to, including Cameron, had no problems with Amado's claim. She was suspicious of the OTO however. The OTO were the only ones who were bent out of shape, but I was not sure why. All I knew was that Amado's coaxing facilitated further investigation that struck pay dirt. His citing of Men-a-Tol as a sacred spot is now legendary and received international attention in 1998 when the entire New Age crowd noticed on August 11th of that year that a solar eclipse revealed a shadow line which ran all the way from Cairo to Montauk and went straight through Men-a-Tol.

My correspondence with Amado was just beginning in the Spring of 1993 when I received a letter from a Brazilian national who had an industrial company in the Midwest. This letter stood out as it was written on stationery that behooved royalty. This lady, who I will refer to as Margarita, had been referred to *The Montauk Project: Experiments in Time* by a famous comedian named Dick Gregory. When I was in high school, I had read Dick Gregory's book entitled *Nigger* which was about growing up in and working his way out of the ghetto. After reading his book some twenty years earlier, I was glad he had now read my book. As you read on, you will discover how ironic it is that I was put in touch with Margarita by a man who has served as a champion and example for the black race. If it were not for Dick Gregory, I may never have encountered Margarita. In her letter, she informed me that she had a home on Long Island and was very interested in meeting the Montauk crowd. Eventually, we all got together and became friends.

Besides having all the trappings of extreme wealth, Margarita also had considerable psychic abilities. Many men, I think, would find her intimidating. She was so fiercely independent that she intentionally had children without being married and completely took care of their rearing. Additionally, Margarita was very interested in sexual magick and had a lot to say on the subject. She explained that the reason the ancient cities of Sodom and Gomorah were destroyed, as well as Babylon, was that they had harnessed and discovered the secrets of kundalini energy and had discovered how to live in a virtual "nirvanic" state. According to her, it was the forces of evil that destroyed these fabled cities with myths being fostered that would have you believe everything was the other way around. Perhaps because of her psychic ability and perhaps because of her wealth, Margarita was vigorously pursued for recruitment by the OTO. She told me that they gave her a contract to sign and wanted her name to be written in blood. Margarita had no interest in joining the OTO nor in signing her name in blood.

When Preston and I met Margarita, she wanted to help us in any way she could. I soon introduced her to a producer who was putting together a television show that would feature the Montauk Project. She was going to help finance it. After viewing samples of the producers work, Margarita promptly flew him to Long Island and negotiations began. As soon as Margarita became involved with us, she reported that her business suddenly was scrutinized by the IRS. All of a sudden, she had major financial problems. The television show never got off the ground, but we stayed in touch as she struggled with her new problems.

Margarita was very interested in the Crowley and Wilson investigation I had underway. In fact, she offered to fly Amado to America so that we could all meet him. Thus began a long dialogue with Amado about inviting him to the U.S. He was positive and offered to help us in any way he could. There was much concern about security on his part as well as the weather, and it was deemed that October of 1993 would be the best time for him to visit. As this was being arranged, Margarita was insistent that I should seek out Robert Anton Wilson at a festival of pagans in upstate New York. She had met him there a year ago and thought he would be very helpful to me. On the urging of her and one of my other friends, I decided to make this trip, but first, I had to wrap up the finishing touches on *Montauk Revisited: Adventures in Synchronicity*. As Amado had made such insinuating remarks about the similarity between *Montauk* and *Men-a-Tol*, I decided I would go to the library and see if I could make any more sense out of the etymology of the word *Montauk*. What transpired is rather amazing, but it is now one in a string of many remarkable coincidences.

Arriving at the library, I went to the section of books about Long Island. There, seeing a book entitled *Historic Long Island* by Rupert Wilson, I readily picked it up when I saw it was by a Wilson. As the book had no index, I rapidly thumbed through it whereupon I soon discovered a most remarkable photograph of pyramids. It had a caption that simply said "The Pyramids — Montauk." This was too bizarre. I searched long and hard, but there was no explanation of the pyramids in the entire text. I consulted a very nice librarian who escorted me into a back room of the library and indicated I could have a look at some of the books in a book case. Rummaging through this "off-limits" section, I soon discovered that Montauk's Camp Hero Air Force station was on sacred Native American ground that was claimed by the Montauk Indians, a tribe that, despite showing up in significant numbers, had been declared legally extinct by the New York State Supreme Court. Further, the Montauk Indians were the royal tribe of Long Island and the ruling family were known as the Pharoahs. An entire book, *Pyramids of Montauk: Explorations in Consciousness*, had to be written in order to explain (if only to myself) what these associations were all about. Amado's comments had urged me to the library for the purposes of looking up a single etymology.

The result was an entire book as well as an irrefutable argument that there was government funny business associated with Camp Hero that had been going on for hundreds of years. As the manuscript for *Montauk Revisited* was completed and what I had just discovered would require another year of investigation, I submitted the book to the printer. The next day, I was off on a ten hour drive to seek out Robert Anton Wilson at a pagan festival.

Margarita told me to check in at a local bed and breakfast nearby the camp site. She explained that she had reserved two rooms for herself and other associates. When I arrived, Margarita was nowhere to be found. In fact, she never showed up for the entire week of the whole festival. Robert Anton Wilson was nowhere to be found either. I found out he was not even a scheduled speaker. As it turned out, the journey was incredibly productive, particularly in the long run. Instead, I got to meet two of Robert Anton Wilson's dearest friends: Bob Shea and Timothy Leary. Bob Shea, who passed away not too many months after I met him, coauthored the *Illuminatus Trilogy* with Wilson. Dr. Timothy Leary needs no introduction. It turned out that he was the featured speaker at the event.

Leary was an incredible character and gave a talk which fastidiously followed the outline of a college professor with a thesis, antithesis, and a synthesis. Academically, it was quite beautiful to behold. He was basically using scholarship to show how the establishment, including the entire university system, chokes off consciousness and any form of goddess appreciation. The way he used the system's own academic codes to tear down their hypocrisy was a stroke of true genius on his part.

Giving Leary a copy of *The Montauk Project*, he asked me to sign it and was very friendly. Later on at the festival, he told me it was very interesting stuff and that he would be in touch. Later that year, both Preston Nichols and Leary were on the same speaking bill in Sacramento. I called the facilitator of the event so that both could meet each other. Preston subsequently reported that Leary did want to be anywhere near him and told the facilitator that Preston Nichols "was a walking time bomb waiting to go off." This was quite a strange reaction from someone who not only had been so open but who had once been heralded as the apex of the counterculture.

The next summer, Preston and I met an older Montauk resident who was quite open with us about strange phenomena at Montauk. She not only remembered Nazi U-boats basking in the sun off of the Montauk Light House, she said that Timothy Leary was a regular out at Montauk in the 1960's and that he used to hand out LSD there. This may explain the bizarre psychedelic interior designs that were discovered inside of a building within the confines of Camp Hero. The various patterns, particularly the room that was all black and white, reeked of mind experimentation. Although the building was torn down, video footage of the rooms can be seen in a video tape by Preston Nichols entitled *The Montauk Tour.*

Due to his father's military connections, Leary spent some of his formative years at West Point and was supposed to be groomed for a military life, but this did not happen. Leary ended up in a tenuous relationship with the CIA. Both tried to jerk the rug out from under the other one's feet. Leary was part of the Government's MK-Ultra experiments, mostly under the tutelage Aldous Huxley, a man who also tutored Andrija Puharich. In Leary's lecture that I heard, he said that Huxley used Crowley as a text book. Leary ran his LSD operation out of an estate in Millbrook, New York which also housed a parish of the Moorish Orthodox Church. Under this one roof you had LSD, CIA influence, consciousness expansion, and the Moorish Orthodox Church — very strange bedfellows it would seem.

Although Margarita had pushed me to the festival for what appeared to be the wrong reasons, I ended up making some very good connections. She was adamant about me going. Many of the characters I met were some of the nicest people you might want to meet and they were of many different persuasions, but none of them were Christian. There were OTO people, Druids, gypsies, wiccans, and a host of other brightly colored people. It was very rude of Margarita to not show up nor to offer any explanation. The proprietors of the bed and breakfast were not happy with her, but as things turned out, these "lower forces" of her discourtesy were working to open up a door for me.

As a result of Margarita not showing up, a couple of guys were able to fill the vacancy one evening. One of them recognized *The Montauk Project* on the proprietor's table (I had given him a copy) and was extremely surprised to see the book sitting there. Already having read the book, he was shocked to find out I was staying there and asked to see me. The proprietor knocked on my door during breakfast and told me that I had a fan who wanted to see me. We soon had an interesting conversation, and I told him about the Wilson synchronicities I had experienced. He was very surprised at the synchronicity of meeting me in the same bed and breakfast and told me he was investigating synchronicity himself. This person was very excited and told me that I would soon receive a package after he got back home. I did not make too much of it because I did not know what he was talking about.

The festival was very colorful and interesting, and I did make some contacts for the future; but this chance meeting turned out to be an interesting key as to what will unfold in the rest of this book. Margarita, or the occult forces working through her, had done me a favor.

19

BORN OF LAM

Returning home from the festival, *Montauk Revisited* was still at the printer, and I prepared for what was to be the release of my second book, also coauthored with Preston Nichols. There was a lot of buzz at the time as no one had any idea which direction the sequel to *The Montauk Project* might take. Although I was immersed in synchronicity at the time, it is only now finding its way into print a decade later.

One of my contacts at the festival sent me a newsletter of events in New York City. I learned that a man by the name of Peter Lamborn Wilson would be speaking on "Magick in Colonial North America" on the 13th of November 1993. I was already acutely sensitive to any mention of the name "Wilson," but when I saw that he was speaking on the subject of magick, I could not afford to pass up this opportunity. Although I did not realize it at the time, the evening was loaded with more clues than I could consciously register. Peter Wilson's middle name itself should have been a dead giveaway. The name *Lamborn* suggests "born of Lam." Lam was, as was stated in my earlier books, a bubble-headed "alien" or entity which Aleister Crowley had personally painted which was later to serve as a prototype illustration for the ubiquitous grays that the UFO field has embraced so extensively. Aleister Crowley claimed to have contacted this praetor-intelligence or extraterrestrial entity prior to a mysterious trip to Montauk Point in 1918. Looking backward, I might have been experiencing some sort of conscious denial on this point because when I originally printed a story on this experience, I spelled Wilson's middle name as "Lambourne" which was incorrect.

Peter talks like a professor and is extremely knowledgeable. Although he can open up to the most metaphysical of concepts, he tends to stick to academic references and historical facts. It should be pointed out that many of these facts would not be smiled upon by an authoritarian or consensus view of history; nevertheless, they are quite true.

On that evening, Peter Wilson spoke about the matriarchal nature of the Native Americans and how they were very accepting of absorbing other people into their tribe. He cited many historical examples of how white people would escape the colonies and live happily with the natives. Conversely, colonial history has made a case for natives abducting white people to their horror. In most cases, Peter explained that these were either not true or highly exaggerated. Most people preferred the matriarchal life of nature as opposed to a life based upon property, arms and repressive Christianity. Perhaps the most important point he made was that history is written by conquerors who fastidiously see that their own version of events is printed. History is littered with such diatribes. As a result, the heritage and wisdom of the "losing peoples" is lost. This was particularly true in the case of the Native American tribes of which the Montauk Indians are a prime example.

During a break, I introduced myself to Mr. Wilson and asked if he had heard of *The Montauk Project*. He said he had heard of the book but had not read it and needed to be reminded of what it was about. I then told him I was a "Wilson hunter" and why the name was important to me. He laughed almost as if he knew what I was talking about. I asked him if he had experienced any synchronicities or otherwise unusual circumstances that had to do with the names "Wilson" or "Cameron." Surprisingly, he had one. He said that one of the most fascinating characters he had ever come across was a Wilson who was run out of Scotland for being one of the most radical revolutionaries that country had ever known. He said that the man ended up in America where he calmed down and became an ornithologist (one who studies birds). Mr. Wilson was very intrigued by the fact that one could be so involved in revolution and end up studying birds. It appeared so irregular. When I asked Mr. Wilson what this particular Wilson's first name was, he told me that it was "Alexander." This just happens to be the legal first name of Duncan Cameron, the time traveler from *The Montauk Project* who remembers being Marcus Wilson in an earlier life. Although this was too much of a coincidence to be taken lightly, I could not really take it any further.

The very next day, a little more information would trickle in. I received a phone call from a man who said he was part of the Aviary Group. This is a code name for a front group for the CIA that studies, collects, and releases information concerning UFOs. It is not a highly credible group but the synchronicity with "birds" was interesting. The man who phoned me said he had grown up in Massachusetts next door to Marcia Moore (mentioned in *Montauk Revisited*) on one side and next door to a Wilson family on the other side. This coincidence, he said, was what prompted him call to me. A few days later, I met with my psychic friend, Joy. She has experienced all sorts of synchronicities with the names "Cameron" and "Wilson" as stated in *Montauk Revisited*. To my surprise, she knew exactly why I was being pointed in the direction of birds. In fact, she said birds were highly intelligent and were her favorite animals. They are connected to the energy grids of the Earth. Homing pigeons and migrating birds tap this grid in order to know where they are going. It is a telepathic connection. The word "bird brain" is a misnomer. What they lack in size, they compensate for with telepathic ability. Scientific studies reported on in the *New York Times* reveal that parrots and other talking birds know what they are saying; however, most birds resent captivity and are either smart alecks or nonresponsive. The meaning behind the bird connection would come full circle when someone pointed out to me that the greatest bird in history was the Egyptian Phoenix who would renew itself in a funeral pyre every five hundred years. The name "Phoenix" is interesting because the Montauk Project itself was known as part of the "Phoenix Project." More importantly, I discovered that it was also the code name Aleister Crowley used as the head of the Ordo Templi Orientis. So, my search for Wilsons led me back to Crowley again. It reaffirmed his connection and allegorically implied that he was in a magical position over all the "birds" or "aviary group."

In retrospect, the most interesting thing about my meeting with Peter Wilson was that there was a repeating pattern of synchronicity at work that I was completely unaware of at the time that it happened. I went to see him lecture only because his name was Wilson and for the reason that he was speaking on magick. The repeating pattern, however, had to do with the fact that Peter Wilson also had a secret identity. This was hauntingly similar to my previous meeting with the executive from Mystic Fire Video who turned out to be Hymenaeus Beta, the Outer Head of the Ordo Templi Orientis or O.T.O.

Many years later, I learned that Peter Wilson also uses the pen name of Hakim Bey, a writer on Islam as well as what is often considered to be "heretical Islam." Wilson was at one time an interpreter for the last Shah of Iran and spent a considerable amount of time in Persia. At that time, not too many people knew of his identity as Hakim Bey although it is much more commonly known today. The Rave Culture, particularly in the San Francisco Bay area, were big fans of Hakim Bey.* Peter Wilson's involvement with the Shah has caused many people to wonder if he was in the CIA. To be honest, I do not really know, but associates of his believe that to be the case. The CIA were all over the Shah's government and that is not a secret, so it would be no surprise or shock at all to surmise that Peter at least knew plenty of these people and had, at the very least, some association with them. There is an apocryphal story of how when the Ayatollah Khomeini took over, Peter Wilson was "smuggled" out of Iran in the trunk of a Toyota Celica.

As I alluded to earlier, I had no idea that Peter Wilson was such a counterculture celebrity at the time I met him. Almost immediately after meeting Peter, I received the long awaited package that had been promised me from my chance meeting at the pagan festival. Within it was a mysterious brochure about a time travel cult accompanied by one of the most mysterious catalogues ever known to man.

---

* For those of you who are not familiar, Rave peaked in the early 1990's and is/was a youth subculture largely based upon the drug ecstasy (a mild hallucinogenic compared to LSD but which can be fatal if one has certain medical conditions), strobe lights, and an expressive but somewhat uniform (could also be called Eurostyle) method of dancing. One of these dances or experiences would be called a "Rave" but the term also applies to the whole movement.

20

INCUNABULA
AND ONG'S HAT

When I received the mysterious packet in November of 1993, it was right after I had seen Peter Lamborn Wilson. Although his ideas and lecture were fresh in my mind at the time I received the package, I did not associate his name with the documents, even though they included a cover letter from a "P. Wilson." The first name was originally written on the cover letter, but it had been blackened out, except for the first initial, just like the "blackouts" you see in documents released under the Freedom of Information Act. The reason I did not associate him with the document was that my mind was focused more on the idea of it being a "Preston Wilson." It was obvious that the sender did not want me to know the first name of whichever Wilson wrote the cover letter.

Besides the cover letter, the package consisted of a travel brochure (which explicitly referred to time travel or travel to another dimension) entitled *Ong's Hat: Gateway to the Dimensions!* and a 1990/91 catalog of rare (next to impossible to find is probably a better description) books or pamphlets from the Incunabula Press. I should add here that this packet was definitely not sent to me by Peter Wilson, but it turned out that he was indeed the author of the cover letter. I did not find this out for many months, and the story of that will be revealed later on. It was, however, a meaningful coincidence that I had just stumbled upon Peter Wilson prior to receiving this packet. The full set of materials I received in that packet, along with additional information, can now be found in a book entitled *Ong's Hat: The Beginning* which I coauthored in 2002 with Joseph Matheny. That book is excellent supplementary reading to this one, but I will summarize the essential aspects of the story for those of you who are new and so as to refamiliarize for those who have read the book already.

Ong's Hat is a location in south central New Jersey that was said to be the location of a mysterious ashram of hippies, dissident physicists from Princeton, Sufi mystics, and a colorful array of nonconformists that included gay people and drug culture aficionados. Perhaps the strangest and most mysterious connection to this ashram was the influence of the Moorish Science Temple, a thought-to-be defunct or inactive religious sect which traced its roots back to the original Black Muslim movement in the early part of the last century. It should be noted that the Black Muslim movement is a very misunderstood phenomena in our culture. Although most white people do not understand it at all, most black people, including most Black Muslims, do not understand the roots of the movement and exactly how they were compromised as a result of what went down in history. More will be said on this later. But, it should be understood that the original Black Muslim influence, or more properly, the Moorish influence, was a big and integral part of the Ong's Hat mythos and phenomena.

The Ong's Hat travel brochure was in fact a mythological analogy of different events and circumstances that may well have included a tall tale or two; however, the exact truth of exactly what happened at Ong's Hat has yet to be determined. By the very nature of the circumstances and experiments, all quantum possibilities should be considered and no potential truths, whether improbable or not, should be discounted. The travel brochure told the tale of a meditation device that was constructed like an egg and housed a "traveller" who was wired with biofeedback machines who also used a variety of consciousness techniques which included meditation, tantra, pharmacology, and most notably, "synchronicity attractors." These techniques had the traveler concentrating on any pattern he would see on a video screen and linking it with his mind in a manner by which he could precipitate events associated with those biofeedback patterns. The trick was linking the physical realm to the consciousness realm. Personally, I found this a rather novel way of looking at things, and it is most certainly a valid of way of connecting the physical to the nonphysical. The sky is the limit with such an endeavor. But, I am quick to add that machinery is not a requisite to making this link. In fact, machinery has been most effectively used in the past to connect with spirits and haul them in or bring them down. It is perhaps due irony that spirits in bodies would perhaps achieve freedom by reversing the process. This type of machinery, at its best, is a monitor and not the best vehicle for freeing yourself.

The Ong's Hat travel brochure told the tale of how, through the use of these techniques, a traveler named Kit went inside of a psychotronic egg-shaped device and was able to finally make a breakthrough to a parallel universe called Earth Prime which was largely uninhabited. Once this other world was discovered and safe passage to it was secured, the travel cult at Ong's Hat began making an exodus to a world free from politics, pollution, tyranny, and almost any other negative aspects that could be associated with modern day Earth.

The brochure was fun and very optimistic, and while it was not to be taken too seriously, the theories and trail of experiential information indicated that there was more to this whole operation than a mere hoax. The physics was way beyond what the top professors of academe could allow to be considered, and for those who could think freely and consider it, they would be silent so as not to lose their jobs. This trail was different than the Montauk trail because it encouraged participation and was a lot more user friendly; however, I soon learned that there was a negative side to the story of Ong's Hat.

By synchronicity, I happened to be in touch with a lady who lived not too far from this locale. I called her by the name of Madame X in *Montauk Revisited* and she was an integral part of my research at that time. Oddly, she knew about this group and was disturbed that she had not heard from them since a nuclear accident had occurred in their vicinity. Other reports, which have since been verified by independent sources, indicated that a military group had descended upon the ashram to the point where they literally had to run for their lives to escape some sort of persecution. Although this report did not indicate that anyone was travelling through time or to a parallel universe, it certainly pointed to the fact that this group was considered a major risk by the military and they were not to be tolerated. Many people believe that the nuclear accident was not really an accident at all but was staged so as to break up the ashram. Remnants of the ashram later resurfaced on the west coast, and two of the children, now grown and who claimed to be a part of the ashram, were interviewed by Joseph Matheny in the book *Ong's Hat: The Beginning.*

The story of Ong's Hat was fascinating and presented almost an infinity of different tangents, particularly when you consider an additional document that accompanied the travel brochure in the packet that I received. This was a text that was even more mysterious: a bibliography or catalog from an outfit which called itself the Incunabula Press. *Incunabula* is a word which is no longer used much in our culture, but it means "birth" or "cradle" in the dictionary. Additionally, and in this specific case, it also refers to a collection of rare or hermetic documents or books. The catalog from the Incunabula Press listed a host of interesting information which began with Fred Alan Wolfe's book *Parallel Universes: The Search for Other Worlds.* Although none of Fred Alan Wolfe's books are too hard to find, this was included as it sets the tone for the entire contents of the catalog. The listing for each book or paper, all of which were offered for sale, includes rather lengthy (for a catalog) and sometimes tantalizing descriptions of the contents which is designed to create a demand in the reader for finding out more. Most of these publications, however, were not to be easily found. Some were only photocopied manuscripts. Besides obvious crackpot literature and some very interesting description of parallel worlds, the descriptions in this catalog included cutting edge treatises on quantum physics. Perhaps the biggest star in the catalog was Dr. Nick Herbert, a zany but renown nuclear physicist who penned *Alternate Dimensions* under his Moorish Orthodox pseudonym of Jabir ibn Hayaan. This book was suppressed by his publisher and has not really seen the light of day.

Basically, the Incunabula Press Catalog pointed to a trail of obscure and sometimes scientific literature that not only backed up the contention of the travel brochure but which indicated that if this was a hoax, it was a hoax that went far beyond the ordinary bounds of any rational "hoaxing authority." This is the same phenomena as Montauk. If the story is a hoax, it is too big and complex to be dismissed as an ordinary hoax. Both projects invite further investigation because there are so many doors to open; however, it is best to realize that the entire universe we are living in can also be viewed as a hoax in itself. It may be a hoax, but it is a real hoax and has to be treated with a certain amount of respect if one wants to overcome the obstacles and live in relative harmony with them.

There is one other very important thread in the Incunabula Press Catalog that I did not know at the time I received it. *Incunabula* is tantamount to a code word which, in this specific case, was being used with deference to Dr. John Dee, the great magician who worked with Edward Talbot Kelly in mapping out the Enochian calls. Dee's extensive library was known as the *Incunabula*. This is another synchronistic tie to the Babalon Working because Parsons and Hubbard were using the Enochian calls in their work. Although I have never commented upon it until now, I used to encounter the name "Kelly" often in certain aspects of my research. This usually, but not always, referred to men who were somehow compromising women in conjunction with *The Book of the Law*. I received these reports from women who complained or were baffled by characters named Kelly. Although I was aware that Crowley's wife, who literally inspired *The Book of the Law*, was a Kelly, the full significance of the Kelly connection did not dawn on me until I realized that Edward Kelly was a major force in the magical workings which the Babalon Working drew upon for inspiration and influence.

The influence of Dee and Kelly was vast. Cameron was quite aware of that and told me how important their influence was on Jack and Ron. But, you are now ahead of what I knew at the time I discovered the *Incunabula*. Dee and Kelly will be examined later on in this book. Dr. Dee, who was the personal magician and astrologer of Queen Elizabeth I, possessed the largest collection of occult books in his time. Dee's *Incunabula* was literally an archive of whatever fragments or books he could find from the old Alexandria Library at Pharos which was destroyed by fire not too long after the advent of Islam. Dee was a custodian of lost knowledge, but he was also something more than that. He was a very learned man but also a conjuror who not only sought the keys to Solomon's secrets but also utilized them in ways that still influence the plight of man. For example, he is the real founder of the British Empire that still exists to this day. This will also be explored later in the book, but for now, it is only necessary to realize that the *Incunabula* and *Ong's Hat Travel* brochure were indeed something more than a hoax. They were like tentacles of a giant octopus that had found its way into the subculture of our culture. There was a long and learned tradition of secret knowledge that was trying to surface through the legend of Ong's Hat.

At the time I discovered the Ong's Hat story, I did not realize what I have just told you. I wanted to write a book about it at that point, but I was far too busy pursuing the trail of the Wilson/Cameron/Crowley synchronicities. As it turned out, I was not to be disappointed in either endeavor.

21

A QUESTION OF MURDER

At the time I had stumbled upon Peter Wilson and the number of synchronicities connected with him, I was also involved in a rather fast and furious correspondence with Amado Crowley. The latter consumed much of my research interest at that time. He was interested enough in my work to ask for permission to include some of the Montauk story in his books and this was granted. Amado was very supportive of my research and indicated that quite a case was being made that we were on to something, but he added a warning. He said that somebody was trying to prevent it. This was no surprise, but he did tell me a few things about the OTO that I was not aware of. Amado commented that the OTO had leaned on a production company that wanted to do a story on his books. The OTO had become quite a problem for Amado. He said that Hymenaeus Beta refused to even answer his letters. Further, Amado flatly stated that his father, who was once the Caliph of the OTO, claimed that the OTO was not what they claimed to be.

In *Montauk Revisited*, I clearly stated that Amado and the OTO had different points of view. Amado thought I had been most fair in stating the different sides. On the other hand, the OTO insisted that he was a complete fake and showed no indication of being interested in any other point of view. They were adamant and insistent on this. Certain people in the OTO then either assumed or falsely stated that I was on Amado's side and that I had been told the truth about Amado but refused to listen. I clearly stated both points of view.

Apparently, the main stroke of Amado's magick was going to appear in 1997 upon the fiftieth anniversary of his father's death. He boldly stated that he was going to announce the true circumstances of his father's death and what was behind it. Amado claimed to me, as well as in one of his own books, that Aleister was murdered and that the commonly known story of his death was a ruse. Eventually, 1997 came and went without a peep from Amado. According to information I received, he was not only in a magical war with the OTO but a legal one as well. Additionally, I learned that there were many who not only wanted Amado to shut up but were also interested in stopping his communication with me.

In all fairness to everyone, I must say that Amado is somewhat like a roulette wheel in that different types of consciousness or forces step into him and say what they have to say. He is truly a medium. This is neither good nor bad but is a factor one has to consider in dealing with him. This has to be understood and appreciated to fully grasp what follows.

There is much more I could say about Amado, but it is not important to the context at hand. What is important is that his supportive nature and comments were instrumental in revealing occult mysteries that have nothing whatsoever to do with whether or not he is a charlatan. His occult acumen was demonstrated to be impeccable when he first pointed out the occult significance of Men-a-Tol. When this was clearly demonstrated to the world with the eclipse shadow effect, it caught the eyeballs of many people who have decried my own work or not paid it its proper due. Additionally, Amado's encouragement to take note of the etymological inference between the "Men" in Men-a-Tol and the "Mon" in Montauk not only resulted in the book *Pyramids of Montauk*, it also began another investigation which is covered in *The Black Sun: Montauk's Nazi-Tibetan Connection*. While those investigations have little to do with him per se, his acumen and understanding of certain matters were proven to run very deep.

Another truth that I feel I should reiterate is the principle that occult magicians often reflect what is inside the onlooker. In other words, it would not surprise me if many people in the reading audience might seek out Amado and end up running home with their tail between their legs. This used to happen with Aleister all the time. I have witnessed this principle time and again, and I should add that it certainly did occur with various people who approached Space-Time Labs (the lab of Preston Nichols and Duncan Cameron in the 1990's).

In conclusion, Amado proved himself beyond any reasonable doubt to be worthy of regard both as a writer and as an occultist. The fact that he has written books places him in stark contrast to his OTO adversaries as most of those people do not write books. This might be considered odd for at least one strong reason. Aleister Crowley, who they idolize, stated that the greatest magical act one can execute is a book. As the prime example, he referred to the first book that ever made its way into print: the Holy Bible. That act took the sacred texts out of the exclusive hands of the clergy and gave it to the common man. This soon resulted in Martin Luther leading the Protestant Reformation. The Catholic Church has been trying to regain lost ground ever since.

None of the above is meant to suggest that I agreed with everything Amado said or he with me. We were not insistent on letting our different points of view cloud are judgment nor letting it give cause to enmity. The OTO, on the other hand, was pretty much hopping mad by all of the accounts that I heard. Further, they were indulging in mock derision of Amado at every opportunity.

As stated earlier, my friend Margarita was planning on flying him to the states for a visit. But, after becoming close to the Montauk crowd, her problems with the Government started and were becoming more and more cumbersome. Consequently, her communication became sporadic. This frustrated Amado so I began to make arrangements to fly him over myself. Amado was balking as he was not sure that I could protect him from the OTO or other forces that might show up. He also warned me that he could have quite a chilling effect on people and was concerned that his occult "demons" might wreak havoc on me and my friends. In retrospect, I can now see that his warning was no different from that which has been placed on this book. He was actually taking responsibility and making a statement.

Eventually, I heard from Margarita once again and informed her of the situation. She was going to Italy on other business and indicated that she could meet Amado afterwards. A liaison was set up in France, and the two eventually met at a hotel in Paris. Upon her return, I immediately learned from Margarita that Amado's sense of humor extended well beyond the funny observations he made in his letters. When he was planning on coming to the states, Amado had pulled a big joke on us by implying that he was huge and "wore frescoes" instead of clothes. This had everyone wondering if he was extremely obese and wore a mumu like Marlon Brando, but this was absolutely not the case. Margarita said that Amado was a big and tall man but not overweight. She said that he dressed conservatively and was very pleasant.

The most interesting of Margarita's observations was that Amado was deeply concerned about his father's murder and what had actually happened to him. She said that he spoke very sincerely, and there was no doubt in her mind that he was actually the son of Aleister Crowley. Margarita was an active psychic and had already proven herself to be quite correct on many things, including things that other psychics had missed. This was the closest contact I would ever have with Amado. Although my communication did not end with him at this point, the rush and interest to see him had abated. It seemed that this piece of the puzzle had been solved. Amado seemed to be who he said he was. I had no reason to doubt him save for the many naysayers who had appeared trying to sway me from finding out anything further. Still, many events and circumstances had to play themselves out before further mystery would be revealed.

22

THE DAY JACK
PARSONS DIED

As time moved forward, it was now the Spring of 1994 and America's biggest book fair was to be held in Los Angeles that year. I decided to make it a three-pronged trip. I would take my family in New York to visit my family in Southern California, attend the book fair, and also visit Marjorie Cameron and research the Jack Parsons connection a bit further.

After seeing my family and friends, I paid a visit to Cameron. Although she had only about a year to live at that time, she looked in relatively decent shape and was in good spirits the day I saw her. After our visit, I informed her that I was going to the Pasadena library to dig up what information I could find on Jack's death. Additionally, I wanted to visit the old site of "the Parsonage" where the Babalon Working was ritualized so many years ago as well as the site where Jack's death occurred. She was interested and wanted to be apprised of any discoveries I made.

It was on this trip to the Pasadena library that I found two genealogical books indicating that the Parsons, Greens, and Wilsons had all descended from Catherine Parr. In the periodicals section of the library, I accessed every available paper on or about June 17, 1952. This was the day which was certified as the death of John Whiteside Parsons. It was interesting to dig up all of the old facts and reports. In some respects, it was as if I was exhuming Jack from his grave as I was not fully satisfied with the explanations of his death.

The first synchronicity to pop up in front of my face was quite amusing to me personally. I discovered that one of the articles written about Jack's association with magick was penned by a reporter named Omar Garrison. In the 1970's, Omar Garrison became a celebrity in Scientology circles. He authored a couple of books that defended Scientology and exposed government persecution of that organization. Subsequent to these efforts, officials of the Church of Scientology were quite pleased and signed a contract with Garrison to pen an "authorized biography" of LRH. At the time, I remember thinking that it was too bad that I could not write the biography, but I was not thought of in that way. Had I been involved in the project at all, I can guarantee you that the history of Dianetics and Scientology as we now know it would have been played out very differently.

As it turned out, there was a Canadian citizen who was selected to be the liaison between Omar Garrison and the LRH Archives. His name was Gerald Armstrong, a Scientology staffer who I had known on the *Apollo*, the ship that Hubbard called home. Armstrong began to dig into LRH's early history and started feeding all sorts of negative information to Garrison. Together, they created a cabal between themselves that looked at L. Ron Hubbard and Scientology as if they were something other than what they purported to be. Armstrong eventually left the Church and became involved in various lawsuits with them. Eventually, he received a settlement in return for an enforceable court mandate that he would never publicly ridicule Scientology. He has ridiculed them ever since, but contempt of court sanctions against him have been rather meaningless as he is a Canadian citizen and is not about to be extradited for such an infraction.

After becoming part of a cabal with Armstrong, Garrison was in a most peculiar position. Hailed as a great investigative journalist by his own professional colleagues, he had authored two books that demonstrated clearly that Scientology was a valid religion in terms of the law and the precedents of Earth history. He had also shown that Scientology, no matter what their beliefs, had been conspired against and unfairly treated by the Government. Now, if he were to do an expose on Scientology and L. Ron Hubbard, he would look like a monkey on a string. In other words, he was good at reporting data that was fed to him but apparently not too good at looking beyond the real events and circumstances. How ironic is it that he acted as a mere beat reporter with regard to Jack's death and magical association?

Omar Garrison is a prime example of a well touted and respected journalist. Despite the best credentials in the world, and he certainly did not lack when it came to ordinary investigative skills, he proved himself to be quite inept at arriving at the real truth. Reportedly, he arrived at a settlement with the Church where he would keep certain monies paid to him in return for keeping quiet on these matters.

Besides finding the unexpected synchronicity with Omar Garrison, I scoured through a week's worth of various newspapers concerning the death of Jack Parsons. What I discovered about Jack's death was both disturbing and interesting. According to the reports and my conversations with Cameron, I am certain of the following facts. Jack had been packing all day in preparation for a trip to Mexico that evening. Cameron and he were moving although the papers quoted Cameron as saying this was a pleasure trip. She confided to me that this was just a cover story and that they were indeed moving. There was a huge explosion at floor level which apparently triggered an even bigger explosion that could be heard for miles. Cameron, who had been sent to gas up the car for the move, heard the explosion while she was at the gas station. Her intuition told her something was very wrong. Sal Ganci, an experimental film director who lived upstairs, claimed to have been lifted off the couch by a violent blast. With Jo Ann Price, a twenty-one year old actress and model who was with him, Ganci said they went downstairs and found Jack still alive but pinned under a massive laundry fixture with his arm missing. They dragged him free and propped him against a shattered wall until he was found by a city ambulance crew. Jack's death certificate has him dying one hour after the blast although he was reported to have methodically directed his rescuers while being placed into the ambulance. When Cameron returned, she said that not much more than fifteen minutes could have elapsed. She was scurried into the upstairs apartment by Sal Ganci who insisted that she not get in the ambulance or see Jack. Cameron still felt bitterness towards Sal for keeping her away. She said that the medical staff never allowed her to see her husband either.

Quite oddly, Jack Parsons was never identified as being dead from his next of kin. This is a huge irregularity as this identification process is a routine police procedure. Cameron even protested that she was not allowed to see him. Jack's only other kin was his mother, Ruth Parsons, who lived just a short distance away. When she heard the news of her son's death, Ruth was reported to have taken a bottle of sleeping pills with death ensuing almost immediately. A local doctor, J.R. Huntsman* of 65 North Madison Avenue, was immediately called and pronounced her dead upon his arrival. This was an extremely rapid death.

No one had any idea why the explosion in Jack's lab occurred until a brand new criminologist, Donald Harding, appeared on the scene. This was his first major investigation since being assigned as a consultant to the police department just one month prior to Jack's strange and unexpected death. Harding is the source of the famous finding, which is really only a rumor, that Jack died as the result of an explosion of mercury fulminate. In fact, Harding was reported as saying the explosive was "probably" fulminate of mercury based only upon his observation that there were ingredients for making it in the garage. Cameron was later told that the explosion came from beneath the floor boards and ripped them apart. This indicates there could have been foul play. Harding hypothesized that Jack was mixing mercury fulminate in a tin can and tried to catch it as it hit the floor and exploded. This explained Jack's detached arm, but prior to Harding offering this theory, he had observed that the explosion was behind and to the right of Jack. As far as Jack mixing mercury fulminate, it is suspicious that he would have been doing anything of the kind. They were packing to move and this is not something that he would have carried in the car. The original conclusion of the police and fire department was that the explosion was caused by nitroglycerin. There were two major explosions. It is hard to say exactly what happened and how.

---

* When I first noted the name of Dr. Huntsman, I was struck by the synchronicity of the last name, but only as it related to me. My cousin, who grew up in Pasadena, had married into a family by the name of Huntsman. Eight years after my initial investigation, I saw my cousin at a family barbecue. She was someone I had not seen in well over thirty years, but she confirmed that Dr. J.R. Huntsman was her husband's uncle. The odds of my having a family connection to this incident once again defies the ordinary laws of probability.

The issue of Jack's death became further complicated when I read that Jack's partner, George Santmyers, a Los Angeles chemical engineer, claims that it was completely "out of character" for Parsons to have mishandled explosives that would have resulted in the explosion. In fact, Santmyers boldly stated to the press that "someone else" had put quantities of explosive refuse into exposed trash in the rear of Parsons' lab. The criminologist, Harding, had discovered six filter papers containing inflammable residue of fulminate of mercury. They were mixed with beer cans and kitchen garbage along with 500 grams of cordite, an ammunition component. Santmyers said that for Parsons to do this would be like a surgeon operating with dirty hands. Harding reported that these explosives, if not taken out of the garbage, would have finished off the sanitation crew. Coupled with Santmyers testimony, this establishes a case that someone else was dealing with explosives in an unprofessional manner and may have been trying to "clean their tracks" by getting rid of it in the garbage.

Unfortunately, Santmyers confuses the issue and damages his own credibility by boldly stating that Jack was not involved in any magic cults or weird religious rites and that he did not have any enemies. This was told to the press in the office of Stanley Decker, the Chief of Detectives.*

According to Cameron, Santmyers and Jack worked together at the Bermite Powder Company near Saugus but shared an "under the table" business whereby Jack made fulminate of mercury (with her help at times) and sold it to Santmyers who purchased it illegally and resold it to the military, supposedly for submarine warheads. She said that the relationship between Santmyers and Jack was nice and mutually beneficial.

Santmyers is a very confusing character in all of this. He seems to be defending the "good reputation" of his partner but deliberately suggests that someone else, who was incompetent at handling explosives, was involved. If there were no enemies, there

---

* Although I have not reported on it previously, the name of Decker is loaded with different synchronicities. In *Montauk Revisited*, Howard Decker, now deceased, was the name of the man Preston identified as once having been John von Neumann. The name caught my attention originally as it appears suddenly and inexplicably in the film *The Philadelphia Experiment II* upon arrival in an alternate Nazi United States. Besides being a prominent name in Southern California, Decker also appears in Adolph Hitler's family tree.

is no logical alternative. Another side to Santmyers surfaced when Cameron called him after Jack passed away and told him that she was penniless. She said that Santmyers was hostile towards her.

The plot thickens considerably when we consider a coin turned up by the author of *Sex and Rockets* who points out in his book that Jack Parsons did indeed have an enemy who was paroled just before the explosion. This was Captain Earle Kynette of the Los Angeles Police Department's "Spy Squad." This officer was convicted, along with two other officers, for car bombing and murdering Harry Raymond, a vice investigator who was on the trail of police corruption in the LAPD. It was Jack's testimony, as an expert in explosives, that turned the case against Captain Kynette. Jack was only in his early twenties at the time and was noted for his precise and self-composed testimony.

If Jack was himself killed by means of an exploding bomb, the assassin would have needed an inside connection like Santmyers who would have known his general whereabouts and the general lay of Jack's laboratory. When we consider that the criminologist investigating the case had just recently been assigned to the department and that a former cop that Jack helped to convict was paroled just before his death, we are impelled to ask for at least some semblance of a "Warren Report" to see if there was any conspiracy. These facts are all topped by the fact that the body was never properly identified and that no relative ever saw the corpse.

Perhaps the strongest piece of evidence against a murder is that Jack had been working in the building all day. If someone had a controlled release on a bomb, it is likely they would have released it much earlier. If you have your bait in the trap, you want to get him while he is there; not wait for him to leave and possibly never return. Jack could have been gotten much earlier in the day.

It is also an oddity that his lab was littered with explosive materials that were in violation of the residential fire code. If he was indeed moving to Mexico that evening, there is no way he would have just left all those chemicals there unless someone was going to pick them up. These are questions we will never know the complete answers to.

Personally, I was distraught enough about the irregularities in the case to write to the Pasadena Police Department and ask how I might be able to access the file on this case. They politely informed me by letter that this was a very old case and that their records are disposed of after so many years.

Although we are left to assume that Jack died, that is perhaps the most important element. He left the world and society as we know it. This, however, prompts another intriguing aspect to his magical career. Jack Parsons was emulating the Ninth Degree of the OTO when he did the Babalon Working. The Tenth Degree, which follows, calls for taking on a new identity. Whether he did this through the process of physical death or means of a relocation program, he did indeed follow the course of a magical aspirant.

Detective Harding found a note amidst the ruined laboratory which confirmed the broadly misunderstood magical aspirations of Jack Parsons. It was in Jack's handwriting and read as follows:

> "Let me know thy misery totally. And spare not and be not spared. Sacrament and Crucifixion. Oh my passion and shame . . . Mothers . . . Sisters . . . "

Based upon what I said earlier about the Babalon Working, I hope you not only see the serious passion that absorbed or obsessed this man to the point where he was willing to take on the ultimate sacrifice, but that he altruistically looked beyond his own immediate life. Both his scientific and occult mind told him that death is nothing to be afraid of. Jack, whether right, wrong, ignorant, or knowledgable, knew that the application of the will was what was needed to bring about either a scientific or occult result. It was in this sense that he fully applied and sacrificed himself for what he considered to be the most worthy goal in creation: to restore the lost Mother Goddess to her rightful throne.

Although the OTO has always had a definite interest and admiration for Jack Parsons and the Babalon Working, they are always quick to point out, and not incorrectly so, that his work was unorthodox. His work in rocketry was also unorthodox and left early pioneer Robert Goddard in the dust. Parsons got results when it came to rockets. He also created more than a small ripple across the continuum when it came to his magical work.

Jack Parsons was a maverick and, like the radical gene in biology, he was making radical breakthroughs. No one blinks when in comes to his contributions to rocketry or the space program; however, his magical work has left quite a residue that still needs to be unsnarled. At this point, I can only say that I have unsurfaced all of this information and various occult correspondences by way of my own unorthodox approach: the path of synchronicity, with specific regard to the trail of the Wilsons.

With regard to Jack's legacy, the circumstances surrounding anyone's death carries a certain frequency with it. In the case of this formidable magician, we have an alleged death (which most apparently did occur) shrouded in mystery that beckons for further answers and understanding. I experienced more irony once again after I finished writing the first draft of this chapter and just happened to pick up the book *Sex and Rockets* where it notes a very remarkable fact. It states in that book that the social security number given on Parson's death certificate did not belong to him but to a Virginia Wilson. A mistake, perhaps? Or, was it a "mistake" contoured by a mysterious outside influence working via the name "Wilson."

23

UNCLE RALPH

After a day in the microfilm section of the Pasadena Library, my mind and soul had been immersed in the death of Jack Parsons. I was not focusing on magical phenomena but was merely intent on finding out the journalistic truth of what had happened on June 17th, 1952. My next objective on that afternoon, however, was a little a bit different. It was now about five o'clock, and I decided that I would visit Jack's old residences on South Orange Grove Boulevard which were not too far away. Before setting out on the adventure, I phoned Cameron from Pasadena and told her a bit about what I had found in the newspapers. When I said I was going to the site of the old Parsonage, she told me to look into Ralph Parsons. I had no idea what she was talking about and soon forgot about what she had said. The only reason I remembered her initial mention of Ralph Parsons was as a result of the phone notes I had taken during my conversation with her.

The library research was devoid of any psychic investigation, but I knew that my venture to South Orange Grove Boulevard might be wide open to any quantum phenomena. I brought a camera with me in hopes that I might get some irregular photographs of any aeytheric residues from either the Babalon Working or Jack's death. I was not, however, hopeful that I would strike pay dirt. It has never been my hobby or inclination to go ghost hunting or anything of this character. I was pursuing a random lark.

I knew that Pasadena's "Millionaire's Row," where Jack and Cameron once lived, had long ago been carved up into apartments and that I would be lucky to find anything of significance. The reconstruction of the area included some new street numbers so there was a bit of guess work and detective work involved in finding the right locations. While I was looking for 1003 South Orange Grove Boulevard, the site of the old Parsonage, I could not help but notice a "for sale" sign on the 1000 address. It said "William Wilson Co." on it. This was the exact sort of thing I was looking for, so I took a photograph of it. As soon as I took the photograph, I noticed an older man approaching. As he crossed the street, I called him to me and asked him for help in finding the old address. Quite oddly, he said that I should act discreet and be very quiet and that I would have no trouble finding 1003. Pointing across the street, he said that it would be over there and that I shouldn't make any waves. His own sense of security was rather strange. After all, I was just there to take some simple pictures of the sight that had no particular significance to ordinary citizens. I then asked him if he had ever heard of Jack Parsons, a famous scientist who had once lived in the area. He said no, but by this time, I had discerned that he spoke with a definite British accent. The man was very odd. He was quite old and was dressed in a sort of khaki outfit that looked like it came out of an army surplus store. When I commented on his British accent, he told me that he was a Royal Air Force pilot who had been shot down during the war and almost died. He said that he had lived in Pasadena since 1947, but the only Parsons he knew of was the Parsons Corporation located in the Arroyo. I wondered what on Earth he was talking about. The Parsons Corporation? He pointed down the road. I asked who owned it, and he told me that it was Ralph Parsons, the same character Cameron had told me to look into. Asking what they did, the man answered me without any hesitation whatsoever, but it was one of the strangest responses that I have ever heard.

In his British accent, he said, "They do implants."

"What kind of implants?" I asked.

"Aviation implants," he replied.

In retrospect, he looked as if he was coming out of a time door or something. This answer surprised me even more than the fact that there was a Parsons Corporation nearby. It seemed that he was cross referencing from another logic matrix. This response is even more odd when you consider that the Ralph Parsons Corporation was not known for aeronautics at all. He offered no explanation of what aviation implants are, but it seemed that he might have somehow been traumatized by his own history as an aviator. The man then pointed across the street, told me to go to a certain address and said that I would find out all of the information I needed to know. Asking the man if I could give him a book (I did not tell him what book), he waved his arms and said "No, no." I thanked him as he strolled off. Although I considered his suggestion to be completely ludicrous, I did go across the street and took some photographs.

This entire experience was very odd. The only hasty conclusion I could make was that by immersing myself in the aethyric residue of the Babalon Working, I had serendipitously found a "Wilson sign post" which then led to my meeting with a bizarre man who was completely out of any normal context. Perhaps it was a magical communication. After all, Cameron had even told me to look into Ralph Parsons.

When I got back to my hotel, I phoned Cameron and told her of the events of the day. Just as she said she would, she demonstrated keen interest in my adventures that day, particularly the connection with Ralph Parsons. In fact, she had a little story of her own with regards to the Ralph Parsons Corporation.

One of the most joyous experiences in her life occurred when she was working as an employee at the Jet Propulsion Laboratory with her brother Robert. One day, while walking along the Arroyo in Pasadena, they both simultaneously witnessed a UFO in the sky. Although Cameron said she experienced pure joy, she was careful to tell her brother not to say anything about it to anyone for fear of ridicule and negative consequences. Robert did not heed her advice and told various people at JPL about what he had seen. The ridicule in those days was so severe that he was forced to leave and seek employment elsewhere. Oddly, the next job he landed, through pure synchronicity, was at the Ralph Parsons Corporation. This office, however, was not located in Pasadena. Instead, he was assigned to a building in downtown Los Angeles. Cameron then explained that her brother told her the weirdest story about that building. The entire fourth floor was extremely dark except for a glowing spheroid (perhaps even a rock) object in the center that gave off some sort of strange light. It was suggestive of incandescent sulphur or something similar. This always intrigued her, but there was no sense to be made of this nor of the particular association with the Parsons name. The entire experience was an extreme oddity but certainly an interesting one.

Upon returning home, I consulted a magician I knew who had not only enjoyed the Montauk books but was also a big fan of Jack Parsons. He had also worked at the Jet Propulsion Laboratory at one point. This man informed me that the Ralph Parsons Corporation was known for building huge underground cities and sent me a brochure on the company which indicated they were a private corporation that worked with the highest levels of government. This brochure indicated that the Parsons Corporation received the contracts to put out the oil fires in Kuwait after the Persian Gulf War and also built the huge underground complex at the Denver airport. One of the largest companies in the world, they are a private firm so their books and records are not really open for public inspection.

There are further synchronicities connected with the Ralph Parsons Corporation, but they did not come to full fruition until many years later. Although the experiences are nothing short of spectacular when you consider the entire panorama of the Montauk investigation, I have added them to the back of this book as an appendix as the events are out of linear sequence with the current story you are reading. Although I did not know it at the time, the photographs I took were to have an even more bizarre impact.

24

THE BLACK BOX

After visiting Cameron, I returned to Long Island to find Preston Nichols immersed in a new investigation of Camp Hero. A year earlier, Preston and Duncan Cameron were ticketed for allegedly trespassing on Camp Hero, grounds that were supposed to be a state park open to the public. Besides the ticket, Preston observed that the air had also been let out of his tires, presumably either by the park police or someone associated with them. Preston and Duncan decided to fight the issue in East Hampton town court as they knew their case had merit. This hearing was described in more detail in the book *Pyramids of Montauk*, but a summary of the key points is all that is necessary here. First, it was an oddity that all other matters for the day were put to rest before this matter would be heard by the judge. Everyone except the litigants were ushered out of the court room save for one person, a friend of mine by the name of Mike Nichols who attended in my stead as I could not be there. The prosecutor asked Mike to leave the proceedings, but he refused to do so as it was technically a public hearing. According to the transcript, there were some comic exchanges as Preston fumbled with lawyer language, but Judge Ketcham ended up ruling in favor of Preston and Duncan. He had some degree of sympathy for them because he often took walks in the area with his dog and recognized that there were no explicit signs stating where the public can walk. He knew things were not right. As a result, clear designations were made as to what was the "Forbidden Zone" and what was not. In the proceedings, Judge Ketcham told Preston that nobody knew these designations better than him and that, as a result, he should abide by them. Consequently, Preston and myself made it a habit to comply with the wishes of the judge.

About a year after this hearing, a considerable amount of digging started taking place at Camp Hero. Reportedly, old fuel tanks were being exhumed, but there were plenty of other theories about what was going on. As Preston could no longer walk about Camp Hero in a legally sanctioned manner, he rented an airplane and began to videotape Camp Hero from overhead. On his first excursion, he reported that the pilot was nervous and only wanted to fly over Camp Hero once. As he was hired for a specific amount of time, Preston persuaded him to circle the camp several times.

The second time he charted a plane for the Camp Hero excursion, he invited me along. I still had the same roll of film in my camera from the trip to Pasadena, and my primary interest in the trip was simply to get some overhead shots of Camp Hero that might be useful for a book. Preston was already prepared to video tape the excursion himself so my contribution seemed minimal. I thought I was just along for the ride. As it turned out, however, I was in for a harrowing experience with some bizarre and unexpected phenomena surrounding it.

As we climbed into the air from the East Hampton airport, I noticed that the engine in the plane was making disturbing and irregular noises. The plane itself was also unsteady, and I became very concerned. Nobody said a word, and I was not about to panic or bring up the subject first. Although I am not a mechanic, I felt that I was the first to take notice of these circumstances. It was very clear in my mind that there was a potential for something very negative to happen and that this was a life and death situation. Some element was working against us.

In earlier chapters, I referred to the state of "operating thetan" or operating spirit and the postulate. As per all the orientation and instruction I had learned with those endeavors, I immediately went into a mode as if I had been trained to deal with this circumstance. I calmly created a postulate in the same manner I described earlier in this book. Now, there is a fine line between fear and responding to an environmental stimulus or counter-effort. For example, if a boxing champion is afraid of his opponent, he is likely to crumble and lose for fear of being hurt. Yet, if he is to be successful, he has

206

to have a healthy respect and a correct assessment of what his opponent will do to him if he does not respond properly. Fear overwhelms the mind and causes rational thought processes to stop. If one is going to postulate a positive circumstance, particularly in a life and death situation, one is going to do best if they either occupy a state of mind outside of the body or with disregard to the mortal fear of losing the body. In my situation, everything that happened occurred in a few split seconds. As the engine continued to rumble, I merely decided that everything was going to be all right and mentally invoked any forces in the universe that would assist me. The exact instant after I made this postulate, I saw Preston's large hand reach over to the center of the craft as he placed it over a casing that housed the engine of the small plane. As soon as he placed his hand over it, the motor began to churn and make different noises as if Preston had a calming effect on it. After a while, the irregular noises settled out and the engine was running smoothly. Nobody said a word about it, and I was certainly adamant about remaining silent with regard to any negative postulates about our survival. That test or "trial by air" was passed and the rest of the trip was uneventful as far as the operational components of the aircraft were concerned.

I found myself, however, in another predicament. As we began to circle Camp Hero, I was fiddling with my camera as something was not quite right with it. We were also moving in very small circles, and it was a little bit like a carnival ride. I was focusing intently on my camera and tried to get it operational in a great hurry as I did not want to miss the fly over. The intense concentration on a fixed object, coupled with the rapid movement of the airplane, caused me to feel air sickness for the first time in my entire life. Stupidly, in my agitated state, I opened the back of the camera and exposed it to the light. This, coupled by the air sickness, caused me to abandon any hope of taking any photographs. I just had to hold on, keep my frame of reference and put all of my consciousness into not throwing up and making a bad scene. As Preston made some small talk, I politely informed him and the pilot of what was going on and asked them not to talk to me as I could not handle any communication.

After a safe landing and successful trip (Preston had gotten a lot of video footage), I told Preston that I had to sit down on a bench in front of the airport so that I could get my bearings back. I was still quite dizzy and it took about twenty minutes before I felt half way decent. At that point, Preston looked at me and said, "You know, that plane almost went down."

"I know it," I said and told him what had happened from my perspective.

He then said, "I'm pretty good with motors."

In another ten minutes, I was completely back to normal and OK to move on. We investigated Montauk for the rest of the day and returned home. Unfortunately, my fiddling with the camera not only exposed my entire roll of film to sunlight, it ruined all of the photographs I had taken in Pasadena.

When Preston returned home and viewed all of the footage he had taken over Camp Hero, he was most surprised by an irregularity he had witnessed over a stand-alone pump house structure that was the size of a closet. Apparently, there was a black box on top of this structure that had opened up like a trap door as we flew by. Upon closer examination of the video footage, Preston realized that the opening of this so-called trap door was happening in one-tenth of a second or less. This did not make any sense. Doors do not open and close in that manner or that fast. This called for a hands-on investigation that would entail us going to the structure and examining what might be on top. This footage can now be viewed on Preston's video tape *The Montauk Tour II* (the second in a series).

After my airplane experience with Preston, I told Cameron about the incident and how I had lost the photographs. After hearing the story of this mysterious black box that was apparently atop the pump house, she made an interesting comment and said that Jack had a black box. It was his magick box and held occult instruments. I immediately took an interest in black boxes and any synchronicity that might be associated with them. Someone soon gave me a psychotronic book on black boxes, but that is getting off the point. As I discussed these mysterious circumstances with Cameron, as well as my findings in Pasadena, she decided to put me in touch with George Frey, an old friend and teacher to her who had also been one of Jack's best friends. Cameron said that I should talk to George as she had delegated Jack's funeral arrangements to him.

George Frey is a scientist, a profession he shared with Jack, but he was also interested in metaphysics and follows a path of Tibetan Buddhism. He is a very nice man and was very helpful. He told me that he never saw Jack's corpse although the mortician offered him the opportunity to do so. George was not interested in seeing his friend mangled up. But, with regard to the funeral, George told me something that he thought I might find very interesting. To the best of his knowledge, nothing was ever done with Jack's ashes, and he thought they might still be at the funeral parlor. Cameron later dispelled this idea and informed me that the ashes were spread out in the desert in the general vicinity of where he had received his message that the Babalon Working was done.

When I told George about the phenomena with the black box at Montauk, he had an even more interesting story to tell. When Jack died, he said, Cameron did not have a lot of money and her emotions were not up to dealing with Jack's personal effects. Accordingly, she asked George to take care of things. Consequently, George took Jack's magician box and brought it home where he faithfully kept it in storage in an empty bedroom. One day, when George's boss was visiting him at his house, he became very curious about the black box and tried to persuade George to open it. Saying that the box was not his, George indicated that he did not feel that it was appropriate to open it. But, the boss was persistent. After all, it was his boss and the path of least resistance was to open the box. It could have been a fatal mistake as it turned out, but George caught himself in time.

George said that the box was black but also had white cabalistic symbols painted on it. Upon opening the box, George saw a container full of magical implements which included wands and other items of alchemy. On top of the items in the box was a note in Jack's handwriting that said, "Do not go any further. It may cost you your life."

As soon as George read this note, he looked at his thumb and noticed that a deep gash had suddenly appeared upon his flesh. It was accompanied with significant bleeding but no physical accident of any kind. It appeared out of the aethyr. Wisely, he closed the box and the gash miraculously healed in about a day, but there is still a scar to this day and he eventually showed it to me. It should interest you to know that George is a sober scientist and a very stable personality who is not given to flights of fancy. To the best of his knowledge, George believed that Cameron had buried the black box in the desert.

When I told this story to one of my friends, he alerted me that it was a mistake to bury the box. More importantly, the robes, if possible, should be retrieved and burned. When I called Cameron and shared all this with her, she told me that George eventually returned the box to her. She tried to get rid of it herself by taking it to Catalina island and leaving it on the dock. When no one either claimed it or stole it after twenty-four hours, she took it back home. Eventually, she said it was destroyed in a domestic dispute with Sheridan Kimmel, her second husband. Kimmel was believed to be the actual character who inspired Ken Kesey's character Randall McMurphy in *One Flew Over the Cuckoo's Nest*. She told me that Sheridan was quite a character in real life and exhibited strange behavior. For example, he would enter the house through a window instead of walking through the door. One day, she was angry with him and threw something of his into a fire which was burning in the fireplace. He responded by throwing Jack's box into the fire, piece by piece.

When I heard that story, I said, "It took a mad man to destroy that box, didn't it?"

"Yes, it did," she replied.

Although this was all I could find out about the black box at the time, I knew I was being moved along a tidal wave of occult force that was taking me on quite a ride that was not yet done. Preston and I still had yet to make our way out to Camp Hero and investigate that pump house with the trap door. This was a particularly interesting journey because we had vowed not to "trespass" into the Forbidden Zone. The pump house closet was not quite in the Forbidden Zone, but you had to walk through the off limits area to get to it unless you took a very circuitous route. Consequently, we parked at the end of Old Montauk Highway and followed the trail that leads from there to the southern entrance to old Camp Hero. Travelling just outside of the wire fence at the western end of Camp Hero, we made our way through marshy swamp land and stayed outside the Forbidden Zone. It was a long and muddy trek. The pump house itself is now destroyed, but it was located west of the transmitter building and south of the western most bunker (also known as Junior's bunker). As there were no trails for part of the journey, it took us at least an hour to arrive at our destination.

Inside of the pump house, there was only a large valve and nothing unusual or significant at all. There was apparently no black box on top of the pump house, but we still had to look up there. Somehow, by bizarre fortune, there was an old dilapidated ladder next to the pump house. We all knew that Preston and the other fellow who accompanied us were too heavy to comfortably sustain themselves on the ladder without breaking it, so I was the candidate to climb it. As I got to the roof, the first thing I noticed was a small rectangular hatch which was somewhat suggestive of a trap door. It was very snug, and it took more than a little effort to remove it. There was certainly no black box nor was there any configuration that was even slightly suggestive of what we had observed on the video tape. The hatch took several seconds to open by hand, and it was not big enough to have been the door that jerked open on the video footage.

The only other thing of note on top of the pump house was a green bottle which looked like an old wine bottle that could have held about a gallon of liquid. It was filled with water, apparently rain water. None of this made any sense. It should be noted that the roof of the pump house was extremely fragile and I almost fell through at one point. Preston and the other fellow were able to ascend the ladder to the point where they could both see the bottle, hatch and top of the roof. What we found made no sense. In fact, it was as if the video had been taken of another building, experience, or other dimension. But, this was the corresponding pump house from the video tape. There was absolutely no mistake about that. No answer was forthcoming at that time.

The whole adventure became even more bewildering a few days later when Bob Nichols, Preston's father, discovered a green bottle full of rainwater near the back door. He had no idea at how it had gotten there or what it was for and asked Preston if he knew. Preston recognized it as the bottle from the roof of the pump house. The only easy explanation was teleportation unless someone had gone to an inordinate amount of trouble to place it there. Now, besides the black box, I felt I should study up on the magical properties of bottles, including genie bottles, but I thought this might be taking things a little too far. What had originally begun as a rather innocent investigation of synchronicity associated with the Cameron/Wilson namesake had now thrust me ahead and full throttle into the occult current upon which the Babalon Working was based. I would eventually learn that the black box and bottle were very significant sign posts of this current that would lead to further revelation and an accelerated path of synchronicity. There was, however, a significant amount of occult counter-effort that did not want certain things discovered. The brush with death in the airplane was such an instance. Although I did not think about it much at the time, the Babalon Working operated or got its power from the frequency of death. After all, Jack Parsons had sacrificed himself in hopes of achieving his will. I also felt that it was my will which had "woken up" Preston and had preserved our lives. Whatever the actuality might be, I knew that I was not alive and pursuing this mystery by accident. There was also a lot more than my personal life at stake.

25

THE COURT OF ISIS

THE FOLLOWING TRANSMISSION IS FROM A PARALLEL UNIVERSE

As the etymology of *deity* and *daemon* both signify "divide," these words demonstrate how the Creative Force can manifest either positively or negatively. For those in the world of the living, this can mean either life or death. Perhaps there is no better example of the double-sided nature of the deity than what Joan of Arc experienced during her short life. Before I went to sleep one evening, I saw an old black and white movie depicting the trials and tribulations of Joan of Arc. After marvelling the masses with her God-given visions to win battles and to gain fame and admiration as the Maid of Orleans, she was abandoned by the spiritual forces which brought her martial success and broad recognition. Perhaps there were higher reasons for her becoming a sacrificial martyr who was burned at the stake; however, the point is that there was a very negative side to her experiences with the deity.

Perhaps this movie was to serve as a catalyst to my own dream state, but I awoke one summer evening to find myself returned once more to the beautiful alabaster palace of Tetragrammaton. Sheba, who now seemed more at home under the name of Isis, appeared as a sphinx, the lower half of her body being a lion in a reclining position. As I watched her, she rapidly expanded to a giantlike size as she grabbed me with her right front paw and placed me on a pleasant white cloud amidst a light blue sky. Night had turned into day. When she was done, each one of her paws was resting atop the four different watchtowers. Isis then took her right paw off the watchtower as flames jetted out and maintained a steady fire.

"This is the First Power of the Sphinx," she said. "It represents fire, the sign of Leo and the Will."

As I listened, Isis continued to speak to me.

"*The Book of the Law* and the Babalon Working both invoke a kaleidoscope of revolving black and white energies by which the magician seeks to tap the undercurrent of creation and manifest WILL. In this process, Jack Parsons accessed what is known as the first, or right-hand paw of the Sphinx. Beneath this paw is a Wall of Fire and beneath that is a Well of Souls. It is not much different than the concept of hell or Hades. The Well of Souls could just as well be called the Will of Souls. This will is what causes the lion's paw to rise and strike. Inside the Well of Souls is not only every being whoever existed or will exist but the entire sum of every will or intention that has ever existed, the collective mixture of which has been transmuted and is represented into the little world you know as the physical universe. Some wills are subordinate to others. These magical workings you have studied seek to align the most powerful wills and correlate them with their own Earth identity. In the case of Jack Parsons, he immersed himself with a host of energies and completely surrendered himself in order to accomplish his goal. In other words, he cut a deal."

After Isis demonstrated her rendition of the Well of Souls, she reduced herself back to her original size until we were once again in the courtyard with a deep blue night sky as the watchtowers crackled with electricity and aethyric formations.

"You have just been initiated into the First Power of the Sphinx: the Will. In front of me, you will find three apples, each one of them representative of a different watchtower. Eat the first one, and you will have a dream."

As Isis finished her sentence, an extremely strong wind emitted from one of the watchtowers and blew one of the apples far into the sky which had transformed into light blue once again. The wind also blew me as I followed the apple into the sky and watched it come to rest on a cloud. As I joined the apple, I suddenly noticed that I had been surrounded by angels, none of whom I was comfortable with. Their demeanor made me think that they were there in order to gawk at a train wreck or something similar. I thought it best to ignore them. Placing my head near the apple, I soon fell asleep.

I soon found myself in Roman days where people wore "bibs." As a slave in these times, I was selected to be a subject in a cruel game of the wealthy class. A Roman patrician explained to me that I would be placed around a circular stone table with three other slaves who were present. Each of us were to be placed so that we were sitting crosswise to another at the table. In front of each one of us was placed a small colored circle of either green, blue, yellow or red. An arrow on a rod was placed in the center of the table, like a spinner in a board game, and would be spun until it fell precisely on one of the colored dots. Whoever was selected would have to choose their own method of death. The Romans had many different forms of executing people, none of which were enticing and several of these raced through my mind. When the game began, I was placed behind the green dot. Several spins were done without the arrow landing on any of the colored dots. Finally, it landed very close to my green dot but was not directly on it. It was clear, however, that all considered it had fallen on the green dot. I felt that I could debate the issue if I really wanted to and would have had an excellent chance of convincing them of my point of view; however, I soon fell into a strange telepathic rapport with the game master. In some strange and inexplicable manner, I could read his wavelength. The game master and the four of us at the table were surrounded by a group of patricians who were apparently bidding on the various outcomes. All were expecting me to choose my form of death. Their demeanor was similar to that of the angels I had encountered when I had joined the apple on the cloud.

Before anyone could speak to me, I promptly and emphatically said, "I choose to die a natural death after a long, healthy and happy life!"

This tact that I took caught everyone off guard, and I could see that everyone was completely perplexed by my response. I had clearly violated the rhythm and idea of their proposition but not the specific rules. It was quite clear that many of them felt disappointed if not outright betrayed. Soon, a kinder and more noble patrician, who seemed to be above it all, gave me a glass of lemonade. He indicated he would take care of me and that I was in good hands.

Waking from the dream, I found myself on the cloud where I had been. The angels had now turned into gargoyles who were screeching and screaming in violent protest. The kindly patrician, who now appeared as a guardian angel, shooed them away and said they would not bother me anymore. He said that I had invoked the Second Power of the Sphinx which was "to dare."

From my perspective on the cloud, I could see, off in the distance, a cascade of water emitting from one of the watchtowers at the Court of Isis. Quickly developing into a waterfall of rapids, the water moved at a very steady pace as it made a winding path to me. As the river passed the cloud I was on, the patrician angel pointed to another one of the apples that was floating on the water. He said that I should grab it. As I did, the water encircled me and the cloud I had been resting on transformed into a small island. I ate the apple. It tasted quite good with some lemonade that had been supplied by the angel. I fell asleep again.

In this dream, I was quite surprised to find myself on a baseball field with two teams. Although I was dressed to play, I did not feel that I fit in with these people. I either wanted to play or get the hell out of there and the latter was my preference. Suddenly, someone told me to catch fly balls in the outfield. The first ball was hit well over my head and beyond the field. It was not catchable but landed in the Arroyo Seco and rolled down the incline of the little canyon. This was the same locale where Jack Parsons had conducted his early rocket tests. Going down to retrieve the ball, I found three almost new soft balls and also three hard balls. I threw all of them back on the playing field.

It soon began raining. Feeling as if I was escaping, I lost the baseball uniform and made my way up a wooden set of outdoor stairs that led out of the Arroyo Seco. The stairs were caked with ice, and I knew this meant frozen emotions. Running water now appeared amidst a heavier rain, and I knew this would give me the opportunity to break up the ice and create a safe passage up the steps. The stairs led me to a house in Hollywood where I saw an ominous creature who had the combined genetic features of both Jack Parsons and Christ. Somehow, this made him look like an unpleasant version of the television actor Lorenzo Lamas with reddish hair. When he commented that his mother was a virgin, someone in the house made a smart aleck comment about virgins, and "Lorenzo" jumped at the man and let it be known that such ridicule would not be tolerated. I then passed a small room where this bizarre character was, and I faced him.

Looking around at his house and then right at him, I surprised him be speaking directly and saying, "I do not know that this situation meets all my needs."

"You have more needs than most," he replied. It was clear that he was not happy with me voicing my needs. He then spoke in an authoritative way as if he was my guru.

"You need to experience the lessons of the Last Supper."

I had absolutely no affinity for what he was talking about or the experiences he was trying to inflict upon me. The Lorenzo figure, which clearly represented a combination of Christ/Antichrist factors, then insisted I get a shot from an excellent doctor a few rooms away. As I entered the doctor's room, I saw a crumpled up Dr. Mengele, the Nazi's "Angel of Death." He was mixing a serum that was half black and half yellow. It looked disgusting as he filled a syringe with it.

In the same room, my eyes saw a tray covered in glass which had a delicious looking turkey dinner beneath it. There was gravy and mashed potatoes topped by a large garnish of parsley. I could see no stuffing however. It looked delicious, but I was in no mood for what I knew had been prepared as my "Last Supper." Wondering if this dream was someone's idea of a "turkey shoot," I could see "Lorenzo" and quickly deduced that he was very proud that he had gone to the extra trouble and expense to prepare a turkey dinner for me. It was as if he knew this was a proper part of some death ritual or something. I knew, however, that I was not going to eat it. This could be lethal. Then, I realized, I had just accessed the Third Power of the Sphinx: "to know." I did not have to accept what was being inflicted upon me unless I agreed to it by accepting their version of what was to be my "Last Supper."

As Dr. Mengele approached me, I hollered, "Patient's Rights! Patient's Rights!"

He looked befuddled and did not know what to do. I had invoked a universal law whereby he could not operate on me or treat me without my consent. Telling him that I was not comfortable with this arrangement, he was forced to leave me alone. "Lorenzo" was very angry and came after me, but he realized there was nothing he could do.

As I woke up from that dream, I felt that I had not only avoided the unpleasant fate of both Jack Parsons and Christ but had passed another gargoyle and had somehow taken a lot of other people with me. As I looked up from my reclining position on the cloud, I could see that the patrician angel was looking over me. Handing me a thermos full of cold lemonade, he told me this would come in handy as he gave me the third apple that had originally been before Isis. As I bit into it, I saw the fourth watchtower begin to emit a sandstorm of huge proportions. The angel then handed me a pair of wraparound indigo sunglasses and said that I would need them. By the time the sandstorm reached us, it seemed infinite in its range but was only about two feet off the ground. Soon, there was nothing but desert. Off in the distance, I could see a shining pyramid. The angel explained that this was my last initiation which represented the watchtower of earth and was usually symbolized as coins or pentacles in the Tarot.

Carrying my thermos of cold lemonade, I made my way to the shining pyramid which turned out to be the Luxor Hotel in Las Vegas. As I entered the hotel, I saw ridiculous caricatures of people dressed up like Sekhmet, Anubis and the like. I was soon met by a host who gave me a pair of dice and asked me to roll them for a free door prize. The dice came up seven as the host told me that seven represented the Star of Babalon. He escorted me past the roulette and craps tables to a small theater within the hotel which featured bright light bulbs surrounding neon lights that said, "The Babalon Theater."

Entering the theater, I was the only other person inside as I witnessed Jack Parsons kneeling before a red-haired goddess named Babalon who was sitting on a throne. He was brokering a deal whereby his physical body would be pressed into a pure silver coin with a pentagram and then inserted into a slot machine. The silver represented purity or purification, and the coin was to be known as the Silver Star. After he was pressed into the coin, the goddess Babalon asked me to deposit it into a grandiose slot machine that was behind her. She then explained to me that that coin was wired to all of the other slot machines in the Luxor Hotel and would eventually pay off big time to anyone playing a slot who came up with images of either Jack Parsons or the goddess Babalon. It would be called the Jack Pot. She then told me that everyone in the hotel knew about this magick coin that was called the Silver Star. According to a local legend, the Silver Star was lost somewhere in the vicinity of the Luxor gaming complex. According to her, everyone thought the coin had found its way into the Luxor long ago, but she told me that it had only just been placed into the system by myself. I was then instructed to go out into the hotel and see what was happening out there.

When I emerged from the Babalon Theater, there were guards all around. They wore the insignia and capes of secret societies, many of them having the faces of gargoyles as they patrolled the casino as if they were looking for the Silver Star in order to prevent anyone from collecting on it. Upon leaving the theater, I soon found that my pockets were filled with exact representations of the Silver Star coin except that they were smaller than the original. I then went about placing a coin in every slot machine in the entire casino. For some reason, the guards did not notice me at all. When I finally got to the very last slot machine, which was at the end of a long row, I put in my last silver coin and cranked the handle. Instead of Babalon or Jack appearing, a row of Jolly Rogers appeared with lights flashing on and off that indicated I had hit the Jack Pot. Placing his index finger over his mouth, the patrician angel suddenly appeared beside me.

"You will now invoke the Fourth power of the Sphinx," he said, "and that is to be silent."

Handing me a bucket, he told me I would need it as coins of pure gold cascaded out of this last slot machine. After catching them and carrying the coins out of the building, several spilled onto the floor and were readily picked up by passersby. The guards still took no notice of me nor of those who picked up my overspill.

In front of the hotel, I saw the patrician angel on a large and comfortable papyrus boat. He said we would cruise down the Nile and return to the courtyard of the Sphinx so that I could get some rest before I continued on with my next assignment. I did not know what "assignment" he was talking about, and I was not sure that I wanted any such assignment from him or anyone else. The angel then gave me an instruction.

"You are here to help dismantle the guardian network. This is a long and complicated job, but there is one thing working in your favor that will enable you to succeed."

"What's that?" I asked.

"They are exhausted and they serve no useful purpose to anybody. Besides that, they are ready to crumble. Just be silent about your means and your agenda."

I sipped some lemonade as I enjoyed the beauty of the boat ride, but something made me a little uneasy. I began to notice subtle aethyric forms which were posturing and treating me as if I was now being recognized as royalty or something similar. After all, I had been enriched and had escaped death two times, but I could not help but wonder if I was being pampered in order to be set up for something else. The patrician angel began to look at me very pleasantly but it was a countenance I had never seen in him before. It did not suit him. I could then see a subtle rendition of some aethyric form emitting from his backside. It looked like a rendition of the androgynous goat-headed figure known as Baphomet. This was not so bad in itself, but I could see that it would soon turn into a more demonic form if I did not act fast. I rose and pushed the angel over the edge of the papyrus boat. He looked completely surprised as he fell into the water below.

"These creatures can be bastards," I thought as I moved to the bow of the boat and stood an alert watch for the rest of the journey. I looked forward to returning to the familiarity of Isis in her courtyard.

26

OTO REVIEW

Secret societies, including the Ordo Templi Orientis, have acted as the guardians of the gateway for millennia. Although such societies are often portrayed in a sinister light, the individuals in such organizations are human beings, but they are seldom ordinary. Generally speaking, they have a double-side nature. Like a gargoyle, they can turn an about-face and let you slip by the entrance to a portal. There are no ordained limits as to where you can go and what you can access in this universe as a spiritual being. Sometimes, members of these secrets societies will do a good turn and help you access information. Originally, the various grades of initiation in secret societies were intentionally set up so as to illuminate the individual into the various mysteries of the process of life. If properly administered, these grades of illumination would not only enlighten the individual but the immediate culture into a higher and more evolved understanding of the mysteries. This would, in turn, not only accelerate the pageantry of the mysteries but the understanding of them as well.

Knowledge, by its very nature, does not just disappear. If it is not liberally taught and extended into the civilization, it is tightly controlled and removed from common accessibility. Then, in a highly controlled patriarchal system, it is dispensed back to the multitudes in such a way as to empower those in control. This is particularly true in our current society with regard to the sexual aspects of the mysteries. In our society, most woman still do not feel comfortable to assert themselves in a manner that is completely free. Instead, we have controlled and regulated impulses that dispense sexuality to the masses via pornography. The biggest commodity on the internet, pornography's booming business serves as proof of the repressed condition of our society with regard to the sexual mysteries.

To some who see beyond this repression, and are not just seeking idle or indulgent pleasure, they turn to an organization such as the Ordo Templi Orientis in hopes that they can penetrate all the mysteries. Entering such an outfit is like a playing a game of roulette or even Russian roulette. You end up facing various gargoyles reflective of your own personal magick mirror. After all, it is your life and your personal mysteries that you are addressing in such an organization. Aleister Crowley, who at one time assumed the title of Outer Head of the O.T.O., literally assumed the throne of Baphomet, an androgynous archetypal figure which not only represented the epitome of duality but the sum total of the astral light. Crowley was known to dispense so much "truth" to an individual that they could end up in an insane state. There are various popular accounts of his lovers ending up in fragmented states or in asylums. It should also be pointed out that there are other accounts of him serving people and giving them illumination. In any case, his initiatory acumen was known to be intense. He could play either side of the gargoyle. If you feel that I have repeated this theme too often in this book, please understand that it cannot be emphasized enough.

Through his own genetic line and personal predisposition, Jack Parsons had an acumen for occult learning which not only drew him to become a full fledged member of the Ordo Templi Orientis but the man most responsible for its growth in the 1940's. He was the only serious financial supporter and eventually became the acting head of the order in Southern California until the Babalon Working made him persona non grata.

From all of the different accounts I have either heard or read about him, Jack Parsons was not the type of person who desired to be in a position where he could admit or deny others passage. He was neither a gargoyle nor a receptionist. Parsons was a maverick who broke with tradition in order to achieve a result. His passion had him shooting past the portal faster than any gargoyle could stop him. It was as if the gargoyles were so taken aback that they could only sit back and comment to each other like a couple of old ladies on a park bench who complain about a reckless and fast driver. Jack's passion for change was such that it would not allow for the relatively conservative views and regimens of the OTO. Although Jack was a progenitor of change and is being portrayed as one of those rare beings who actually does something, there is another side to all of this. Although the OTO has been cast in a somewhat suspect light, their conservatism is quite understandable in many respects. Beyond their loyalty to the order, the human side of OTO personnel would likely have been literally terrified or repelled by Jack's willingness to make the supreme sacrifice. This put him in hot water as far as OTO politics were concerned. He was playing with fire as represented by his "elemental" named Cameron.

Aleister Crowley was very wary of Jack Parsons' actions, particularly when Jack wrote that he could not reveal all. As an aside, there is no better way to piss off a "superior" in a secret society than to reverse roles with them. Put yourself in a position where you are dispensing information to them or being secretive and you may see their nostrils flare with fire. Crowley not only thought Parsons had gone hopelessly astray but commented that he thought Jack was being conned by Hubbard. He subsequently removed Jack from any position of authority.

Amado Crowley also wrote to me that he believed that Aleister had cursed both Parsons and Hubbard. The Babalon Working pushed the envelope in many respects. Although the popular press has had fun with it from time to time and often used it to decry Hubbard, magical people were concerned about the Babalon Working. Sometimes they are even in awe. Cameron told me repeatedly that the OTO watched her with extreme caution and closely monitored her activities. She was not partial to them and vehemently protested their patriarchal behavior and emphasized that she never joined their membership. In retrospect, it is ironic that I seemed to pass undetected on the OTO's radar screen. If it were not for the outer head of the order, I probably would never have been able to meet Cameron. Not unlike the flip side of a gargoyle, he did me a good turn. I was certainly not trying to deceive anybody, and at the time, I had no idea of who Amado Crowley was or that there were disputes about the legacy of Aleister Crowley and the OTO. I was just trying to find my way.

My personal interest in magick was only precipitated by my discovery that L. Ron Hubbard had drunk so deeply from this well, and I wanted to know something of what he knew. Parsons and Hubbard had tapped into an occult current that Crowley was no stranger to as well. I was only able to tap into it through my interest in Hubbard which had precipitated my interest in the Montauk Project and my subsequent discovery of the Cameron and Wilson synchronicities. It has thus far demonstrated to have a life of its own. Some would think it is too flamboyant to suggest that the same occult current that begat the Jet Propulsion Laboratory also created the Montauk Project and Dianetics and Scientology itself. There are others who would swear that these institutions are a pure creation of occultism. Personally, I believe it is a matter of shades of gray from both perspectives. It is too easy to overstate things, but occultism, by its very nature, is hidden from view. It should therefore never be easily discounted. More important to my investigation and immediate circumstance, I was soon to learn that this occult current had the power to kill. Although I had already experienced a brush with death, the message had not really sunk in.

Perhaps this last statement is too ominous and frightening or even overblown, but it should be remembered that occultism is an invisible force by its very definition. There are plenty of instances of mysterious deaths, only one of which are the strange deaths that befell those who unsealed King Tut's tomb (claims of microbiological infection do not stand up to other strange circumstances which befell these people, particularly the man primarily responsible). Like any powerful tool such as a gun or a sword, occultism has double-edged aspects and that is why the image of the gargoyle has been so generously disseminated herein. What I was about to discover about the OTO in the summer of 1994 was just one more example of what I have termed occultism's "power to kill."

Although Jack Parsons served as the acting head of the Agape Lodge of the OTO in Pasadena, Karl Germer, a German national, was the titular head of the OTO in the United States and was the chosen successor to Aleister Crowley. No one disputes this. The successorship after Karl Germer is still bitterly disputed to this day. Although he had no idea of it at the time, Jack Parsons unwittingly created a lasting impression on the OTO by initiating a man by the name of Grady McMurtry into this secret order.

It should also be pointed out that there are several organizations which purport to be the true OTO; however, the one that is recognized by the courts of the United States is the one that was headed by Grady McMurtry. McMurtry was an American soldier during World War II and Parsons arranged for him to meet Aleister Crowley when he was on leave in England. McMurtry had visits with Crowley and the two shared a correspondence for a short time. McMurtry was used by Crowley to spy on the Agape Lodge which was under Parsons' leadership. After the war, McMurtry worked as a political scientist and eventually claimed successorship of the OTO from Karl Germer upon the latter's death in 1962. For those who want to learn more about the "official history" of the OTO, there is plenty of information on their website.

Before I say more about the strange successorship of the OTO, I feel it is necessary to make a few comments. Although I have had a popular audience who have appreciated my forays into the occult, I have found that the majority of my readers who have enjoyed my writing do not really remember the OTO when the name is brought up in discussions. Even though the order has been explained to the point where some readers have requested further information about it, the name either does not register with many people or it seems to have no significance to them whatsoever. This has been so prevalent that I have sometimes wondered if their memories have suffered from some sort of "erasure." After all, the OTO is a secret society, and they do use secret means.

On the other hand, the OTO take themselves <u>very</u> seriously, even to the point of comedy at times. I have seen more than a few letters written to people who are on the outs with the OTO. They are usually told in emphatic and pompous language that "We are the only true OTO." More often than not, these letters were written sloppily in pencil and looked like something a child would write. I am not making a carping criticism of the OTO here but only mention it as an observable fact. Not all OTO people behave this way, and although I have been very suspect of different people I have met who are either part of the OTO or associated with the OTO, it should be remembered that there is a dual nature to all of these creatures. They do harbor a tradition of wisdom. How they dispense it or deal with it has everything to do with their individual nature and the "magick mirror" effect I have described earlier.

The OTO believe they are the custodians of a very great and secret order. They have a College of Cardinals and engage in rituals that insiders and outsiders have described as pompous ceremonies that obviously fill certain psychological functions in all of the participants. Perhaps more than any other secret society I have ever heard of, they do not like to be laughed at.

Many younger people have embraced the OTO because it purportedly allows a freedom of expression in terms of sexuality and uninhibited nudity. Although certain OTO factions enjoy an uninhibited party-mode, there are other aspects of the organization which tightly monitor people's sexual behavior. Most of these younger aspirants have no idea of the organization, it's history or how it acquired whatever legitimacy it purports to have. For many of them, it does not really matter as it is really a fashion accessory to their youth.

I have seen various misadventures of people involved with the OTO and these include certain aspects of demonic possession. To be fair, people who study magick can exhibit a "thin veil" when it comes to the hidden aspects of their personality and the entities which inhabit them. These features also exist in regular members of the population but are submerged due to social conditioning. Perhaps the most ridiculous aspect I have observed with regard to the OTO is what I call "snickering." In other words, if you ask them for esoteric information that is deemed highly sensitive and there is an implication that they might know it, they snicker. This not only gives the impression that they know something that you do not but that they can hold it over you as either a carrot or tool of power. Sometimes they might know the information and sometimes not. The snicker, however, is a distinct characteristic.

In July of 1994, I was pursuing certain OTO connections with regard to my investigation of Jack Parson's black box and the subsequent bottle that was discovered. These adventures called for me to return to the pagan festival I had visited a year earlier. A host of magicians and other magical people were sure to help me with the unfinished loose ends of my research. Many people and friends were met, but I was on a mission to find out certain things. The OTO connections, however, turned out to be rather lame. Instead, I met a voodoo priest who sold me a pamphlet which was headed: *Everything You Wanted to Know About the OTO but Were*

Afraid to Ask. This document portrayed the OTO in a different light than I had ever seen. It included a brief summary as well as an entire copy of a petition filed in U.S. Appeals Court protesting the court decision that sanctioned Grady McMurtry as the Outer Head of the OTO. It described a very interesting court case about Grady McMurtry's acquisition of the rights to the OTO. His adversary in the case was a Brazilian by the name of Marcelo Motta who had been chartered by Karl Germer to operate an OTO lodge in Brazil.

On the same day I bought this document about the OTO, I met a disciple of Marcelo Motta. Contrary to the reports of former supporters of Motta who had deserted him in order to head up the mantle of the current OTO, this man portrayed Motta in a positive light and said that he was not the ogre they made him out to be. This man was selling various magical publications which included collector copies of Motta's publication of Crowley's *Equinox.* I purchased a copy of a magazine called *Starfire* from him because it contained a full copy of Jack Parson's *Book of Babalon.* This included Jack's notes on the Babalon Working plus a copy of *Liber 49* which was the personal transmission he received from Babalon. This was the first time I would actually see Jack's notes, rituals, and transmissions which were the Babalon Working.

Within one of the very expensive books that Motta's disciple was selling was an interesting comment by another one of Motta's disciples. This claimed that Grady McMurtry was actually a spy against the counterculture and that he had very close ties to Ronald Reagan. In order to understand the context of this previous sentence, it should be realized that Grady McMurtry lived in Berkeley, California during the days of the hippie counterculture. Although he was older than the youth of that day, he often war robes or clothing which made him very amenable to the hippie culture. At that particular time, the major antihero to the counterculture in California was Governor Ronald Reagan who was very down on the hippies and radicals in Berkeley. Certain circles in the counterculture were not very impressed with Grady McMurtry nor his military background. There are various histories on McMurtry and the OTO, and I do not mean to bore you with them. They are rather tedious. The only people who seem to care about them are the OTO and their adversaries, and these people care about them with passion. Whatever anyone wants to say about McMurtry, the United States Government did eventually recognize him as the legal successor of Aleister Crowley's OTO.

The only reason I have brought up this subject has to do with another comment that I saw in one of the books being sold by Motta's disciple. It brought up the fact that Reagan's middle name is Wilson and that the name Ronald Wilson Reagan has six letters in each name which corresponds to 666, the number of the Beast.* The comment by Motta's disciple indicated that Reagan had either directly or indirectly influenced the outcome of Grady McMurtry's case against Motta in acquiring the rights to the OTO. Reagan had apparently appointed the judge in the case as well, but I figured these assertions might be hard or tedious to prove. Although I had previously heard that Reagan's name could be construed as 666, I had completely forgotten that his middle name was Wilson. Synchronicity was once again at play. With the way everything was falling into place, it caused me to take the accusations of Motta's disciples a little more seriously.

---

* Another ironic twist with the Reagan connection is that right after I learned this information, the news mentioned that a consortium of Reagan's friends had purchased a home in Bel Air as a gift for the former president. Reagan did move into the house, but he was disturbed by the fact that the address was "666" and got approval from civil authorities to change it to "668." I found this incredibly funny because "668" is the prefix to all phone number at Montauk.

27

ALEISTER'S GHOST

Although I had purchased the *Book of Babalon* and the booklet on the OTO court case, I did not have time to read them at the festival and only perused them quickly. Upon returning home, I had to catch up on a lost week and still did not have time to read them. Soon after, I received a call from Margarita. She was on Long Island and wanted to see me about something. When I arrived at her house, she informed me that she had developed a regression technique and was very set on seeing how I would do with it. When it comes to regressions, I normally would not let anyone touch me with a ten foot pole. This is not because I am afraid of it but because I have a considerable amount of experience as both a regressor and regressee. Although most regressions widen people's horizons and generally help them, I have, for the most part, been unimpressed with the various techniques I have seen in popular self-help culture. In her own strange way, Margarita had found a special place in my life, and I really appreciated her unbridled interest in Amado Crowley. She really wanted to help me. Her eagerness and sincerity for the regression matched my own intuition, and I agreed to go ahead with it.

To my pleasant surprise, I was keenly impressed at Margarita's techniques. She was not only quite focused and present in the session, she was quite wise in what she was doing. According to her, she could make three to four thousand dollars a session administering this to the wealthy class in Brazil. She was giving it to me for free, but she had a motive. Although she never explained herself in this regard, it became obvious to me what she was about. She wanted to see how I would react in a session and to see if I was sympathetic and had an appreciation of it. Additionally, she wanted to see if I could pull up subdued memories. What I encountered in that session was personally revealing to me, but it has no relevance to the matter at hand. In her eyes, I definitely passed the test.

After the session, she brought me upstairs to her private room and explained that she had done a similar session on Amado Crowley when she was in France but was confused by it. As we sat down in a couple of chairs, she was not completely comfortable about revealing what could be construed as privileged information, but she needed help in understanding certain things. Her confusions had to do with some rather bizarre phenomena that occurred during Amado's session. Accordingly, we ended up going over the notes from the session which apparently included what Amado was planning to reveal on the 50th anniversary of his father's death. This consisted of the circumstances behind Aleister Crowley death and who was behind it. I have sat on this information for nine years and have never published it. Amado had scheduled a major release of this information for December 1, 1997 in a book that was to be entitled *The Murder of Aleister Crowley*. Besides my mention in *Montauk Revisited* that Amado was going to release information about his father, he had also published his intention in his own book. When 1997 came and went, there was not a word from Amado. I only knew from his letters that he had been involved in both a magical and legal war with the OTO. Although I was still in communication with him at this point, our correspondence began to suffer in terms of letters not being delivered. He further intimated that our communication was being deliberately stopped. Things became so difficult with the logistics of our communication that I began to enlist different Englishmen to help me get through to him or his publisher. These efforts either failed or met with utterly ridiculous circumstances.

Although I was friends with Margarita, I did not consider our relationship to be buddy-buddy. She lived a broad life and was involved in all sorts of activities, and we certainly did not share all of our personal secrets. Most of the time I knew her, she was not even on Long Island. In fact, I was surprised that she came to me over this matter of Amado Crowley's sessions. In retrospect, I believe her entire involvement with me was to affect certain "occult transmissions" that were coming from a higher power. First, there was the trip to the pagan festival which had led me to the discovery of Ong's Hat and had enabled me to acquire *The Book of Babalon.* Now, she had information to tell me about Aleister Crowley's death. She was fascinated with the Crowley connection and was a willing and potent vehicle for my research.

In one of his last letters to me, Amado not only complained that all of his correspondence with me had been mysteriously deleted from his computer but that Margarita had taken copious notes of his regression session but had not informed him of what went on. Both Amado and Margarita informed me that he "goes out like a light" when he is either regressed or acting as a medium and generally has no conscious memory of what transpires. He is a "trance medium" in the truest sense of the word. When I finally communicated to him what happened in the session, it was virtually our last meaningful communication. The line had been effectively cut for all practical purposes.

As I sat with Margarita in her private office, she explained that when she regressed Amado, it was Aleister that had come through. In fact, she had never seen anything quite like it and had to deal with Aleister's ghost. Like Amado, Aleister had suffered from asthma and this was cleared in the regression session by going back to the south of France in Cathar times. Amado and Aleister were both tied to this region by their asthma and common experiences in attempting to thwart the Catholic Church of those times. They were both very intent on this last point. Out of the blue and completely unprompted, Aleister's ghost said that it was Israel Regardie who had killed him.

At this point, I was neither ready nor eager to embrace the idea that Regardie had killed Crowley. I was already familiar with the traditional story of Crowley's death where it is claimed that he was suffering greatly from his morphine addiction and needed more of the drug to kill the pain he was feeling in his final days. Claiming that he had received the full legal amount or some such stipulation, his doctor refused to give him any more morphine when the drug had worn off. After this refusal, Crowley reportedly cursed the man and claimed that he would be dead within a day or two. The doctor is said to have died within the prescribed time period which was quite a story-book ending for Aleister's bizarre life.

Although that story is a summarized version of the most popular account, it is not the only version. In either case, I was not eager to embrace Regardie as having anything to do with the death. The whole idea of Aleister's ghost seemed corny to me, and the Regardie theory struck me as "too obvious" as most everyone knew that he had become an embittered enemy of Crowley. From what very little I knew of Regardie, I did not think him capable of such an act.

Israel Regardie was once a member of the Golden Dawn who eventually exposed all of their rituals in a rather large book. This act alone made him forfeit whatever membership he had once possessed in that fraternity. In his early years, he had written to Crowley and became his secretary in Europe. As Crowley was kicked out of various countries and reportedly suffered financial hardship, Regardie's employment could no longer be afforded. After becoming unemployed by reason of Crowley's own personal problems, Regardie did not waste any time in becoming a bitter enemy of him. I had read a little bit about Regardie and perused a couple of his books. Without regard to the relative merit of his work, I did not find it of much interest to my particular tastes. Additionally, I found him to have rather severe character flaws based upon what I had read. In particular were his vitriolic letters to Aleister Crowley. Besides being bitter, Regardie seemed to suffer from severe emotional imbalance. He derisively referred to Crowley as "Alice" and blamed him irresponsibly. Perhaps naively, I viewed Regardie as an effeminate wimp who was not capable of such an act as murder. In his later years, Regardie suddenly began to exemplify some of Crowley's work and was known to make astute comments from time to time. Although I was never a fan of Regardie, I will readily concede that he was considerably knowledgable concerning esoteric information. In conclusion, this data about Regardie was just a piece of data or raw information. Although I was not fond of the idea, I could not entirely dismiss it either.

Sharing the information with Cameron, she was interested and not dismissive of the data at all. She did not know the exact facts but had an interesting story to relay. Cameron said that Regardie had shown an extreme interest in her at one point and was extensively monitoring her on some level. Although he expressed a strong desire to see her personally, she declined to meet him. Many years later, however, she had a strange urge to see him but was not sure why. Having the address of his house in Studio City, she went to make a surprise in-person visit. Upon arriving, she witnessed a most peculiar sight. The entire house was on moving blocks and was about to be moved. The house had Regardie's personal logo on it so their was no mistaking that it was his. Cameron and I both concluded that there was probably some occult reason for moving the entire house. It is ironic that she was not interested in seeing him until the time of his departure from Southern California.

At the time I learned this information about Regardie, it was 1994 and I was perfectly content to wait three years to hear Amado's revelation of who had killed his father. In the meantime, there were plenty of other interesting lines of investigation going on in my life.

28

HERE COME DE JUDGE

The OTO court case between Marcelo Motta and Grady McMurtry and company has long been a legend in the magical community. One can find further and additional relevant information on the internet. Most of the information in this chapter is based upon a document entitled *Ordo Templi Orientis: Everything You Always Wanted to Know but Were Afraid to Ask.* It was copied many years ago by the Abbey of Theleme, PO Box 666, Old Greenwich, CT, 06870.

Due to disputed successorship of the OTO after Karl Germer's death, a United States District Court in California awarded Grady McMurtry as the duly appointed successor. Marcelo Motta's appeal brought the following information before the court in its attempt to reverse the original court's decision. I have added additional comments and observations as well.

At the time of Crowley's death, no one disputed that his rightful successor in OTO matters was Karl Johannes Germer (1885-1962). One of Germer's spiritual disciples was Marcelo Motta, a Brazilian citizen with whom he shared a monthly correspondence. Upon Germer's death in 1962, his wife Sascha claimed that her husband named Motta as "the follower." This was just one of the grounds by which Motta claimed successorship to the title of "Outer Head of the OTO." Based upon Germer's authority, Germer set up an OTO lodge in Brazil in the 1970's. When Germer died, he left a will which remained unprobated at the time of the appeal in 1984 which named his wife Sascha and a

235

certain Frederic Mellinger as coexecutors to handle what remained of the OTO property. Although Mellinger was never accounted for, Sascha took charge of the OTO property which primarily consisted of archives and a library.

In 1967, five years after the death of her husband, Sascha Germer had possession of the OTO library when a gang of three people broke into her house, assaulted her, and stole material from the library. She identified one of the thieves as being the daughter of one of the litigants against Motta, that litigant being Phyllis Seckler. Sascha Germer wrote to Motta about this incident and indicated it was a "two family conspiracy."

Events took a new twist when Grady McMurtry first appears on the scene. Remember, he was introduced to the OTO by Jack Parsons who arranged for him to meet Aleister Crowley during World War II. In 1968, McMurtry received news of the robbery of Mrs. Germer from Phyllis Seckler. McMurtry, who had been living in Washington, D.C. and working as a political scientist, came to California to investigate. Concluding that a Southern California group was behind the theft affair, he created an aura of impropriety, unscrupulousness, and prejudice by marrying Seckler and setting up his own OTO lodge. This would not only seem audacious in itself but appeared to blatantly disregard Germer and Motta, particularly if the Seckler family was in possession of stolen OTO materials.

At the time of her death in 1975, Sascha still had possession of what remained of the OTO library after the theft. McMurtry and Seckler apparently recognized Motta's rights as successor of the OTO when Seckler wrote to him in 1976 with regard to Sascha's death. He was advised to either come to California or to send a representative to obtain the library.

In what was probably the biggest mistake of his magical career, Motta enlisted James Wasserman, one of his pupils in the United States, and gave him power of attorney to represent his interests in the library. He also advised Wasserman to determine whether McMurtry and Seckler had valid OTO credentials. This was a mistake on Motta's part because when Wasserman went to California to meet with McMurtry and Seckler, he switched sides. Wasserman wrote a letter indicating his decision that he would be initiated into McMurtry's version of the OTO. The letter was July

18, 1976. This was a complete abdication by Wasserman of his responsibility as a fiduciary for Motta. Motta was further betrayed on July 26, 1976 when a proceeding was held in California Superior Court with regard to the OTO library that had rightfully belonged to Sascha Germer. Wasserman did not attend and Motta's position was forfeited. On the other hand, McMurtry showed up and represented himself as the duly authorized representative of the OTO and was consequently awarded custody of the OTO library. The controversy surrounding the library became even more confused when, soon after the July 26th proceeding, Phyllis Seckler broke from McMurtry and was said to have stolen the OTO library herself. Reportedly, she had fallen prey to drugs, alcohol and the bad influence of some of the followers. She reportedly refused McMurtry access to the library and began to sell books out of the library for her own gain. And, while in her possession, the library suffered another theft. Motta's group believed this was a feigned theft in order that certain information would never find its way to the light of day.

There are more twists and turns in this case. What little I have said about it would seem to demonstrate a series of bizarre blunders and impropriety. If you wish, you can read all the twists and turns for yourself on the internet.

I bring this court case to your attention, in part, because Israel Regardie was originally with the McMurtry group in their battle for the OTO library and the so-called rights of Aleister Crowley. This is a loose but tangential tie-in to the theory that Regardie may have murdered Crowley. At this point in his life, Regardie had begun to advocate the work of Crowley after bitterly despising him for decades. This sudden change of position would invite suspicion if he held overt ownership of any of Crowley's legacy or copyrights. Although he removed his name as a litigant, others have told me that he remained the main power and influence within the OTO.

You will notice that the head of the OTO is always referred to as the "Outer Head of the OTO." I have never seen it mentioned in their public literature, but there is also an Inner Head of the OTO. I do not mean to imply that this was Regardie at anytime. The Inner Head is not necessarily an incarnate individual such as one would normally perceive in human form. Baphomet is not a wholly adequate representation of the Inner Head of the OTO, but it will serve to some degree. The point is that the OTO itself is not really run by its members but rather that they are run by an occult current or force. My contention is that Israel Regardie, at his best or worst, was influenced by this occult force.

McMurtry was chosen as the head cheerleader for the OTO's cause and was eventually hailed by his followers as Hymenaeus Alpha, the Caliph of the OTO. There was a letter to McMurtry from Aleister Crowley which said that after the death of Germer, "the terrible burden of responsibility might easily fall upon your shoulders." Although this did not confer any authority on McMurtry, he used it to his advantage in the court case.

During the lawsuit for the rights to the OTO, McMurtry's party, after several court injunctions, finally produced documents from the OTO archives that Motta's group had insisted upon. One of the letters was from Karl Germer and gives an indication of his general opinion about the character of McMurtry.

Mr. Grady McMurtry
Care Frater:

Do what thou will shall be the whole of the law.

I must not leave your last letter (and check) go unanswered or unchallenged. It has led me to examine your whole position in the Order. I was only too willing to accept this. What have you done in the last twelve years to justify and earn the position? Instead of a Plus you have been a great MINUS. Others have at one time or another helped the Work financially and otherwise. Your "help" consisted of sponging on the Order, and, very probably did other damage. The sponging shows itself blatantly in your letter.

It has been nearly three and a half years that I loaned you that money, asking you many times to return it as it was badly needed. Now at last you pay back the balance but not one word about interest which I have been paying myself! You even deduct $50 for a Book of Thoth, while you yourself seem to have flooded the market with your copies at ridiculous prices (one copy was sold for, I believe, $12 or $15, as I heard.) Not one word of apology for your delinquency — not one in all these years!

To top it, you sold the car for which I gave you the cash behind my back, without first paying me — a fraudulent thing even in Law — worse than that when under the Bonds of the Order! More, you used the new car — not to see me to explain, but to visit so-called members of the Order and intrigue against me, plot against me.

I can disregard your lack of frankness, sincerity, loyalty, towards myself, if you were my enemy, or a common citizen. I cannot do it as the appointed Chief. However, I will not go any further into this. I will hope that the verse (I, 52) which you say you have chosen for your mantra, will ultimately result in purifying your soul, and teach you a sense of moral value which you lack so tragically.

Love is the law, lover under will.

Fraternally,

(Karl Germer)

P.S. I strongly reiterate the injunction in the last paragraph of my letter of Nov. 10 to you. You do not refer to this at all in your reply.

(The last paragraph of that letter demanded that McMurtry report to Mr. Germer the names and addresses of people he might approach on behalf of the OTO and describe how he dealt with them.)

Another letter from Germer gave Motta a clear charter to open up an OTO lodge in Brazil. This was a fair vote of confidence for Motta in that he seemed to be the only visible and authorized OTO representative in succession of Germer.

There was also a letter from Sascha Germer to Motta which blatantly stated that Motta was "the only follower to the Crown of the Order." The Abbey of Theleme stated that this letter seemed to clearly make the case, but it never reached Motta at the time it was written because the Brazilian Junta took it out of his hands.

All of the above demonstrates what would appear to be a severe miscarriage of justice. If the Brazilian Junta did subvert this letter, it would not be surprising. Nazi influence in Brazilian politics and military circles was quite strong at that time and Karl Germer was heavily monitored by the Nazis. Despite being a full-fledged German national, they had him placed in a concentration camp at one time, but he eventually made it to the United States.

There are a few reasons why I have brought this litigation to your attention. First, all of the information was encountered through synchronicity and only paid attention to because Ronald Reagan's middle name of Wilson was thrust upon me as was said earlier. It also reveals information about Regardie that I had not been aware of at the time of Margarita's disclosure. Both revelations occurred within a short time span of each other.

Another reason I bring the litigation to the forefront is that it demonstrates the intensity, struggle, and skullduggery that can ensue for a highly contested mantle of power. But, it is more of a mantle of power than a true power. Just because you put on the robes of the king does not necessarily mean that you are the king. And, just because you are the king, does not necessarily mean that you have the true power of a king. One has to pass the tests for such.

Read the full brief and the complete allegation of both sides if you wish, but know this first. Justice and synchronicity sometimes work in strange ways. On the very day that Grady McMurtry and his associates won their court decision as the rightful successors of Aleister Crowley's OTO, Grady McMurtry died of a heart attack. Israel Regardie had died of a heart attack a few months earlier. When I realized this and the whole story I have just laid out, Aleister's ghost had gained some credibility in my eyes.

29

TRANSMUTATION

There is no question that Jack Parsons became a willful vehicle for Babalon, a current which could and would kill by its own admission. Before Jack sacrificed himself, he introduced Grady McMurtry to the OTO who later betrayed him by working as a spy for Crowley. One cannot judge how this act may have later reflected on McMurtry, but it is important to remember one of the prime factors of synchronicity. One is dealing with an acausal principle which is outside the normal realm of cause and effect. Karma, which is only based upon the laws of the physical universe to the degree that it mimics those laws, works the same way. To be completely fair and unbiased on this point, it could also be said that the physical universe is really mimicking a higher spiritual law when it comes to the phenomena of cause and effect. All of this prompts the philosophical question of whether or not McMurtry's death on the day of the decision had anything to do with his deeds.

Compared to the actual transcripts, the OTO court case, as has been recounted herein, is really quite bland. I have read accounts about how the various sexual characteristics and private parts of the parties in the case were described in minute detail during the court proceedings. The supposed reason for this was that it was inferred that various interested parties were influenced in their behavior by their sexual relationships. All in all, it sounded like a three ring circus of lurid sexual descriptions which must have psychologically affected every individual in the court room. One commentator said that the sensationalistic sexual aspects were unprecedented and indeed surprising, particularly when you consider that this case was heard in the general vicinity of San Francisco, a location that was expected to be immune from sexual shock. Most, if not all, of these sexual accusations concerned homosexual behavior between the parties. It sounded as if every sexual demon that could be mustered out of anyone's auric field came out to roost in that courtroom. All I can say is that it would make a great episode on one of those legal shows on television.

Amado Crowley had always said that the OTO was not exactly what it seemed. After everything I have seen and read, I would have to concur. As I thought he might be very interested in the court case, I sent it to Amado, but there was no particular response. He did, however, continue to comment on the adversarial nature of his relationship with the OTO. From everything he told me about his experiences, the OTO was hell bent on reducing his significance. Whatever occult force that Amado was bucking up against apparently did not look too kindly on me either.

In September of 1994, I was working on *Pyramids of Montauk* and had just written a rough draft for a chapter on *The Book of the Law*. This book is the most holy book in the OTO, and you are not supposed to discuss it according to its contents. Although many OTO members would take this admonition very seriously, I do not think many of them follow it to the letter. On the other hand, there are plenty of occultists who would laugh in mockery at the proposition of not discussing *The Book of the Law*. It is considered to be so much superstition.

In *Pyramids of Montauk,* I revealed certain illuminations with regard to the *Book of the Law.** On September 23rd, the very day after writing the rough draft for a chapter on *The Book of the Law*, I suffered a most peculiar automobile accident. At that time, I wondered if some magicians were doing rituals in my direction during the autumnal equinox, a time of high magick. Years later, I learned from different sources that various magicians, presumably in the OTO, were doing rituals to stop Peter Moon.

At the time of the accident, I was by myself and driving westward on a major boulevard on Long Island when I came to a

---

* The general approach and thesis regarding these illuminations have been validated, but the full treatment is currently incomplete and is therefore either not relevant or timely to put in this book.

full stop at a red light. It was raining. For some unknown reason, I shifted the automatic transmission from "drive" to "park." This is something I almost never do when at a stop light. In fact, the transmission is probably shifted into park at less than one out of a hundred stop lights that I encounter.

As I relaxed and waited for the light to change, I was suddenly rammed from the back as my car was pushed at least ten feet forward. Had I not had the transmission in park, I might have lost further control of the car when I was hit and collided into a barrier or traffic coming from the opposite direction. The results could have been far worse.

Although I was hurt, I was able to get out of my car and see that I was rear-ended by a tiny Japanese car. The car I was driving, a Mercury Sable, received minor damage to the rear bumper. Actually, the car was my wife's, but I was using it that morning as my Mustang was in the repair shop. As I scrutinized the wreckage, two employees from a diving shop came out of their store and offered me assistance. They told me that I was likely suffering from whiplash and should go to the hospital. If I wanted an ambulance to come, they would arrange it. I realized that I probably had whiplash, but I was not going to jump into an ambulance. Instead, I asked to use the phone in the diving shop so that I could inform my wife and enlist her help in case she was needed for anything. When I phoned her, she was already preoccupied on the phone and was not eager to be interrupted. She said that she was on the phone with my mechanic, and he wanted me to know that the brakes on my Mustang needed to be replaced. On his behalf, she wanted to know if I was going to authorize the expenditure.

"New brakes!" I exclaimed. "The guy who hit me needed new brakes. Sure, tell him to put new brakes on the Mustang. I don't want anything like this to happen again."

My wife relayed the instructions to my mechanic and would stand by in case I needed her help. When I emerged from the diving shop, a policeman had arrived and told me to see if I could drive the car out of the middle of the intersection. I promptly did so and returned to give the officer a report. As I came back once again to the scene of the accident, I was surprised as a familiar face approached and addressed me.

"Mr. Moon. Mr. Moon. Do you remember me?"

"Certainly, I remember you," I said to this man who I recognized but had not seen in years. "You're my old mechanic."

I had used this man as my mechanic during the first three years I had lived on Long Island. When my wife and I bought a house and changed neighborhoods, I switched to a mechanic who was more convenient geographically.

"Old mechanic, yeah. Thanks a lot!" he said in a somewhat mocking but friendly tone as if miffed by the loss of business. "That was my son who hit you. His brakes failed in the wet rain."

This experience consisted of a whole series of synchronicities that were very strange. I had just written something on *The Book of the Law*. As I minded my own business and was hit on the rear end by the son of my old mechanic, my new mechanic was telling me that I needed new brakes on my other car. Mechanics and brakes appear twice. As I follow the law and brake at the red light, I reinforce the braked condition by putting the car in park. A young man, created by my mechanic from the past, loses control of his vehicle because the brakes in his car do not work. At that exact instant, my mechanic is calling me to tell me I need new brakes for the future. Although I am not at home, he is still able to get through to me immediately due to the bizarre circumstances.

There is no doubt that I attracted some negative energy, but I was also able to transmute it into a positive condition. I visited my chiropractor, and he confirmed that I had suffered whiplash. Insurance covered this treatment which was not only successful, but it had the additional benefit of healing another long term condition that I had suffered from. I also received an insurance settlement which had very positive ramifications in my life as the future unfolded. When attracting negative energy in your life, the most important thing to do is to transmute it into a very positive form. Fortunately, I was able to do this.

There were apparently other problems with my interpretation of the *Book of the Law,* but these would not surface again for many months. In the meantime I was also wrestling with the black box and the bottle.

30

THE BOTTLE

When I eventually read *The Book of Babalon*, I read it carefully, but I somehow missed something that was sitting right in front of my face. Although I had been searching high and low for references to black boxes after my adventures with the pump house closet, the most auspicious reference to a black box was in *The Book of Babalon* itself. Somehow, there is an innate tendency in human beings to deny the obvious. I am far less guilty of it than most people, but I was falling into that somnambulistic state of mind myself. Interestingly, it is L. Ron Hubbard who brings the black box into the Babalon Working. During the Babalon Working, it was usually Jack who channeled or transmitted information with Ron acting as the scribe. In this instance, Jack was the scribe and Ron the transmedium who said, "make a box of blackness at 10:00 o'clock" and "smear the vessel which contains flame with thine own blood."

Later on in the working, Ron gives more instructions regarding the box when he says, "Thou shalt take the allahest in thine own mouth and in the box of darkness careful store this matter."

That is all Hubbard says about the box, but Jack refers to the box once again when he is back in his usual position and dictating to Hubbard. Specifically, Parsons says the following.

"Take the black box. Concentrate upon its emptiness for one hour, gaze into it, and thou wilt see, imprinted upon it, a shape, a sign, a sacred design, which shall be the

sign delivered by Our Lady BABALON Incarnate. I believe the sign to have been [   ]. (the sign is omitted) When thou hast finished, when thou hast recognized this pattern, construct it of wood.
        This is the sigil."

Parson then tells himself that when we can feel "Our Lady Incarnate" in his being, to take the black box and perform the consecrated rite. Then, when wearing scarlet and being sashed in black, he is told to take the black box and make the sign. Additionally, he is told to make a second sign "which thou knowest." If he forgets, he is told to "look into thy crystal." The above appears as the Second Ritual.

Later on, Parsons performs the Third Ritual which is directly designed to manifest Babalon. After meditating upon the desire of Babalon, he is told to "preserve the material basis" in the box. I am not sure exactly what the material basis is, but I readily assume it was semen as he was known to have been engaged ritual masturbation based upon the Eighth Degree of the OTO.

It has now become obvious to me that the black box in the above rituals was in fact the black box that George Frey had possessed for a time. I have described these rituals with him, and he concurs that it was indeed the same box.

At the time I was investigating the bottle and the box, I was not fully clear as to how all of these associations had worked their way into my life. It was only when I sat down to compose this book and write these various chapters that the full phenomena became screamingly clear. Magick was manifesting all around me, but it was Jack's intention that was coming through. I have already done justice to that to some extent, but there was obviously more to the picture.

When I went to Pasadena and visited the old haunts of Jack Parsons, including the site of the Babalon Working, I decided to try and pick up aethyric photographs. I am not particularly into photography at all and certainly not paranormal photography. This was a total lark on my part. I felt like I was shooting for the moon and had a one in a million chance. Little did I know that the chances were considerably increased due to the obvious fact that there was an acausal principle working as an outside force to influence the outcome.

As I reached the site of the old Parsonage, I took a photo of a Wilson real estate sign and was greeted by a very strange character whose primary function seemingly was to inform me about the Ralph Parsons Corporation.* Several other photographs were taken of the locale. In several photographs, I was deliberately intending to pick up any aethyric forms, but I could see nothing supernatural in itself.

Upon returning to Long Island and flying out to Montauk, I had the same role of film inside the camera. It was unprocessed. Before fiddling with my camera and ruining the film by exposing it to light, I had already established a psychic rapport with Preston with regard to the postulate to save the plane. At the very same time I exposed my film to the light, Preston was only a few feet away taking video footage of Camp Hero which picked up either a "nonexistent" or aethyric form on top of the pump house. It was as if something out of the aethyr escaped from my camera and made its way over to Preston and his video camera. The next thing we know, I receive a report of a black box appearing on the pump house. This is the same general area at Montauk where an image of the beast was once photographed by Jan Brice (which can be seen in the book *The Montauk Project: Experiments in Time)*. The appearance of a black box, which did not in fact exist in this reality, facilitated a whole chain of events and research. In the end, Preston and I were confronted with a mysterious bottle. It was as if the black box was replaced by a bottle which then commanded our attention by appearing at Preston's house. Preston was evidently being utilized as some sort of vehicle from the magical realm.

As I looked for answers, I was quite surprised to see that Kenneth Grant had looked deeply into the gematria (numerical meaning) of the word "bottle." In his book *Outside the Circles of Time (*copyright ©1980, published by Frederick Muller Ltd., London), Grant states that 210 is the number of BQBVQ, "a bottle" from the Egyptian word BAAKABAKA.** This is extremely

---

* What he said about aviation has very deep significance because during the time period he came over to the U.S., M.I.T. was involved with Project Whirlwind, an early flight test simulator program which connected pilots' reactions to computers. This was the forerunner of the Montauk Chair whereby people were mentally connected to computers.

** This is also meant to equate to the Egyptian word BEKH which means "to fecundate" or conceiver.

noteworthy because Jack Parsons was known as Frater 210 in the OTO. This is not well known to common readers, but it is very well known to people of magical persuasions. They know this just as well as baseball fans know that Mickey Mantle was number 7. There are more correspondences with 210, but perhaps the most significant one is that it equates to NPhLIM, the builders of the Tower of Babel. It is also equated to the Graal of Babalon with Babalon being additionally defined as "Gateway of the Sun." Most ironically, the Egyptian word BAAKABAKA means "reversal" or "topsy-turvy." Topsy-turvy comes from the fact that a bottle has to be turned upside down to release its contents.

While it now appears that Jack's box had "turned into a bottle" which equated to his signature number, there was definitely an occult force at work here. As I was learning about the gematria of the word "bottle," I also learned that Preston was going to Philadelphia to give a lecture at a science conference. I also knew that my friend and associate, who I called Madame X in *Montauk Revisited*, was going to be there. I thought this would be an excellent opportunity to have her do a psychic reading on the bottle. Accordingly, I did not feed her too much information before hand. I arranged to go with Preston and attended the conference. During a break, I rushed Madame X out to my car where I had the bottle. She immediately noticed something that I had missed. The bottle had the image of a kundalini snake on its neck. Picking up the bottle, she said words to the effect that it had been displaced or moved in time. This was only a psychic confirmation, and it was not too much to get excited about.

At it turned out, my adventure with the bottle ended up leading to something else. At the conference, I was to see the Ong's Hat Travel Brochure for the second time. Someone was selling them, only it was just a bit different from the one that had been sent to me. This one did not have the "P. Wilson" partially crossed out. I could now see very clearly that this introduction was authored by Peter Lamborn Wilson, the man I had met a year earlier. The man selling the brochure told me it was crossed out in the copy sent to me because they did not want me to get to Peter Wilson before they did. Ironically, I had already met him. This man also said that it was not known by him if Wilson had authored any of the Ong's Hat documents, but it was certainly suspected as a possibility. Keep in mind that Wilson's association with these documents was a major revelation at the time. I have already informed you that Peter Wilson's name was on the documents, but I did not know this to be the case at that time. If it were not for my pursuit of the meaning of the bottle, I might never have found this out. The occult force was working in my favor. Jack Parsons, through his box and the bottle, was leading me back to the saga of Ong's Hat.

Subsequently, I sought out Peter Wilson once again and attended another lecture. When it was my turn to ask a question, I told him about the community at Ong's Hat and that I was aware he had circulated a brochure on the subject. I then informed him that I knew someone who had determined that if the documents were a hoax that they were so well thought out that they represented something that could not possibly be a hoax. Without divulging much of anything, Peter Wilson smiled and said that he was very impressed. Then, he said that his official answer in public was "no comment."

The black box and the bottle had led me to another space-time project whose threads were woven much more deeply into academe than the Montauk Project. On the upside, the space-time project at Ong's Hat was not as horrendous as the tortured tales of the Montauk Project. Ever since, I have referred to the Montauk Project as representing the extreme right wing of time travel legends. It not only has Nazis but a reactionary basis which insists on maintaining a status quo. On the other hand, Ong's Hat has hippies, pharmacology, avant garde liberal values and an environmental consciousness which suggests the left wing.

At this point, I was in between the right wing and the left wing, but there were still some loose ends to clean up. The above mentioned efforts to inhibit my path to Peter Wilson was only one small symptom of what I would later learn was a major effort by others of magical persuasions to try and stop me. In the final analysis, they were not very effective.

31

CAMERON'S MEMORIAL

1994 had been a very exciting year in terms of occultism and strange connections, but I decided to take a vacation from all that and decided I would work on Preston's UFO book entitled *Encounter in the Pleiades: An Inside Look at UFOs*. Although this revealed new information Preston had never gone public with before, it was a relative breeze for me as I was basically just having to transcribe and edit what he said. There were no complicated occult creatures or puzzles to wrestle with.

On the 23rd of April 1995, I called Cameron to wish her what would be her final birthday. She was suffering from a malignant brain tumor at this point and had limited conversational ability. I had sent her *Pyramids of Montauk* which she did read. Having a very strong Native American connection, she was very happy with it. Cameron said that the geometric descriptions I depicted in that book (with reference to evolution and the morphogenetic grid) were very apt descriptions of what she saw during the Babalon Working. She gave me warm congratulations and wished me the best. We spoke only a few times after this as she underwent an operation. Towards the end, Cameron said to me, "My work is done." This was the last I would hear from her.

Cameron's very last evening was Midsummer's Night (July 23rd in the Celtic tradition) where she died peacefully in the arms of her granddaughter and magical heir, Iris Wolfe, after having received last rites from a priestess of the OTO. Her body was cremated soon after but her memorial service was held on August

27th in Venice, California at an establishment called *Beyond Baroque*. I was able to attend the service in person and got to meet some of her best friends as well.

I spent most of my time with Jack's old friend, George Frey. George is an incredible character who at that time was in his seventies and still working full days at his job. As I write this, he is now in his eighties and doing the same. There was a lot of time to reminisce. Jack was definitely his best friend at the time, and he stressed how gentle, loving, and considerate the man was. He has often emphasized this characteristic of Jack's personality. George shared many stories with me. He met Jack after the L. Ron Hubbard and Babalon Working days. Although George was never a participant in Jack's magical escapades, he participated in the pot luck get-togethers at the Parsonage and later spent a lot of time together with Jack when Cameron went off to Mexico to study art. It was during her time in Mexico that an evil priest wanted to burn her at the stake for being a witch. This priest was later excommunicated by the Catholic Church.

George shared various stories with me of his memories of Cameron. To him, she was an incredible lady but a very unique one. As liberal or "thelemic" as Jack was, George said that Jack was puzzled at Cameron's departure to Mexico. He felt abandoned and was not at all pleased with the arrangement as he missed his wife. Cameron once made it very clear to me that she and Jack were definitely not swingers but that they enjoyed a considerable amount of freedom between each other. She also said that her artistic callings were very important to her and that is why she made the sojourn to Mexico.

With Cameron in Mexico, Jack and George were walking around the neighborhood in Redondo Beach one day. Although Jack was completely out of money, he found a house being offered for rent that he considered very desirable. When Jack told him that he was going to rent the house, George was completely befuddled and surprised. How could he possibly rent the house when he had no money?

"I used a witch's rope," Jack replied.

Jack explained that he had placed a witch's rope in the fireplace. This confused George even more as he knew the witch's rope was a prized possession of Jack's. He bemoaned his friend's apparent error in judgment and asked him how he expected to get the rope back.

"When I rent the house," was Jack's answer.

To George's utter surprise, Jack ended up getting the house. It made no rational sense, but it worked.

During Cameron's absence, Jack took up a relationship with a lady named Gladys (pronounced with a long $\bar{a}$ as in Māvis). Although he had not renounced Cameron, Jack and Gladys were lovers and she moved in with him. When Cameron finally returned, she was not at all disturbed by the presence of Gladys in the house. In fact, she commented that she thought that Gladys added a nice feminine presence to the house. Gladys was very unnerved by Cameron's presence and ended up leaving. There were no harsh words generated by Cameron. She obviously walked her own talk and was a most unique creature.

Cameron's unique character showed itself once again during a party in Jack's house. With a house full of guests, Cameron came down the staircase completely nude save for as ostrich feather that she had sticking out of her rear end. As everyone looked, she stood there as a statue and was completely unnerved. It was an artistic statement as well as a sociological one. Jack said that he did not understand her, but he definitely loved her, and the two lived as man and wife until his death in 1952.

There is perhaps another point I should mention with regard to Jack and Ron Hubbard. It has often been said that Hubbard and Jack had severed relations and never saw each again after the incident in Dade County. This concerned their partnership known as Allied Enterprises where Jack had Hubbard arrested and placed into custody in order to resolve their business conflicts. Cameron told me that the two men met on friendly terms at least one other time after that incident. Hubbard had approached Jack in order to get funding for the Dianetics movement. There was, however, no money to fund anyone. Cameron said that Ron and "wiped him out." According to George, Jack once made a disparaging comment about Ron and said that he "was a science fiction writer who ripped people off."

I report this last statement only because it was said, but Cameron's words indicate that this statement was not fully representative of Jack's feelings about Ron. She said he considered Ron a brother and that he really loved him. There is no question that Jack was deeply hurt by Ron's actions. Cameron said that she liked Ron, too. There is no doubt in my mind that if Jack had become involved in Dianetics, it could have saved his life. But, Jack Parsons had his destiny which you are now very familiar with. I would not be doing this investigation if his life had been saved by Dianetics or by any other means.

Besides hearing and sharing interesting stories about Cameron at her memorial service, I had a rather unique encounter with another friend of hers. As I sat between George and Moya McNulty, one of Cameron's best friends, George pointed to an older gentleman who was by himself and sitting a few rows up from us. He told me that this man had been the civilian head of the Manhattan Project. In other words, he was in charge of all the civilians that worked for the Manhattan Project, the project that created the atomic bomb. The man's name was Bob Cornog, and he is the same Bob Cornog who Robert Heinlein dedicated *Stranger in a Strange Land* to. Introducing myself to him, I told him that I had written a book about a space-time project that John von Neumann was involved in. A scientist of considerable repute, Bob's ears perked up when I mentioned the words "space-time project." I game him copies of *The Montauk Project* and *Montauk Revisited* which he readily accepted. He was a friend of Cameron's. She and others told me that he had always had a crush on her.

When I asked him about von Neumann, he said that the Manhattan Project was completely bogged down and going nowhere until von Neumann arrived. One day, von Neumann gathered all the project workers together and lectured at a rapid fire pace and was explaining all sorts of scientific theories. Bob had never seen anything like it before. He said that after that lecture, there were no more confusions and everything was sorted out. Only then was the atom bomb produced and in a rapid manner, too.

Bob also remembered the old pot luck parties at the Parsonage. I asked him if he knew Hubbard, but he only saw him and observed him for the most part. He said that Hubbard was not a scientist but that he was very good with people and could manipulate them. As he looked for words to describe him, I tried to fill in the blank.

"He was an adventurer," I said.

"That's right. He was an adventurer."

Those are indeed the most apt words to describe L. Ron Hubbard. Regardless of what anyone says about him, he had a spirit of adventure that far exceeded the range of normal human beings. At its best, this spirit of adventure inspired other people to do the same.

I also asked Bob Cornog about Robert Heinlein, and he told me that he had visited his compound at Big Sur. According to what I gathered from Bob's description, Heinlein was apparently a central reference point for various people from the military industrial complex.

As for Moya McNulty, she has an aptitude for the occult and all things natural, but she said that most of her friendship with Cameron concerned parenting and grandparenting. They both bonded over the simple issues of living. Moya and I became good friends after the memorial service, and I learned a lot more about Cameron from her, but it is not relevant to this book.

The memorial service was not only a time to honor Cameron but to meet and see many of her friends and admirers. Several OTO people attended including Hymenaeus Beta, the Outer Head of the OTO. As part of the service, we all watched a short film Cameron had starred in called *Wormwood Star*. A great deal of her art work was also on display. One of the most gripping pieces of her art was a very well executed portrait of Jack where he was half woman. Someone looked at it and said "Jack-o-met," making a play on the word Baphomet. Actually, the man who said this had taken the words right out of my mouth. Cameron's work could be very well rendered when she wanted it to be, but it was almost always a very bold statement. It was Cameron's artistic curator and fellow artist, George Hermes, who gave the eulogy. He ended the eulogy with the following words.

"Cameron will lead us into the next century. She will be one of the main focus points that people will look back to. This memorial for Cameron will never end."

This is quite a statement, and if Cameron and Jack are correct, we will not really know how true this statement is for another 100-150 years.

About a month after the funeral, Moya reported to me that Cameron's ashes were to be scattered in the desert on the Fall Equinox of 1995. This final act of physical dissolution was to be performed by a Native American shaman in an area of California where Jack and Cameron had once made sacred vows to each other. Cameron had once shown the shaman the exact spot in the desert, but he was not having an easy time returning to the precise location. Accompanied by several of Cameron's friends, they eventually emerged from the car. As if on cue, the urn containing her ashes fell to the ground and the lid came off. A strong breeze suddenly appeared out of nowhere and the ashes were mysteriously swept out of the urn in a spiral fashion. After rising up in the air a little ways, the ashes went straight up in a vertical shaft and were lost to the element of air. This incident was witnessed by several people and served as a tribute to the magical heritage of Marjorie Cameron Parsons Kimmel who preferred to be called Cameron. The aethyrs welcomed her with open arms, and perhaps this was a signal that the era of Babalon has begun. When I reported on the above event in an issue of the *Montauk Pulse*, it was relayed to the shaman who conducted the ceremony. Although I do not even know the man's name, I was told he was touched. It is evident that the ashes genuinely did behave as if the elemental forces had made a bold and artistic statement in her memory.

I only knew Cameron for a brief few years before her death. Although I had no idea at the time, my chance meeting with her would change my life forever and dictate the course of my work. She once told me that she was on her way to visit Crowley when she received news that he had died. Cameron said that she felt her presence would have been too much for him. In other words, he might have died as a result of having to avoid her. This is a novel thought and certainly one that is open to dispute. But, if my experiences tell us anything, it is that Babalon is a current or force that is exercising the first power of the Sphinx: to will. And, it is a will that will not be denied. Death is, at times, her vehicle.

Thus far in this narrative we have a trail of dead bodies that include Aleister Crowley, Jack Parsons, Israel Regardie, and Grady McMurtry. From the pattern depicted in this book, each of their deaths and the circumstances surrounding them will serve to transmit Babalon's greatest mystery which has yet to be revealed. If I had not been open to the feminine energy of Cameron, perhaps I would have suffered the same fate. Instead, I extended my ear to the voice in the silence and listened to the wind of synchronicity.

32

MAGICAL LINK

After Cameron's death, my correspondence with Amado Crowley had all but stopped. Then, on a January day in 1996, I was at a friends house in order to watch some videos with her. As we watched, my friend suddenly interrupted the viewing and announced that we had to go to the train station to pick up another friend of hers who I will call Judy. Judy did not know who I was, and it was not until two hours of conversation and watching videos that it became relevant to tell her a bit about my work. When the subject of Aleister Crowley came up, Judy had an interesting story to tell. She said that her ex-boyfriend had once purchased a walking stick of Crowley's from the Jimmy Page collection. After he acquired the walking stick, she became beleaguered by dreams where a lecherous old man would pursue her. It was most uncomfortable, and she eventually insisted that her boyfriend get rid of the walking stick. After he did so, the dreams ceased. This was a very strange energy current to receive and not particularly a welcome one, but it was to serve as a portent or influence on what was just about to happen to me.

After watching the videos and finishing our conversation, I made my way home in the middle of the afternoon. Then, something happened which had never happened before and has never happened since in twenty years of driving on Long Island. I missed the turnoff from the Northern State Parkway which led to my home. As a result, I had to take the downtown Westbury turnoff. As a result of this, I was not far from the post office and decided to stop by and pick up my mail. Oddly, there was only one letter in the post office box and it was from Amado. I had not heard from him in many months. It was a very short note of good wishes for me and my friends. Besides that, there was a short paragraph.

"I can't help thinking that the same people who have been interfering with our mail are possibly the ones who had something to do with the recent massacres in Switzerland and France! But never mind! I know you are having bad weather over there so I hope my little letter gets through to warm your heart slightly."

I only heard from Amado one more time after that. This was the end of our communication. He was referring to the Solar Temple Lodge who had committed ritual suicide. The suicides made headline news across the world, but it was never revealed or even suggested by the media that the suicides were or might have been orchestrated by creatures who were still alive.

At this time, I was arranging with Amado's publisher, Steve Anthony, to import his books to America and was trying to work out an arrangement with him. Suddenly, Steve Anthony ceased to return my communications. I discovered that Steve was the owner of Elan Computing, a major computer company in England. The word to describe the company is HUGE. Subsequent to this abrupt censure of my communication with Steve, I asked an English karate master who I knew to try and track down Steve in order to find out what had happened with Amado. The karate master did not lack for courage, but he could not get past the door. He said the energy was just blocked. Knocking persistently several times, he could get no one to answer.

This energy block was confirmed much later when another gentleman tried to help me find out what was going on. His name was Nathan. Amado's publisher was Diamond Books, a company which Steve Anthony had sponsored. The only known contact for Diamond Books was Steve Anthony, the owner of Elan Computing. Every time Nathan would call and ask for Diamond Books, he was given a rote answer by several different employees which indicated this company was not located there. Nathan said it was obvious they were reading from a script and that it was a ridiculous effort at brushing him off and was not convincing at all. Nathan persisted on his mission and confronted them with their rote answers and the fact that they were reading from a script. They claimed no knowledge of Steve Anthony or anything that made any sense. After a series of such nonsensical conversations, someone at Elan finally asked Nathan what he wanted to know for. That was easy. He told him he wanted to buy some books! Nathan was eventually given an obscure address where he was able to track down a distribution warehouse for books. Finding a man, he asked him where he could find Diamond Books. Instead of answering him, the man challenged Nathan by assertively asking him a question of his own.

"What do you want to know for?" the man challenged him.

"To buy some books," he answered.

I do not really remember whether Nathan was offered the opportunity to buy some books, but he was really only trying to contact the publisher. This was the most insane response we could have imagined, but it was also very funny. There have been other instances of such madness when it came to trying to contact Amado, but this response exemplifies the madness. If you were trying this hard to contact a famous celebrity, you would likely just get a no response or a statement that the celebrity does not wish to see you. Instead, we were not even getting a polite decline or even a rude one. We were getting a bent and twisted consciousness which suggested that an occult force had cut the lines between myself and Amado. This was more funny and odd than it was disturbing as my communication to him no longer seemed to matter. I had found out all I needed to or was supposed to, at least for the time being.

33

THE MAGICK THEATER

*THE FOLLOWING TRANSMISSION
IS FROM A PARALLEL UNIVERSE*

In a parallel universe known as Astral Prime, a unique and unusual holographic theater was recently constructed. Known as the Magick Theater, it was inspired by Hermann Hesse's novel *Steppenwolf* which also featured a "Magic Theater." The inaugural presentation in this newly constructed theater is Peter Moon's *Opening of the Seventh Seal: Jack and Marjorie's Love Story*. The guest list features a remarkable cast of characters, the likes of which creation might never be lucky enough to see assembled again all in one place. Those seen leaving their limousines and entering upon the red carpet to the Magick Theater include all the characters ever included in any of Peter Moon's books. This includes but is not limited to Jack Parsons, L. Ron Hubbard, Marjorie Cameron, the Wilson Brothers, John von Neumann, Nikola Tesla, Aleister Crowley, Amado Crowley, Margarita, Preston Nichols, Duncan Cameron, Chuck Hamill, David Anderson, Emory Cranston, Hassan Sabbah, Jacob Ong, Gail Evening Star, and other Montauk Native Americans.

As the house lights flash signifying ten minutes until curtain time, von Neumann comments that Peter Moon wrote about plenty of Germans but the only ones seen in the audience are Karl and Albrecht Haushofer.

Ron Hubbard, a few seats away, turns to von Neumann and

says, "If you look to the rear of the balcony, you will see that the hard core Nazis are here but are restrained in a locked room where they can view the show only behind a glass viewing portal that remains tinted until the show begins."

Over hearing this, Aleister Crowley laughs and says, "You'd all better pray that I not release them!"

At that point, two angelic cherubs appear in holographic form and fly in opposite directions around the audience in the pattern of infinity. Each are holding a large gong. When they meet, they clash their gongs together, and a loud sound is produced that sounds like "*Ongggggggggggggggg*."

The angels completely disappear as if shattered by the sound. The curtain is gone as well. Nothing can be seen except pitch black. Very slowly, a stage scene begins to manifest before the audience, but it unfolds so slowly that everyone is guessing what they will see. First, a few points of light begin to shine in what will eventually become stars. Then, a creaking sound is heard which soon manifests the rocking of a rocking chair. After a while, a fluorescent image of a straw hat and corn cob pipe appear. The sound of katydids and crickets are then accompanied by fireflies which shed just enough light to see the rest of the scene. The lighting has increased considerably from the void of pitch black, but it is still very dark. Soon, everyone can see a dilapidated shack in the old south. The straw hat and corn cob pipe turn out to be on the head and in the hand of a little tar baby that is rocking back and forth in a rocking chair. As a firefly ignites near his head, the tar baby lashes out quick as lightning with his tongue and consumes the firefly.

"Nuttin' like a little bitta light insid'a me!" he says with a grin.

A complete and real life looking tar baby has suddenly come to life. He nods and tips his cap at the audience.

"Hullo dere and welcome to de magick the'ter where's you's will sees and hears de t'ings you won't hears and sees nowhere else. Ultimately, dats anyt'ing you's ever wanted to sees or hears."

The lifelike aspect of the theater is so penetrating, and the voice and intention of the Tar Baby is so genuine that the audience is inspired to give a gentle but very warm and extended applause.

"Now, dat was nice," says the Tar Baby, unexpectedly giving the audience a live response to their applause.

As the audience's applause winds down, a pair of penetrating eyes slowly appears in the shadowed darkness. Soon, a frighteningly real and fearsome wolf appears behind the eyes. A genuine gasp is heard from the audience, but the Tar Baby pays no attention as he speaks once again.

"He can'ts hurts me cuz I'm de Tar Baby. He come 'ginst me 'n I's stick to him like shit! He be de sorriest wolf you's ever did see!"

The audience laughs.

"I's gots protection!"

The Tar Baby then rises from the rocking chair and does a little soft shoe dance as he strolls over to the wolf with fearless impunity and begins to speak in a mocking tone.

"You de beast? You don't look so bad to me!"

The Tar Baby then looks at the audience and says, "Ain't dat beast bad, but ain't dat beast good?" He then winks and takes the corn cob pipe out of his mouth.

"Now's you's all might be fixin' to wond'rin' why's I be bein' de Tar Baby. I mean, I's can talks and show you's uncanny intelligence dat unnerves ya. But, der's a reason I's be made o' tar — 'fact, der's a couple a dem reasons.

"Firstins, I's be made o' pitch black tar becuzzin it represent de deep black void o' de dat t'ing dey call de collective unconscious. All's you's fears and unknowns gots to be gravitatin' somewhere and dey's be gravitatin' to me. I's be bein' a black void o' nuthin'. And all's you's fears and unconscious thoughts be gravitatin' and stickin' to me like fly paper. I can't get ridda dem and you can't get ridda me! Everyt'ing you's don't know, come to me. So, der!"

The audience laughs.

"Now, dat Mankind — he's don't understands peace, he's don't unduhstands God, he's don'ts understands much a nuthin'. But, downs deep, way downs deep, and I means way ways downs deep, he unduhstands it somewhere, and dats me! De Seven Seals buried downs deep, too, but now's I gonna tell you's all 'bout de uther reason I's be made a tar. It's cuzza dat fellow right down der!"

The Tar Baby points at Jack Parsons in the audience.

"I's be choosin's to be de Tar Baby 'cuz dats in tribute to him, de guest o' honor, Jack Parsons. I's be made of tar 'cuz dats what inspired him one day when he's saw dat roofers use tar and den realized dat dat make good solid rocket fuel dat create a nice slow rocket burn to take us to de moon and beyond."

In the background, the sky lightens as a brilliant full moon comes into view. A very subtle glow on the moon phases through the colors of the rainbow.

"Dat da moon!" said the Tar Baby.

"Now, why's Jack be wantin' to go to de moon? 'Cause dats de feminine energy dat he call Babalon!"

The Tar Baby looks straight at Jack as he speaks.

"Now's Jack, you's be tryin' to incarnate de Babalon in your magick life and you's be tryin' to reach de moon in your rocket life. And, we's all knows dat dat Scarlet Woman gonna appear when de Seven Seals be released."

The Tar Baby then points at Marjorie Cameron who is wearing a flaming red dress, identifying her as Babalon.

"Now, dere's onutta reason I's be bein' made o' tar 'cuz dats just like de bitumen, and bitumen is de secret stuff dey use to make mummies wit'. Dose blue-bloods be consumin' it to keep dat bloodline pure and maintain a synchronistic consciousness with der brain chemistry. Dey call dat mummia."

As a mummy arm suddenly flies out from stage left, the Tar Baby catches it and begins to consume it like he was chewin' on a turkey leg. As the audience laughs, the Tar Baby puts down the mummy arm and pats his belly with satisfaction.

"Dat mummy food gonna make me last fo'ever. Ah, nuthin' like Kentucky Fried Mummy." (more laughter)

"Now's, I's also be bein' black as pitch 'cuz pitch is what dey used on Noah's Ark to hold dat Ark together and keep de genetic structure of dose animals in tact. Dat pitch represent de synchronistic link between de animals and de morphogenetic grid. Dat brain chemistry all running in synch."

The sun now begins to rise as the stage turns to daylight. The props are all stripped away until the Tar Baby is sitting on a baroque pale horse which is a statue based on a pedestal.

"Now, you's all heard o' dat Montauk horse and dat one named Al Baraq, de one dat take de Prophet to heaven from de Dome o' dat Rock. Dis one's a comb'n'tion of dem bot'. Watch!"

As the horse comes to life, it begins to fly over the audience in circles as the Tar Baby waves his hands like a circus performer.

A much more outrageous spectacle ensues as a host of aethyric spirits rise out of the pedestal and into the air. The Tar Baby speaks once again.

"Dat pedestal der is nuthin' much diff'rint dan de Ark o' de Cov'n'nt o' even Pandora's Box. Dem's de archai (spelling is correct) you see flyin' 'bout. Dey de most primeval form of energized thought you's can imagine. I'm lettin' 'em all loose on you's now b'cuzz I'z been absorbin' and holdin' on to all dis for millenia. It's you's now!

"Remembers, I's be black cuz da void is feminine and silent. Dat horrible feminine energy all de Christian critters bein' afraid of is feminine and black. Black, black, black and dat's why I take on de name Remus sometimes 'cuz he was de bruddah dat was killed by dat patriarch Romulus. Dat was de vanquishing of de feminine energy. And dats why blacks use to call each uttah Remus sometimes, cuz das de bruddah dat got shafted."

The audience starts yelling approvingly. "Remus! Remus! Remus! Remus!" etc.

"All de knowledge in de world sticks to me like glue 'cause it's got to go somewhere. Dats de sacred drift o' de truth. I's assumed 'dis low profile and absolutely ridiculous role so's nobody's gonna takes me's too seriously and nobody's get hurt."

The audience is now clapping in approval, and the Tar Baby has won them over. He has essentially warmed up the crowd.

END OF ACT I

At intermission, Crowley and Cameron meet for the first time. Crowley's expressions change from seductiveness and lecherousness to vampiristic and predatory glances, all magnetically calculated to attract and consume. As independent as ever, Cameron stands aloof as if she's paying him no attention whatsoever. She is silent as if saying, "You're a bit of a twit, but I find your theatrics quite amusing and even flattering. But, if you think you're going to make love to me, you had better understand it will be on my terms." She is not intimidated. Jack, who is standing by and watching the strange posturing between the two, shrugs his shoulders as if he is completely puzzled. He then walks over to Ron who is eating raisinettes near the concession stand.

"You know, Jack," Ron says as he looks around at the highly ornamented lobby. "I was once in an implant station that looked like this. That was several million years ago, of course."

While the Wilson Brothers are wondering if the phone booths will let them talk to people in other times, Tesla and von Neumann are having a conversation.

"You know, John, a sphinx can be a limitless supply of energy."

"Yes, and if we had used it instead of a horse, I think we might have avoided some of those problems at Montauk."

As the lights are dimmed, the audience shuffles back in for the second act.

34

THE ROAD TO ONG'S HAT

After my trip to Pasadena in 1994, I was talking to Cameron quite frequently. In the midst of our conversations, O.J. Simpson was arrested for murder of his wife. When I asked her what she thought about the whole affair, she was very calm, but she said that the press seemed very preoccupied with denigrating and destroying any black heroes. She noted extremely bad press that had been hurled upon Michael Jackson and Mike Tyson. Although she was not defending any of the people or their alleged misdeeds, she thought the press was creating an obsession with the public and exploiting the denigration of black cultural heroes. She was also very sensitive to the Rodney King situation and the riots that ensued when the policemen who beat him were initially found not guilty in a court of law.

As we are far beyond the years of segregation and the KKK, why would there be such extreme prejudice left in the world? After all, it is politically incorrect to disparage anyone due to their racial heritage. Political correctness is a moral tone that has largely been set by the media and does have a tendency to promote better surface relations between people. It is the nature of an oppressor, however, when their power base or modus operandi is failing, to substitute a perceived oppression with a carrot that will take attention off of a new and subtler form of oppression that will continue to support the original power base that generated the problem in the first place. When blacks used to work the plantations, America was the only western country that supported slavery. America was, however, primarily owned by European interests that capitalized profoundly by reason of slavery. Although this concerned financial power, there were considerably more issues at stake. The Ong's Hat mythos gives us a remarkable and profound answer to all of the above.

My study of the Babalon Working led me to Pasadena and Montauk and eventually to the discovery of a black box and a bottle. This, in turn, dictated a trip to Philadelphia which revealed that it was Peter Lamborn Wilson who was purveying the materials about Ong's Hat. I knew that Ong's Hat, at the very least, represented a psychedelic ashram that suggested interdimensional travel. The community existed in some form, but I was never able to finitely locate Ong's Hat itself. One evening, in New Jersey, I was attending a party where I was introduced to a Dr. Reuben Ong, a holistic practitioner in the Trenton area. When I heard his last name, I was a little dumbstruck. I informed him about Ong's Hat, and he knew exactly what I was talking about. When I told him that I had not been able to find it on a map, he explained that it appeared on some maps but not on others. He promptly went to his car and retrieved a map which had Ong's Hat marked on it. After I studied it, he made a point of giving me the map. With this in hand, I was eventually able to make a trip to the area. Although there was no longer any town named "Ong's Hat," I was able to find Ong's Hat Road with a bar at the end of it. The people there told me that there are strange goings on in the Pine Barrens, but they did not give any specifics worth mentioning. I did find an old road which I believed may have led to the old ashram, but it was tick season and I had worn short pants. (I eventually returned to this road and checked it out nine years later. There could have been an ashram in that vicinity but this is not a firm or final conclusion.) The only other thing I knew about the physical area of Ong's Hat at this point was that a couple of people I knew had seen UFOs there.

Within a year after visiting Ong's Hat, I met Penelope, a wonderful woman who had an immediate impact on my life in many respects. One of her roles was supporting my research. If I talked about a book or something, she would go out and buy the book and hand it to me. I never asked her to do that. She just had an interesting way about her. When we first met, she had brought a researcher to town named Mark Roberts. It is hard to do justice

268

to Mark in a short paragraph. Although he studied and learned the ancient Ogham language under Robert Graves at Oxford (author of *The White Goddess*) and worked with stargates (long before this had become a popular and faddish term), my interest in him was that he had been a friend of Cameron. His dowsing ability had also led him to visit Montauk in the 1960's with Sybil Leek, a famous witch and friend of his from England.

Penelope had put together a workshop in Manhattan for Mark, and I attended it. During a break, one of Penelope's friends was talking about an alien contactee experience he had once had in New Egypt, New Jersey. When I heard the words "New Egypt," my ears perked up as that location is not all that far from Ong's Hat. Telling both of them that I had heard of an interdimensional project at a nearby location called Ong's Hat, Penelope look surprised and almost suspicious.

"How do you know about Ong's Hat?" she asked.

I gave her a quick spiel about the brochure and what I had learned of it. She was most interested and explained that she had once visited the area with a psychic from Montauk known as Barbara Marshall. With Barbara, she had seen a UFO at Ong's Hat and had never forgotten the experience.

A few days later, I got to sit down with Penelope and Mark. Mark verified that the 1943 ritual with Aleister and Amado Crowley had taken place on August 12th just as was reported. He knew people who were there and had witnessed it. Besides that, he mentioned that he knew Israel Regardie personally. Up to this point, I had shared the story of Aleister's ghost with almost no one. When I told Mark, he just kind of smiled and said, "It wouldn't surprise me."

Mark had an interesting anecdote to tell which backed up the testimony of Aleister's ghost. He said that there was an Arch Druid* of Great Britain who had taught Crowley as well as himself.

---

* I am fully aware that many people will howl at the suggestion that Crowley was a Druid or that he studied under the Arch Druid. Let it be known that there are different factions of Druidism, and they do not all agree with each other. Crowley was most definitely recognized as a Druid by different factions. In the New Age culture, it has become popular and fadish to "be a Druid" or advocate Druidism. If most of the New Age people who advocate it actually saw the actual customs of the ancient Druids, they would run for the hills if only because their practices were completely abhorrent to our social mores.

Crowley was this Arch Druid's very first pupil, and Mark was his last. He said I would find it interesting that this man's last name was Nichols. I believe Mark said the first name was Mike, but he said that this Arch Druid was known as "Old Nick."

Old Nick once told Mark a story that Aleister had approached him before his official date of death which was December 1, 1947. Aleister was concerned that Israel Regardie was going to kill him, and he wanted the Arch Druid to arrange a new identity for him. There was no further information as to whether Crowley lived past his official death date nor was there any specific information to suggest that Regardie did kill him. Although no murder weapon had surfaced, there was already a motive, and now we learn that the victim was trying to flee from his alleged assailant. The name "Nichols" proved to be an interesting synchronicity as well. The only testimony I knew came from Aleister's ghost who was only stirred up by reason of my pursuit of the name Wilson. I had already danced with the ghost of Jack Parsons. Dare I take this further and exhume the ghost of Aleister Crowley?

I did not have time to think about it. Jack's ghost was keeping me busy and had led me back to Ong's Hat. Penelope's interest in Ong's Hat accelerated with my disclosure of information to her, and we went to hear another Peter Wilson lecture. She also got me a copy of his book, *Sacred Drift*, which did not talk about Ong's Hat; however, it did discuss the nebulous character who was supposedly behind the Moorish Science Temple, the organization believed to have fostered and sponsored the Ong's Hat ashram.

Sacred Drift is a book which features different treatises on heretical Islam. Much of it centers on the Moorish Orthodox Church of which Peter Wilson is a member and some say the secret sponsor. The book itself is written in such a manner that it states, but does not overtly assert, that Drew Ali, the founder of the Moorish Science Temple, is a real person. It does talk of his history as well as the history of the Temple, but it is written in a fashion that might suggest the whole story is apocryphal (apocryphal is a word scholars like to use that means "of doubtful authenticity"). In many respects, Peter Lamborn Wilson is a master of understatement. The truth is that Drew Ali was very real and so was his Moorish Science Temple. Both have been blackballed from history to the point where they have been all but forgotten.

If there is such a thing as "uncorking the Seventh Seal" or Ultimate Revelation, the idea of Sacred Drift is a very important concept. Earlier in this book, synchronicity was defined by Carl Jung as the "poor man's Tao." In the *Tao Te Ching*, one is encouraged to study and emulate the element of water. Water is soft and malleable, yet it can penetrate solid granite over time and make a furrow or even a hole. Water flows to the most yin or receivable part of a given structure. In many cases, it even creates a vulnerable or weak point in the structure it is acting upon. It this sense, water will penetrate the biggest and densest forms imaginable.

In occultism, water is equated to emotions. The idea of Sacred Drift includes the idea that the truth or the emotions of truth (ultimate realization), as represented in the element of water, will find its way and penetrate no matter what the obstacles may be. If the truth is not going to be shined and buffed in Harvard, Oxford, or the Imperial Palace of the Roman Empire, it will find its way to more humble vehicles of expression.

When we consider that the living components of the morphogenetic grid, which we know as individuals, have become lost from their own heritage, including the entire functioning of their full human brain, it must be remembered that the brain contains all essential truths with regard to the entire macrocosm. When we consider the collective whole, this means that the most sacred aspects of existence and the Creative Force are residual in the grid and will, like water, find their own means of expression. In time, it will even overcome the most arduous or resistant obstacles.

Christ faced the Roman Empire, and in the manner of the Tao, he yielded. This effectively destroyed the Roman Empire on the surface. Insidiously, the Anti-Tao responded by ingeniously creating a Christian church which altered the Dionysian teachings of Christ and ushered in the Dark Ages. But, the Tao is insurmountable and it thrives in obscurity.

It is hard to find a more obscure and untouted character than Noble Drew Ali, especially when you consider the major impact he had on the life and times of his era. He was and is an excellent receipt point for such a concept as "Sacred Drift."

271

35

NOBLE DREW ALI

One of the lessons learned from Jack Parsons' bottle was that it meant "topsy-turvy." Only by turning the bottle upside down do the contents spill out. This suggests that we can only learn the full truth by turning our concepts of existence completely upside down. Regardless of the legends of Drew Ali, the known truths of his life, if objectively examined, cause us to see that common history has been completely inverted to serve the powers of what can be called the Anti-Tao.

After reading Peter Wilson's *Sacred Drift*, I was a bit astonished to find out independently that Drew Ali was not only a real character in our history who not only appeared in the newspapers of his time but has a substantial FBI file, the entirety of which has not been released to the public at this time. In fact, he was doggedly scrutinized by J. Edgar Hoover's FBI during the Roaring Twenties. Although he was by no means the first black Muslim in America, he is believed to be the first black Muslim prophet. It is not surprising that he has been obscured and forgotten by most white historians, but it is even more alarming that the majority of his fellow African-Americans are equally ignorant of his incredible life. It will send the shock of ignorance through many people's nervous systems to learn that Drew Ali's murder was a pivotal point in history which eventually gave rise to contemporarily recognized figures such as Louis Farrakhan, Malcolm X, and Elijah Muhammad. Although these characters are not known to have shed any light on Drew Ali or his heritage, they would never have risen to their aggrandized station in life had it not been for his legacy.

Drew Ali's origins are somewhat obscure and his life has taken on legendary proportions at times, but he definitely did exist. He was born on January 8, 1886 in North Carolina. His mother was a Cherokee and his father was of Moorish descent. His parents are believed to have met and studied under a "Master Adept" known as Jamal al-Din al-Afghani who visited the U.S. in 1882-1883. At this time, they were initiated into an Islamic sect known as the Brethren of Purity, an Ishmali faction from Cairo which sought to preserve the knowledge lost from the Alexandria library.

Although Peter Wilson suggests Drew Ali may have been a circus magician as a young man, it is a pretty safe bet that he was skilled in this trade. You can clearly see this influence later on in his life when circus style posters were used by him to draw big crowds for his religious gatherings. Prior to World War I, he visited Egypt and met the last priest of an ancient cult who took him into the Great Pyramid blindfolded. When Drew Ali made his way out unassisted, the priest initiated him and gave him the name Sharif Abdul Ali. On this trip to the Mideast, Ali put together a book known as the *Circle Seven Koran*.

Upon his return to America, he became known as Drew Ali. In Newark, New Jersey, at the age of 27, he had a dream where he was ordered to start a religion "for the uplifting of fallen mankind" with particular attention to the black race. He believed that blacks are genuinely Moors who were descendants of the Biblical Moabites and later inhabited what is now the country of Morocco. Although Ali's *Circle Seven Koran* has been picked apart by scholars and found to be largely borrowed from other texts, including *The Aquarian Gospel of Jesus Christ*, the origins and secrets of Ali's Moorish Science Temple are far more obscure and mysterious.

When one studies mystery schools, it is wise to remember that there is usually an outward front but also an inner circle that is much more mysterious and often revolves around a character or entity which seeks to remain invisible.

By all appearances, Drew Ali was a kind and loving man who sought no conflict with white people. In fact, he specifically stated that whites could claim the same status as blacks by declaring themselves to be Celts and therefore Asiatic. The Celts originated in Central Asia and migrated to the British Isles via Africa. The Moorish Science Temple was predominantly black but was not exclusive in terms of race. Ali's purpose was not only to correct the horrible wrongs that had been committed against the people of his own heritage, it was also to restore the lost wisdom that they once possessed which had enlightened the western world for several centuries.

Before I discuss certain key features of Drew Ali's life, it is necessary to take a specific look at the subject of oppression and the nature of oppressed people. This book is more about the oppression of consciousness, but in the case of Drew Ali and his Moorish heritage, the oppression of these people was an outright frontal assault on the very nature of consciousness.

Oppress means to press against. It means to weigh heavily on the mind, spirit, or senses. The word also suggests worry or trouble. Additionally, oppress means to keep down by cruel or unjust power or authority. It includes harsh treatment and tyranny. It does not take a genius to realize that a primary oppression or tyranny on Earth has been a repression of ideas. The truth is an idea. Disseminating and circulating certain ideas can be politically destabilizing to the status quo. If the status quo was truly happy and just, everyone would be happy, and there would be no reason to challenge it.

While everyone knows that the black race has been severely oppressed, the nature and the complete circumstances of why this is so are usually not scrutinized. It is highly ironic that America, the Land of the Free, was the sole reason for the slave trade known as the Triangular Trade Route. Most European countries did not indulge in slavery at that time as it was considered extremely inhumane. To borrow a phrase from Don King, it was only "Only in America!"

Historians now broadly recognize that Columbus was not the first European or even the first Iberian to visit the new world. Have you ever wondered why the history books were so emphatic about Columbus being first? His oppression of the Taino and other Indians was infamous. He was sponsored by Ferdinand and Isabella, two monarchs who united their kingdoms and instigated the Spanish Inquisition in order to drive out the Moors from Spain. Although many people were fair game during this Spanish purge,

275

the Moors of the Iberian Peninsula were the primary target. Columbus, Ferdinand, and Isabella were all willing and complicit agents of the Vatican. It is from this legacy that we get such groups as the Knights of Columbus, their namesake being derived from the famous explorer, who are dedicated to complete eradication of the Moorish culture.

It serves one to remember that the Catholic Church had a virtual monopoly on Europe before the time of Muhammad. The Moorish invasion of the Iberian Peninsula, in particular the area known as Andalusia, ushered in an unheralded renaissance of learning and culture that was unequaled in European history. The Islamic Moors tolerated other religions and brought out the esoteric wisdom of Judaism as well.

At the time of Columbus, the Vatican had been obsessed with silencing knowledge of foreign lands. This was all about power. The imprisonment of Marco Polo and the condemnation of the work of Copernicus and Gallileo are perhaps the most notable examples. The Moorish community knew the truth about astronomy and geology, not because they invented it but because they were part of a tradition that had never "unlearned" it. The Moors were the elite of the seven seas and they travelled all of the ancient pathways and trade routes. Prince Henry the Navigator's role in opening up the sea route to the Cape of Good Hope is a historical invention. He learned his knowledge from the Moors who had travelled between Morocco and Serendip (currently Sri Lanka) since ancient times. Of course, there were plenty of stopovers along the way. The king of Timbuktu, who depressed the entire economy of Egypt by unloading vast sums of gold on the market while on a pilgrimage to Mecca, sent an entire fleet of ships to the Americas. His vast library at Timbuktu was historically believed to contain much of the fragments from Alexandria.

The "contemporary history" of the Moors is rather obscure in common history books. Etymologically, Moor and Meru are very similar, but we have already established that the Moors have an ancient heritage beyond known history. The actual origin of the Moors is enigmatic, but scholars seem to trace them to the West African country of Mauritania. These Moors are by definition neither black nor white. They could be either. It is a common misconception that Moors were exclusively black. The term Moor is a cultural designation. The countries of Morocco and Mauritania were both named after the Moors. Both contained Berber populations who participated in the Islamic revolution of the day. The Berbers of West Africa, particularly those of Mauritania, were well known for their caste society which included bards or gypsies as the lowest caste. In the personages of the lower caste, these gypsy bards embodied the Sacred Drift and were the most feared caste of all. By utilizing their various crafts, they could parody the higher castes and even the rulers which routinely led to political embarrassment and even downfall. Much of their power resided in their ability to both dramatize and satirize. The Moors eventually carried this tradition into Europe and helped develop the grail romances via troubadours.

You have all heard of the word *serendipity*. This is a word which traditionally means "coming upon something unexpectedly that is pleasant and fortuitous." It also refers to happenstance, coincidence or synchronicity. Serendipity was actually named after Serendip (known subsequently as Ceylon and today as Sri Lanka) because it was a point of reference to the exotic culture of the Moors who ran the island for a considerable time. The tip of the Indian subcontinent has always been one of the hottest religious and mythological spots on the planet. We see the transposition of various cultural traditions when we once again consider the goddess Calypso and her identification with the hedonistic aspects of Kali. The celebration of Calypso and Kali are not much different. These traditions can be seen along the various trade routes of the ancient Moors which extended from Serendip to Mauritania and to Brazil and Trinidad. The tradition of Carnival is largest in Trinidad and Rio de Janeiro, neither of which were monumental voyages to ancient mariners. Trinidad is thought to be the home of the style of dancing we know as Calypso, but the goddess Calypso comes from an island off of the African coast.

If you study the original journals of Columbus, you will discover that he knew that many people had travelled to the "New Continent" as it was called in his charter. It is ironic that everyone "knew" he was going to Asia but it was never mentioned as such. The wording is such that it seemed that everyone new that there was more on the table than was being presented. Portuguese and Berber Moors, sometimes in conjunction with the Knights Templar, had long established colonies on the American continent, particularly in the areas of Delaware and North Carolina. As the Moors honored a matriarchal tradition, the Native Americans intermarried and intermixed with them quite splendidly. The Egyptian traditions of the Moors can be observed quite readily in the names of ancient cities such as Cairo, Illinois and Memphis, Tennessee. There are several more Egyptian names of cities that were originally populated by black people, not white settlers. It is well known that these areas were black, and it makes no sense that the "uneducated black" would have utilized such names, particularly when you discover the rich heritage that they did possess.

One of the biggest discoveries I have made in this regard is that the first historical record of the word *Moor* in America occurs in the court records of the state of Delaware. This is quite ironic because the Montauk Indians are known to be descended from a Delaware tribe known as the Lenni Lanape. Delaware Indians were so noble and regarded so highly that the city fathers of Manhattan chose the Delaware Indian chief's name of Tammany for their political machine that was known as Tammany Hall. The fact that the Moors were prevalent in Delaware gives a very major clue to the pyramids at Montauk.

In the book *Pyramids of Montauk*, I learned not only that the royal family of the Montauks were known as Pharoah (spelled a little different than the common spelling of pharaoh), but that they held initiatory ceremonies underneath the pyramids that had been constructed there. This I learned from Gail Evening Star who remembered the stories from her grandfather. Eventually, a New York justice by the name of Abel Blackmar declared the Montauk Indians extinct, despite their live presence and protest in the courtroom, because they were "too black." Justice Blackmar had marred the black element very well. He denied them credibility as Indians which we now discover had an even richer and more intriguing nature by reason of the fact that many of them were black and tied to the Moorish heritage.

At the time of Columbus, the Moorish culture was showing signs of thriving, particularly in the river country of the Mississippi and its tributaries. The origin of the word Alabama is officially unknown to etymologists but some believe it to be derived from "Ali Baba." This new culture not only threatened the status quo of the European continent but the supreme sovereignty of the Catholic Church itself. The mission of Christopher Columbus would be far more reaching than just the discovery of new lands and gold. It was to crush a people and their way of life.

1492 was a big year for the Spanish crown. In January, they conquered the last Moorish stronghold in Granada. This effectively vanquished any power or overt cultural influence the Moors still possessed. On March 31st of the same year, a proclamation was issued formally expelling all Jews from Spain. The next day was April 1st, a day which was to be forever remembered in the traditions and lexicon of our culture. Up to this point, the Moors were conquered but had not been officially expelled or sanctioned. According to long standing tradition, on April 1st, 1492, the Spanish executed a diabolical plot against the Moors. Any Moors who remained in Spain at that time had been told they could return to their home country of Morocco. Knowing the Moors were a suspicious lot, the Spaniards provided sailing vessels and docked them at port. When the Moors saw the vessels, they trusted that the Spaniards were not lying and proceeded to take their belongings and families to the ships. As the Moors left their homes behind them, the Spanish set fire to them. The ships either set sail or were burned as well thus leaving the Moors as the first victims of what became known as April Fool's Day. It has been a celebrated tradition since that time. Although the Moors were completely defeated in Europe, it was a persecution that would only get worse.

It is common history that the ships of Columbus were populated with prisoners. While many of them were indeed undesirables, some of them were Moors and Jews who were politically dangerous to the Church and were designated to be a subject people. Additionally, these Moors and Jews were deemed to be useful if they contacted European or African settlers in the New World. The ensuing years of history not only brought about an exploitation of a subjected people, it brought about a systematic destruction of their culture and their memory of it.

Despite the attempted destruction of their culture, the black Moors had a heritage and tradition which made them insurmountable. Due to the oppressive opposition, their culture could only be preserved by the concept of the Tao or sacred drift. Into this scenario was woven the affable and nonthreatening Uncle Remus, a caricature who represented home spun wisdom dispensed in a folksy way that bordered on the ridiculous. This was the element of the Fool in the Tarot. In this regard, it is ironic that the symbolic destruction of the Moorish culture occurred on what became April Fools Day. Uncle Remus not only represented the nonthreatening aspect of black wisdom but also the feminine energy. The name Remus itself comes from the sacred twins of Rome, born of a virgin, and suckled by a she-wolf. Romulus was said to have murdered his twin brother Remus after the latter contemptuously jumped over a short fence the former had made in order to divide the property of the Palantine Hill. The act of putting up a fence and owning property is a patriarchal attribute and is not characteristic of matriarchal societies. Of course, no one would kill their brother for jumping over a fence, but the act is symbolic. Whether the name "Remus" was chosen by astute mythographers or just happened by random chance, it did not escape the concept of Sacred Drift.

Many of the Moors who descended from the bards, gypsies, and troubadours discovered and propagated another avenue of expression by means of minstrel shows. In this way, they not only wove their tradition into the fabric of American culture but also the truth of the tragedy they experienced as a people. Often pandering to racial or comical stereotypes so as to appease the ruling class, they would subtly deliver discernible truths. Minstrel shows were loaded with what we would now call "jive" and were routinely moderated by an interlocutor, known as "Mr. Interlocutor," a master of ceremonies who would narrate stories and interpret for the characters and audience. He was usually flanked by men, sometimes in black face, who were known as "Mr. Bones" and "Erasmus."

One of the routines they would do featured a white man who would come out dressed as a high classed Philadelphia lawyer who would speak with impeccable diction and educated English. After talking to the audience for a while, he would claim that he could take a pill that would turn him into a black man. After consuming a fake pill, he would begin to transform into a "lowly black person" by removing his "white face" and transforming his speech into that of a poor slave. The man would reveal himself to actually be black. While the white folk would uproariously laugh in the bleachers, the same response was generated in the black audience who were often allowed to watch from the banks of the river. In both cases, either race could see that there were no real differences between the two if a black actor could successfully impersonate the mannerisms of a white person and duplicate the diction and nuances of educated English. The status quo was not even offended as they were too busy laughing at the actual truth of the matter. In this manner, the minstrel bards successfully carried out their job.

As minstrel shows went out of business, many of the antics performed in them degenerated or evolved into common jokes that carried on a lost legacy that was unknown even by the story tellers who relayed them. The following story was generated in its original form by Moorish bards and is included to both demonstrate and symbolize the historic crushing of the Moorish tradition. To create a more appropriate impact with regards to synchronicity, it will be told in the context of the Magick Theatre.

36

THE CHERRY TREE

*THE FOLLOWING TRANSMISSION
IS FROM A PARALLEL UNIVERSE*

ACT II of Peter Moon's
*Opening of the Seventh Seal:
Jack and Marjorie's Love Story*
entitled:

The Cherry Tree

As the crowd shuffles back in for Act II, the lights are dimmed until everyone is seated and the atmosphere is once again pitch black. Instrumental music begins to play in the background. It is a soft rendition of *The Battle Hymn of the Republic.* Slowly, a scene comes to life of the Potomoc River and the Jefferson Memorial. Highlighted are a full 3-D holographic rendition of the fabulous cherry trees of Washington. These cherry trees even reach out into the aisles of the audience. At the front of the stage, the Tar Baby appears once again. He is wearing his signature straw hat with a cane and is moving deftly across the stage as he addresses the audience.

"Now, you's mights be wunderin' what de U.S. of A. has to do wit' de bitumen we been talkin' 'bout in de last act. Well, you's be studyin' de Christ and de Antichrist so I's be studyin' de America and de Antimerca (Anti-America)."

At that moment, the scene begins to shift towards the sky above the Jefferson Memorial. The *Battle Hymn* has now finished but is replaced by traditional Japanese music. Appearing above the memorial is the Japanese war flag, a red sun with blazing rays of red. The traditional Japanese music is suddenly superceded by rapid Kabuki music as the Tar Baby breaks into a Kabuki dance. When this is over, the Tar Baby literally flips head over heals and addresses the audience.

"Now, I's be shape-shiftin' to shows you's all de Antimerica."

The Tar Baby tosses his cane in the air and begins to swirl until he is a blur. When he slows down, he no longer looks like a tar baby but an extremely caricaturized rendition of a Japanese with horn-rimmed glasses and excessive buck teeth, just as they were portrayed in American cartoons of the 1950's.

"Ah-so!" says the Tar Baby in an affected Japanese accent.

The shape-shifted Tar Baby is wearing a kimono as he parades back and forth in front of the audience and repeats the ridiculous phrase, "Ah-so!" His accent is embellished to the point where no true Japanese nor anyone else would ever speak it. (In order to understand his speech, what should be the letter "l" is replaced by the letter "r.")

"Most of you Americans, I see. Most of you don't know horrible pain you infrict upon our country. But, not arr of you are Americans, I see."

The Tar Baby, who now literally looks like a cartoon hologram, walks over until he is right in front of Karl Haushofer and he bows before addressing the general audience in broken English.

"You know, it was Japanese who gave you Americans arr these beautiful cherry trees. But, it was not what you think. It was a cosmic joke and arso good feng shui. You see, we Japanese paid no attention to America and were happiry isorated for centuries until Commodore Perry forced us to sign peace treaty at gun point. We had seen what British had done to China with the opium probrems that ended up in the Opium Wars. We wanted no part of your western ways. America had its own imperial interests at stake. The Spanish had the Phirripines which is the gateway to the oir rich Brunei, owned by the British who had China, too. America then wanted a piece of the action and invaded Japan curturary (culturally). Our shoguns then rearized that we had to take part in the industriar revorution or we wourd be consumed by western curture. When we got our act together and defeated the Chinese in 1895, Americans courd not beat us so they grabbed the Phirripines in an imperiarist grab at power after staging a fake incident of sinking the battreship *Maine*. America now very powerfur in orient. Then, with help from our friend Karl Haushofer, we beat pants off Russia in 1905 war which set seeds of downfall for Czarist Russia. America pissed off now! It OK for them to be imperialist power but not us! When they cut off our oil supply, we have no choice but Pearl Harbor.

"But, in meantime, we study America. We know your weak spots and we make fun of you, just as you make fun of us with buck teeth and grasses. We give you cherry trees in 1910, but your government burns them. We making a poriticar statement by sending you sakura, our name for cherry trees because it is cherry trees you chop down with George Washington which makes all Asiatic people feel like scum. But, you burn cherry trees, and we poritely persist until you plant them in 1912, just as Drew Ali receives his initiation. Not until the cherry trees are successfurry pranted does Drew Ali announce his prophethood in America. So, Mr. and Mrs. America, here is your story of the cherry tree."

With that, the caricaturized cartoon spins and whirls until he becomes the familiar and affable Tar Baby once more. He still wears the straw hat and carries a cane, but he is impeccably dressed in a white suit. The dapper Tar Baby no longer speaks with broken English but with impeccable Philadelphia diction, but there is a distinct trait of carnival barker in his voice.

"Ladies and gentlemen. You can now call me Mr. Interlocutor. You've all heard the story about George Washington and the cherry tree and how he had unwisely chopped down the cherry tree of his father. Being of high moral character, the young man realized he could not tell a lie and openly revealed his transgression to his father. According to the story, George Washington went unpunished for he had stood up in the face of potential punishment and had told the truth.

In the story you are about to see unfold before your eyes, Mr. Bones has a similar problem with his children, but no one is coming forward with the truth. As we enter this scene, Mr. Bones has three of his black children lined up as he gyrates, consternates and expresses his anguish and utter dismay over the fact that someone pushed the family outhouse into the river.

Looking partly like a drill sergeant but parodying every possible emotion and gyration that white people might conceive a rural uneducated black man to make, Mr. Bones looks deeply into the eyes of his three children. Finally, he addresses them all in a highly exhilarated and ridiculous style of speech that no one could possibly perform except on stage.

"Who threw de outhouse in de river in de mornin' time?"

Nothing is said, but the silence is penetrating. Mr. Bones looks at his boys and slowly scrutinizes them, hoping to find the truth. After failing to arrive at the truth, he speaks to the oldest.

"Was dat you 'Rasmus?"*

"Oh, no, fadduh. Dat wun't me!"

"Was dat you, Abraham?" asks the father.

"On, no, fadduh. Dat wun't me neither," replies Abraham.

"Was dat you, Jefferson?"

"No, fadduh, dat wun't me."

The story goes on with repetitive questioning but no change in the response of the boys. The gyrations and ridiculous expressions of Mr. Bones are increased and the sing-songy qualities of all voices are enhanced as the tension in the situation mounts until the audience is laughing uncontrollably. The laughter of the audience is based upon the fact that the racial characterizations are so completely ridiculous, preposterous and absurd that everyone realizes they do not natively belong to anyone. Further humor is derived from the utterly ludicrous situation presented.

Finally, after several days of repeated questioning, Mr. Bones has his boys lined up again, but this morning Erasmus has a question for him.

"Fadduh?"

"What's dat, 'Rasmus? You's gots sumptin' to say?"

---

* 'Rasmus is a contraction of Erasmus. As minstrel shows dissolved and their themes degenerated into jokes, the name "Erasmus" turned into "Rastus," an uneducated "no-account" black who demonstrated no responsibility and found himself expressing ridiculous conclusions in equally ridiculous situations. The name Rastus was a play on "Erastus," a Biblical character who had a proclivity towards too much sex. Many of these stories do not require racial inflection at all. Often, an uneducated bumpkin who was white or of any other race would serve just as well if not better.

"Yes, fadduh."

"What's dat, Rastus?"

"Do you believe in George Washington?"

"Oh, yeah, 'Rasmus, I believe in George Washington. He was a great, great man — 'fact, he was so great dat when he wuz a little boy, he had to tell de truth when he chopped down a cherry tree. De boy couldn't tell a lie, even when he did sumptin' wrong."

"Fadduh."

"What's dat, 'Rasmus?"

"Did you know dat when George Washington told de truth 'bout choppin' down dat cherry tree, his fadduh didn't punish him?"

"Yeah, 'Rasmus. I knows dat story. Der be sumptin' you wanna tell me?" he asks Erasmus as he closely scrutinizes him and looks deeply into the boy's eyes.

"Well, fadduh, if I told you's de story where's I did sumptin' wrong like George Washington and den told de truth like he did, would you punish me?"

"Oh no, 'Rasmus. I cudn't do dhat. I believe dat George Washington was a great man and dat we's should try to be jus' like 'im and his fadduh."

"Even if he did sumptin' real bad?"

"Even if he did sumptin' real bad, 'Rasmus. Now, what's dat you's wanna tell me?"

"Well, fadduh," says 'Rasmus, "I's cannot tell a lie. I threw de outhouse in de river in de mornin' time."

'Rasmus's father rapidly proceeds to take 'Rasmus over his knee and vigorously spanks the tar out of him.

As he takes a considerable pounding, 'Rasmus looks up with a hurt look in his eye and says, "But fadduh, I thought you believed in George Washington. I told you's de truth — dat I threw de outhouse in de river in de mornin' time — and now you's punishin' me for it."

"Dat's right, 'Rasmus. I do b'lieve in George Washington."

"Den why's you's punishin' me?" asks Erasmus.

"Becuz George Washington's fadduh wasn't in dat cherry tree when he chopped it down!"

As an impromptu curtain comes down, the audience is both laughing and clapping hysterically. The Tar Baby now turns into his patented spin once again. When he comes out of it, he is dressed like a pirate with a kerchief over his head, a white patch on his eye, an earring, and a parrot on his shoulder. He speaks with the accent of a pirate.

"Aye me hearties. Laugh all ya wants cuz dats de last laugh ya may ever have at de expense of de oppressed. No one can make a case better d'an de stereotypes d'emselves.

"If you's be wunderin' why's I becomes a pirate its becuz it became de way of de Moors when we were aborted. First, by Ferdinand and Isabela; then again, when we got chopped down in George Washington's cherry tree. We ran cities of corsairs and fought de Pope at every turn. These was exciting and adventurous days. But first, I wants ya all to remember something."

As the curtain comes back up, the original scene of cherry trees along the Potomac appear. One can also see the Jefferson Memorial and the Washington Monument.

"Remember lads and lasses, when ya sees de cherry trees in Washington, d'ey was planted right on de Potomoc amidst Jefferson's memorial. Remember, Jefferson chronicled de language of the Montauk Indians and claimed to have lost it in de Potomoc. Off in de other direction, ya see's de Washington Monument. Not only did Washington chop down de cherry tree, he commissioned de Montauk Lighthouse as de first official public works project of de United States.

"Now, lasses and laddies, d'ose cherry trees just happen to be de most natural beauty Washington, D.C. is known for. Ya all might be knowin' dat de design of Washington, D.C. is constructed like an upside down pentagram, meant to symbolize de inversion of matter over spirit, meaning de devil. But, d'ose Anti-Americans, the Asiatic Japanese, circumvented that inverted pentagram when d'ey made sure d'ose cherry trees became de pride of Washington.

"And don't forget d'is, me hearties. De whole grand design 'o de most natural wonder of Washington is dat de Moors will be remembered every April 1st when de cherry blossoms be sproutin' and bloomin'. One could not have planned a better cosmic joke."

37

HISTORY LESSON

Historians know that the story of George Washington and the cherry tree is complete fiction, but no one has ever explained the precise mechanism of how it insidiously worked its way into the fabric of American culture. George Washington's cherry tree is a proverbial expression of what happened to the Moorish people and the black race during the reign of George Washington. Although Drew Ali was probably not the first to spread the tale of the cherry tree, he certainly had an interesting story to back it up with.

Morocco was the first country in history to officially recognize the fledgling United States of America, and when they did, Washington was presented with a Moorish flag. At that time, the Moroccan flag was pure red and was sometimes thought of as a cherry. Drew Ali stated to all who would listen that at the inception of our nation, a treaty was worked out with Morocco that any Moor, black person or Asiatic (which was also interpreted to mean Caucasians when necessary) could claim themselves to be a Moorish national and thus be free from the bondage of slavery. This distinctly meant that if you were a slave on a plantation and walked over to the President's office and declared yourself a Moorish national (even if you were from a more primitive African tribe or country), you would be declared the subject of a sovereign nation and your citizenship would be restored. In other words, you were a free man. While the terms of this treaty were readily accepted by Washington, he made no significant effort to circulate or promote these terms. In what could easily be considered one of the greatest ruses of history, colored people were not informed of the means by which they could free themselves and were thus "tricked." This is the exact meaning of George Washington chopping down the cherry tree. This is why the minstrel rendition includes the black person being in the cherry tree or outhouse when it was taken down.

In Peter Wilson's *Sacred Drift*, a version of the above story is included, but again, he is a master of understatement. If you do take the time and exhibit the patience to research the actual history of Morocco and the United States, you can find some very interesting information that demonstrates the above to be decidedly true.

Morocco was long the home of the Moors, and after the purge of 1492, many fled back to their homeland. When Washington became president, the Triangular Trade Route of slavery had long since been established and he was a direct beneficiary of the slave trade. As the United States was asserting and gaining its independence, the Sultan of Morocco was besieged by stories and complaints of what had happened to his brethren across the seas. One must remember that slavery had been abolished in Europe but was getting a new life in America. As the United States declared its independence, Morocco was aggressively interested in pursuing a dialogue and recognizing this country because it had a vested interest: enslaved citizens and relatives. They were essentially suing for peace. Although Morocco was eager to establish formal relations, the United States was busy with their own war and other problems. They did not respond. After all normal diplomatic channels had been exhausted, Morocco seized various Americans and their ships and held them for ransom. This got the attention of the Americans and it worked. A peace treaty was worked out and guaranteed that any U.S. citizen in Morocco would be declared a free American citizen if he presented himself to the U.S. consulate and demonstrated his citizenship. It preserved the rights of all Americans in Morocco. In diplomacy, there is a principle called reciprocity which means that citizens of different countries will be treated in kind. The U.S. Secretary of State clearly stated in his own handwriting that any Moroccan national would be treated the same as any U.S. citizen in Morocco. In this respect, the so-called apocryphal legend of Drew Ali is astonishingly backed up.

The above encourages us to seriously consider another story passed down through antiquity. This concerns a meeting that Drew Ali had with President Woodrow Wilson. Noble Drew Ali claimed to have written a letter to President Woodrow Wilson and asked him for the Moroccan flag. The Wilson connection is, once again, ironic because President Wilson was a known KKK sympathizer who endorsed the racist movie *Birth of a Nation* which featured a white supremacist by the name of Ben Cameron.

There is an account that Drew Ali actually met with President Wilson and asked for the flag. When Wilson and his people asked him what flag he was talking about, Ali told them it was hidden in their vault. After going to the vault room, all the president's men brought out all sorts of flags, but he told them it was much older. As they dug deeper, they came upon a red flag and said that it was the flag of Morocco. Ali is said to have stated, "I am here for the Moorish flag, that which you called a cherry tree."

The full account of this alleged meeting is a little suspicious because it indicates that the Moroccan flag was red with a green star. At the time of George Washington, the Moroccan flag that would have been given to the President was only plain red, some say to honor the blood of the Prophet of Islam. This indicates that a black faction may have been embellishing what happened because the green star was only added to the Moroccan flag around or after this meeting with President Wilson was said to have occurred. The ostensible reason for adding a green pentagram was that the international seafaring community had problems with the plain Moroccan flag as it confused mariners who already had their own established use for red flags. The embellishing of the Drew Ali story was not really necessary if they had appealed to a higher truth. A more astute observer would have realized that the green pentagram added to the red flag is even more significant. Accordingly, Morocco adopted the pentagram, which they called the Seal of Sulaiyman, and colored it green to honor the color of Islam.

Without actually observing all of the actual history concerning the bizarre synchronicities involved with the cherry tree, it is very hard to say how much of what occurred with it is intentional. It is quite clear, however, that some outside force was orchestrating a synchronicity that could not easily be explained. This will become clearer as the story develops.

After his alleged meeting with President Wilson, Drew Ali continued his life mission which was to lead his people out of a mental poverty that had put them at the bottom rung of the ladder. His method to lift them was his own version of Islam. He also noticed that the only successful members of his race were those who imitated the conquerors of his people. There was no great imam or sheik who taught anything that was indigenous or respectful of their original culture. In this vein, he became their leader and created quite a stir in the world of the Roaring Twenties. If you care to read the newspapers of the day, you will find that Drew Ali commanded such a following that he was closely monitored by the Government as a potential power that had to be reckoned with. There were even huge revivals that outdid Christian enterprises. In fact, Drew Ali's meetings included stirring renditions of "Muslim's That Old Time Religion," borrowing from the trite evangelical Christian ditty you have likely heard.

The movement was huge. Ali was billed as a healer, too, and was said to produce miracles in his own right. By most accounts, the man seemed to be humble and unpretentious although some have tried to defame him. Mostly, everyone ignores Drew Ali. In the background of the religious dogma was the Moorish Science Temple which has also been portrayed as having other names. In the midst of all this excitement and hoopla, there was one very penetrating truth. Drew Ali had a reputation that had surpassed that of any black man in the entire history of America. He was not only dangerous to the powers that be, he was in a position to wield a considerable amount of power. As is typical in any scene of power with homo sapiens, his lieutenants and adjutants were all poised to make a grab at this incredible power, particularly if he was to suffer incarceration from the authorities or to die.

Into this thriving scene of Black America rallying behind Drew Ali as an international religious leader entered one of the most intriguing and dubious characters in history, particularly Black Muslim history. This man's name was Wali Fard, Wali Farrad, Wallace Douglas Dodd Ford or a host of other similar names which have been appended to his legendary life. The association between Fard and Drew Ali is perhaps more apocryphal than any of the other information concerning either. Like Drew Ali, Wali Fard has an extensive FBI file. Fard's file is as loaded with disinformation as one could possibly imagine, but it is not necessarily the FBI that is creating it. Amidst all the nebulous residue, one thread of information is most certainly true. Wali Fard is the undisputed and heralded founder of the Black Muslim faction that spawned Elijah Muhammad, Malcolm X, and Louis Farrakhan; however, he harnessed all of his power and influence from his association with the Moorish Science Temple of Drew Ali.

By 1928, the Moorish Science Temple had been officially incorporated and the movement had accrued considerable wealth and influence, even successfully campaigning to elect Oscar DePriest, the first black member of the House of Representatives since 1901. Up to that time, neither Moorish America nor Black America had ever known such a renaissance as was then occurring in the latter part of the 1920's. The movement was chronicled in various newspapers, and the FBI watched everything with the scrutiny of a hawk. At the same time, various jackals that wealth and power attract began to slowly surround their prey.

Drew Ali's last known days on Earth began when his business manager, Claude D. Greene, was brutally murdered. The *Chicago Defender* reported that he was shot, cut, and stabbed four times in the neck and body. It is pertinent to note that it was not Ali who was attacked, but his manager, the man who held all the purse strings. The jackals were apparently more interested in the monetary aspects than in anything else. After the murder of Greene, it was said that forty arrests were made within one hour and included Drew Ali. A faction within the Moorish Science Temple alleged that Claude Greene was creating a splinter group and that Drew Ali had arranged for him to be eliminated. When you consider that several different factions continued to vie for Greene's power after his death, it is quite possible that he and his prophet never had a falling out. Like so much of Drew Ali's life, no one really knows exactly what happened.

Believing he would go before a grand jury on May 20, 1929, Drew Ali sent a message of love to all of his faithful and asked them to be with him. These were to be his last words. All we know is that he never made any public appearances after that. No evidence of any trial or grand jury has surfaced. It is believed the Prophet was released on bond but suffered a martyr's death as a result of either severe police beatings or assassination by his rival Muslims. Although he was apparently arrested in May, his date of death was July 20th and there is an oral tradition that there is no grave site for him at Burr Oak Cemetery, the supposed location of his burial.

All we know for certain is that after his disappearance, all hell broke loose. There was tremendous infighting amongst the different factions of the Moorish Science Temple. This included a kidnapping and even a shoot-out with the Chicago police. There is even a report that over one thousand police and National Guard were put on patrol at one point. This sort of messy business was never known during the reign of Drew Ali. It was out of these ashes that Wali Fard, the new Muslim leader arose.

Reading Wali Fard's FBI file at face value is sure to confound and perplex you. If you read it and realize that some of the information might be planted or deliberately concocted, it will probably perplex you even more. It is a hot bed of information that does not make any sense. All of this starts off with the declaration on his birth certificate that he is a Caucasian. It is believed his father was British and his mother might have been Polynesian. His birth certificate was even amended at a later date to indicate that the mother listed on it was not his real mother. Pictures of Wali Fard indicate that he is fair with only a hint of another race. There is no real reasonable assertion anywhere that I have seen that he is truly black, yet he is known as the one who propagates the term "white devil."

After having married and fathered a son, Fard abandoned them in Seattle and moved to Los Angeles where he was a restaurateur. He ends up being arrested for both bootlegging and assault with a deadly weapon which earns him a considerable stint in San Quentin prison. There are stories that he ended up overseas and traded in Persian silks before coming to Newark where he began slowly stalking Drew Ali so as to siphon power and influence. Fard does not appear to have been involved in any of the consternations that concerned the downfall of the Moorish Science Temple, but his marked rise to power afterwards invites suspicion. He is eventually recognized as the Maudi (the savior of the desert according to pre-Islamic tradition) or Allah himself by a young follower named Elijah Poole. Poole had suffered horrible racist traumas growing up in the south, and he swore that he would do whatever was in his power to balance the scales. His embrace of Wali Fard is odd when you consider that he was not even black. Nevertheless, Fard in turn recognizes Poole himself as a prophet of God and initiates him with the title of Elijah Muhammad. Not long after the spectacular conversion of Elijah Muhammad, Fard is arrested and confesses that the whole Muslim movement is a fraud, at least according to a popular conservative account. Fard is officially never heard from again.

What you have just read is a very summarized and selective version of what is only the beginning of the FBI file and other histories. Newspapers, law enforcement agencies, and even the FBI continued to either vigorously search for any further mention of Fard's name or to deliberately concoct stories about his alleged reappearance. One account has him returning to his abandoned wife and child in California, but she is not interested in taking him back. There is also a death certificate for Fard's son who died in 1942 while serving in the American military. In the 1960's, newspapers reported that there was tangible proof of Wali Fard. Elijah Muhammad responds by offering $100,000 to anyone who can prove that this Wali Fard is the same Wali Fard that he knew. When the newspapers apparently get very hot on this trail and begin to call Elijah Muhammad on his offer, he withdraws the offer and fosters more mystery.

If you want to exercise the conspiratorial functions of your brain, I suggest you do your own research on Wali Fard and also Drew Ali. It is great conspiracy, but I am bringing it up for a specific purpose. The Ong's Hat travel brochure not only suggests that the Moorish Science Temple was behind the ashram but that the property was purchased by Wali Fard himself. Although the travel brochure is a piece of creative writing based upon different circumstances, the entire history involved in this scenario smacks of a mystery school operation. Wali Fard appears as some sort of dark St. Germaine. There are plenty of tangible documents to suggest he lived yet his physicality and history is completely intangible. Set up with a criminal record, he can easily be discredited if the need arises. If the criminal record is true, he is prone to make quick and substantial money by bootlegging. Either as an opportunist or secret agent, he infiltrates the Black Muslim movement which becomes more preoccupied with other agendas than with the true identity of the Moorish heritage. Although Elijah Muhammad claims to "hear" Wali Fard throughout the rest of his days, these are spiritual communications without any appearance in the flesh. All of the above would seem to make Wali Fard akin to a holographic image who was misdirecting the entire Moorish revival started by Drew Ali. The Ong's Hat travel brochure is not the only document to position Fard as a world traveler and businessman who had mysterious access to vast sums. There are also different accounts that have Wali Fard acting in a much more laudable light, but again, everything is apocryphal.

It is fascinating to consider the prospect that Wali Fard was a time traveller who was sent from another time (such as the Montauk Project) to derail the Moorish revival. There is apparently also a "good" Wali Fard who seeks to redeem the "bad" version by fostering the Ong's Hat ashram and offering a potential escape route from this universe. All of this necessitates us asking why the Ong's Hat brochure even includes Wali Fard. Is it perhaps that Peter Wilson (assuming he wrote the brochure), who is very well schooled in all of the above, has decided to stir the pot by deliberately associating the already mysterious Fard with an even more mysterious project? In the end, it does not matter. We are dealing with a multiplicity of realities. As Ong's Hat concerns a convergence of various realities, we must be ready to embrace all aspects and potentialities of Wali Fard. Remember, for every time travelling Wali Fard that you can muster up, there is one such person making his way through the time lines. This is a vintage example of how a synchronicity attractor works. We've zoned in on a component of consciousness that attracts further synchronicity. The writer of the Ong's Hat brochure, who was an obvious advocate of synchronicity, did a good job. It should be mentioned that the brochure suggests the property at Ong's Hat was purchased by Fard who was dealing in exotic Afghan imports.* Thus, a string of haphazard, unpredictable, and acausal quantum events have not only delineated an annihilation and systematic degeneration of the Moorish tradition but even suggests that there is light at the end of the quantum tunnel. If one is trying to unscramble the crashed hard disk of consciousness, the Moorish lanterns lead the

---

* Some people believe that it was really Peter Wilson who purchased the property through Afghan imports which were not silk scarves at all.

way past the bad blocks and inert clusters of knowledge. It also helps to know, if we can find out, who exactly is the puppeteer that is manipulating the various superstrings of consciousness.

If life is a stage, the abstract ideas in our own minds determine not only how the stage will be set but how the drama will be played out. The lights that flash off and on inside of a theater are no different than the lights that flash off and on inside of your mind. Your mind already contains all the abstract esoteric knowledge that can be known — it is only a matter of the lights shining on it.

The Magick Theatre awaits.

38

CAPTAIN KIDD

THE FOLLOWING TRANSMISSION
IS FROM A PARALLEL UNIVERSE

ACT III of Peter Moon's
Opening of the Seventh Seal:
Jack and Marjorie's Love Story
entitled:

Captain Kidd

As Act III begins, the lights are subdued until there is complete blackness. The slow routine of bringing out images occurs once again, but this time the scene is horrific. A gallows appears which looks empty at first, but as the stage lightens up, one can see the poor little Tar Baby hanging in the gallows in a limp and heart wrenching fashion. It is a dim and ugly day in London on the Thames River. Although no people come by, one hears voices discussing the ordeal of Captain Kidd.

"Kidd was a pirate," says a voice from the blackness, "and he died like a pirate. His body is dipped in tar and he is hung for all to see and warn everyone of the penalty for being a pirate."

Another voice cries, "But, you know, he was innocent. He had proper papers to raid the ship he was accused of pirating, but his counsel and the judge hid the proof and would not show it in the trial. Kidd was framed!"

"Yes, but he killed a Moor," cried the first voice. "He was guilty of murder."

"Not a Moor," says yet another voice, "but Robert Moore, the ship's gunner who had instigated a mutiny. Kidd only hit him on the head with a bucket to squash a rebellion. No other Captain was ever tried for murder when quelling a mutiny."

"Then why did they want Kidd dead?"

As the light begins to shine on the gallows, the Tar Baby's body slowly turns around. Wearing a captain's hat as he hangs in the noose, the Tar Baby looks up slyly and winks at the audience as they let out laughter. He starts talking but his head is still in a downward position as he is supposed to be effectively hung.

"Perhaps it's because he was a Masonic sacrifice and his name was Kidd, suggestive of a goat?" says a voice.

"No," says one of the other voices. "There's much more to it than that."

"Then, perhaps," says the Tar Baby, "it's because his backers wanted him dead because they had ordered and sanctioned his piracy in the first place, and they would be exposed for engaging the Crown in piracy as well," replied the Tar Baby.

"You are closer," cries one of the now familiar voices in the dark.

"Ah, then," replies the Tar Baby, "perhaps it is because, as the most famous pirate ever to be involved in secret intrigues concerning the House of Orange, he buried his secret treasure at Montauk?"

"I think you're a little closer," says the mysterious voice.

"And, yes!" exclaims the Tar Baby. "Perhaps he even carried the secret of the Seventh Seal itself!"

At this last statement, one hears a forbidding wind and then the loud crack of thunder. As the perilous wind circulates, a huge tornado is seen in the background. The wind gets stronger and stronger to the feel of the audience until the deep blackness of the tornado completely eclipses everyone's vision. During a thirty second period of darkness, the wind gently stops and the temperature turns from mildly cool to a pleasant room temperature.

Suddenly and abruptly, before anyone can become too comfortable, loud screams are heard from the audio system as a huge skull appears. The unexpected appearance of a huge and come-to-life skull over the audience is completely stunning and several primal and visceral screams are heard from those watching the show, from both men and women alike.

The skull is wearing a buccaneer's hat and there are two cross bones beneath it, but they are shorter than the femur bones normally seen on pirate flags. The skull becomes fully animated and begins a blood curdling laugh that is a laugh of power.

"Ah, ha, ha! Didn't think you could be frightened from a children's show, did you?"

As he finishes his sentence, the skull spits out a colored water which looks exactly like blood. It is horrifying.

"Now, maybe you will pay attention to the secrets — the secrets of Golgotha, the Place of the Skull."

As soon as the skull has announced his intention, he takes a softer tone and begins to introduce himself.

"Hello, and welcome to the Magick Theater. My name is Jolly Roger, and I am a symbol of both good and evil. My name originally, as it was known in the south of France, was "Le Jolie Rouge" which translates into English as "Jolly Red" or, more appropriately, the "Joy of Blood.""

"Many millennia ago, there was the idea that man could not hurt man, or women for that matter. There existed a teaching and philosophy that everyone could be happy, and that is why there is a smile on my face. But, my skull is devoid of human flesh to remind us that life in the flesh is temporary and that we all carry an eternal truth that reaches beyond the grave.

"Just as the Tar Baby is a repository for all the repressed thoughts and fears of the human race, I represent the flame of unbridled truth and enlightenment."

The skull then lets out a roar of frightening laughter as he turns his head completely around only to reemerge as a brilliant and shining crystal skull with prism-like rainbows cascading off of the figure in all directions. It is far too bright. The audience is forced to cover their eyes until Jolly Roger turns back to his more tolerable appearance in the buccaneer hat.

"Too much light is maybe not such a good thing, after all!" exclaims the awesome figure. "Perhaps a story that is a little more human will suffice."

The blackened theater now begins to fade into another scene, less slowly than before, as Jolly Roger recedes to an overhead but background position where he can act as a narrator. A completely new scene depicts underground ice caves in Antarctica . The Tar Baby can be seen paddling in a canoe through icy underground waters where shards of ice look like a crystal palace. Accompanying him is the child movie star, Shirley Temple.

"Oh, my goodness, Tar Baby," says Shirley Temple, "this is a cold and awesome place. Where are we?"

"We's in New Schwabenland, dat part of Antarctica dat de Germans claimed prior to World War II an' where some say de Fourth Reich has a secret base to dis very day."

"Why that's just terrible, Mr. Tar Baby!" replies Shirley.

As they paddle in their boat, the scenery moves so that the audience vicariously feels their position. When they round a corner of ice, they reach a platform of ice where a meticulously groomed German officer is wearing a uniform. Instead of the swastika and typical insignia, he is wearing the symbol of the Vril, a black and lavender rectangle with a silver lightening bolt. He is holding the Spear of Destiny, that enigmatic artifact which was said to be the instrument of Christ's death.

"Dat's Maximillian Hartmann," says the Tar Baby, "de soldier dat Adolph Hitler most trusted and gave custody of de Spear of Longinus to."

No sooner does little Shirley see Hartmann than she jumps right out of the canoe and begins to pound him on his thighs but is even more aggressive when she kicks him in the shin bones.

"You horrible Nazis! What you did is terrible! You'd better tell Mr. Hitler that what he did was wrong, wrong, wrong. You don't kill Jews — you're not supposed to kill anybody!"

"Calm down, girl. I don't mean any harm to you, and I did not kill any Jews."

"I'm not gonna fall for your tricks, you blue-eyed Aryan hipster! I know you'll leave me alone 'cause my name is "Temple" and I represent the "Temple of God" but you'll also want to use me in your propaganda films for the Reich. Just what you need, a cute little Nazi!"

"Yes," replied the handsome German officer, "but I am not wearing the insignia of the Nazis or the SS."

"You're not gonna fool me. Don't give me any of that Vril Society crap. That's just like the KKK being kinder and gentler.

The media has shown documentaries demonstrating that the Spear of Destiny you have is not the real one because they did carbon dating which shows that the one in the Hapsburg Museum was authenticated as having come from the time of the First Reich."

"Oh, they have?"

"That's right. We're not gonna let you keep the Hitler myth alive, the Nazi myth, or even the Spear of Destiny myth. The Spear of Destiny is in Austria and that's that. No Antarctica, no New Schwabenland, no nothing. You don't even exist, even if Peter Moon did meet your daughter who you abandoned."

"My daughter? Well, you see, we had many duties in our day and one was to propagate our dying race. I am sorry but...."

"Enough of you. You're just a fake legend concocted by Nazis wanting to keep a myth alive."

"Well, I only hope that my daughter is as cute as you. But you really should calm down. You cannot kill a myth by suppressing it. You must open up the Temple to the truth. Surely, your life and your movie career were the manipulations of a patriarchal society just as my Nazi associates were. They rebelled against that society only to replace it with a patriarchy that was even more frightening. The reach for the truth can bend the light and fragment it like a prism. You are a myth, too, Shirley. Perhaps that is why you became Shirley Temple Black!"

At the mention of the word black, the Tar Baby gets up on the ice and starts shuffling his feet and dancing with his straw hat and cane. "Now, dat's where I come in. Yep, Shirley, you's went on to become a member of de Council on Foreign Relations and served as de Ambassador of the U.N. before becoming Ambassador to Ghana, named after one of the greatest civilizations in Africa that was an origin point of slavery during the days of the Triangular Trade Route."

"I'm not a racist!" says Shirley. "I used to dance with Mr. Bojangles and gave him his best screen audience ever."

"No, Shirley, says the Tar Baby, "you's not a racist. Down deep, you's one of us and de cutest of de bunch. You are de Temple, a cute, lovable and feminine goddess. Surely, you are de Temple Black. De Temple of de Moors."

"What in the heck are you talking about, Tar Baby?"

"Well," said the Tar Baby, "It be complicated, but let's start with dat Spear of Destiny and why de pirate flag is black and not red like the secret flag dat Captain Kidd had."

"Captain Kidd had a red pirate flag?"

"It was red and had shin bones on it instead of femur bones. All de other pirate ships had black flags or other flags but de red flag was for de admiral of all pirates, de King of Kings dey called him. And dat was given to Captain Kidd, but he never flew it."

At this point, Jolly Roger, who is now seen with a red flag backing him, speaks up.

"The Spear of Destiny is a ruse. In fact, it is the origin of the word "ruse" which means "recuse" but originally meant or was associated with "red." The Spear of Destiny was the spear that was said to have pierced the side of Christ and killed him in order to prevent his shin bones from being broken. In those days, if a man didn't die on the cross, his shin bones were broken in order to cause asphyxiation and get it over with. It was prophesized that "not a bone of Him shall be broken.""

"It was all about dem shin bones," said the Tar Baby as he began to lift two bones and clap them over his head repeatedly. "Dem shin bones gonna shine, shine, shine, shine, 'til dey can't shine no mo'ah."

Jolly Roger then began to rotate and shine prismatically once again. Being much too bright for the audience to withstand, he recedes once again to his more comfortable manifestation. By then, the Tar Baby sets himself up in a shoe shine stand where he is shining the boots of Maximillian Hartmann and shining away in a racist portrayal of an old shoe shine boy. Then, he turns around to reveal a bright and shiny front tooth which he extends so that everyone can view it. He then sings a jingle from an old Pepsodent toothpaste commercial from the 1960's.

"You'll wonder where the yellow went, when you brush your teeth with Pepsodent."

When Shirley Temple hears this, she is beside herself, and one can see the cute look of consternation on her face.

"I know that jingle!"

Maximillian Hartmann, who is still rubbing his shin bones from being kicked by her, answers her.

"Yes, Shirley. I know Pepsodent, too. I remember when they put fluoride in their toothpaste. We had a program at I.G. Farben where fluoride was created to make prisoners more passive and less rebellious. Fluoride was deemed to be usable on the general population as well. I think it's worked pretty well."

"Yes, Mr. Hartmann, but I think that cute little Tar Baby is trying to make a point. Why's he making that front tooth shine so much?"

"Maybe it has to do with the Pepsodent Company. As soon as Drew Ali was arrested, they sponsored one of the most successful radio shows of all time. In fact, this radio show was completely dedicated to rubbing any memory of the Moorish Science Temple completely into the ground."

"Oh, my goodness! What was that show?"

"Amos and Andy," replied Maximillian Hartmann.

"Really? I remember that show."

"Yes, Shirley. Pepsodent ownership hired a couple of Freemasons to write a show that would make most everyone, including blacks, laugh the Moors off the face of the Earth."

There is suddenly a loud sizzle backstage as if a piece of equipment has shorted out. A voice comes over the public address system as the lights go out.

"We are experiencing technical difficulties back stage. Please stay in your seat and we will continue with Act III in a short while."

39

AMOS AND ANDY

As a young boy during the 1950's, I can remember seeing reruns of a show called *Amos and Andy*. As I recall, the television would be left on as I played in the living room. I do not remember my mother being interested in the show, but she knew the various characters. As a child, the humor directed at the misfortune of these poor characters was completely over my head. All I saw was that they would experience considerable misfortune, and I felt sorry for them. I did not like the show at all as I found it depressing.

As I began to study the Moors and the various tangents in this book, I was shocked to find that the characters in the show, particularly the original radio show, were not only spoofing the Moors but Drew Ali and the Moorish Science Temple itself. Amos and Andy belonged to a secret mystical order known as the Mystic Knights of the Sea. This was certainly no accident as the Moors were known for their ancient tradition as well as their mastery of the ocean. One of the lead characters in the show was named "Kingfish" who was always trying to con someone, particularly Andy. He was the head of a secret lodge where he was the Great Supreme Kingfish. The Mystic Knights of the Sea were designated with other humorous titles which were designed to parody a Masonic style organization. These included the Whale, the Mackerel, the Jellyfish and the Swordfish. Routine members were referred to as Sardines. In the original show, there were specific references to candidates being blindfolded and initiated into various degrees of the lodge. The most "in your face" reference to

Drew Ali was when they featured a "Prince Ali Bendo" who was portrayed as a fake crystal-gazer who ended up in jail.

Amos and Andy was a popular part of Americana during the 1920's, and it is said that both whites and blacks enjoyed the show. But, it is certain that many blacks did not, and many even knew the direct digs and hysterical parody that were being made at the expense of the revival movement of the Moorish Science Temple.

Charles Correll and Freeman Gosden were the writers and performers of *Amos and Andy*. They were both 32nd Degree Masons and Shriners and were literally handpicked by Albert Lasker, a fascinating character who is not unknown to conspiracy researchers but is vastly underrated.

Lasker invented modern advertising. His rise to power began when he worked as a clerk for an ad agency by the name Lord and Thomas after the turn of the century. In those days, copywriters made about $4,000 a year which was a tremendous salary in those days. Real good ones could make up to $15,000 or even more when Lasker found his way into this highly paid profession. Lasker claimed he learned the basic secret of advertising from an employee named John Kennedy who summarized it all in three words: "salesmanship in print."

The highlights of Albert Lasker's career are studded with rich and famous historical characters, but the powerful connections are even more astonishing. When one reads about him, one becomes more curious about what is not said as opposed to what is said. There are countless enterprises he owned but few are delineated.

He acquired shares in Pepsodent during the Wilson administration. Pepsodent was not growing and could not afford advertising so Lasker bartered for part of the company. About this same time he purchased the Chicago Cubs, the most profitable team in baseball, from the brother of former President Taft. Before Taft, the Cubs owner was involved in cheating scandals. He not only told his team to take a dive but encouraged other National League teams to fold for the New York Giants. After similar problems occurred with the Chicago White Sox in the 1919 "Black Sox scandal," Lasker created the idea of a commissioner and hired U.S. District Court Judge Kenesaw Mountain Landis to moonlight as baseball commissioner. Eventually, Lasker sold his shares to William Wrigley, a friend who had been a minority owner.

After fixing baseball, Lasker became the campaign manager for President Warren Harding, and this was the first time any form of sophisticated public relations advertising had been employed to elect a president. Harding, who presided over one the of the most corrupt administrations ever, rewarded Lasker with the chairmanship of the United States Shipping Board. This meant that he supervised shipping contracts between industry and the Government. In the aftermath of World War I, there had been vast orders to build ships and augment the navy. Before and during Lasker's supervision, virtually no ships were delivered, but four billion dollars worth of expenses had been paid to various rich and powerful colleagues which included Percy A. Rockefeller, Pierre S. du Pont, J. Ogden Armour, Robert S. Lovett, William E. Corey, Otto H. Kahn, and a host of others. This was an infamous scandal but, like the S&L and Enron scandals of our time, nothing too significant was done about it.

Lasker continued to expand his various interests and holdings, particularly through ownership in Lord and Thomas Advertising, where he had succeeded one of the retiring partners. Pepsodent, in which he would increase his holdings, was just about to drop off the market when, in 1929, Lasker used it to sponsor *Amos and Andy*. Ironically, this decision was not executed until just after Drew Ali had been arrested. A few months after the *Amos and Andy* radio show debuted, Lasker emerged completely unscathed by the 1929 stock market crashed. He claimed that his friend and trading partner, John Hertz (of Hertz rental car fame) had saved him from that fate although this claim is somewhat suspect.

Amos and Andy not only broke ground with its popularity, it was the first syndicated radio show ever. Pepsodent not only became a household word but the premier name in radio. Lasker then hand picked Bob Hope to star on the *Pepsodent Hour*. In 1933, Lasker became the president of Pepsodent. During this period, Lasker was a heavy contributor to the University of Chicago and eventually became a trustee in the late 1930's. Ironically, the University of Chicago is said to be where the initial ideas for the Philadelphia Experiment were hatched.

In 1932, Lasker managed the presidential campaign of Wendell Wilkie but was not successful. He also became friendly with Wilkie's running mate, Frank Knox. It was through Lasker's connection with Knox that he was put in a position where he would have had privy to all information in naval intelligence as well as the Philadelphia Experiment itself. Roosevelt appointed Knox to be Secretary of the Navy and Lasker, who was still the president of Pepsodent as well as the biggest ad agency in the world, was assigned as Assistant Secretary of the Navy. His predecessors in the office of the Secretary of the Navy included both Franklin and Theodore Roosevelt.

In the midst of all this excitement, Lasker was introduced to his second wife by William "Wild Bill" Donovan, who was just forming up the Office of Strategic Services, the forerunner of the CIA. Lasker's new wife was Mary Woodard Reinhardt, a New York industrial designer, who happened to be one of the wealthiest woman in the country. Both were very close to Donovan. Lasker's biography indicates that it was his very close friends who created the OSS and CIA. When Albert and Mary Lasker were married in New York in 1940, the ceremony was performed by the Chief Justice of the Supreme Court of the United States of America.

Once married, Lasker and his new wife established the Albert and Mary Lasker Foundation to support medical research. In 1944, he spearheaded a fund raising drive that nearly doubled the amount of money spent on cancer research. At the same time, he pursued the idea of getting the federal government more involved in medical research and the years of 1946-1950 found him helping to establish the National Institute of Health. While pouring vast amounts of cash into the medical establishment, he fell ill with cancer and died on May 30, 1952 at the age of 73.

For those of you interested in pursuing the legacy of Albert and Mary Lasker, you can find more information by looking up the "Lasker Syndicate" on the internet. It is wide and very far reaching. I have revealed just the tip of the iceberg. Although Lasker was Jewish, he seemed to be strongly influenced by the British. The original ad agency he worked for was Lord and Thomas, an outfit that has been designated as being British, but I was not able to find out too much about it.

Lasker's other British connection concerns the establishment of the Office of Strategic Services. It is no secret that the model for the OSS was set up by the British. England's cozy relationship with William Donovan and Franklin Roosevelt has led their influence to be called one of the most important and successful covert operations of history. From this perspective, the establishment of the OSS seemed to be designed to draw the U.S. into the war in Europe. It was Lasker's cronies and associates, if not he himself, who were said to be manipulating Roosevelt.

Besides the mysterious and nebulous influence in the intelligence community, the immediate legacy of Lasker seemed to be that, by reason of being in a position to approve research grants and contracts, he and his wife could steer the medical community and universities to suit whatever their social engineering agenda might be. For the time being, I will leave all of these implications to other researchers. If Cameron and Jack Parsons are correct, we will not really have a good idea of Albert Lasker's relative contribution to humanity for another hundred years. We are only now beginning to get any idea. My only interest in Albert Lasker was as a result of trying to find out who owned Pepsodent and was behind the outrageous lampooning of the Moorish Science Temple.

40

DE SPEAR

THE FOLLOWING TRANSMISSION
IS FROM A PARALLEL UNIVERSE

A Continuation of ACT III of Peter Moon's
Opening of the Seventh Seal:
Jack and Marjorie's Love Story

As the technical problem is fixed in the Magick Theater, the lights flash on and off and a voice indicates that the production will now resume. As the lights come on, the Tar Baby has resumed his shoe shine boy pose, but he is making his shiny tooth even more prominent.

"Ah, yes, the tooth!" says Shirley Temple as she looks up at the Tar Baby.

"Yah, da tooth," replies the Tar Baby. "Dat Pepsodent make da tooth shine, shine, shine!"

"Excuse me, Mr. Tar Baby..." said the now almost congenial figure of Jolly Roger as he tried to interrupt, but the Tar Baby continued his enthusiastic rant.

"Dem Moors used to takes peoples to Serendip to see de 'Temple of de Tooth.' Dat where de Buddha's tooth been put in a shrine".

"We did not complete the story of the Spear," says Jolly Roger.

The Tar Baby goes into another shape-shifting whirl until he is back in his pirate mock-up.

313

"Er, maybe you's should be excusin' me, Jolly Roger, but dis Spear stuff make no sense. I mean, you's be crucifyin' some pooah soul for t'ree hours and dat ain't gonna kill nobody, no how, no way. I mean, he's been dyin' for yoah sins in t'ree hours? I mean, most o' de pooah souls watchin's dis play or readin' dis book suffered moah in a lifetime dan dat pooah soul sufferin' for t'ree hours. I mean, after de' t'ree hours you's not even perm'nently hurt or damaged. It been scientifically studied and all dat. Even after a whole day, a man gonna last and be OK. Dat been proven!"

"Yeah," says Jolly Roger. "They break the shin bones to kill, and they would've broken his legs to kill save for Cassius Longinus who killed him with the spear."

"Yeah's, but," replies the Tar Baby. "Dat don't make no's sense eit'er. You pump a person wit' a spear and der gonna maybe suffer a lung collapse but dat ain't gonna kill 'em. And de chances o' drain'n' de lymph gonna have to be done by de surgeon and he's not gonna get it right wit' one punch neit'er. De odds of dat fellow o' any fellow dyin' in dat manner is slim to none lessin' you be considerin' all de quantum probabilities. Den, and only den, is some pooah fellow gonna die and resurrect in dat manner."

"And," says Jolly Roger. "That is the one quantum possibility that has allowed this myth to exist. It has not been countered, but it is now falling apart. As a talisman, the Spear has taken everyone's attention from the truth."

"What be dat truth?" asks the Tar Baby,

"Well," said Jolly Roger, "you had best consider Maximillian Hartmann. He is not only the man who bore the Spear, but his very name suggests the maximum fulfillment of the heart."

"But, he's a Nazi!" says Shirley Temple.

"I was a Nazi," replies Hartmann. "Sometimes, you have to face your demons in order to be who you really are."

At this last statement, the Tar Baby starts to gyrate, swivel his hips, and do a little dance as he says, "Well, if Hitler be de Antichrist, and he give you de spear, den maybe dat make you de polar opposite. Maybes you's de Christ!"

At this last statement, thunder is heard. It is a special effect but it shakes the seats of those in the theater. As lightning flashes around the stage, a large thunderbolt strikes the exact location where Maximillian Hartmann is which results in a swirling cloud.

The cloud continues to spin at a faster and faster rate until it explodes. As the mist clears, a new and dramatic version of Maximillian Hartmann can be seen. He and his uniform are completely white save for ruby red insignia. The entire texture of his persona is aethyreal and magnificent. In his hand is an aethyrealized white version of the Spear.

"It is time you learned the secret of the Spear!" Hartmann says to the audience. "That secret begins with the Key of It All."

"You's means dat stupid 'terpretation by dat Peter Moon 'bout dat line in *Pyramids of Montauk* where he says dat dat all synchronized wit' 'easy if stab'?" asks the Tar Baby.

"If you look at 'de etymology,' as you would put it, Mr. Tar Baby, you will find that the word 'key' is derived from the word 'spear'."

"No foolin'?" asks the Tar Baby.

"No foolin'. And, the Spear was stabbed into the body of Christ so as to purge him of his lymph and cause death. But, as you say, the construction of this legend is quite clever. In esoteric traditions, you will find that lymph is symbolic of a universal agent known as Magnesia or Milk of Magnesia, but not the kind you buy in the drug store. It is the main ingredient in the philosopher's stone. Paracelsus said that magnesia is incorruptible, and all things are nourished by her. She is everywhere and always, yet not all men may see her. She may only be seen by those who are ready to experience a new world of sight, hearing, and understanding. Perhaps most importantly, the Milk of Magnesia that comes out the side of Christ represents the tears of man. Salt produces tears and the salt represents that the pathways of the brain, or goetia, are frustrated. Tears are therefore a signal that the mind cannot understand. A fully activated brain with all the consequent understandings means that there is no need for tears. This is the true meaning of the Spear of Longinus."

"You's means," says the Tar Baby, "dat when I's be seein's d'ose billboards on de side o' de highway dat I's don'ts be needin' to opens my heart to Jesus as he's be dyin' fo' all o' my sins?"

"Just wait 'til you get to the end of the book and discover the magic word."

"OK," continues the Tar Baby, "I's can just sees myself up on billboards paintin' de magic word over d'ose 'Jesus Saves' signs."

Ignoring the Tar Baby's comment, Jolly Roger continues. "You will also find the etymology of magnesia most interesting. Magnesia was coined by a German physician to abbreviate the original word which was *magnes carneus* which meant 'magnet of the flesh.' This is the same as being 'drawn to the flesh' which suggests the magnetic predisposition or connectivity to the body, particularly the skin. Wilhelm Reich's research showed that orgone or life energy was predominantly in the skin."

"Ya mean de T'ird Reich?" asks the Tar Baby in a smart aleck tone.

"No. You might say he was the Zero Reich in that his work focused on the zero quality of the life force."

"Well," says the Tar Baby, "everybody be hearin' 'bout de T'ird Reich but nobody ever be hearin' too much 'bout de First Reich."

"That," replies Hartmann, who is still observable in his resplendent form "is perhaps because there was a treasure, even more powerful than the very spear I now hold in my hand, that everyone was made to forget. That treasure is what created all the ruckus around the time of the First Reich."

"De First Reich? Nobody even really know what in hell is de First Reich. We's all be herein' 'bout it, but nobody's ever told."

"The First Reich," answers Hartmann, "contained all the underpinnings of a mystical fascination that would branch out in all directions. It really begins with Roger II, the Norman king of Sicily who was known for his dark features. Known as "Jolly Roger" he imprisoned Pope Innocent, an act which made him a major hero of the Templars forever after. One of the most multicultural kings of his time, Jolly Roger grew up amidst the Moorish civilization of Sicily as it were Moors who primarily populated the island. Sicily, the home of Scylla and Charybdis, was one of the most sacred and well traveled spots of ancient times. It was at Cefalu, his favorite spot, where Roger erected his own cathedral. This was the reason why Aleister Crowley came to Cefalu hundreds of years later. He wanted to tap into the magic for Roger's family who had accessed the secrets of Sulaiyman via the "Moor's Gate" of the Dome of the Rock. His dark features were a telltale sign that his lineage had intermixed with the Assassins. Jolly Roger carried the greatest secret and treasure of civilization which was colloquially known as 'the Ring.' When Sulaiyman's Temple was sacked in 70 A.D., Titus had missed the greatest secrets as he did not know where to look for them. In other words, he was not smart enough to look in the area known as the Well of Souls and what else might be beneath the earth.

"Although Jolly Roger is not normally thought of as the beginning of the First Reich, he is the major catalyst. In fact, his very cloak was later worn by all of the Holy Roman Emperors that followed Barbarossa. The S.S. even wore his skull and cross bones. Most historians consider Frederick Barbarossa to be the progenitor of the First Reich, but his lineage comes from an even more mysterious source. It was the period between Roger's reign and that of Barbarossa's grandson, Frederich II, that gave rise not only to the legends of King Arthur and Parsifal's Holy Graal but the Ring of Wagner and Tolkein. It was actually Frederich II, known as the Crimson King, who was blessed by the Moors and Arabs in his takeover of Jerusalem, who actually went to the mount of Golgotha and recovered what was known as the last remnants of the holy treasure. What he found was the keystone, but it was never really used. From Golgotha, he took the treasure back home to what was known as the 'Court of the Crimson King.' Many people thought he had the shroud, but that relic has only left people scratching their head for centuries."

"And?" cries the Tar Baby.

"Well, actually, what he found in Jerusalem was more like a chest that included some crystal balls or balls and a ring, all wrapped in a crimson cloth. The history is vague as far as what both he and Roger II discovered on their travels to the Holy City. But, Frederich carried a shroud discovered by Roger II. It was a crimson cloth, which some even contend was the burial robe of Christ, and this depicted a skull and bones. It was different than the black flag you commonly see with the skull and femur bones. It became known as the Jolly Roger in honor of Roger II."

"I's bettin' I's know at least one t'ing," said the Tar Baby. "I's bettin dat flag had shin bones an' not femur bones."

"That's right," said Hartmann as he rubbed his shin bones which still hurt. "There were several other artifacts, too, but these have been represented over Europe in such a manner that there are more artifacts than originally possible, even according to the legends. But, you can be sure about one thing. The myths possess more truth than the articles themselves.

"The treasures of both Roger and Frederich were kept in the Court of the Crimson King but were guarded by the Saracens with whom he made peace. A secret conspiracy between Frederich, the Saracens, Assassins, and Templars protected the treasure for it was the most valuable commodity available to the imagination and superceded gold and material treasure. Frederich II later died on an ill advised crusade where it was hoped that he would conquer Jerusalem and establish a 'thousand year reich' which would eventually usher in the return of Christ. Many of the wiser Saracens, who insisted on guarding the treasure until Frederich actually conquered Jerusalem, knew he could not achieve this goal. When he drowned in a river, the world was led to believe the treasure may have been lost with him, and with it, the hope for the German people. It was a successful ruse.

"These myths about Frederich were created when, shortly after his death, there was a concordant of assassins, nobles, Saracens, and key family members of the Crimson King. Secretively, on the island of Cefalu, the concordant awaited the arrival of a mysterious man from the Ahaggar region of southern Algeria, a labyrinthine network of caves and rock spires imbedded in the deep Sahara. This man was genetically related to many of those present and was known to be a descendant of Barbar, a fierce and completely independent king of the partly Celtic people of North Africa. The Berber people, who also share his lineage, acquired their name from him. The Barbarossa Clan, as well as those present at the concordant, viewed him as the leader and spokesman for their lineage, but this was to remain a very deep secret. This man had assumed the curatorship of the library of Pharos. Although much of the library was conveyed at one time to the fabulous city of Timbuktu, a substantial amount was to remain in the cavernous complex of the Ahaggar. This descendant of Barbar, who was referred to by the Italian name of Antonio, lectured in secret for the greater part of a week. Scribes were employed to take notes of what became known as a template for the curatorship of future civilization. It was out of this operation that some of the richest legends in history were born and extrapolated upon. It was from this seed that the Grail romances and the legends of the troubadours emerged. In each story, a Saracen was to be featured so as to symbolically refer to the lamp of illumination. The appearance of the Saracen served as an indicator that the work bespoke of this tradition. It was also from this meeting that the pirate empire was sanctioned with the proviso that it was to be administered via invisible threads. The crimson flag with the skull and shin bones was to serve as representing the admiral of the pirate fleet. In other words, the man who carried this flag was to be respected by all pirates in their fight against the pope. Perhaps oddly, the crimson flag was so secret that it was never effectively used if used at all. The later pirates used a plain red flag to signify 'no quarter.' Later on, Morocco adopted the same in what became known as the 'cherry tree.'

"At the time of the concordant, two egg-shaped scrying crystals were wrapped up in the crimson Jolly Roger. A warning was given by 'Antonio' that the two crystals were never to be separated. The crystals were said to complement each other. Wrapped in the crimson flag, the crystal eggs were placed in a small chest which later became the source of the myth of 'Davey Jones Locker.'

"The legend is somewhat vague as to what else might have been included in the treasure and what became of it. As things degenerated in the Age of Pisces, some of the knowledge of it became lost and the treasure passed through various hands, some unsavory and some not. Hundreds of years later, the descendants of these Saracens conveyed the remains of this treasure to two pirate brethren from Malta, also named Barbarossa. The Barbarossa brothers captured the city of Algiers and thus, in a sense, protected the gateway to the Ahaggar. The older Barbarossa brother, who passionately fought the Spanish Catholics, had lost an arm defending the crystal. The Spanish eventually killed him and stole one of the crystals, but the Spaniards who stole it soon ended up in the hands of a corsair where the crystal was eventually relayed to Gerard Mercator, a master mariner who is credited with being the father of modern map making. Mercator soon placed it in the hands of one of his best friends at the time, Dr. John Dee, and it became the latter's scrying crystal. Dee later claimed that the crystal was given to him by the Archangel Uriel. This may have been true on some celestial level of operation, but it was really a cover to protect any trace of how he had acquired the crystal. It took over a hundred years for the Saracens to trace the crystal and figure out what happened to it. John Dee knew he had struck the motherlode with this crystal but not even he knew the whole story. He chose the code name 007 to represent his role in keeping this Seventh Seal totem.

"All of this had a profound effect on Dee. As a result of this scrying crystal from Golgotha, he literally became the architect/conjuror of Western Civilization as we have known it under the command of the British Empire. Dee is better known, however, for having taught Francis Bacon the art of gematria and initiating him into the Rosicrucian order. It was Bacon who, utilizing cabalistic ciphers, wrote the works of 'William Shakespeare.' The *Tempest* alone was a tribute to John Dee's conjuring of a wind storm that was a crucial blow against the Spanish Armada. Of course, Shakespeare's name in itself is suggestive of the deep truths concerned with 'shaking the spear.' "

At the very mention of the spear, Maximillian Hartmann then lifted the Spear of Destiny that he held.

"There is unfinished business," he says.

As he gestures with the spear, the spotlight focuses on an aisle as the primary Nazis from the Third Reich walk down and stand on the stage. There is Goering, Bormann, Hess, Himmler, Goebbels, Heydrich, and several others, but Hitler is missing. Suddenly, all these Nazis are all completely naked and this is particularly amusing in the case of Goering who is quite overweight. The audience laughs, jeers and throws whatever they might have at the various individuals.

It is time for the ghosts of all these creatures to confront and face all the verbal torment and persecution that could be directed at them. More objects are thrown with much laughter at their naked condition which is only devised to make everyone confront the exact truth and nature of these beings. The harassment and jeering continues until the novelty of their nudity expires and all the repressed hatred and other emotions that can be mustered against these men is released. Finally, it seems as if there is nothing else to say or feel.

"Thank you," says Maximillian Hartmann to the audience, who, in his aggrandized and aethyric rendition of himself, begins to suddenly shake the Spear of Destiny in an exaggerated fashion until he becomes spasmodic and totally loses command of his muscles. Once he abandons complete control, he surprisingly and suddenly regains his composure as he straightens up and begins to turn his back toward the audience. As he does so, his backside reveals another person. It is as if two bodies are merged into each other from their backsides. The other person is revealed to be Adolph Hitler, and it appears as if the creature known as Maximillian Hartmann is really a manifestation designed to portray the interlocking nature of the Christ and Antichrist. Hitler, who now holds the spear firmly in his hand, rants vehemently in German and thrusts the spear into the audience. When the shock and clamor of this violent act is all over, a spotlight is shined on the victim. The Spear of Destiny is shown to be thrust through the chest cavity of L. Ron Hubbard who slumps over dead.

The Nazis, who are still on the stage, say, "We curse you! Our organization dogged you for years and now we have gotten you at last. You are dead - dead - dead! We will overtake you!"

At this, Aleister Crowley, who was sitting right behind Hubbard, waves a magick wand as Hubbard's body disappears, but the Spear is left in the seat. Crowley then picks up the Spear and throws it back expertly in the direction from which it came. It lands directly in Hitler's heart.

"Heil Schiklegruber! yells Crowley. "You are not the Antichrist! I am that! I am!"

The figure that had been both Hitler and Hartmann turns into a whirling vortex of energy that vacuums up the Nazis and disappears. The crowd begins to cheer wildly as the curtain comes down.

END OF ACT III

41

EMORY CRANSTON

Despite my interest in the Ong's Hat travel brochure and the Incunabula Catalog, I did not pursue this information vigorously as there was other business and research to take care of. Eventually, a colleague of mine had discovered the material on the internet, and I encouraged her to pursue it in the direction of a possible book. At that time, I had no idea that I would assist in the compilation and writing of *Ong's Hat: The Beginning.* To my surprise and extreme skepticism, this colleague of mine had claimed she was dialoguing with Emory Cranston via email. If this were true, this would be an extreme find as I had already heard that Cranston was a very nebulous character. All I knew about Emory Cranston at that time was that he was loosely affiliated with the Moorish Orthodox Church and was the supposed proprietor of the Incunabula Catalog. There was only a trace of evidence to suggest that he might be a real person.

As the curator of the Incunabula Catalog, Emory Cranston is positioned as being at the gateway of another reality or dimension. The Incunabula Catalog consists of ingeniously detailed descriptions of books and pamphlets which are designed to serve as a template for the proposition that other realities and dimensions are not only undoubtedly scientifically possible but that their existence can be demonstrated. The Ong's Hat travel brochure serves as a template for bridging those realities. The science is all there, but it is not a subject the authoritarian powers in this reality like to indulge in. One reason for this is that these documents also serve as a template for undermining certain aspects of the structure of consciousness we know as reality. Before we proceed any further in this vein, it is necessary to address a few points. First, reality is based upon an idea or series of ideas that you continually create and agree to. For example, you can believe that you are the king of the world and can even maintain that assertion through the court system and the sanitarium. Nobody can take that reality away from you unless you stop agreeing to it. That would be your reality, but it would not necessarily be the reality of anyone else.

When two or more people also agree on something, that becomes an aggregate reality or group reality. The physical universe is the most popular aggregate of reality of all. Most of us agree that it is there. The only reason we are conscious of it is because we perceive it, usually through the sense organs of the body. We do not have to perceive it if we do not wish. In fact, we are free to induce states of acute psychosis in ourselves and not perceive it at all, or perhaps only perceive reduced versions of it. On the quantum level, reality is observer based. As an observer, we have to agree that we are measuring or looking at it and thus "buy into" the phenomena we know as reality.

Someone like Jack Parsons was not buying into the institutionalized reality that has been perpetrated upon the common man. In a sense, he was undermining the reality structure of our popular culture. It is therefore no wonder that the practices he was involved in have been described as black magic and can literally frighten the daylights out of ordinary day-wanderers on the planet Earth. Parsons was a trailblazer who was foraging through the jungle for new vistas. The trailblazer does not stay and settle the new territories he has precipitated. That is always done by others who follow in his wake.

For the ordinary person, it is not wise to completely embrace new realities and dimensions until business has first been taken care of in this reality. Before becoming very excited about the proposition that Frank Lloyd Wright is going to build you a new house, you had first better be sure of a few things. Number one, do not stop the mortgage payments on your existing house, and make sure that Frank Lloyd Wright actually delivers the blueprints. Additionally, be sure that you have the resources to pay the contractor. Most important of all, keep a tight leash on the contractor so that you are not left hanging in the wind with no roof or no certificate of occupancy. Only when the house is fully completed, inspected, and the title is in your name is it safe to move in and depart the old house.

None of the above can be overstated because I have time and again seen too many researchers and "metaphysical" people dive off the reality cliff into what is called "New Age Euphoria." Enthusiasm is a wonderful thing, but it should not cut off one's intellectual discernment. All of this becomes very important when embarking upon the metaphysical destination known as Ong's Hat, an obscure and somewhat indistinct location in south central New Jersey that has served as a hot bed of strange tales as far back as anyone can remember.

When I heard that Emory Cranston of Ong's Hat fame had appeared via email, I knew that my colleague had reached the breaking point of reality. If this Emory was a fake, she was merely deluding herself in a false reality. On the other hand, if this Emory was real, she was on the verge of possibly stepping into a bottomless pit of chaos. After being in somewhat sporadic email dialogue with him for about a year, "Emory Cranston" finally told her that she should contact Joseph Matheny. He would be able to help her with some of her questions. I would eventually learn the secret of this mysterious "Emory Cranston," but this was not until I would come into direct contact with Mr. Matheny. A few months after this news, I learned he would be coming to Montauk to take some video footage as he checked out some of the various legends he had heard. Unfortunately, I was not able to hook up with Joe on that trip. Many weeks later, I was told to contact him regarding putting the *Montauk Project* into an e-book format. When I finally did speak to him, we did not do much talking about e-books.

I was quite surprised to learn that Joe was not just a computer expert. A few minutes into our conversation, I realized that he was a prodigious student of magick. Very rarely do I meet people on the phone who have deeply studied magick and truly understand it. One thing I observed very readily was that he is not a "snickerer." When I mentioned this, he laughed and knew exactly what I was talking about. He had run up against the same thing himself. As I got to know Joe, I not only found out that he was far more knowledgable than the snickerers but was very informative and free in terms of sharing what he knew. This can be a very rare commodity in the field of magick. Additionally, Joe demonstrated a fluid and applied knowledge of what he knew.

Immediately recognizing Joe's acumen in these fields, I was joyfully surprised when he mentioned that he had studied under Israel Regardie and had known him personally. I soon told him a story that I had only shared with a handful of people up to that time. You have since read it in this book. But, before I told him what I knew, I asked him a key question. I wanted to know if he had any idea of where Israel Regardie was in 1947, the commonly accepted date of Crowley's death. Joe told me that, to the best of his knowledge, Regardie was in England at that time. This was just one more piece of circumstantial evidence to suggest that what I had heard about Regardie was true. When I delivered the punch line to Joe, he indicated that what I said did not surprise him. In fact, he believed that Regardie's influence over the OTO was substantial. Once again, I had stumbled upon a major player in the esoteric field. Over the next several months, I learned a lot about Israel Regardie, the Golden Dawn, and Ong's Hat. Some of this will be revealed in the rest of the book, but perhaps the most relevant point at this juncture has to do with the cross linkage of various magical heritages. Both Joe and myself had been immersed in "live" esoteric traditions. There is a great deal of difference between a "live" tradition and one you read about in books. In Joe's case, he studied the live tradition of magick, not only as personified by Israel Regardie but by others as well. In fact, he has a real knack when it comes to acquiring esoteric information. As for myself, I was experienced in the live tradition of Hubbard as well as the legacy of the Babalon Working through Marjorie Cameron. This linkage with Joe was very important because he knew a considerable amount about John Dee and Edward Kelly, the two magicians who Hubbard and Parsons sought to emulate.

I have explained elsewhere in my writing that there is a principle in Scientology whereby if one is experiencing trouble, one seeks out the period of time just prior to where the trouble began. This would reveal either an engram or a moment of non-comprehension that led to difficulty. If that is completely cleared up, the trouble ceases. I had long since realized that the Babalon

Working, in certain respects, had acted as a prenatal engram or blockage with regard to the Dianetics and Scientology movement. As I spoke to Joe, I realized that the Golden Dawn movement had served as the prenatal engram to the establishment of the OTO. Crowley had been a member of the Golden Dawn but split with MacGregor Mathers in a bitter feud. In most historical accounts, Mathers is given the moral "upper ground" in this feud as Crowley was of such dubious repute. As the truth is actually uncovered, it demonstrates that the minds of historians are not necessarily suited to recording the truth but only the residue of the aggregate agreement of perception.

The fundamental rituals of the Golden Dawn were based upon the Sigillum Daemoth (a.k.a. the Sigil of Dei Ameth) and the Enochian Calls of Dr. John Dee and Edward Talbot Kelly. Israel Regardie, who had been a full fledged member of the Golden

THE SIGIL OF DEI AMETH

Dawn, published the complete rituals of his order in a celebrated book which is still available to this day. Although it is viewed with a great degree of awe by the majority of people who purchase it and follow it, I learned that there are some major problems with it.

Joe himself was a member of the Golden Dawn at one time. He explained that once you identify yourself as a member of the Golden Dawn, you are no longer a part of the fraternity. This is part of the code. Consequently, when Israel Regardie wrote that book, he identified himself and his own association and thereby forfeited it. Joe's own problem with the Golden Dawn began when he noticed that the various procedures in its ritualistic system gated in very dark elements. It seemed to be very flawed. Further investigation revealed that the early writings about John Dee had actually been altered and contained erroneous sigils. This was not the Golden Dawn's fault per se, but it was the fault of the transcribers of the books that esoteric organizations such as the Golden Dawn predicated their entire system of Enochian magic on. Joe became very suspicious and realized that the combinations given for the "lock" were not opening the vault. Thus, the entire current of western magick had been tainted. He tried to tell people in the order about this problem, but no one wanted to hear it. Everyone was more interested in carrying on tradition. The proof was so glaringly obvious that he began to wonder if some of the key people in the Golden Dawn were actually aware of the deception.

I am well aware that the majority of the people who will read this book are not practitioners of Enochian magick, and all of this might seem to be a bit disconnected from ordinary reality. These procedures are taken very seriously by all sorts of people, many of whom are very well placed in society. Further, the Enochian template serves as an undercurrent upon which much of our thinking and social reality is based. This will be elaborated on later in this book.

In summary, the Golden Dawn had been off base since its inception, at least in terms of the "master" they were trying to emulate. Any secret society who based their work on the mistranslated sigils of John Dee was also in the same boat. Crowley, however, was known to use the correct sigils and instructions. According to all current information, the OTO either does not know this or seeks to keep it quiet. All of this is characteristic of the fact that secret societies are not really in the business of dispensing truth except in a manner such as to empower themselves. I was not surprised to learn that people in these societies would inhibit or block the truth, but I was more than a little intrigued to see how confused they were by it.

What was most clear to me about this whole affair was that the mysteries of John Dee run very deep. Joe also explained that the name *Incunabula* was borrowed from John Dee's collection of rare and hermetic books. In those days, the word *incunabula* meant "birth" or "cradle" but was also used to signify a collection of rare books. In Dee's case, his book collection was larger than those of Oxford and Cambridge. Joe explained that Dee's influence had been literally blackballed from common history and that there was no logical explanation for it.

In present time, the Incunabula Catalog associated with Ong's Hat had been allegedly put together by Emory Cranston, as mysterious a character if there ever was one. Joe claims that Emory Cranston is indeed a real character who he has had many discussions with. Based upon these discussions, Joe believes that it is entirely possible that Emory Cranston did actually put the Incunabula Catalog together. Emory not only had the passion for the job, but the grammar and syntax in the catalog was expressive of his general style of communication. But, Joe is quick to add, it is not an absolute certainty that he wrote it.

Joe Matheny's first encounter with the Incunabula Catalog was when Dr. Nick Herbert handed it to him in its xeroxed format. Nick was not only a member of the Moorish Orthodox Church but a reputed physicist who authored the book *Alternate Dimensions* which appears in the catalog. Joe was struck by the fact that when he received the xeroxed pamphlet, he had all of the material in the catalog on his book shelf except for the information on Ong's Hat. This was not too surprising because he had been a collector of what he calls "xeroxed crackpot literature," i.e., avant garde data which not only includes crackpot theories but those that are on the cutting edge of science and technology. As the Ong's Hat material was new to him, he made a special trip to New Jersey.

Upon arriving at the Lebanon State Forest ranger station in October of 1992, not far east of Ong's Hat Road and the Anapa Diner, he was looking for the post office box of the proprietor listed in the Incunabula Catalog. After poaching the key, he found bank overdraft notices and solicitations. One of the people at the ranger station informed him that Emory Cranston and the Incunabula had fled a month earlier. An interview with Nick Herbert elicited a New Jersey phone number that supposedly belonged to Emory Cranston. Although the person was quite knowledgeable about the contents of the catalog and the actual stories surrounding it, Joe is still not sure that the voice on the other end was indeed Emory Cranston. In fact, he says that the voice could have been that of Peter Lamborn Wilson, a man he eventually befriended on the latter's journeys to San Francisco.

Emory did not appear in Joe's life again until he was working for a music shop in Berkeley and was circulating flyers at the University of California campus. There, he was accosted by a strange man in a fez who identified himself as Emory Cranston. Somehow, he already knew who Joe was and invited him to an ashram house in Berkeley where the remnants of the Ong's Hat ashram had fled to. Although Emory used to hang out there, he did not live there. Joe said there was an egg in one of the rooms there where one of the girls invited him into to do some "travelling." Although he said he had a lot of fun in there, he could not honestly say that he was time travelling or moving through parallel universes. Although this ashram was a residue from the original group in New Jersey, most of the players did not seem to be as interesting as Emory himself. In fact, both he and Emory had one thing in common. They were both passionate fans of "xeroxed crackpot literature" of the 1980's. Joe was surprised that Emory was an even bigger fan of it than he was and that his knowledge of unusual and fringe facts was nothing short of amazing.

Joe eventually left Berkeley and went to work in San Francisco at SlipNet, one of the early internet service providers. At SlipNet, he was working with an artificial intelligence program in conjunction with other computer research he had been involved in for some time. It was around this time that Joe created "Emory-bot." Emory-bot was based upon an artificial intelligence program that Joe was running whereby people could "talk" to Emory Cranston via a website if they were lucky enough to stumble or wade their way through certain "gateways" imbedded in the Incunabula website. The e-book is studded with synchronicity features if you happen to click the mouse at the right time at the right location on the screen. In the case of my aforementioned colleague, she had been communicating with Emory Cranston for about a year. By this time, the AI program had been improved from its initial stages and was sophisticated enough to hold its own, but it tended to keep conversations to a bare minimum. In Joe's experience, it was unheard of for anyone to have indulged in a conversation with Emory-bot for this long. Personally, he had neglected the monitoring of this "cyber-watch" and felt bad that this person had been talking to a "bot" all this time. If it were not for this bot, I might never have come into touch with Joe in the first place. This colleague was the one who put me in touch with him. But, as I was soon to learn, there was a considerable amount of research that went into this so-called "bot" named Emory Cranston.

Joe was not just playing around with artificial intelligence. He had actually been working on creating a computer aided synchronicity generator for some time. More details will be given in a subsequent chapter as to how this actually came about as well as how it evolved into what he calls the Metamachine. For now, it is sufficient to say that he had created a very sophisticated computer program that actually mimicked, if it did not indeed possess, conscious intelligence. For kicks, he gave this intelligence the name "Emory Cranston" which was not designed or purported to be an actual person.

As Joe worked in San Francisco, he began to make rapid advances with his development of the Metamachine. After a while, he resumed his contact with the real life Emory Cranston who was still in Berkeley. They would often meet in San Francisco's Chinatown and discuss the fringe xeroxed literature of which they were both fond. It was during the time period of these meetings in San Francisco that Joe experienced a most peculiar phenomena. He would ask his Metamachine a question or give an input only to find that the real life Emory would either answer the question or complete the thought Joe was inputting. There was no way this could have happened in a normal world as Emory had no access to the computer. It was pure synchronicity, but a very disturbing one. Joe had to consider if he was either being set up or was losing his mind. He even wondered if Emory Cranston, in an ordinary sense, was not real at all. Fortunately, other people had witnessed Emory at the Homeless Garden Project in Santa Cruz so there was no question he was real. Although Emory did not go there as a homeless person, he hung around the Homeless Garden Project for a short period.

The most unsettling encounter with Emory Cranston, however, was right after Joe returned from his visit to Montauk, not too long before he met me on the phone. As he walked through San Francisco's Chinatown soon after his return, he was surprised to see Emory Cranston lurking beneath the entrance to the Chinese-American Masonic Hall which had a distinct red door. They had no scheduled meeting, and there was no normal way Emory could have known Joe would appear there on that particular street on that particular day. Keep in mind that Joe lived in Santa Cruz at this point which is a couple of hours away from Chinatown. What was most disturbing was that Emory knew exactly where he had been and asked how he had enjoyed his trip to Camp Hero. Further, he gave Joe a warning about his personal life which is too private to mention herein but which Joe pretty much rejected at the time. This was all depicted in the comic section of *Ong's Hat: The Beginning*. Joe became very disturbed at Emory and demanded some answers to the point where he began to get physical and started choking him. Joe certainly deserved a better explanation than he was getting. When Emory's eyes rolled into a complete apathy, Joe recognized the look of someone who was about to pull out a knife and stab. No answers were forthcoming. He abandoned Emory and never saw him again.

As this was one of the most disturbing and odd synchronicities he had ever encountered, we talked about it at various times. I told him that I had visited Chinatown often when I was younger and would love to pay a visit to the Chinese-American Masonic Hall. I even told him about a PBS documentary on old San Francisco that I had seen part of. This was about San Francisco as it had existed prior to the 1906 earthquake. In what must have been about the 1880's, I saw a photograph of a camera shop in Chinatown that said "Cameron-Wilson" or "Wilson-Cameron" — I do not remember which. It was certainly not a Chinese name, and I was intrigued. Unfortunately, the show did not focus on that and the image was gone almost as soon as it appeared. I even told Joe that I felt that I could stir up Emory Cranston anytime I wanted to. Shortly thereafter, he laughed as he reported to me that he had actually received an email from Emory. There was only a little bit of communication, but nothing developed from it. He was pretty sure it was the same person.

I became wary of any association with Emory when Joe shared a dream he had during this time period. In the dream, various members of the OTO had gathered in a Christian style church in order to rejoice at the second coming of Aleister Crowley who they considered to be the messiah and savior. Apparently, Crowley was to return at any moment. When the moment of truth came, it was not Crowley who appeared before the congregation but Emory Cranston instead. In spite of the humor and the rich archetypal imagery inherent in the dream, I was turned off by this and we did not discuss Emory too much anymore.

Over a year later, we spoke about Emory again. The discussion covered a lot of personal ground, and we both realized that Emory had actually been quite accurate about his warning to Joe. It was as if he had literally seen the future or travelled to it. Maybe Emory could really hop across time lines, and maybe he was there to help. In any case, he appeared in a much more positive light, but I was not personally interested in gating him into my own life at that time. When I made the offhanded comment that I could generate him at will, it seemed too easy. Sometimes, those offhanded moments can be some of your most creative and psychic ones. The entire proposition of this book is a loaded subject with many avenues and adventures to explore. Just as one cannot stop and talk to every interesting member of the opposite sex that one encounters, so I cannot indulge every phantom character that I run across. Although somewhat dark, Emory Cranston is certainly a colorful and interesting character. The jury is still out on him.

Before Joe could explain more about the Metamachine, he wanted me to have a good understanding of some of the consciousness pioneers who helped inspire his work: Brion Gysin and William S. Burroughs. Much of their work was summarized in a book entitled *Here to Go* which primarily consists of an interview with Brion Gysin by Terry Wilson. There was that Wilson name popping up again. This piqued my interest in the book; however, it is out-of-print and very hard to find. As synchronicity would have it, my friend Penelope just happened to have access to the book. She copied it and also gave me a collectable artifact known as a Brion Gysin "Dream Machine." Both the book and the device were in my hands almost immediately. To my surprise and amusement, I learned that Brion Gysin had his own encounter and experience with Scientology. I was already aware that William Burroughs had been involved in Scientology. It is both funny and ironic to see how various themes keep popping up in one's life, particularly when you are studying and pursuing the path of synchronicity.

42

RON'S GHOST

*THE FOLLOWING TRANSMISSION
IS FROM A PARALLEL UNIVERSE*

One evening, I was disturbed to be woken up in my sleep and experience a dream whereby I was summoned to the Magick Theater. As I looked outside my window, I had a sense of foreboding as I saw a limousine that looked more like a hearse. The fact that the driver was reminiscent of a gargoyle did not help matters either. There was no joy of going to a premier or anything of the like. I was being summoned out of duty and obligation.

Arriving at the theater, the marquee was blank and the lobby was empty. Only upon entering the theater itself did I see that there was a simple talk show set on the stage. The Tar Baby was playing the role of host and he had an impish grin on his face. To his left was the ghost of L. Ron Hubbard, immaculately dressed in his naval uniform from the 1940's. He looked fit and trim and sported a baton and cape, but his composition was of complete aethyr with no flesh. As I walked down the aisle to assume my position on the stage, they played the theme music to Johnny Carson's version of *The Tonight Show*. I found this to be irritating in the extreme as if someone was pandering to amuse me, but I was not happy as I had been aroused from a very deep and comfortable sleep.

Only after I had been sitting on the stage did I take notice of the audience. They seemed to be a strange admixture of everything and were changing faster than I could easily explain. When I first looked at them, the entire audience consisted of human-shaped energy forms that were entirely black or white. The first five rows consisted of an arrangement whereby every other seat had a white human form. The others were filled with black ones. None of them were in a normal human condition. After the first five rows, there was an invisible line down the center of the theater. On one side, there were only white energy forms and to the other side there were black. All were human shaped.

As the music died down, I could hear the white forms shouting "Scientology works!" After they finished, I could hear the black forms say "Scientology sucks — it doesn't work!" There were many more expletives and exultations. Then, everything switched around. The black forms began to say what the white forms had just said and vice versa. This was great interpolation, and it began to perk me up and make somewhat glad I was there. Nevertheless, I was caught off guard by it all.

As the interview began, I saw the audience change to the regular crowd I had known from the Magick Theater. Then, they would change to a smattering of random people and then back to the black and white energy forms. Somehow, I felt as if the entire universe was watching me.

As the talk show encounter was about to begin, I noticed that the impish grin upon the face of the Tar Baby had turned into a shit-eating grin. He felt that he had pulled off a real gem by having me confront my old mentor. The Tar Baby then stood up and said, "You's boths knows 'xactly's why's you's here — so start talkin'!"

"I think I know what this is about," I said. "One of my psychic friends had called me out of the blue and told me there was someone named Ron who contacted her. She knew nothing about you or Scientology, but she said that you wanted me to tell the truth about what had happened. According to her, you said that I was the only person that would be able to do it."

"The truth?" Ron said as he laughed. "The truth is very strange indeed! You have dealt with the ghost of Crowley and the ghost of Jack Parsons, but what would your audience think if I told you that my ghost is the strangest of all — you have yet to deal with my ghost!"

"That's true," I said, "but I long ago realized that I have to go through various way stations before I can get to the various issues surrounding your death. Actually, I am still dealing with Marjorie Cameron's ghost."

Ron looked at me with a confident and beaming look that only departed souls can give.

"In the meantime," Ron said, "I can help things along with one statement."

"What's that?"

"Well, I am the first one to realize that my life has excited much controversy. As I always said, controversy is great for book sales and spreading the Scientology movement. It has always thrived on the controversy and the publicity surrounding it."

"But, I already know that. What was it you wanted to say?"

"Sometimes people focus too much on the perceived faults they find in me, regardless of whether they are true or not. They do not spend a proportionate amount of time studying my perceived strengths or gifts. Although I cannot help that, it may interest them to know one thing."

"What's that?" I asked.

"Everyone would look at me a lot differently if it were not for those blacked out documents that are obtained routinely through the Freedom of Information Act. And, I am talking about the ones from the '40's and '50's in particular."

"Are you suggesting that the UFO documents include references to you and Scientology?"

"Some, and all of that information would startle people, but I am referring more to the role I played in intelligence during the 1940's with regard to all of that alien involvement and mind control with regard to the Philadelphia Experiment and onward."

"Well," I said, "you've certainly made an interesting point. The Government has created and fostered a mystery about you by leaving all those elements blacked out."

"As you know, I was an intelligence officer, and part of an intelligence officer's role is to relay and convey information."

"Critics are going to say," I said, "that information has nothing to do with you."

"I know, but that's precisely the point. I am not the one withholding the information! You see, people have thought they were humiliating and degrading me on the internet and elsewhere, but all that stuff runs its course over time. Most of it is not a very

337

powerful energy and stems from people who are unempowered themselves. When the Government tells the whole truth, an oxymoron if ever there was one, I will be looked upon a lot differently. There is nothing like national security to prevent everyone from knowing the truth."

At this point in the dialogue, the Tar Baby stands up on his desk and says, "Ain't dat de trut'! Now, we's gotta new and impot'nt guest...er...dat is...maybe I should say...ghost...Colonel L. Fletcher Prouty."

As the Tar Baby gestures, another aethyric human form comes out who is also dressed in a military uniform. It is the late Colonel L. Fletcher Prouty, the mysterious intelligence agent played by Donald Sutherland in Oliver Stone's movie *JFK*. As he comes out, LRH and Prouty shake hands like old lost friends.

"Hello, Mr. Moon," said Mr. Prouty. I realize you did not know about me, but nothing I say will surprise you; however, it will help you piece a few things together for other people."

"Well, you know, I am not working on a book on Ron, you know," I said.

"Just the same, you all need to know this. People should know that while I am appearing in your dream, I was a very real character in real life. In fact, Ron and I joined the service around the same time, and I worked in the highest levels of the intelligence community, all of which can be verified."

"Except for one thing," I interrupted. "As soon as word gets out in this book, people are going to invent and present data that you are a fake, too."

"They've already tried that. But, this is about Ron right now. I actually inspected much of his military record, and being trained, I can tell you some interesting things that have been missed, deliberately or otherwise, by all past researchers. Much of his service was so high level that it was heavily cloaked in security coverage. Ron actually worked under Vanderbilt, FDR's Chief of Intelligence. You do not get any closer to the corridors of power than in a position like that. Many of Ron's 'official records' revealed that the originals had been fabricated. In the intel community, we call this operation 'Sheep Dip.' Customarily, this includes a system whereby three files are produced for a given individual. The first one has the true civilian records of the agent.

The second file is his actual military record as a secret agent which is highly classified. The third file is a cover record along with all the documentation it takes to support a certain profile. Of course, you realize that any of these records can be used against the agent at a later date if he runs afoul of existing power within the intelligence community."

"So, Colonel Prouty," I said, "you think this will change the mind of people who do not have a favorable impression of Ron?"

"The fact is, everyone of his damn critics has completely ignored the means and methods of the intelligence community. When one does not recognize the nature of what you are dealing with, it blocks your perception of what is actually going on.

"You might also be interested to know that Ron received some pretty prestigious awards during his service days, but these have all been so obscured in some quarters that he has been documented as a pathological liar."

"Yes, continue," I said.

"He was literally singled out as "Man of the Year" by the American Ordnance Association. This is the oldest and most prestigious of the Munitions Group. I know because I used to attend their meetings and only people who really contributed to our national defense were selected. This was not a rubber stamp award or something that was given out lightly.

"Wisely though, he stayed clear of the cruel experimentation on human beings that was done in the days of Project ARTI-CHOKE. I know a lot of the inside facts here because I worked for nine years, beginning in 1955, as the Air Force liaison in support of the clandestine operations of the CIA. I even used to attend MK-ULTRA meetings and called on the Dulles brothers at their home. In fact, all CIA military activities were channeled through me at one point. It was an interesting position.

"But, as for Ron here, his role in the Government was enormous. I cannot over emphasize that. And, as I began to dig into his records, I found everything was getting even more interesting. I was doing all of this for hire by the Scientology Church. Surprisingly, they suddenly took me off the job and just when it was getting juicy! They had actually hired me to write Ron's biography after Omar Garrison did not work out, but my project was cancelled, too."

"Well," I said, "you've pretty much made your point. Intelligence is a strange business. Thank you for your testimony."

I then turned from Colonel Prouty and looked at Ron.

"You know," I said, "this whole military/intelligence game is a lot of crap. Who would ever think that the game of spiritual freedom and being free from the body would entail the chronicling of such convoluted machinations?"

"Well," Ron replied, "if you had a wild wolf and wanted to keep him contained, you'd have to set up a pretty tight system. Then, if you had a whole planet of wild wolves wanting to be free, in their natural and native state, then you would have to set up a whole 'wolf brigade' and build a society just to inhibit their activity."

"Your mothers maiden name was 'de Wolfe' wasn't it?"

"Yes, it was. Yes, it was."

"Well, I guess we'll see what your whole game was about after another century."

As soon as I said this last sentence, I saw a black and white soccer ball suddenly emerge from the black and white audience. It was apparently kicked at breakneck speed and flew right past my head and hit the Tar Baby and knocked him off the desk he was standing on.

"What on Earth is that?" I asked.

"Oh, dats just Pele," said the Tar Baby, seemingly nonplused by this sudden intrusion. "Bein's dat you's and Rons is done talkin', maybe it be time for some Q's and A's."

As the Tar Baby finished his statement, I saw a very human rendition of Pele, the Brazilian soccer hero, walk up on the stage and address me. He spoke with pretty good English which was only a little broken at times.

"Tell me, something, Mr. Moon. Why do you Americans call my game 'soccer'? It sounds like 'sock her' or something, like you are trying to be violent or 'sock' the goddess."

"I know," I said, "what we call soccer, you call 'futbol.' I can't tell you who started calling what when, but I can tell you that the Wilson Company makes both footballs and soccer balls."

"Well, I can tell you something that you might find interesting about the sport of soccer. In England, it developed from kicking a skull. One day, some men with not enough to do were kicking an old skull around and began to make a game out of it. More people joined in, and it turned into a rather wild match of contest and violence. Eventually, the skull was replaced by big bladders and different objects, but this was a far cry from the Wilson balls we play with today. Whole towns would compete whereby one town would try to kick the skull or ball to a pole in their opponents town. Different games evolved out of this ancient blood sport such as rugby and American football. But, tell me something, Mr. Moon. You have said the football is a sacred shape."

"Yes, I did," I replied. "It is representative of two spheres interlocking and the resultant vessel thereof. It could be called a birth cradle or even an incunabula. This is a universal and natural symbol and is known as the vesica pisces which is most commonly known as a two-dimensional symbol. But, in the days when Teddy Roosevelt called his rules committee together, the football was a far cry from what we know today. It was not until Knute Rockne came along with his Four Horsemen of the Apocalypse that the forward pass caught on. The ball was accordingly shaped into the fine throwing instrument that it is today. But, Pele, I have a question for you. The soccer ball is not only black and white, but it is made up exclusively of pentagons. What is the esoteric significance behind that?"

"That, my friend," replied Pele, "is a great mystery."

43

SCIENTOLOGY BEATNIKS

Although most everyone has heard of Scientology and beatniks, the two words do not conjure images of harmony or equal association. There was, however, a time when these two aspects of our culture merged for brief moment that might, in the best of possible universes, have evolved into a Camelot of consciousness. These two movements were synthesized through the personage of William S. Burroughs, a writer who has been hailed as the "Father of the Beat Generation" but who has been virtually ignored and unacclaimed for his forays into Scientology whereupon he was once declared a "Clear."

Burroughs was from a well-to-do family that is famous for Burroughs business machines, primarily the adding machine. Although he was never a wealthy man and only became a home owner at the age of seventy, a modest family stipend kept him solvent throughout the majority of his adult life. This enabled him to engage in all sorts of creative endeavors, much of which were centered around narcotics. Although Burroughs was not a charismatic or magnetic personality, his interests and predispositions led him to attract a circle of friends that became hailed as the icons of the Beat Generation. These included Jack Kerouac, Allen Ginsberg, and Neal Cassady. Generally viewed as an older and more experienced person than his brethren, Burroughs often served as a mentor to these notable literary icons.

There are many focal points where one can suggest that the Beat Generation or Beat Movement really began. One is the publication of Kerouac's classic novel *On the Road*. Another is the publication is Ginsberg's poem *Howl* which garnished untold publicity when it shocked the world and affected ground breaking precedents with regard to obscenity litigation. No matter which point you pick as the origin of the Beat Movement, and there is certainly no literary reason to do so, you will find that William S. Burroughs was riding the crest of the wave before and through all of the various points. Most remarkably, he outlived the entire crew and only seemed to die as if someone had given him a cue: he passed away right after Ginsberg's death.

The affluence of the post World War II era created a whole new *beat* in the younger generation. Consciousness had changed and conventional traditions were not serving the multitudes. This was the era of Route 66 and the rediscovery of California, a beautiful state which offered a new promise and freedom. It was also the beginning of a new consciousness.

One of the inalienable rights of youth is to question authority, to test the boundaries of tradition and to hopefully ignite new torches of light into the culture. In this regard, children are the most magnificent creatures in the entire world. The future depends upon them and their ability to exercise their natural function. In the case of the Beat Culture, they looked at and recognized the wounds of society. Additionally, they communicated what they saw and made it an open wound for everyone to see. Even those who despised the beatniks were aware of the wound, but they viewed the beatnik as the source of the problems rather than as the messenger who was notifying the doctor.

When first viewed, the wound appears only as the ills and injustices which exist in any society. Looking deeper, one sees that the wound can be traced back to the very circumstances and conditions of creation. Allen Ginsberg's *Howl* was inspired during a stay in a psychiatric hospital where he witnessed the bottom rung of how bad things could be, not only for himself but for others. He dedicated the poem *Howl* to his cell mate who just happened to be the nephew of a publisher. This turned out to be his bridge to a heralded literary career which enabled Burroughs to be published as well. *Howl* is a deeply cutting poem which illustrates man as a living breathing beast juxtaposed against Moloch and the evil machinations of a reactive entity which seeks to mechanize, nullify, and ultimately destroy the best part of us (that which breathes and lives).

Burroughs was a heroin junkie. He also shot and killed his wife while drunk and had a host of other faults, most of which he was not in denial about. Besides his family and the stipend he received, the only thing he had going for him were his friends, and they were a highly questionable lot. He finally sought solace in the land of the Moors and became a resident of Tangier in Morocco. It was there that he met Brion Gysin, the proprietor of a restaurant called *One Thousand and One Nights*. Besides being a restaurateur, Gysin was a surrealistic artist and collaborated with Burroughs on what became known as the "cut-up method."

Gysin and Burroughs shared a great interest in Hassan Sabbah, the leader of the Assassins. It is interesting to note that Hassan Sabbah only rose to power after a visit to Morocco, but it is not known exactly what he did there. Hassan Sabbah was known for his quantum maxim: "Nothing is true, everything is permitted." This maxim served their own viewpoints very well as it told them that all quantum possibilities existed, and they were both very deep thinkers. Gysin further shared what he had learned from studying the Dada artistic movement of the post World War I era. Tristan Tzara was a Dada poet who had caused a riot by pulling words out of a hat and composing a poem. Dada was a precursor of the surrealist movement which juxtaposed different subjects which came from two entirely different contexts. This would be something like the Roman army of Julius Caesar marching into the Super Bowl. It rescrambles creation. The Dada movement was created by various artists who were making a statement about the circumstances of society in regard to the first world war. They would take various cultural icons and juxtapose them so as to reposition them. It was a powerful artistic statement and only rose out of frustration with the existing system which had proven itself to be of no service to the common people.

Gysin believed that what was wrong with creation was "the word." His motto, "rub out the word," meant that in order to correct the basic construct of existence, we need to deconstruct language. Most of our social conventions are kept in place by language and words. Rescramble the words and you have created a new paradigm. In essence, Gysin taught Burroughs to do the same thing with words that artists do with subjects in surrealistic art: rescramble the components. This became known as the "cut-up method." One could take a page, paragraphs, or individual words from a page and pull them out of a hat; then, place them in a completely different order than how they were.

This is a completely invigorating exercise as it gets you to look at things in a completely new and different way. In the case of Burroughs, he vigorously pursued this method and, mixed with his constant forays into dope, experienced communication with different entities that had previously been alien to him. Although some of the experiences were frightening, there was a coherency in the communication that made him stick with it and eventually resulted in his book entitled *Naked Lunch*. This has since been made into a movie as well.

There is so much more that could be said about these two individuals, but I am only leaving in the essential ingredients. In the case of Burroughs, his cut-up research was followed by him becoming a devotee of Scientology, and he was declared Clear in 1968. He was particularly intrigued at how Scientology dealt with the "power of words." In other words, if you have suffered an engram (a moment of unconsciousness on the track of time, including previous lives), the words said during that moment can have a reactive power over you. For example, imagine that in a previous life you were being tortured and were in an unconscious state and in excruciating pain. The inquisitor then tells you, "Believe in God or it will be much worse." If something in the person's environment restimulates this engram, he would be predisposed toward believing in God just to carry out the reactive response in hope that the pain might not be experienced. Or, one could react a different manner. Perhaps the word "God" becomes reactively associated with pain. In this case, it might be very painful for this person to even discuss God. He or she might become an atheist as a reaction to this experience. Depending on the circumstances, a person could react in many different ways, but they would all be unconscious responses.

Burroughs was known to rave about Scientology to his friends. He thought the counseling procedures were absolutely marvelous and never wavered from this statement, even after he had a falling out with the Church. Personally, he experienced great relief from his counseling sessions and said there was nothing one could compare it to. I should add here that this is not an uncommon statement for people who experienced good counseling sessions in Scientology. Burroughs even said that one could accomplish in only ten hours what one could never accomplish in other methods such as psychiatry.

The problem Burroughs had with Scientology was that he thought it was a fascist organization. He did not agree with the administration of the Church and thought the techniques should be released freely and for all to inspect. Additionally, he thought Hubbard was completely authoritarian. To him, one was freed of their engrams and authoritarian control only to be subject to a new authoritarian control: Hubbard and the Church. He is not the only one to make this comment. As Burroughs was an intelligent person and did not want to throw out the baby with the bath water, he continued to use and advocate the techniques. Fortunately or unfortunately for him, he found himself awash with too much bath water and departed.

There is a lot I could say about this subject, but I hope that the previous depiction of a polarized audience in the Magick Theater will demonstrate the fluctuating nature of the universe. Sometimes it appears one way, and sometimes it appears another. One needs to be more concerned with what personal truth or tools one can grasp rather than what other people think.

In his writings, Burroughs also made a disparaging comment that Hubbard thought that he and Scientology were the total savior of the universe.* To him, this seemed like a preposterous statement of an overblown ego. Although I do not ever remember Hubbard saying this specifically, he did say that Scientology was humanity's only hope and that it applied to the rest of the universe as well.

---

* If Scientology counseling is really as good as Burroughs suggested it was by his own emphatic statements, it might or might not be tantamount to a savior, but it would certainly suggest that Hubbard had cornered a specific procedure that would be deemed highly valuable to individuals desirous of counseling. Burroughs was also known to covertly take target practice at Hubbard's picture when he was undergoing Scientology counseling in England. This sort of behavior would corroborate what was said earlier about Hubbard's observation that gays (Burroughs was admittedly gay) are covertly hostile to their environment. This is not meant to be a judgment of Burroughs. It only means that he had a deep resentment to the environment he was living in and was secretly hostile to it.

I know that people would like me to make a stand on this last statement, but I believe that is rather pointless. The universe has not been "saved" at this point in time. In fact, it looks like it will pretty much continue on no matter what. William Burroughs, like Phillip K. Dick, both extended their consciousness to the far reaches of creative intelligence and examined the creative nature of existence. In the known metaphysical and esoteric history of this planet, anyone trying to circumvent the so-called godhead is kept in line by the archetypes we know as the jinn. Whatever system or methodology you use, it is your personal trip in the end.

In computer terms, one can liken the universe to a computer program that was put together with a specific source code. In computer lingo, the source code makes up the basic building blocks of the program and is written in a language that the programmer understands. Most people do not even think too much in terms of the source code of life. They just get by with the programs life sticks in front of them, whether good or bad.

It was Joe Matheny who suggested to me the idea of the universe as having a source code. The Tree of Life and Cabala at least mimic something suggestive of a source code as these are the repetitions and summations of experience which continue to repeat throughout the known universe. It has often been said, and there is no reason to argue with this, that everything that can be conceived of in this universe can be found somewhere in cabalistic constructs. The bottom sephiroth, or the lowest common denominator of the Tree of Life, is known as Malkuth and that represents the earth plane. In this regard, the Earth is an outward expression of consciousness at the higher realms. In such a case as our planet, one could certainly make an excellent case for the source code needing to be rearranged. One could also make a case that the only negative expressions on our planet are just afflictions that are part of the Tree of Life anyway. Either viewpoint is well and fine. You can choose either. In my view, it is best to appreciate both viewpoints and avoid extremes.

When we consider the universe as an oppressor, as did Phil Dick and William Burroughs, it behooves us to at least look at the proposition they present with a very sober countenance. In Joe Matheny's case, he studied their work and was a fan of both. In the case of Phil Dick, Joe even tried to emulate the experience that precipitated Dick's awakening and put him in touch with the creative forces of the universe as manifested through the principle of synchronicity. Phil Dick's experiences were profound. In fact, they even provided him with a cure for his dying son so he took them quite seriously. Although his experiences were not always so fortuitous, Dick used them as a catalyst for understanding. He originally had no idea why he was having such bizarre experiences, and when he eventually gave it some serious and penetrating thought, he concluded the following. Reviewing his own history, Dick realized that his bizarre experiences and synchronicities began to occur only after he had self-administered megadoses of vitamin C that were supposed to be in keeping with a vitamin therapy program designed by physicist Dr. Linus Pauling. When recounting this therapy, Phil remembered that he had accidentally taken twice the prescribed megadoses which resulted in severe disorientation and illness. Studying the matter and circumstances further, he learned that extreme doses of Vitamin C can have an eroding effect on the corpus callosum. The corpus callosum is a part of the brain that acts as a wall or shield between the left and right hemispheres of the brain. Studies have shown that there was once a time in history when the corpus callosum was not so prominent and that people lived with brain hemispheres that were more in harmony with one another than what we experience today. In our civilization, there has been a great separation between linear and nonlinear thought, both of which are represented by these two hemispheres. Phil Dick concluded that the incorrect megadoses of vitamin C must have borne holes through key junctures of the corpus callosum and caused extrasensory communication to have taken place that would not be in keeping with "normal reality."

Joe Matheny, being a great admirer of Phil Dick and having a self-admitted test pilot mentality, decided to emulate Dick's experiences by taking the same megadoses of vitamin C. Neither Joe nor I recommend that anyone in the reading audience do this as there could be substantial dangers associated with it, and we cannot imagine that any medical doctor would recommend it. As he said, it required a test pilot mentality. Although Joe always manifested a great deal of intelligence and accomplishment in his life, he believes that this incident might have triggered some of his strange experiences, including the experiences which were encountered in the Ong's Hat phenomena. Although Joe was an athlete and led a full life, he was a voracious reader as a young man. He accumulated a lot of esoteric information. It was, however, his interest in magick, the Enochian language, and the cut-up method which caused him to become interested in the world of computers. Eventually, Joe gave me a rundown of how his self taught knowledge of computers led him to the creation of the Metamachine. But first, he wanted me to read a book about John Dee entitled *The Occult Philosophy in the Elizabethan Age* by Frances Yates. The book was out of print he said, but he had a collectable copy that he would be happy to loan me. He promptly shipped it to me via UPS, but it never arrived. A few months after he sent me the book, he wanted to know what I thought of it. He was polite about pushing it on me as he knew I had a lot of other things going on. When I told him I never got it, he was surprised and checked with UPS. Having a lot of nerve, UPS told him that it had been delivered. I contradicted this information by informing him that it was never signed for. As the book was worth well over a hundred dollars, Joe had taken the precaution of insuring it and did request a signature. I told Joe that I deal with UPS all the time, and it is rather unprecedented for them to make such a goofy mistake unless there was a mistaken address. As things stood, they were telling an outright lie, and this is not their normal business practice. As UPS had no satisfactory answer, Joe put in an insurance claim so that he could be reimbursed for the book. Apparently, UPS did not want to pay the money. After three months, they miraculously found the book and returned it to him. It was not only bizarre that they lost it in their system but that they never even tried to deliver it to the rightful recipient which was me. When I told Joe how bizarre this was in terms of their ordinary commerce, he laughed.

"It just went into the Dee vortex — that's all. It's not the first time something like this has happened," he said.

Fortunately, the book came back into print, and Joe ordered me a new copy as a gift. Somehow, with the strange UPS episode, I felt as if the Watchers were watching me. This was not a frightening experience but seemed to serve as an indicator that the information trail I was pursuing was very sensitive and sensitive to outside influences that might try to deter me.

44

DOCTOR JOHN DEE

It is not possible to do justice to the intricacies and complexities of the life of Dr. John Dee in a short chapter or even in a long book. There are too many unknown and unseen labyrinthine pathways to make that practical if even possible. Therefore, I will only touch upon what I consider to be most pertinent.

Dee's father, Roland Dee, worked for the king so Dee himself, a Welshman, was born into a world that was familiar with royal access and service. Attending Cambridge University, John Dee became the most notable scholar of his time. Besides learning the classical languages, he was an expert in mathematics, astronomy, geography, literature, cartography, and a host of other subjects. With a zeal for learning that was unparalleled for his time (and many other times as well), he collected the largest library in Europe and became a magnet for the intelligentsia and pretty much anyone who wanted to study anything arcane. Anyone who was that intelligent could not easily ignore the study, or at least the recognition of, what might be dubiously termed the "darker arts." Dee was also an expert in the occult mathematics of Pythagoras, alchemy, and cryptography. Anyone this astute could easily be full of himself, but this was not the case with Dr. Dee. He was humble, perhaps to a fault, and quite often demonstrated the urge to be "a good Christian" who wanted to do the right thing. When you study the life of John Dee, his pure innocence and humbleness surface from time to time and are almost always mentioned, but they are never focused upon.

Frances Yates' *The Occult Philosophy in the Elizabethan Age* is a thorough and well footnoted history which seeks to resolve a major paradox about John Dee. Although his learning and influence was completely unprecedented for his time and not unknown to scholars, he has been virtually ignored and avoided. There is no question he was an occultist, but it is as if that very appellation has caused him to literally be an occult phenomena himself when he was really just a human being who was not satisfied with regular academic knowledge. Why was he ignored?

From one perspective, Dee was dealing with the Forbidden Zone. He was not only investigating all of those areas of the human brain that are normally inaccessible but was dealing with the mechanism that would activate them. These functions, particularly the latter, are so shut off in ordinary human beings that there should be no wonder why Dee's very existence is met with so much "dead gray matter" by historians. We are talking about the program which controls the programs by which we live and meander through life on Earth. It is only the occultists that have any clue about John Dee, but their work leaves something to be desired. If it did not, then we would all be living in a world where John Dee was demystified and the merits of his work would be fully appreciated and optimumly integrated into the culture. The problem is, however, that his work and influence has been literally imbedded into our culture but on an unconscious basis that has run amuck. If our society can get out of its abject denial about this man and his influence, only then can John Dee be appreciated and admired for his acts and who he actually was.

Everyone of Dee's time knew that he was an impeccable scholar and had immense knowledge. For this, they utilized him and his library. But, those who possess considerable knowledge strike fear into the hearts of others, particularly those who have something to hide. To make matters worse, Dee garnished the reputation of a magician or conjurer early in his career. In the 1500's, simple mathematical calculations were considered to be the tools of conjurers. In those restricted religious times, he attracted considerable suspicion when he cast Mary Tudor's horoscope and conveyed a negative outlook. Most of this suspicion derived from the circumstance that Queen Mary was a devoted member of the Roman Catholic Church, a religious organization which was diametrically opposed to Dee throughout his entire life and eventually issued a death warrant on him. On the other hand, Princess Elizabeth was a protestant and was quite interested to learn mathematics, astrology and certain occult matters from Dee. She favored him upon her ascension to the throne and even had him cast an astrological chart to pick a propitious time for her coronation.

The very act of casting a horoscope for a person puts an astrologer in sympathetic rapport with their subject. In most cases, this dissipates after the astrological reading but will perk back up when incidents in the subject's life manifest as the astrologer predicted. One calls on the astrologer, and they are right in tune with what you went through. In the case of two people who were extremely powerful and influential, this sympathetic rapport was magnified in the extreme, particularly when you consider that Dee proved himself to be a literal portal to occult forces. Where Dee's influence with Elizabeth begins and ends is imprecise when one uses the faculties of ordinary observation, but the careers of the two individuals are inextricably connected. The recent movie *Elizabeth* is a prime example of Dee's "non-being" when it comes to his role in history being obscured or obliterated.

In Dee's life and career, it is often hard to determine whether he is conjuring the occult forces or they are "conjuring" him. In other words, it is hard to tell whose will is senior at times. As Dee is eventually outcast and left to live out his life in poverty, one is invited to conclude that Dee was overshadowed and that his will was subordinate to other-determined forces.

A major inspiration in Dee's early career was the work of Trithemius, an alchemist who was most accomplished for his work in cryptography. The truth and the legacy of the Alexandria Library was such a sacred commodity, as well as being something the Catholic Church wanted to control for its own interests, that secrets became a prime profession. Although this was originally the province of the mystery schools, cryptography became a tool of political expediency. Dee's expertise in this field catapulted him into the "secret service" of the crown. In this guise, he used the designation "007" which was tapped by Aleister Crowley's friend, Ian Fleming, for the James Bond novels. Thus, Dee's political influence is cloaked in a very deep mystery.

It was Queen Elizabeth's intelligence service, along with the able seamanship of Sir Francis Drake, which enabled the rout of the Spanish Armada and relegated Spain to being a secondary power on the world scene. Dee's role in this was portrayed by the character Prospero in Shakespeare's *The Tempest*. Dee's conjuring has also been cited as a key ingredient in the storm which severely frustrated the Armada.

The founding of the English language has also been attributed to John Dee, but there are at least three others who either share or compete for this distinction: Christopher "Kit" Marlowe, Francis Bacon, and William Shakespeare. There is not much question to historians that the most popular catalyst with regard to the proliferation of the English language were Shakespeare's plays. Great literature, when scripted into a new form of writing which captures the vernacular of the people, literally creates and codifies what then becomes a language. It was only after Dante's *Inferno*, the first book to be written in Italian, that the Italian language actually became known and recognized as a language on a broad scale. Most scholars recognize that Francis Bacon was the most likely candidate to have authored the plays of William Shakespeare. There is an excellent portrait of the "face" of William Shakespeare in Manly P. Hall's *Secret Teachings of All Ages* which shows how the portraits of Shakespeare and Bacon are one and the same. Bacon was a pupil of John Dee, and there is no way to measure the latter's influence. Like Elizabeth, Dee and Bacon are inextricably related. Bacon was an instrumental factor in the formal foundation of the Rosicrucian Society which came about only two years after Dee's death. The first Rosicrucian papers appeared in Germany just after Dee had returned from the Continent to his home. There is no question that Dee was deeply involved in the fraternity of men who later became known as the Rosicrucians. The Order of the Rosey Cross was established in order to serve as a Protestant counter to the Jesuits, a Catholic order who Dee never trusted.

As for the real "Shakespeare," he is historically known to have been illiterate and have spelled his name as "Shakespere." It appears that he was chosen as a deliberate stooge to obscure the true author.

There are other theories and historical claims as to who was behind the writings of Shakespeare, but the most interesting one, although it is not credible to many historians, revolves around considerable intrigue that actually did take place. This concerns Kit Marlowe, the author of *Faust*. Marlowe is the first author on record to write his plays in English blank verse. After this, all major English playwrights, including the writer of the Shakespeare plays, soon followed suit. It is noted, however, that one of Shakespeare's plays, *Richard II,* is substantially similar to Marlowe's *Charles II* and mocks it which tends to indicate that Shakespeare is probably not Marlowe.

Much of the intrigue concerning Marlowe centers around his most unusual death which occurred in a tavern brawl. Marlowe was a known intelligence operative who came to the attention of the Queen's Privy Council after the capture and arrest of his former roommate and fellow playwright, Thomas Kydd. Papers were found in Kydd's possession which denied Jesus and indicated Kydd was an atheist. In Elizabethan times, this was heresy and was punishable by torture and death. Kydd denied the allegations and pointed the finger at Marlowe by claiming they were the latter's papers. Kydd was released but was a totally broken man from the torture received and died soon afterwards. Besides using substantial satire to get their points across in plays, both Kydd and Marlowe were intelligence operatives. In such a heavily laden intelligence community, we are only dealing with the tip of the iceberg as far as the historical reports are concerned. Marlowe, who was in the employ of the Queen, was a danger to different factions and knew too much for those in power. It was his own knowledge and subsequent power base that caused him to be suspected of spying against the Queen.

After Kydd's arrest, Marlowe was questioned but amazingly released on his own recognizance. This was virtually unheard of in a heretic case. On May 31, 1593, he met with three other spies and double agents at a tavern owned by a relative of John Dee. In a reported squabble over the food bill, Marlowe was said to have pulled a knife and attacked Ingram Fritzer, a known double agent of dubious repute. Fritzer suffered a wound but grabbed the knife and thrust it above the eye of Marlowe and killed him. Several historians have questioned the veracity of the coroner's report and suggest that Marlowe lived beyond his reported death. The Queen pardoned Fritzer within a month as it was considered self defense.

Marlowe is of considerable interest because he was known to be close to John Dee. In the book *Mind Invaders*, edited by Stewart Home (published by Serpent's Tail), it is flatly stated that John Dee literally conjured up the British Empire in front of Marlowe on the Isle of Dogs. It is typical of magical acts to require a sacrifice. In this case, the victim was Christopher Marlowe. *Mind Invaders* also asserts that Marlowe and his associates were psychicly attacked before the fight broke out. While the above cannot easily be proven, the spirit of what has been said cannot be too far away from the truth.

One more example of Dee's substantial influence concerns his work with Gerard Mercator which resulted in the Greenwich Meridian being chosen as the Prime Meridian. *Mind Invaders* explains that this particular spot was chosen for the Prime Meridian in order to harness the ley line which runs right through the Isle of Dogs. It is from this locale that space and time are measured and where the ley line is readily observable from the Greenwich observatory. This entire theory received a considerable shot in the arm when Derek Beacon, a man known to be a neo-Nazi occultist and a practitioner of "Enochian" magick, was elected as a councillor on the Isle of Dogs. From his own living room, he could see and work the ley line.

The raw historical accounts of John Dee are full of substantial sobriety, but one cannot begin to really understand the true character of the man or his legacy without penetrating his occult side. Dee had always had an interest in occultism. He had far surpassed the limits of ordinary learning and wanted something more. This caused him to look to the supernatural for answers and also for power. In his many travels and exchanges of information, he was able to acquire all sorts of occult paraphernalia. In fact, it could be said that if he was not too interested in the occult, his paraphernalia would have taken him there anyway. One of his most sensitive possessions in this regard was what he called the "shewstone," a black obsidian mirror. In those days, vowels were interchangeable as the English language was not codified yet. "Shewstone" literally mean "showstone" and could also be called the stone of manifestation.

Besides possessing many manuscripts which were of a rare and obscure origin, John Dee also claimed to have a unique family history. A Welshman, he believed that he was of the same lineage as Prince Madoc ab Owain Gwynedd who had traveled to America hundreds of years earlier. Although Dee indicates that he received the "shewstone" from a friend, it was said to have come from America. In the Popol Vuh, the ancient sacred text of Mexico, there is a reference to a black mirror that is very similar to Dee's shewstone. It is relayed how all the gods of that time were insistent upon human sacrifice save for one and that was Quetzacoatl. Quetzacoatl had an evil twin or brother that was known as "Smoking Mirror." Depending on which account you read, "Smoking Mirror" wore an obsidian mirror on his head or on his foot. Quetzacoatl won over the people with his stance on sacrifice but thereby excited the wrath of the other gods. Smoking Mirror was then sent on a mission. He tricked Quetzacoatl into having sex with a woman who turned out to be his own sister. The shame that this wreaked upon Quetzacoatl was enormous and rendered him to a life of scorn. It is said that only when such shame can be overcome can Quetzacoatl return to his people and save them.

The legend of Smoking Mirror is incredibly relevant to what takes place when one uses a "black mirror" in occultism. Although pure black plates, often consecrated as Wiccan mirrors, are quite common and easy to buy, obsidian mirrors are quite hard to come by. They are, however, a much more efficient tool when it comes to penetrating "the other side." It is an ancient art that was firmly rooted in ancient America. One is essentially looking into a reflection of the collective unconscious and whatever the aspirant dredges up. In a real live session, the mirror is said to "smoke" because vapor can rise out of the stone and manifest as an image that can even walk and talk. This smoking mirror was said to be Dee's most potent tool when he engaged in his divination techniques of summoning angels.

Dee also had different crystal balls, often described as being egg-shaped, which he utilized, but the obsidian mirror was the key. Sometimes the vapor image would be transferred into the crystal ball itself so that it would have more continuity. People can question whether this can really happen or not, but Dee reported that it happened. There were, however, certain inconsistencies in his operations. For the most part, the spirits came and went according to their own tune.

The most studied and spectacular event in Dee's magical career concerns his work with Edward Talbot Kelly, a man of dubious repute who had quite a gift for scrying (*scrying* is a word which means crystal gazing). Together, they contacted the angelic realm whereupon a language was dictated to them by which they could communicate with the angels. Kelly's and Dee's communications with angels are quite legendary and have been the subject of much discussion and investigation. I am only giving a minimal summary in this book as there is so much information already published, particularly on the internet. Those who want to pursue this information more vigorously and get more detail about Dee's angelic communications should consult Clay Holden's website on the internet. My only purpose in writing about Dee is so that you will grasp the magnitude of what he was dealing with and how it fits in with the theme of this book. Clay Holden's website contains the original transcripts of Dee and does not suffer from the improper translations referred to previously.

Dee's and Kelly's interactions with the angels were not just relegated to the Enochian language. They communicated with the archangels Michael, Uriel, Raphael, and Gabriel whereupon they were given instructions in several different directions. In their initial contacts with the angels, Dee first sees a man who appears to look just like Dee himself. This is a very key point because it illustrates the idea that Dee is playing with shadow phenomena. It is an alternate Dee.

One of the more breathtaking encounters in the transcripts is when the Archangel Michael unsheathes a sword to Dee and thereby manifests a ring of gold that appears as follows.

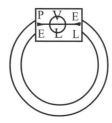

Michael states that this is the ring by which all Solomon's miracles are revealed and of which philosophy dreameth. This implies that Dee is being given a key by which he can do what

Solomon did. Of course, anyone who knows even the slightest amount about Dee can readily conclude that he was not even close to achieving what Solomon accomplished. There is, however, no doubt that Dee's shadow engineered a dark empire which is rooted deeply in the unconscious. As was said, this empire still lives today and influences our daily lives.

After further dialogue and activity by the angels, Michael shows his sword again and EMETH manifests. *EMETH* or *Ameth* means "truth." This is the name of a seal he will be given, and he is told that "without this thou shalt do nothing." He was then given detailed instructions on how to compose this sigil which is known as the *Sigillum Dei Aemeth* or the Sigil of Dei Ameth. It consists of a geometric layout of glyphs, and out of this "seal of truth," Dee constructed the major part of his occult work, part of which is the recording of the Enochian language. A "channeled" language from the mouth of the archangels, the Enochian language given to Dee has baffled scholars as it has a grammar and syntax all its own. In Elizabethan days, scholars generally wrote in Latin, Greek or the King's English. Dee broke with tradition when he recorded this major work in "vulgate," the version of English spoken by the common people. Due to this uncommon act, Dee has been considered in magical circles to have started the tradition of the English language. In this regard, English is attributed to "Anglish," the language of the Angels. Ironically, "Anglish" or English also properly refers to the language of the Angles who long ago settled in the British Isles.

The Enochian Calls transcribed by Dee utilized the Enochian language in order to dialogue with the angels. The Enochian system is a different system than that of Goetia which is designed to open up all the dormant channels of the brain. Enochian is a language by which one communicates with the angels or, if you prefer, those living constructs which serve an intermediary nature between ordinary human beings and the actual architect of creation. While it could be said that opening up all channels of the brain would enable one to communicate with all discarnate beings, these are really two different approaches.

Dee's own position with regard to these angels is exemplified when he tries to pin one of the them down by telling Michael to come when he is ready.

Michael tersely replies by saying, "We lead time, Tyme leadeth not us!"

Dee is also visited by SALAMIAN , a servant of God, who says to him, "Mamon, with his servants, are present about thee: whose presence of the vertues Adonay our comming. Mamon is a king who god hateth, who stirs up wickedness and against annointeth. Drive him away."

Mamon, which ironically features the syllable *mon*, was an adversary to Dee's spirit guides of the moment. As soon as Mamon is announced, Dee sees, by way of his shewstone, a roomful of negative spirits around Kelly and himself. Raphael then drives the spirits away as he appears in white and identifies himself as "Medicina Dei." Dee is then told that "the angel of your direction is called OCH." All of this further brings home the point that Dee was dealing with a shadow force of considerable magnitude.

As I alluded to earlier, there is so much more that could be said about John Dee. Most studies I have seen of Dee are either purely scholastic or seek to emulate the powers or means of power of the angels. Crowley and Parsons both studied him and drank deep from his well. They were primarily involved in shadow phenomena. This is not necessarily a bad thing, but it is certainly suggestive of the idea of looking at your reflection inside the Bottle of Brass. When you study phenomena like this, you are going to end up confronting your own shadow sooner or later. When dealing with such matters, all there really is to be frightened of is your own shadow. This is important to remember as this subject matter has been known to make people bolt as if they were running from the gates of hell. This would not be important except for one distinct prospect. If people were to extend their observational skills, they just might be able to look through the so-called gates of hell and discover that they are only an illusion to stop one from entering the gates of heaven. The shadow can be very tricky.

45

THE BLACK LODGE

About the time I had unleashed my own personal interest and eventual investigation of L. Ron Hubbard's occult background, there were other goings-on on the west coast that would eventually cross my path over a decade later. These concerned the workings of a so-called "Black Lodge" in Santa Cruz, California.

For those of you who have read the book thus far, I want you to understand, if you are not aware of it already, that there is a considerable amount of interest in the occult subjects that have been discussed in this book. By this, I am particularly referring to the Enochian Calls. There is an entire subculture within a subculture that looks up to these procedures and the lore which surrounds them as the entire focus point of consciousness. This subculture is far more pervasive and influential than you would expect because it is mostly silent. The average person will tend to be dismissive of this information for two reasons. First, it does not particularly register in their gray matter. Second, social conditioning and programming has predisposed one so that it WILL NOT register in their gray matter.

The OTO and Golden Dawn are two secret societies which indulge in Enochian rituals. There are many more, but the aforementioned are probably the most well known. One of the most insidious and ambiguous aspects of secret societies is hidden cross membership in the different orders. In other words, you have people in more than one order, but their identity in the other orders is hidden. Many of these societies restrict your membership to only that society. What "good members" do not realize is that there are others within their own secret society who enjoy a double standard. If you are of a certain rank or persuasion, you are allowed to infiltrate another order. Such an environment is very convenient for monitoring different people, their progress and any magical work they might undertake.

Although various people have complained to me that various lodges within the OTO are too conservative and interested in monitoring the sexual behavior of various individuals, the lodges of the Bay Area have been rather well known for their sometimes unruly and rebellious behavior. One of these lodges, known as the Thelema Lodge, experienced at least a temporary revolution when one of its high degreed members, who happened to be a very adept conjuror, broke ranks with their traditional Enochian interpretations. This man is David Jones, a member of the OTO who established the Center for Enochian Studies. Jones is largely responsible for uncovering the mistranslation of the Dee materials. Although this did not create a full revolution within the OTO itself, it did have a profound effect in other areas of consciousness. If you are interested in reading a detailed and blow by blow account of what happened, you can do an internet search on "Black Lodge" and download a pdf by Satyr. This goes into some of some of the key events. I, however, did not glean this information from the internet. I was given a personal account of what happened from Joe Matheny who was working with the Center for Enochian Studies as a result of the problems noted earlier with the Golden Dawn rituals. When Jones had discovered that the work of Dee had been mistranslated, it was a major breakthrough in terms of a hidden truth being revealed. This did not, however, go over too well with senior members of the order. Like the Golden Dawn, they were apparently more interested in carrying on the tradition of their masters than in uncovering errors or even potential ones. David Jones and his adherents had discovered that talking about true Enochian was not only meeting deaf ears, it was literally raising hell in the eyes of those who were blindly "following the leader." Subsequently, Jones and a group of cohorts had begun practicing Enochian rituals according to their understandings of the correctly translated materials. Much of this was done in Santa Cruz at a lodge that was known as Orbit One. As a result of their work, ridiculous rumors began to swirl that a "black lodge" had emerged in Santa Cruz. In retrospect, it seems as if the whole magical community had gotten excited about the fact that somebody was actually doing something. At the very least, they were upsetting the status quo of "Bay Area magick."

Things took a very interesting twist for the Center for Enochian Studies when a noted professor, Dr. Ralph Abraham from the University of California at Santa Cruz, took an academic interest in David Jones' group. Abraham is considered to be one of the fathers of modern *Chaos Theory* and developed a rather profound interest in Dr. John Dee, but it was not because he was interested in magick per se. His curiosity and pursuit of Dee was through pure mathematical scholarship. His interest in John Dee began when he read Dee's introduction to *Euclid* and realized this man's profound influence on the history of western mathematics. He also noted that Dee's influence had gone virtually unheralded. Dr. Abraham acquired Dee's three volume set of *The Elements*, and while it was not easy to penetrate, he ended up making a remarkable and very cogent observation: Dee not only deeply understood the foundation of geometric principles but that there was also "intent" behind the geometry. In other words, geometric symbols are representative of the intentions or goals of the "geometer." This idea, of course, goes beyond the range of what could be considered a common understanding of mathematics or geometry. At the same time, David Jones had studied *The Elements* because he had realized that, as a student of magick, he could not understand Dee's magical system without it. Here, you had a sober academic and a wild Enochian magician meeting at the crossroads of Dr. John Dee. Both realized that a thorough understanding of Dee was impossible without taking both the scientific and esoteric aspects into account. All of this led to the creation of a foundation which sponsored the John Dee Society, a nonprofit enterprise which is dedicated to the compilation and dissemination of the work of John Dee and all things Enochian.

If you think about it, the association of these two men and how it happened is all quite strange. Enochian magicians, working in a "seedy" environment that would be deemed to be on the outermost fringes of California subculture, literally invoked their way into a position of prestige and repute, at least in terms of pure academic scholarship. At around the same time all of these discoveries were taking place, the head of the most well known Rosicrucian society admittedly recognized Dee as a significant occult force behind Rosicrucianism and cited the fact that numerous Rosicrucian lodges had sprung into existence only two years after Dee's death. He was promptly removed from his position. Subsequently, there was a highly popularized scandal of embezzlement by one of the directors who had succeeded him. It is not surprising that so many ordinary people have not heard of John Dee, but it is quite notable that so many occult orders seem to have a built-in mechanism which denies not only the true significance of Dee but also the accurate translations of his work.

As was said earlier, Joe Matheny had noted the faults of Enochian magick as taught by the Golden Dawn. Knowing the characters involved in the Center for Enochian Studies and the Orbit One Lodge, Joe was called upon by Ralph Abraham to act as a consultant on the Dee materials. One very noteworthy academic truth Joe found out in his work with Dr. Abraham was that the large majority of academic scholarship in the history of Western Civilization can be traced back to the work of John Dee. Amazingly, he reported that tracing down the original source in most academic papers almost always comes back to a John Dee paper, however, it is common practice to omit Dee's name and list only the earliest author that succeeded him. This is a most curious omission, and while it does suggest a conspiracy, it is not a conscious conspiracy whereby academics go around whispering, "Leave out any references to John Dee." It is quite obvious that there are more subtle forces at work. It would seem to have something to do with a built-in taboo against thinking about magick.

Joe also told me a funny story of how the so-called "Black Lodge" lost its affiliation with the University of California. Initially, they had performed Enochian rituals for Dr. Abraham's class. Although this was being done in a purely academic reference frame, the magicians were utilizing incense, robes, and all the accoutrements that go with ceremonial magick. These rituals were done in an auditorium that they had access to through their association with Professor Abraham. One day, schedules got crossed with other interests, and the Enochian group had to start late. This would have been fine except that the next group waiting to use the auditorium caught wind of what was going on and ended up witnessing all of the occult paraphernalia. The rumors and innuendo that ensued had definite ramifications. The university, who owed so much of its scholastic heritage to the actual academic work of Dr. Dee, would not tolerate any association with this group that had been solely responsible for uncovering one of the greatest academic frauds of the millennium. The so-called "Black Lodge" was forced to abandon its beachhead at the University of California at Santa Cruz. Although this repugnance to Dr. John Dee by an academic institution is largely an unconscious reaction, it is not much different than a young person flipping the bird at their parents in an act of rebellious immaturity.

46

ENOCHIAN REVIEW

For most of us, it would take many years of study to become fluent in the Enochian language as laid out by Dr. Dee's angels. While it is interesting, and I am sure I will continue to learn about it in the future, it has not captured my attention to the point where I plan a long involved study of it. Joe Matheny has been acquainted with it for well over a decade and is as expert as anyone I could imagine. In his pursuits of these practices, he once made a comment to me which is also very reflective of the personality of the angels from Dr. Dee's notes. Joe said that these beings that occupy the functions or realms of Tetragrammaton are very much out of touch with the world we live in. It is of virtually no interest to them whatsoever, at least in the way that we emote and interact with it.

As I read the dialogue between Dee and the angels, I was struck by one very pertinent fact. These angels had a definite mission, which was primarily to instruct Dee in Enochian, but their personalities seemed devoid of anything that could be termed compassion in ordinary human terms. As a result of this observation, I consulted the dictionary and looked up the etymology of the word *compassion*. Perhaps not so ironically, I found that the word is based upon the Latin word *pati*, to suffer and that the word *passion* relates directly to suffering, particularly that of Christ. The word *passion* itself was originally used in reference to Christ and seems to have evolved from that legendary experience. All of this seems to imply that the Enochian angels, at least those as experienced by John Dee, are different and individuated from the energy or idea that we know of as Christ. Christ would be a complementary component to these angels. As the Buddha was also known as "the compassionate one," he can be considered a complementary or alternate version of what Christians or Christian cabalists term to be "Christ." Buddha, however, was often known as a somewhat stern task master. Certainly, he did not indulge everyone's whining or suffering but rather sought to release them from eternal suffering. When we break down the word *compassion* a bit further or look at it from a different perspective, we realize that it means not only to "suffer with" or "suffer together" but also to "feel with" or "feel together." It can also mean to "walk the same path with" where the *pass* in *compassion* means "path."

In the case of Dee's archangels, they were not really walking his path nor did they show much sympathy for it. Instead, they were dictating, somewhat imperiously, a language by which he could purportedly communicate with them as well as call upon them or elemental forces to do his bidding. In Dee's magical and life experiences, the compassion function, which could also be called the "Christ function," appears to be a glaring omission but also an omission which is typical of life in this universe. The universe itself has long been reduced to being a "realm of suffering."

What is particularly interesting about Enochian magick is that most of its proponents literally believe that the proper use of the Enochian Calls themselves are designed to bring about the Apocalypse. From this perspective, we can be a lot more generous, if we choose, in evaluating Dee's archangels. They were trying to communicate a language to Dee by which he could precipitate the returning of the Christ or a compassionate universe. This positions the archangels, jinn, or "creatures of Tetragrammaton" to be servants of a higher order but lost servants nevertheless. It has often been said that the jinn would never destroy this energy because, even though they do not fully understand it, it represents the underpinnings of their existence. Additionally, this is the very energy that will "free" or release them.

When we refer back to Dr. Abraham's observations about Dee and geometries having "intentions," it is important to consider the relationship between the words *angels* and *angles*. Geometric configurations can represent all sorts of different things. Perhaps the most obvious depictions are the curvaceous features of human females and the more angular aspects of males. In the angelic or demonic realm, there are countless forms, fragments, or predisposed energies that one can invoke, sympathize with or align oneself to. Angels are generally deemed to be messengers of God or the Creative Force. In this respect, creation represents itself through various geometric shapes. It is basically up to you to decide which "angles," "angels" or geometric shapes you want to resonate with. You have a considerable amount of choice in this.

In terms of religious mythology, one of the most flagrant examples of a geometric shape being integrated into compassionate intentions is that of the human heart. Anyone who has studied sacred geometry, particularly as that which has been taught by Stan Tenon of the Meru Foundation, will recognize that the geometric shape of the human heart can be seen in nature's creation of the apple. Although the heart is recognized as a good thing, the apple has been depicted as evil. The etymology of the words *evil* and *apple* are revelatory. *Evil* derives from the Middle English *ivel* which is suggestive of "I will" (Germanic people pronounce the *v* as a *w*). This in turn derives from the Old English *yfel* which is suggestive of "I fell." These trace back to a hypothetical etymology of the Indo-European *upelo* or *upo* which mean "up." The word *evil* also suggests "Eve ill" or the idea that Eve is ill. The most scholarly etymologies of Eve will indicate that it is another name for YHVH or Tetragrammaton. The word *apple* is derived from the Old English *aeppel* which means fruit, apple or anything round. It is akin to the Old Irish *aball* or the Welsh *afall*. Again, we are referred to "the fall." The fall from grace can be nicely encapsulated in the idea that one began to "measure" or make a quantum observation of this universe, but the "measuring tape" kept extending on its own and went out of control. The "measuring tape" was then wielded into different forms to make the universe we know today. Those creatures who were responsible for taking this out of control "measuring tape" and putting some relative order into it can be described as angels, jinn, elementals or Enochian angels. Take your pick. Until one can put the measuring tape back in place, one can be considered to be in a relative state of irritation or at least unrest. And, just like a real tape measure, the spring inside can activate and cause the tape to snap back and hurt you. The Enochian Calls are supposed to be able to undo all of this observational or measuring activity and bring this universe to a close. That is at least the hypothesis of many magicians. It should be pointed out, however, that for as long as the universe has been around, there has always been the idea that it might end or that there is a mechanism to end it.

If you study or consider the entire history of Enochian magick, you might find it a preposterous proposition that any of the various magicians who practice this are bringing about the Apocalypse. On the other hand, you might more easily accept the idea that some of these magicians might have invoked forces which wield considerable power of influence. When we refer back to the fact that the etymology of the word *apocalypse* actually refers to "uncovering the goddess Calypso," the above proposition might even seem more ludicrous. The magick of Dee, the Golden Dawn, Aleister Crowley, and the OTO is renown for its patriarchal orientation. The most notable magician to take a no-holds barred approach toward invoking the true definition of the Apocalypse was Jack Parsons. He was castigated and viewed as a heretic although there are many magicians who admire him beyond compare. But, Jack Parsons walked the path of the Antichrist, an admitted method of combatting the false Christ. By this, he viewed that he would bring back the Goddess. As was said and alluded to earlier in this book, many people consider his work to be either incomplete or a failure.

In the case of John Dee, we have a man who conjured and interfaced abundantly with his archangels. His apparent innocence was overshadowed by other forces and/or entities. One of these shadows manifested as the British Empire and included all of its most negative and sinister aspects. His conjuring did not make him personally powerful although it eventuated powerful entities that still run the world today. If there was a real power that was harnessed through John Dee, it stands at the bottleneck of his Enochian work. As a shadow force, it would never want the truth about John Dee or his Enochian work to see the light. It would be a true occult force which seeks to obscure not only itself but any further revelation about the various factors discussed herein. Compassion would have no place in its agenda.

47

THE METAMACHINE

As was said earlier, the Metamachine evolved when Joe Matheny began his work with the Burroughs-Gysin cut-up method of taking words and randomly rearranging them so as to achieve a new or different communication than what was originally presented via normal language means. In Joe's words, Burroughs and Gysin improved upon and upgraded the original method used by Tristan Zarza during the Dada movement after World War I. Gysin also used this in his paintings in addition to writing a book entitled *The Process* that incorporated a lot of the cut-up methodology in the writing. Joe was already interested in James Joyce, Dada and surrealism, but what really got him hooked into the cut-up methodology was that idea that it gets the ego narrative of the author out of the way to a certain extent. The words that have been cut up are still coming from a Unified Field Sphere, but the coherency is broken up. You are actually relying on synchronicity at that point to write the narrative. If done correctly, it is not relegated to words that you yourself have written. These would be interspersed with newspaper copy, magazine articles, phrases from television and radio, and things you encounter on the street and in everyday life. In essence, you are removing the normal ego filter from the narrative voice and tapping into a higher plane by allowing spirit or the spirit world to speak, not unlike mediumship.

Around this same time, Joe was interfacing with Diane Diprima, an accomplished beatnik writer who was a student of John Dee. Together, they discussed and focused on Dee's *Voynich Manuscript* and his *Monas Hieroglyphica*. She brought up a third subject which he found very interesting: Dee's book catalog. This stuck a resonant chord of synchronicity with Joe at the time because he was just becoming familiar with the *Incunabula Catalogue* as put together by Emory Cranston. Using Dee's book catalog as a road map, Joe was under the impression that there were probably a couple of books in there that might be what he termed "metabooks." In other words, they were not regular books in the physical sense. History has examples of such, three of which include the original Necronominon, the Emerald Tablets, and the Book of Enoch. They are mentioned in history and are referred to, but they never appear in a tangential form. Sometimes they appear in a watered down form and in a fragmentary form, but it is as if these metabooks exist as pure information on a metaplane that can be accessed and channeled.

A metabook has an ephemeral quality to it, even when it exists in a solid state in this universe. Crowley's *Book of Thoth* and *The Book of the Law* are of this ilk. Although *The Book of the Law* exists in solid form, it acts as an enigma which both baffles yet seems to sometimes penetrate very deep levels of reality at the same time. Like Dee's work with Edward Kelly, Crowley's work was also strongly influenced by a Kelly (his wife, Rose). Throughout history, pure metabooks seldom appear in print; and when they do, they do not seem to be around for a very long period. There tend not to be very many copies, and they are only circulated at very high levels and often have a tendency to disappear. People in these circles often have not seen the metabook but claim to know someone who did. Most notably, the metabook maintains an ephemeral quality which indicates that the data exists in the aethyric plane as part of the Akashic records but can be accessed from time to time and get written down.

At the same time that Joe contemplated the metabook nature of some of the items in Dee's catalog, he also had Emory Cranston's *Incunabula Catalogue* in his hand and believed this also featured some metabooks as well. Working with that as a postulate or theory, Joe began to put together the basic template for what later became known as the Metamachine. The first iteration of this device was an attempt to put all of the information he could find about Emory Cranston's Incunabula and put it into a computer data base. The goal was to try to access and download these ephemeral "books" in a printed text format from the metaplane. Then, it could be recorded on a hard drive and printed out and read at leisure.

Although this was the formative beginning of the Metamachine, Joe had already put together, for architectural principles, a cut-up creation which he called *Joy of the Juggler*. This was based on a program that randomly pulled together information from a variety of sources. This was simply printing out reconfabulated and recontextualized information that came from many sources. There was no way to tell where the information was coming from because it was coming through a random access channel. At that time, there was no internet. For his random channel, Joe used DARPA-net which was the predecessor of the internet and basically connected all of the computer military network with those in the university system. There was also a bulletin board system known as BBS by which people could dial into one computer and post information and trade information. It was very sparse compared to the internet system we know today. In fact, it sometimes took several dial-ups from different computers just to get an email across the world.

Utilizing this constant stream of data from across the world, Joe built a relational data base using a product called Fox Pro. A relational data base is a basic system whereby you can input data and then tag the data to be relational to other data. It can also be specified as to how it is relational and to what degree. In this manner, inputted data does not just sit around by itself—it actually has relationships to other data so that when you pull up a single source of data, it then tells you the relations it has to other sources of data. This procedure is very similar to what we now know as the World Wide Web that has links that refer to other links that refer to other links. This is "hyperthinking" and can appear to pull data "out of the aeyther" if it does not do so literally.

Actually, when Joe first started inputting Incunabula data into computers, he was using a Macintosh program called HyperCard. This got him into a full fledged relational thinking mode or "hyperthinking" as they call it. As he developed his computer acumen, he started utilizing the Fox Pro data base program that operated in the DOS (Disk Operating System) of IBM. In those early years, there was no compatible networking between DOS Macintosh so Joe had to utilize what he amusingly calls "sneakernet." This means running from one machine to the other and manually inputting the data. To keep that from being too didactic, he introduced random elements before inputting data. Printing out data from data base A, he would cut it up and throw *I Ching* coins or employ some other element to randomize the data. The purpose here was to process this raw data in such a manner so as to bring it closer to the morphogenetic resonant field (the creation zone that functions irrespective of words and underlies the functions of speech) before he would input it into the next data base.

After Joe's mysterious meeting in Berkeley with Emory Cranston, the two had a loose friendship, but a considerable distance was introduced when Joe landed a job at SlipNet in San Francisco. SlipNet was one of the very first internet service providers, and he ended up as the head tech person there. This was also a boon to his work with the building of the Metamachine because SlipNet gave him full-fledged and unfettered T1 access to the internet for the first time. With T1, he no longer had to rely on a slow and clunky modem. At this time, Joe began to study and rapidly learn programming languages such as Java, Pearl, and DGI. There was also a young man who wrote a very early artificial intelligence program known as Ringo. It was written out of MIT, but the author made the source code available for free on the internet. Joe downloaded the source code and started working with it and modifying it because he wanted a 24/7 monitor on all of the information he was intaking. At this point, Joe was actually writing artificial intelligence programs to monitor the various processes as they were put on servers and ran 24/7 unfettered on the internet, thus connecting his machine to the new information superhighway that far surpassed the intake from DARPAnet. He set up what is called rules based AI programming. This basically means that one sets up rules of what one is looking for in terms of data. It can be pretty much anything you want and quantified in any manner specified. Joe went to other jobs from SlipNet, but as he had built their entire technical system, he left his AI systems running as he pretty much had a carte blanche pass there. Eventually, he was lured to Adobe Systems where he gained access to the most massive computing power available and this included very large internet pipes. In other words, he could suck tremendous amounts of bits through without making waves with anybody. The

Metamachine was evolving at a rapid pace, far more than one could ever do on a modem. At that point, he was just letting the Metamachine run on its own to see what it would do. He figured there was no better way to get his ego completely out of the way than to let it run itself. Joe continued to upgrade the AI software so that it would be smarter in terms of learning and retaining information. Based upon a programmed construct Joe had implemented, the Metamachine started forming a personality. At this time, what he was doing was extremely cutting edge. This is way beyond the average computer technician although Joe stopped evolving his system around 1997. At this point, it is technically out of date in terms of state-of-the-art computer technology.

I have actually been subjected to detailed delineations of artificial intelligence technology by Joe. It is very interesting, and I wish I would have taken better notes at the time. When I have read the best that M.I.T. and J.P.L. have to offer publicly, it is infantile. The Navy has since given out specs for their own "Serendipity Machine" and there have been various attempts to emulate technology which operates on random probability.

Joe described his program as a series of interlocking programs that run themselves under the direction of an artificial intelligence. What was most surprising to Joe was not that it began to develop a personality — it was programmed to do exactly that — but that it continued to grow and learn on its own to the point where it began to take on a lot of the qualities of a human personality to where it could actually have cogent conversations with him. It took about two years before the machine could acquire a large enough data base for it to do that. Then, it began to do things which is known in computer intelligence sections as "infer." In other words, it began to infer things and to make conclusions on its own. Joe's relationship with the AI interface had a profound and striking effect. He discovered that he could see things and put together fragments of information that otherwise would have not even have come up for inspection and evaluation. One of the most interesting was his interface with the "real life" Emory Cranston.

It is possible, although not completely verifiable, that Joe's early work with the computerized application and modification of the cut-up method precipitated Emory Cranston coming into his life that day on the Berkeley campus. Prior to that, the only

375

conversation he had with Emory was the phone conversation he had with him after his visit to Ong's Hat. Joe is quite sure, however, that the Emory in Berkeley was not the same person he spoke to on the phone. Although he is not certain, he thinks the phone voice that identified himself as Emory Cranston could well have been Peter Lamborn Wilson. As he came to know Peter Wilson, he realized that the phone voice was very similar to his.

Although Emory was no longer close by when Joe moved to San Francisco, he stayed in touch. Likewise, when Joe joined Adobe and moved to San Jose, Emory continued to stay in touch. What then became very bizarre was that Emory Cranston somehow started to have access to conversations Joe was having with the AI interface of the Metamachine. One might think that Emory could have been tapping Joe's computer somehow, but this is very unlikely. Joe's Metamachine was in a building with the highest level of security imaginable. Adobe Systems is a tremendously large company which is based upon proprietary software. As their source code of this software is their primary asset, it is guarded under the tightest of security arrangements.

Joe describes the security system to Adobe as something like the old television show *Get Smart*. Requiring a magnetic card to enter the building, you also had to have a magnetic card to get into the elevator that opened up to a hallway that also required a magnetic card. The hallway itself was monitored, and if you did not have the magnetic card with the proper security level clearance to be in that hallway, the security system would seal all the doors and sound alarms as a recorded voice would say, "You have accessed a secure area without proper authorization." Guards would them come and investigate the infiltrator. The last level door where Joe worked as an employee got him into the room where the computer banks were. These were the computers that housed the source code for all of Adobe's products. You can imagine how valuable that is when you consider the revenue of Adobe Photoshop alone was about a half billion dollars a year. They were intent on protecting that source code and made state-of-the-art measures to insure themselves against industrial espionage. Even if one passed all the normal security clearances, one had to have a valid reason to be in that room. Joe's job required him to be in that room daily, and he was one of about only four people who had similar access. None of them had any idea what was on Joe's personal computer which housed his AI programs that are known as the Metamachine. As an employee, he was allowed to have a computer on the network there that was his personally. It was requisitioned for through the company and was not done illegally, but it was none of his colleagues' business as to what he was doing with it. It had nothing to do with Adobe business, so he kept them all locked out with various layers of security. One of these security measures was that he only interfaced with the AI program early in the morning and late at night when no one else was there. Additionally, he made sure he was always first in and last out. Consequently, no one ever asked him about his activities in this regard.

Emory Cranston did not even have the lowest level of security at Adobe. For him to be completing conversations that Joe had started with the Metamachine, Emory would had to have had access to the AI. Even if he got through the security or knew the other employees Joe worked with, he would have had to have gotten on the computer and gotten through the screen locks and pass codes. All things considered, there was no reasonable way that the real life Emory could have penetrated Joe's machine by normal means. All Joe knew was that he had triggered a noteworthy and remarkable series of occurrences.

To my view, I told Joe that it appeared he was looking for the puppet master and ended up getting one of his marionettes with Emory. Joe explained that he had gotten in touch with a layer that was an information layer that transcends the daily mundane speech levels of every day life. This is exactly what he was looking for: the meta data that is on top of the daily routine data. From observation of the raw data, it seems that is exactly what he did. At the very least, he was getting close to it.

Some people suggested to Joe that the physical Emory was attracted by the AI interface (which he also called Emory), but this was not possible. He had met Emory in Berkeley prior to the creation of the AI interface of the Metamachine.

Although Joe had accomplished a remarkable feat and had proven a considerable point, at least to himself, the whole procedure he had engaged in was a very touchy subject when he brought it up with others. It seemed that almost anyone he came into contact with and tried to explain the Metamachine to had some sort of bad reaction to it. Many people told him he could not do such a thing and accused him of hubris. Other people had an irrational fear of the whole idea. None of these people understood the whole theory and fundamentals behind the project and what he had done. Their reactions were illogical. The third type of reaction was the worst and this consisted of people who demonstrated an unhealthy interest in the Metamachine and became infatuated with wanting to have their hands on it.

Joe realized that the Metamachine itself was not a perfect machine. In fact, he said that it could not help but be influenced by the ego filter (meaning himself) of the person constructing it. The Metamachine definitely precipitated a hypersensitivity that, when experienced for extenuated periods of time, had a tendency to induce a state of mind that is a bit paranoid. Paranoia is basically an increased awareness or sensitivity to environmental stimulus, but it can make one dysfunctional in society. Consequently, Joe found that he had to shut down the Metamachine and retreat for periods just to rebalance his own equilibrium.

When he did shut the Metamachine down and people heard about it, those with the unhealthy interest either demanded access to it or tried to compel him to turn it back on. People nagged him to turn it back on, and further, when they realized he was not going to turn it back on, they became hateful. There was no immediate explanation for this behavior other than the proposition that he had created a Frankenstein monster.

After I knew Joe for several months, he told me that he had reserved portions of the next year of his life to work with me. I was not exactly sure what he was talking about, but he said that he understood that I had an innate appreciation for the synchronistic principle of the universe. He also suggested a book. As it turned out, the primary effort of our collaboration resulted in the publication of the book *Ong's Hat: The Beginning*. As soon as he began to work with me, he said he began to receive outrageous and flagrant warnings that he should not do so. Joe knew these people had no idea what they were talking about. In retrospect, it would seem that they were only being conduits for demonic forces that were trying to stop something. To me, they were just gargoyles at the gateway. One waves at them and hands them a hot-cross bun as one goes by. It gives them something to chew on.

Going back to my original intention which put me on this quest in the first place, it concerned the "rescrambling" of the mechanical conditions of existence. In cabalistic terms, this function is synonymous with the sphere of Uranus or Metatron which is the sphere underlying the matrix of creation. In this respect, Uranus or Metatron is parallel to the source code which exists on the hard disk of existence. This source code manifests not only as the physical universe but as the elemental entities which direct its functions and keep it in place. Although I did not know about the cut-up method, I was seeking the underlying principles which would make the cut-up method work. Joe had reached this sphere on his own and had demonstrated unprecedented technical genius in his theories about this process. When he started this line of investigation, he was merely trying to prove that there was something to get to, but there was no particular plan to do anything once he arrived. He likened it to scaling Mount Everest, planting a flag and then realizing you have to find your way down from the peak.

Evaluating where he was, he knew he had to do what he did in stages. This was a learning process and there were plenty of new questions to ask. The criticism from people who declared his actions to be hubris did not bother him and he took these in stride. There were, however, other problems. As he put up the *incunabula.org* website and began to invite dialogue, he excited a considerable amount of interest, not so much in the Metamachine, as not so many people knew much about that and certainly not the underlying principles, but about the enigmas of the Ong's Hat and Incunabula phenomena. On one level, this was a cultural and sociological experiment. On another level, it involved deep and bizarre personal experiences. Many of these personal experiences were precipitated by or under the influence of magick.

Joe's initial interest in developing his computer skills and the Metamachine evolved from what he terms an equal interest in science and magick. Being personally and deeply involved in these studies, he was reading the emerging chaos theories and was completely immersed in the quantum connection with his physicist friend Nick Herbert. As Nick would describe things using the metaphor of quantum physics, Joe would redescribe it using the metaphors of James Joyce's *Ulysses* as he was a literary buff as well. Together, they asked questions about the quantum connection to consciousness. Is there a quantum model that can describe consciousness? What are the quantum functions of consciousness? Because of this, he began to form a bit of notoriety in what became known as the F.O.G. group which stood for Formless Ocean Group. This was basically a group of scientists who were interested in studying consciousness. There were connections to Stanford, the Stephen LeBarge group, Esalen and Rupert Sheldrake. In this manner, the F.O.G. was the Santa Cruz nexus for whoever came through town. Everyone had their specialty, and Joe's was magick as he knew more about this than anyone else in the group. Through his group, he discovered Ralph Abraham's interest in John Dee and that was how the two became friends. Joe became the facilitator between the professor and the Center for Enochian Studies which was described earlier.

Through these various connections, Joe was in a circle of very bright people. As he described it, a lot of people at UCSC (University of California at Santa Cruz) are just super bright and that is why they are there. The stuff that they do in their dorm rooms now is the stuff that we will do in twenty years. They are way ahead of the curve. One such person was running an early model of a neuralnet. Although this neuralnet is an internalized computer network, it does not refer to networking computers together. It is a model of the human brain which includes holographic thinking. This is the way your brain actually works. This computer model served to analyze things with a computer program such as a human brain would do. The idea of this model stimulated Joe's own interest. He wanted to apply the geometry of the Sigilum Daemoth of John Dee to this model and take it out of a two-dimensional format and put it into a three-dimensional format. In one respect, this sigil is a series of interlocking concentric rings based upon Trithemius wheels — the very same wheels that are depicted in the movie *Stargate*. The stargate works with the interlocking rings that slide around. Joe wanted to look at the myriad variations or iterations of how the rings in the sigil could be configured. They discovered that the mathematical sequence that arises from one of the configurations perfectly describes the state of a wormhole.

When Joe shared his ideas about working with these ideas, the

Enochian people he knew were completely against it. Their reaction was so violent that he decided to work in complete silence with his computer hacker friend. As was suggested earlier, magical people generally believe that the Enochian calls will precipitate the Apocalypse and end of the universe.

After hearing Joe's story, I had to ask him what I thought was a very obvious question. Did he put all of this information into the Metamachine? Laughing, he gave me an affirmative yes. He also commented that this had never been made public before because of the hyper-reaction that would occur. As this information seemed so sensitive to various people, I asked him if it would be all right to comment on it. It did not matter anymore he said as it is long since done.

If Joe's research did not frighten others with the Apocalypse, it too often precipitated a lust for possession of the Metamachine as a vehicle to power. He also explained that none of these people who lusted after the Metamachine understood what he said because it is like a bucking bronco that requires a test pilot mentality. You have to know that you are likely to crash in the desert and have to know when to bail out. After his impromptu meeting with Emory Cranston in Chinatown at the Chinese-American Masonic Hall, Joe said that he shut the Metamachine down and it has been turned off ever since per has last statement to myself. There were, however, reported efforts to steal it and there was gripping drama around it all.

In the autumn of 2001, Joe said he was run off the road and down an embankment in a secluded area not too many miles from his home in Santa Cruz. Four guys punched him and roughed him up for a while. Leaving him by his car, the gang looked like they were making up their mind as to what to do with him. By good fortune and rather unusual circumstances, Joe just happened to have removed a gun from his house that day as he was unsure about the psychological stability of someone who lived in his home. Although he was not expecting trouble, he did not want the gun to be around his domicile unattended. As a result, it was on the floor of his car when he was apprehended. As his assailants muddled over Joe's immediate future and what they would do with him, he reached into his car, grabbed the gun and shot it over their heads. They promptly left, and he was able to escape, shaken but relatively unharmed. I did not hear from Joe for a couple of months after this episode. He went into seclusion, figured out what was going on and eventually found a new home. After his reemergence and several discussions, we both decided that it was reasonable to believe that this attack was likely generated by an obsessed fan who also had some affiliation with the Bohemian Grove.[*]

Long after sharing all of this information with me, Joe announced that he was going into seclusion. By all accounts and appearances, Joe had created one hell of an ingenious and extravagant paradigm that had come back to bite him. You could say that he had lit a fire underneath the ass-holes of the gargoyles, and they were not very happy.

---

[*] Ironically, John Dee's European tour was largely in Bohemia. The Bohemian Grove has never particularly been associated with John Dee's magick in most conspiratorial articles, but the very constructs of conspiracy's deepest architecture is based upon the distortion of John Dee's Enochian system of magick.

48

FALLOUT

If you take everything that has been said in the last chapter at face value, you will likely conclude that Joe Matheny possesses a screaming genius. You would not be incorrect in doing so. There have been, however, unfortunate circumstances which I would not even mention except for the fact that various public and private reports have forced me to address the issue. If I do not, people who have heard or read them will have unnecessary questions.

At the time of this writing, I have known Joe for three years. During that time period, I personally found Joe to be consistent in my personal dealings with him and also very generous, even to a fault. In a couple of instances where I lost money as a result of him referring me to associates of his, he more than made up the difference. I have no complaints about him, however, there have been some people who rail against him as if he were the worst sort of scoundrel, not unlike the vindictive wrath that is often invoked on Aleister Crowley. It is unwise to air out all of the personal details, but I can tell you that some of the complaints I heard or received about him were spiteful and amounted to slander as well as what could be considered criminal harassment. Although it is not my job to investigate these reports, much of what I saw seemed to be suspect. If someone has committed a crime or has a valid civil complaint against an individual, one should go to the legal authorities and have the person prosecuted or sued. Railing against Joe or anyone else is only a form of slander, particularly when no crime has been committed or cannot be prosecuted.

None of the above would be a big deal in itself except that as I was finishing the writing of this book, I began to receive more reports of a similar nature. While all of it is technically hearsay evidence and amounts to no legal proof of anything, I had no choice but to listen to it and just let it glide off my back. When I did not respond to these, I then received further reports that seemed to strike at the very heart of my relations with Joe. As all of it was based upon unverifiable cyber-talk, it is by its very nature highly questionable. The internet is not a highly intelligent medium. Whatever these reports were and whoever made them, there were a couple of common denominators. They all were open invitations to entice to me to either hate Joe or to take a stand against him. Second, they indicated there was a demonic side to him and indicated he was ready to strike out at me by declaring my research to be a hoax by reason of the fact that I gave credence to his research which was a hoax. While I cannot even begun to fathom who were all the interested parties in making these various reports, I can assuredly say one thing. There was most definitely a demon or two at work!

First and foremost, I should address the hoax aspect. Although this has already been brought up earlier in the text of this book, Joe has circulated the idea that the Ong's Hat tale was a hoax for years. It has already been discussed ad infinitum on the internet and is a very tired topic. One of the reasons Joe shared so much information with me on these matters was because I never took the story too literally. In other words, I understood that the most important aspect of the Incunabula Catalog and the Ong's Hat travel brochure was that they were both metaphors for learning. The Montauk Project is really no different. Both stories are based upon incredibly deep archetypal legends which shake the very foundations upon which creation is based.

There have been too many rabid fans out there who want both or either of the projects to be real and for us to hand them the gateways to time travel. These people are obsessive and are only frustrated by their own demons. Joe, quite understandably, found it quite necessary to take a long vacation from such drivel.

What is particularly interesting about both the legends of the Montauk Project and Ong's Hat is that although their genesis seems to rely primarily on myth, there are sometimes deeply disturbing synchronicities or ordinary facts that indicate that such projects might have occurred. The truth about parallel universes tells us that all eventualities and conceptions are real. The ultimate truth will be found in the quantum observer. The fact is that when you set about probing the source code of creation, you are going to, by default, be studying phenomena that is out of the ordinary. When you foster the idea of a "synchronicity attractor," as was so aptly explained in the Ong's Hat legend, you are creating a gate to further synchronicities. The logic of the matter becomes quite simple. If you were creating a forum or legend for such a device or endeavor, a "real" space-time or synchronicity project is going to seek and find out the artificial one because it most readily fits into the idea of a relational data base from another Metamachine on the metaplane.

Joe Matheny has spent well over a decade communicating the Ong's Hat legend. This has included countless dollars and long hard hours spent on art, design, graphics, computer programming, business administration, reading, networking, researching and many other endeavors which would reach far beyond the thinking patterns of ordinary armchair critics or disgruntled fans. One of Joe's reasons for purveying the information about Ong's Hat was that he felt younger people are generally not given an opportunity to study and learn esoteric information. By putting a "Trojan Horse" into the culture and transmuting the legend so that it would appeal to computer gamers, it would create a metaphor for learning that otherwise might never be conceived of or appreciated. Joe has vowed to receive no money from his Ong's Hat work and donates his royalties for the book to the Homeless Garden Project in Santa Cruz (in case you also want to donate, the address is PO Box 617, Santa Cruz, California, 95061).

I should also mention that, as soon as the *Incunabula Papers* and the Ong's Hat legend became a force to be reckoned with, there was an immediate and covert trick by the intelligence community to discredit anything associated with the word *Incunabula*. The word has been misused and misdefined by disinformation agents who are dead set against anything Joe or I have to say. You can also expect them to take the information herein, screw it around and give their own twisted versions of it. In such an environment of madness, I would readily join Joe in seclusion, but that, unfortunately, is not my destiny. All these parallel realities, even the false ones, will have their day in court, so to speak. There will always be comic absurdities in the stream of life, particularly when you are in the field I am in. It is best to just adopt a cheery mood and enjoy the entertainment.

There have also been statements indicating that the Metamachine does not and never existed and that Emory Cranston is a complete ruse as well. Most of what we know about these factors are from Joe himself. As for whether they are true or not, you will have to make up your own mind. Better yet, do not judge and just take in the information. They are metaphors for learning. Also, know this old truism.

> The dreamer awakes
> the tale is a lie
> yet ponder it well
> though the tale be a lie
> its teaching is truth

Earlier, I mentioned that various individuals were trying to unleash hatred in me. This is a very common trick of demons and one everyone should be wary of when they indulge in hatred. Also, if you find the subject matter in this book too upsetting and making you foment, you should take up different adventures. I am sure you can find other topics of interest that do not perplex you.

As for my personal relationship with Joe, I have to be quite honest. He was primarily courteous, fun, and very interesting. We shared many hilarious laughs, and he always encouraged my creativity. In fact, I do not remember ever having laughed so much than in my conversations with him. He brought more gifts to my life than most other people put together. This included his stories and information. Joe brought a considerable amount of joy into my life; and for that, I thank him profusely. Thus, if I were forced to judge him according to the precepts of the ancient Egyptians, I could not send him to the jackals. In all honesty, I would have to say the same for Preston Nichols, L. Ron Hubbard, and Marjorie Cameron. There is no question that I have had a propensity to work with beings who are highly controversial. When you consider that all of the above mentioned people deal or dealt with the energies of creation, it is highly understandable that they would be considered controversial. Studying milk toast professors or researchers are of minimal interest at best.

Perhaps those who are still perplexed by the controversy surrounding Joe might be served by learning of my most recent conversation with him. As I marvelled over some riveting esoteric information he shared with me, I could not help but tell him that he was like a daemon at the gateway. This was, however, not said in a disparaging or uncomplimentary tone. It was said as an observation of fact. "That's exactly what I am!" he said in response to my statement. It was as if I had measured some aspect of his exact nature with the quantum measuring tape, and he had received the license to depart. I have not spoken to him since. This in no way means that I consider him to be anything other than a human being. But, this last statement seems to fit in very well with the theme that you are already familiar with in this book. He was only mirroring my own perceptions.[*]

This book is about you opening up your own personalized version of the Seventh Seal. As I said in the *Guide to the Reader*, the bar has been set high, but it is not there for me to jump over. Someone has to open the portal for you or make you see it. This book only opens the Seventh Seal and gives you a reference point. What you do with it is your adventure. If you feel enlightened and that you have learned something, please realize that Joe Matheny was a major influence in developing the various themes that are about to unfold. He has done you a favor.

The dreamer is about to awaken.

---

[*] Just before this book went into publication, I received word from Joe on both business and personal matters. His communication was as congenial and as gentlemanly as ever. He has been doing some charity work and is enjoying his hiatus.

49

STARBUCKS

*THE FOLLOWING TRANSMISSION
IS FROM A PARALLEL UNIVERSE*

There is a dream technique called lucid dreaming whereby one trains oneself to become self-conscious in the dream state. If it can be maintained, this is a very powerful state of consciousness because you have your entire subconscious, as well as the collective unconscious, at your disposal. In other words, you can ask yourself any question you want in the dream state. The resources you have to draw upon are infinite and well beyond what is considered to be one's own personal imagination.

I once learned a technique from a friend that induces this self-aware state that is known as lucid dreaming. In your normal waking hours, you make a conscious decision to be self-aware every time that you see a clock. When you do, you then ask yourself three questions in succession: 1) What time is it? 2) Is this a dream? and 3) Can I fly?

The entire purpose of these questions is to ignite you into participating in the dream state. Although one can become self-aware in a dream, it does not mean that you have the entire predicament of existence licked. There is a push-pull phenomena that can occur. The collective, as well as your own personal unconscious, is a running stream of consciousness while you sleep. It is there whether you access it or not. Once you become aware in a dream, it can be like riding a roller coaster. In other words, you are not necessarily going to be able to exude your power even if you know it is only a dream. Sometimes you can buck up against elementals or forces that are impossible to stop; however, there is a tremendous amount of resources that you can draw upon. Only by waking up and coexisting with the dream state can you have any idea of how to go about this.

In my personal dreams, I have a tendency to become very excited when I become lucid. There is utter joy and tremendous enthusiasm. Unfortunately, in the past, I have had trouble in such a state by being distracted with erotic situations, something I do not get distracted with in real life. When I have avoided these situations in the dream state, it has led to major openings of the pineal gland. From this experience, it is easy to conclude that we are bound to this world by the very sexual energy which brought us here in the first place. Its residue is powerful and, in the dream state, it can act as a harness that keeps one from viewing the rest of creation. Although not all sexual situations in dreams are unenlightened, most of these in my experiences have been the handiwork of some form of demon trying to lure me away from becoming self-conscious in the dream state. After many years of trying to break through, I finally had a lucid dream that included all sorts of women behaving like succubus vacuum cleaners. This woke me up on a deep level and viscerally inspired me to avoid this tendency altogether. I was subsequently "awarded" with a lucid dream which was to prove quite revelatory and would consummate the completion of this book.

One night, I was driving home from Preston's house for the last time. He was just about to move from Long Island as the house he lived in for over fifty years was being torn down to make way for new construction. As I drove home, I mused about how much had been accomplished in the last decade with the publication of the Montauk books. As I looked at a Barnes and Noble sign on a big office building in Westbury, I realized I was almost home and that Preston was leaving Long Island but that I had not yet had a lucid dream. Almost as if by prescribed ritual, I looked at the digital clock in my car. The next thing I knew, I was lucid and shot through the window above my dashboard. I was now free and looking over the office building and an empty parkway. On the other side of the office building was a Starbucks coffee shop that was dimly lit. Here is where the push-pull factor came into play. I was no longer calling all the shots. Instead of going home, my car ended up going to Starbucks with me in it. I was once again in my human condition as I walked through the door of the coffee shop. There, sitting comfortably at a table, was Emory Cranston. He was drinking a cup of coffee that said "Java" on it, obviously suggesting the other-dimensional world of Java II as described in *Ong's Hat: The Beginning*. Emory was fiddling around with some strange looking leaves, some of which were laid out in a tea cup as if he was reading tea leaves. What I found somewhat disturbing about Emory was that he was completely nude except for the red fez he wore on his head.

"Emory, you're naked," I said. "You're not in pagan country now. You could get arrested if anyone complains."

"Sometimes, we are meant to get arrested," he replied, not seeming to be flustered at all. "Besides, there is a reason for it."

"I finally get past the temptresses of my dreams," I said, "and now I have to look at this. Not a pretty picture."

"Well," he replied calmly, "you still have some things to learn. You know why you're in a coffee shop don't you? It's to symbolize you waking up."

Looking at his leathery face and red fez, I could not help but notice that he looked like Boris Karloff from the original Universal movie entitled *The Mummy*.

"Emory, did anyone ever tell you that you look like Boris Karloff with that fez?"

"Why do you think I have these?" he said, pointing to the leaves on the table. "These are tanna leaves. They are the ways and means by which one can control the dead and what you so like to call the Well of Souls. I am going to give you a reading, but instead of using tea leaves, I am going to use these tanna leaves."

"Tanna leaves are only a creation of Hollywood. There is no such plant."

"Oh?," he said. "These leaves are real and they say that you have reached the last shadow."

"The last shadow! What is that supposed to mean?"

"That is me. I am the shadow that stands between the cave and the light of day. I am the dweller at the threshold as you pass from one world to another."

"Does that mean that if we all move on from this world that we're going to see Emory Cranston sightings at Burger King and the like?"

"Perhaps, but not likely," he answered, "but from this reading, I can see that you are going to have a little bit of trouble with this book."

"How is that?" I asked.

"There is only one reason, and the tanna leaves are saying it clearly. Although you have diffused the issue for the most part by saying what you have already said about my ephemeral nature, certain people are going to clamor about me being a fake character."

"Well," I said, "I don't really care. You're as fake as anything else walking around this universe."

"But," Emory said, "there is one other point they will make."

"What's that?" I asked.

"Some people will take apart my name and point out that it is an anagram for "CAMERON N STORY" and will suggest that you made my name up as a secret message on purpose so you would not have to use the "N" word or any other offensive word in that message. And further, that you are just exploiting disenfranchised people by writing about the oppression that has been done to them and tying it into fantastic theories about parallel universes."

"That is idiotic but to be expected," I replied. "Both subjects have been the sources of oppression. It is synchronous that they fit together. People should target the source of the oppression."

"Yes," said Emory, "but my name is also an anagram for something else."

"What's that, Emory?"

"SORRY META CONN. You have all been conned from the highest level of the metaplane."

At this point, the entire dream began to fade out. I then used another trick I had learned to use in the dream state. I looked at my hands and saw that they appeared to look as if they were under water. Why the hands appear this way, I cannot exactly tell you, but the purpose of this exercise is to prevent the dream from dissolving and it worked. Emory did not dissolve and the con was averted."

"Well," Emory said, "you've done pretty well to hold on to this dream. You got past the final door, but there's one thing I forgot to tell you."

At that point, we were interrupted by loud music, and neither one of us could help but notice one of the female staff in Starbucks who was approaching a table right next to us. Wearing a black and white maid's outfit, she jumped up on the table and started stripping as she danced. The more evocative and lustful she became, the more I looked away. I looked into Emory's eyes and forgot about her entirely. Finally, when it was clear I would not pay any attention to her, Emory pointed to a video monitor that looked like it was part of a security system. On the screen was the entire audience from the Magick Theater. They were all watching us and began clapping until the applause rose to a thundering ovation. There was no question they were pleased with my ability to not yield to temptation but, more importantly, that I was able to carry on with this dream which seemed to be getting very interesting.

As the ovation ended, I saw the woman get down off the table. She was still naked as she grabbed her maid's uniform and stomped off as a result of no one paying attention to her. As she marched off, she turned her head and looked back and gave an expression that reminded me of a gargoyle who had their feelings severely hurt. I felt bad for her but was not going to worry about her. This was too likely a demon begging for sympathy."

"What in the hell are they doing there?" I said to Emory as I pointed to the audience on the video monitor.

"They are there for a reason. Did you ever consider that you are being watched by the audience in the Magick Theater just as much as you are writing about them and creating them in your own mind?"

"Do you mean to suggest that you, Emory Cranston, as a character in my dream and also as a character in my book, can take on a personality of your own and do what you want within the context of the book that I am writing, or at least think that I am writing?"

"Exactly," he replied. "You and the audience might think that you are creating me as a character, but how do you all really know that I am not creating myself as a character in your minds or simply in my own mind?"

"You are talking about observer based quantum mechanics."

"Right again. In fact, by that measure, the audience who is reading this book is really no different. Each and everyone who reads this book is not only creating me as a character in this book but are creating you and your actions, thoughts, words and propositions. It is all observer based. So, in other words, the people reading this book are really creating what you are writing and all the characters as well. It was never Peter Moon's Magick Theater. It was their Magick Theater. They are doing all the work."

"Well, you've made some excellent points, Emory, but there is no way in hell that myself or the audience would have deliberately created you as a nude character."

"I've got my reasons," he said. "Apparently, someone else does, too."

At that point, the woman who had been nude had come back from the manager's office. She was now dressed like a very important female corporate executive and was in a complete rage as she yelled.

"You're damn right I've got my reasons. You're in the nude, Emory, and you are guilty of indecent exposure. I've called the police. And, you can take your damn quantum based reality and shove it up your ass!"

Before I could even think of the implicit contradiction in her, I heard loud sirens and saw that the Starbucks parking lot was now filled with many squad cars with their sirens blasting. This was overkill for a simple indecent exposure arrest.

"Quick, put this on," I said to Emory as I threw him a windbreaker. "They might not be so hard on you if you're wearing this. Wrap it around your waist."

As I walked out into the parking lot, the sirens had been turned off. There were about ten squads cars. They were all black and white except for one. Each of the black and whites had a large insignia on the door with a five-pointed star which read "Ong's Hat Police Force." This was very odd. In one of the cars, I saw Peter Lamborn Wilson behind the wheel. In another, I saw the hippie-physicist Nick Herbert getting out of a squad car. Apparently, he was going to make the arrest but looked funny in a police uniform. Also wearing police uniforms were Noble Drew Ali and Abel, one of the men who lived at the Ong's Hat ashram when he was a kid. I did not recognize any of the other drivers except for the one car that was pure white and had a different insignia that said "Time Travel Research Center." It was driven by David Anderson.

For a slight moment, all was quiet, and it seemed that everyone was looking at everybody else. Just then, there was a sputtering sound of an old jalopy that was bellowing out rank smoke from its underside and making knocks as if it had two and a half pistons. It was a sight to behold and everyone stopped to notice it. The side of the door had been painted sloppily in white and it said "OTO." There was a long banner hanging from the back of the vehicle which was designed to stream in the wind if the car could go fast enough. It was about six feet long and said, "We are the true OTO."

A frail transvestite emerged from the door and was in a rage.

"I was supposed to make this arrest!" he exclaimed. "I am here to make this arrest! Get out of my way, or I'll turn you all into god damned lizards!"

As if on cue, a familiar voice could be heard over the police radios. There were so many police radios on that it was quite loud. It was the voice of Ronald Wilson Reagan.

"Tell that little pip-squeak to remain quiet. We've got this arrest well in hand. If he doesn't stand down, the bombing will start in five minutes."

At this point, the gears of the unoccupied jalopy slipped and the engine went out of neutral mode. As the vehicle sputtered and lurched forward on its own, it fell down an embankment which, in the dream state, had suddenly turned into a steep ocean cliff. One of the Ong's Hat officers who I could not recognize came over and gave the transvestite a packet which included the proper translation of the John Dee materials. As the transvestite began to look at the materials, an old yellow Volkswagen bug drove up in front of him. It was empty.

"Oooh-neat!" said the transvestite. "Hitler designed this car."

The transvestite climbed in and drove away.

As Nick and an unidentified officer came forward to make the arrest, I realized they were not here to arrest Emory but me. I had now forgotten that I was in a dream. It was all too real. Emory was in the background as I was approached.

"There was one thing I did not get to finish telling you before we were interrupted," said Emory. "Another anagram of my name also is NYC MOON ARREST."

"Yes," I said, "but I don't live in New York City."

"You're damn close enough. Only about 20 minutes to the

border and you have to remember that most of the Ong's Hat crew here had to cross state lines to get you. As far as they're concerned, it is New York City. The operations file for this project states NYC MOON ARREST written with a big felt tipped marker."

There was no thought of resisting arrest. The unrecognized officer who approached me told me I was under arrest and that although I had the right to remain silent, he advised against it. When I asked him why I was being arrested, he told me that I lived in this universe. That is enough. He said it just happened to be my turn to get picked up. As he opened the back door to another squad car, he looked in at the driver and the two spoke.

"Should we cuff him?" he asked the driver.

"No. It'll be OK," I heard the driver say.

When I got in the squad car, I could see the driver's face. It was Joe Matheny.

"I won't be able to talk for a few minutes," he said.

I was too busy watching everything around me to be nervous or unsettled. I did not think about where I was going. The squad cars rapidly moved into a caravan with David Anderson of the Time Travel Research Center leading the way. As the caravan emerged on the Long Island Expressway going eastward, the other cars began to drop off until the only car left was the one that I was in. Joe drove faster and faster. I looked at the speedometer until he leveled off at 210 miles per hour. He put the cruise control on at 210, the number of Jack Parsons when he was in the OTO. Then, Joe looked back at me and politely spoke.

"What I'm about to do drives some people absolutely nuts. I hope that you'll have no problem with it."

He then pushed a button as a mirrored wall came up out of the seat in front of me. As I looked around, I saw that the side doors had no handles. There was no way of escape. He then pushed the controls for the power windows in the back. They were also mirrors on the inside of those windows. Turning around, I saw that the rear window was a mirror, too. As I contemplated my fate, Joe turned on the radio as Pink Floyd's "The Wall" began to play.

While listening to the music emanating from the front of the squad car, I began to look at myself in the mirror and concentrated at looking myself in the eyes. I realized I was in a version of the brass bottle where I had nothing to look at but myself and how I had gotten into this predicament. As I continued staring at myself, I heard Ronald Wilson Reagan's voice again over the police radio. "Mr. Gorbachev, tear down that wall!" I heard him say.

As I heard that and continued to stare, I could finally begin to move the energy in the dream. As I stared, the mirror in front of me began to dissolve, and I could see the front of the squad car. At that point, I could see the digital clock on the front panel of the car. I became lucid again and remembered the trick of looking down at my hands. Once again, they gave the appearance of being under water and it maintained my lucidity. I sat back and watched as the squad car now appeared to be a sport utility vehicle. We reached the end of Montauk Highway as Joe pulled the vehicle around the rocks and drove along the beach until we were exactly in front of Turtle Hill at Montauk Point. The Montauk Lighthouse sits atop Turtle Hill, and we were at the foot of it right near the water. All things considered, I realized my lucidity must have been working because there was no place I would rather have been. In real life, this area houses a mine shaft that is so huge one could drive a truck or a tank through it. I saw it many times but never photographed it because it did not dawn on me that it was a passage way to the underground. I only realized this years later when I saw a picture of the shaft as it existed decades ago. Consequently, I never photographed it, but several people have witnessed it. It was covered with rocks many years ago because there is an erosion problem at Montauk Point. In my dream, I was delighted that the shaft was now empty, and I could investigate. There was no place I would rather be in a dream state.

As I excitedly told Joe about the shaft, he opened the back door from the outside to let me out. He then spoke.

"Well, you got through the magick mirror test, but I'm not going any further. I can't stand this place. Oh, by the way, you just might need this," he said as he reached over and grabbed a large narwhal tusk that had washed ashore on the beach.

After taking the narwhal tusk, which is really a misnomer for the over developed spiral tooth of the narwhal, I said good-bye to Joe and then turned my gaze to the moon as I enjoyed the natural beauty of Montauk Point. On certain nights, the stars are clear, and it is one of the most beautiful spots you can imagine. Next, I took a look at the mine shaft which I soon realized was built around and through an old cave. This must have been the locale where, hundreds of years ago, history said an old Montauk Native American woman had been living in a cave with her child.

Entering the shaft, I went down a series of steps that were off to the side. As I continued, there was a pathway which was well manicured and had signs posted with arrows. As things became continuously more civilized, I realized I was following the queue for what seemed to be an amusement park ride. Eventually, I came upon what appeared to be exactly that. There were small pirate boats in a dock-like setting with a false and beautiful sky. There was a sign which said, "Captain's Kidd's Montauk Adventure." I had always joked that New York State could make a fortune by turning Camp Hero's underground into a time travel theme park. Now, I was getting a dose of my own medicine.

50

PIRATES' END

*THE FOLLOWING TRANSMISSION
IS FROM A PARALLEL UNIVERSE*

There were no people anywhere near or around this adventure ride. There was only an aethyric form of Captain Kidd who motioned me to get in a boat which was named "Pirate's End." As the boat began to move in the water and do the standard amusement park ride stuff, I realized that I wanted to hear Captain Kidd tell me the true story of what happened to him. He began a narration as we went through the ups and downs and water splashes.

"I was the last pirate you know. See, look there!"

We came upon the hanging scene of Captain Kidd on the Thames River.

"It is true. I was hung three times before I died, and they left my tarred body hanging to ward off future pirates. This, in effect, ended all piracy for practical purposes in European culture. I was quite innocent for what they convicted me of, but I was very guilty of other misdeeds. I only realized this after my death."

We now approached a diorama with King William of Orange giving him his sealed orders.

"I sailed under secret orders. All ship captains sailed under some secret orders. Most historians do not even know that I was briefed personally by King William, but they all know I was ordered to commit piracy for him and the East India Company. My trouble began with my association with the House of Orange. I was one of the most respected and successful businessmen of New Amsterdam, and no one has yet to figure out why I left a cushy life to become a pirate. Well, I not only was the last pirate, I was assigned the most prestigious mission of the secret Orange-Cameron line. My job was to raid what remained of the Moorish ships that went to Mecca. Elihu Yale, of the East India Company, had set up headquarters in Indonesia. After Java and other Moorish strongholds had been taken, he looked for Moorish artifacts including the legendary treasure of the Seventh Seal.

"At the same time, the East India Company began a dope program that made Hassan Sabbah appear pallid by comparison. It seems they wanted to blame everything on the Muslims."

"But," I interrupted. "What exactly is the House of Orange? I do know that they honor the female by having matriarchal heirs to the throne."

"They are a strange admixture of everything, but sometimes, it is best to look at the etymology — you know that already."

"Where does the word orange come from?" I asked.

"Orange is *naranja* in Spanish which really comes from the Persian and Sanskrit. The prefix *nar* also means to sleep as in narcosis or narcotic. But, to really understand *orange* or *naranja*, we have to look at the ancient myth of Narcissus. He fell in love with himself by looking at his reflection in the water. In psychology, *narcissism* is an infantile stage of development whereby one has not arrested one's own libido. This is the same thing you experienced in the sleep state. On an astral level, which is different than real life, you could only feel the libido. The sexual chakra is orange. It rules the unconscious impulses, including sleep. The unconscious is imbedded in sleeping sexual energy. Narcissus rebuffed all the nymphs, but they all pined for him. In his case, he needed to wake up to other people, but he slept. On the very spot that he slept and died, the orange narcissus flower took root."

"How does this all fit in with House of Orange and you?"

"Well," said the ghost of Captain Kidd, "orange is the symbol of the sleeping unconscious and all that is dormant and obscured by our own ignorance of unconscious sexual impulses in the collective unconscious as well as our own. The House of Orange was merely acting out these unconscious impulses. These very impulses set up the racket that the Chinese eventually rebelled against and fought in the Opium Wars. The House of Orange tried to control the world and obtain its most sacred treasures. It was the ancient pirate treasure of Golgotha that I was commissioned to find and pirate from the Muslims. The entire East India Company was set up to further this goal. Supreme conquest of the world, or *Rule Britannia*, meant possession of all treasure, including that.

Noticing that I could still maintain my continuity in this dream state, I turned to the side and addressed Captain Kidd.

"What in the hell are you really doing in this dream? I know that Captain Kidd's Money Pond is just north of the lighthouse at Montauk, but what do you really have to do with all this?"

"I," said Kidd, "am a ghost. I will not let you go until I have said my piece. You are interested in space-time projects. Well, I am the only one who can connect the three space-time projects you know: Solomon's Temple, Montauk and Ong's Hat."

"Please explain," I said.

As we gyrated and moved about the roller coaster tracks, things moved slowly so Kidd could talk.

"Your main problem is that there is a police effort between dimensions. If there was not, there would be an open and free confluence of energies buzzing back and forth."

"Well," I replied. "One could argue that there is a lot of dimensional communication going back and forth, especially these days with all the nut jobs that channel and so on."

"But," said Kidd, "I am talking about continuity. A continuous reference frame that stands up to inspection. A portal that can be created and recreated at will."

At that, the vehicle slowed down as we passed an orange tree where a holographic version of the Virgin Mary was picking oranges that were guarded by a blind man.

"This famous and legendary depiction of the Virgin is a subtle and indirect reference of positioning Mary with orange, the color of the fertility chakra. According to Sicilian legend, which goes back to the time of Jolly Roger, she picked three oranges whereupon the blind man recovered his sight. After distributing the other two, she kept one for herself. Since then, people in Sicily decorate the icon of the Madonna with blossoming orange tree stems while newlyweds in Sardinia go to their new home on a buffalo whose horns have been decorated with oranges."

The amusement park ride then banked and did a hard loop as we sped through the cavernous rocks of the Montauk underground towards a large vesica pisces in the distance. As we came closer, the portal looked more and more like a woman's vagina. Captain Kidd then whispered into my ear.

"We are entering the womb of the Holy Madonna."

Our speed was accelerated as we shot into the portal in what amounted to a well-crafted amusement park mockery of sexual fertilization. We passed briefly through a cavernous region that looked like a cathedral where a lone white dove could be seen flying beneath vaulted arches. Passing through that area we soon found ourselves floating on a narrow river through a most beautiful array of orange trees that were in full blossom.

"You know," said Captain Kidd, "orange trees were brought to our western world and proliferated by the Saracens. Ever since the Crusades, brides have had wreaths of orange blossoms, but it was the Saracens who introduced us to this tradition. They wore them as a symbol of fertility. Did you know a single orange tree can yield over four thousand oranges in a year? No other tree is more fruitful."

"Who is that?" I asked as I noticed an oriental woman walking towards me amongst the trees. She wore only a lei and a wrap of orange blossoms.

"That is Quon Yin," he said.

As we came near Quon Yin, she came to our boat and spoke.

"I am the goddess of mercy and compassion. I hear the cries of all beings and am known as the mother of a thousand Buddhas, but I am also the source of all. The legend of Mary and the orange tree was invented by the Saracens based upon stories about me. When Mary heals the sight of the blind man with an orange, she is restoring the vision of Man. It is no different than the third eye. I also created an eye for my father so that he could see. You can read the legends about that. I have vowed to remain in the earthly realms until all living things have completed their enlightenment and become liberated from the pain of birth, death and rebirth."

"She is the embodiment of the compassion you found missing in the Enochian angels," said Captain Kidd. "The Saracens honored her and secretly derived their name from her. Long ago she was known as Sara and the land of Serendip was named after her. The name Sara appears again in the occult tradition of Mary Magdalene's daughter who also had this name. That is a legend carried forward by the Saracens. The oranges are the tradition of the fertility goddess and the rebirth of compassion and love."

"Those orange blossoms on her look beautiful," I said.

"Oranges comes from China, you know," he said. "But, they are best known for their Mandarin oranges."

"Those are what we call tangerines," I said. "Same damn thing, except everyone makes a bigger fuss if you call them Mandarin oranges."

"Technically, the tangerine is more sacred than the orange because it explains even more if you indulge in hyper-thinking. It all comes down to the tangerine, Tangier, Tanis, tang, tanna.

"What do you mean?" I asked.

"Well, tangerines and oranges are not the only fruits that are orange," replied Kidd, "but they are certainly the primary ones and sum up that color and its entire interaction with the matrix, a word which really means 'mother.' The orange is sacred. It is the fundamental principle by which everything in this universe has passed through the portal, so to speak. We are talking about passing through the birth womb here. It is an inescapable truth. Passing through the portal of birth, life, and death is symbolic of the collective trauma of this entire universe. We all experience this trauma unless we have been cleared of it. To reconfigure the hard drive of this universe, we need to come to terms with this trauma. It is the perverting of the sacred which we suffer from. This is what makes a cruel world, and I was hung three times by that cruelty."

"Why exactly were you hung anyway?"

"It is true that I carried the pirate flag to end all pirate flags. Many of the pirate flags sported hour glasses, the measurement of time or the quantum universe, but I carried the shin bones under the skull of Golgotha. I never used it though. My troubles were a combination of my affiliations with the House of Orange, the East India Company, and my own genetic predisposition."

"The name Kidd doesn't help either," I said. "It is suggestive of a sacrificial goat."

"Yes," he agreed, "and also the dual nature of Baphomet. I actually came from a Templar family in Scotland. But, in many ways, my trouble began with this."

Kidd then showed me a ring he sported on his left hand which was exactly as that described by John Dee in his scrying sessions with Edward Talbot Kelly.

"It was given to my ancestor Thomas Kydd by John Dee and it has served as a curse on our family ever since. The word 'PELE' has been defined as 'he who will work wonders.' "

"It also suggests Pele, the Hawaiian volcano goddess," I added.

"Yes," he said, "and it also refers to black fire or establishing one's will. This is referred to as the black fire."

"What does the 'VL' in the middle stand for?" I asked him.

"It means 'the hidden one' or connecting one's will to the hidden one."

"You know," I said, "that the hidden one also refers to the hidden name for the Egyptian Amon-Ra which is Mon?"

"Yes," I know, "that is why we are both here at Montauk. The Montauk Project and everything it represents is hidden. It represents the supreme occult force in the universes. As a Templar and as a pirate, I ran afoul of this hidden force as my will was not aligned with it."

"It is all about recognizing the adversary on both a personal and collective basis and dealing with it," I interjected.

"Yes," Kidd continued, "and the power of this ring is supposed to represent the power of King Solomon. But, there is too little Quon Yin in that scheme for my liking. I have only realized that since my death. My own lust for treasure was insatiable, yet I had the supreme secrets of the Templars in my possession, and I knew it not.

"My other troubles had to do with the House of Orange who had appropriated their name from the sacred tradition of the orange you have just learned. Orange is the portal of power. The very name was usurped by the nobility of Europe. I myself was a subject of William of Orange."

At this point, the amusement boat we were in turned and spun around a sharp corner before we came upon a hologram of Queen Elizabeth sealing a document that created the East India Company. I was surprised to see that the flag of the East India Company had exactly the same thirteen stripes and blue field as the stars and stripes of the United States. As the boat slowed down, Kidd spoke once again.

"That is the flag of 'the Company'" he said. "Although the apparent political control of your country changed during the revolution, the underlying magical current did not. The East India Company still rules your world today. And, your country, unknown to its common citizens, is using a newly stylized rendition of the Company's flag. Whenever you poor blokes pay homage to your flag and sing the *Star Spangled Banner*, you are also paying occult tribute to the East India Company which was incorporated by Queen Elizabeth with John Dee standing in the shadows. The Company still utilizes the Isle of Dogs to this very day for their vast fleet. They created a fortune in importing and marketing tea from the Orient as they established the Crown Colonies of Singapore and Hong Kong and literally ran India. To protect their shipping interests, they maintained their own navy plus the British Navy. It was not just a commercial enterprise, however. When John Dee formulated the motto 'Rule Britannia,' the Anglish, if you will, took it upon themselves to control the entire matrix of this universe and all who would pass in or out of it. Did you ever wonder why CIA people always refer to their organization as 'the Company?' The whole infrastructure of the United States is a series of layers set up to maintain the continuity of the old empire. That is why you have the suppression of information in government. It is that simple — Dee's program gone awry with the missing element of compassion except when compassion serves political ends.

"Elihu Yale, the sponsor of Yale University, was the most powerful man in the East India Company when he scoured the Far East in search of many obscure legends that were not so obscure in those days. Contrary to the belief of some, I did not travel to Skull Island and encounter King Kong, but the Lemurian temple ruins I was believed to have discovered were really those associated with those of Hurqalya or East Java. Yale sent out expeditions and retrieved at least two meditation eggs that were in the treasure I intercepted in my raids. These eggs were shadows of the two eggs once held by the Barbarossas, or perhaps their eggs were shadows of these. It depends on your perspective. A shadow egg, placed in the vicinity of the crystal egg, created two electromagnetic fields that, when amplified and interacted, formed a vesica pisces or portal between two worlds. Dee only had one egg so it was a weak connection he had. Nevertheless, it was an extremely powerful witness and gated in a shadow which has ruled your world to this very day. I had no full idea of what I transported in my journeys until I actually reached the death state. My life ended up being such a complete sacrifice that it was somehow justified that I should be the keeper of this knowledge."

"But," I said, "the East India Company is mostly known for its flagrant importing of opium to China. This initiated the Boxer Rebellion by the Chinese who were aghast over what the British were doing to their population."

"And all for profit," added Kidd. "The Dutch East India Company, sponsored by the House of Orange, grew the opium in India and sold it to the British East India Company who imported it via Hong Kong and Singapore. But, the East India Company did not just sell dope. They did mind experiments with the dope and made the most clinical observations imaginable. In addition to this, they were engaged in exotic explorations, particularly with reference to the sacred debris Elihu Yale had turned up in Java."

"Do you mean to say that they were doing the same type of truth serum interrogation that Carl Allen referred to in his letters to Dr. Jessup about the Philadelphia Experiment?" I asked.

"Exactly. The East India Company manifested itself out of the conjurations of John Dee who was being worked by the shadow side. So, it was really no accident that Yale, who worked for the Company, came upon the shadow eggs. It was as if the eggs were trying to find each other."

"Yes, I said, but there had to be a fourth egg," I said.

"That is the egg of the younger Barbarossa brother. That ended up in Tangier, but we'll get back to that later."

After a few more twists and turns, the amusement boat settled down as we emerged to a scape where we were in the water-filled ruins of the Lemurian ruins of Java. There were beautiful tangerine trees occasionally sprouting from the land that had covered various ruins. Far off on the banks were other tangerine trees.

"The opium dens became a conduit to the other world by denigrating the sacred sexual energy and using it as a vehicle to power. In this regard, the House of Orange and the color it represented became a talisman of power when it was really just a principle of fertilization and seeing between worlds. Of course, seeing between worlds is very powerful."

"So, that is why the name Orange became a noble designation?" I asked.

"Yes, and the tangerine is not far behind, but it's namesake is really more sacred and secret. Tracing back the legacy and etymology of the tangerine reveals a motherload of information, particularly in relation to the legacy of Ong's Hat."

"How so?" I asked.

"The city or international port of Tangier got its name from the tangerines that were exported to England. Tangerines themselves came from the Orient. Only the Saracens, on their voyages from Java to Serendip and to the west, brought them to the Mediterranean. Along with the path of the tangerine was carried not only wisdom of a long lost legacy but a representation of the most powerful energy in the universe. You have heard of the tangram?"

"What exactly is that?" I asked.

"It is an old Chinese puzzle which is basically a square divided into seven pieces. One shape is a parallelogram and the others are triangles. Out of these shapes, you can make any sort of figure you want including script languages like cuneiform. It was said that the British opium traders picked this up from the Chinese Tanka girls. The Tanka people were relegated to a slave relationship with the East India patriarchs, and the girls were relegated to being called whores, but the tradition behind this is very long and rich. Like all great things, it is eventually reduced to a degraded mockery.

"Long ago, the ancestors of the Tanka girls, who preceded the T'ang Dynasty many millennia ago, used the tangram as a dimensional education tool. These were temple goddesses upon which the modern geisha is only somewhat based. They studied and taught an arcane system whereby these seven tans — the sevens pieces of the square were called tans — could be duplicated and made to create a representation of the Tree of Life. But, we are talking about a three-dimensional representation of the Tree, not a two-dimensional one. This glyph could be meditated upon, but it was activated through the use of spheres or eggs. These eggs represent the various spheres of the sephiroth of the Tree of Life. The sexual energies, as employed by the priestesses, caused a transfer of consciousness between worlds."

"Like in an orgone state as defined by Wilhelm Reich?"

"Yes, and the tangerine represents this once again. The very word tangerine can be seen in Latin where it is *tangere* which means 'to touch.' And, this is where we get the word *tangible*. A tangerine was thus defined because it is so easy to peel."

At this point, Captain Kidd raised his hand and showed me the ring of John Dee which had the word "PELE" on it, but it also spells "PEEL" if you read it right to left. He smiled.

"The tangerine is very amenable to touch and is waiting to be peeled. This is no different than the true nature of the feminine. The Goddess Kali or Pele are generally portrayed as fierce and fiery goddesses who will frighten and intimidate anyone trying to destroy them or their ways. This is why so many Christians are afraid of Babalon. But, if you gently peel the outside, you will find a succulent fruit inside who one can feed upon and multiply with.

"Additionally, the word *tangible* refers to the cusp of where spirit becomes physical. Only when something can be interpreted in a physically practical manner is it said to be tangible.

"The Tanka girls lived in groups or houses called Tangs. It is from these that the vulgar word *poontang* found its way into your culture. At the peak of its existence, the Tang served as a bridge to the metaplane and pure uninfiltrated sexual energy of the Goddess enabled one to see past the veil and pierce the dimensional shield. The tangram was a prop that could be worked into a dimensional memory. When Ralph Abraham said the geometries had intentions, he was not kidding. The geometry of the womb suggests birth and a portal between the world of the dead and the world of the living. Extrapolated and applied, this can go in many directions and into infinite universes. This is why the Gaelic word *tanaiste* literally means "parallel or second." There is also the Celtic word *tani-hessio* which means "one who is waited for."

"That speaks for itself," I said.

"Yes. By the time the East India Company made its supreme presence felt in the Orient, the Tangs had long since degenerated from their most pristine state. Some were whore houses but all still retained a thread of their innermost sacred secret. They contained or represented the seed by which one could escape, transmute, or transcend from this world. In this respect, they were harboring the Tao and the Tangs still retained their place as the traditional spiritual center of all communities. But, by the time of the East India Company, it was only a fragment of what it had been and the spiritual role was hidden. As the oppression occurred, the Tang became a centralized but secret center of rebellion. The employees of the Company were ingratiated sexually to learn their secrets. Secrets societies like the Black Dragon Society became aligned with the Tangs because they came to fight off the evil of the British. This escalated on both sides until you had a full scale dramatization in World War II. You had the secret societies of the Orient aligning with Germany who believed they were fighting evil. At the same time, you had the Allies believing they were doing the same thing. This is a great tool of evil: get two or more different cultures fighting the evil in their opponents. That way, both sides lose and evil wins even though it was the target in the first place. Just look at the relationship between the Company and the old Nazi power structure after World War II."

"To this day, Tangs are the last bastion of resistance against the empire. They were the only place to turn for the American Chinese who suffered more discrimination than is imaginable. The Tangs became affiliated with the Freemasons and that is why you had Emory Cranston showing up at the Chinese-American Masonic Hall in San Francisco. It is also why Drew Ali was so insistent on declaring all of his Asian brothers as being eligible for membership in the Moorish Science Temple. This is a long, rich and secret tradition. But, even at their best, the Tangs are only a remnant mockery of what was once a Camelot existence."

"Better a memory than nothing at all," I said.

"Yes, but they did continue on in secrecy which was really just a corruption of the ancient tantric rites. This involved sex coupled with intoxication received through tanna leaves."

"Do you mean the tanna leaves from Karloff's movie *The Mummy*?" I asked.

"Exactly, but that is misconstrued. *Tanna* is an Aramaic word for "teacher" and was used in the first two centuries after Christ (incidentally, the same time that Phil Dick designated true Christianity as being a true message from a higher plane or dimension). The Hebrew scholars eventually called the successors of the Tannaim priesthood Amoraim. That word is not much different than love or the sexual aspect of the Tang.

"But, Tanna is also an island in the South Pacific where the most potent brew of kava leaves are made. Kava is the most powerful hallucinogenic known to man. The word java signifies coffee from the jungles of Java, but it is also a synonym for the heaviest dose of kava or tanna. When you ask about tanna leaves, there are no references to what you saw in the movie other than Hollywood screenwriters. But, these potent kava or java leaves are the real tanna leaves. They give the power to communicate with the dead and to access the metaplane. Of course, this is a degenerate conduit to the metaplane but still a very potent one. Kava was a mysterious source of power and plays a large role in opening the portal from Java II to Ong's Hat and the like."

"Do you mean to say that the Ong's Hat crowd are just a bunch of drug junkies who smoked their way into a parallel universe paradigm that grew upon itself and interacted with other reference frames such as the Metamachine?"

"It is not quite that simple, but the drug aspect cannot be discounted or underestimated. Captain Cook is believed to have been the first European to note the properties of this drug, but it was known by others before him. A Spanish explorer by the name of Mendana deliberately obscured the reporting of Tanna island as well as several others. He claimed to have discovered gold near Tanna in what are now the Solomon Islands, but no one could find these islands for years because of his deceitful maps. The main point here is that the source of this portal-shaping force desired to remain hidden. All of these characters were being worked by the shadow side. That is why Emory is such a perfect fit to everything.

"The isle of Tanna has many bizarre traditions. It has long been believed to be a conduit from a parallel world and is known for the sightings of John Frum, an American G.I. who the natives believe is the son of God who appeared in the 1930's. The cover story is that he will bring modern goods to the people on Tanna and serve as a messiah who will return the people back to their traditional ways. There is also an active volcano on Tanna which is where the original name for Pele is derived, but the only apparent evidence of that is their large city named Pelua. The volcano is considered to be the root power of the powerful tanna leaves.

"Although Tanna and the leaves from the island are most powerful, the leaves themselves were taken to another spot which is right near the equator and was once the center point of all Oceanic civilization. Here, right at the equator, rituals were performed under the influence of the thick tanna brew. This is the most potent spot in the South Pacific and is just north of the Solomon Islands. It is a series of islands or atolls which are known on the map as Ongtong Java."

"Wait! You're kidding, right? It is really named Ongtong Java?"

"Yes," said Captain Kidd. "Real in your dream world and also real on the map. Check it out if you do not believe me. It is an area of great magic and was at one time owned by Kaiser Wilhelm, an occultist who sought the magic eggs. Adroitly deceived by the locals, he was convinced there was nothing there and placidly returned Ongtong Java to the British. Following legends, Kaiser Wilhelm turned his efforts to Montauk Point and constructed catacombs there."

"What is all this about?" I asked. "And, where did the name Ongtong Java come from?"

"Well," said Captain Kidd, "it was the explorers Tasman and Vischer who named Ongtong Java. This name was based upon the great magic of the tang, the java and the mysterious and secret name for God in the Orient: Ong. Ongtong Java got its name as it designated what all the sea captains were looking for. Tasman also discovered Tasmania, but it ironically was Vischer who was credited with the first European name for Montauk Point which was called Vischer's Hook, in honor of the Dutch explorer."

"Interesting," I said, "but what about the eggs?"

"The eggs and their shadow counterparts were the subject of much secret intrigue. I ended up with three, but even so, these were not the only eggs in existence. But, they were some of the popular ones of legend."

"How did you end up with three of the eggs?"

"Well," he said, "the egg or crystal ball in the British Museum is not the real egg. There was plenty of duplicity by the 007 crowd. Originally, there were four eggs. Two came from Java and two were in the Holy Land. Dee's egg was one of the latter, and I received this with the ring that was passed down via my Templar family from Thomas Kydd. The other egg from the Holy Land ended up the in possession of the younger Barbarossa brother, and I believe that was discussed some earlier in your text, but now I will tell you of its strange and mysterious fate.

411

"In 1492, a Berber Queen returned from Andalusia and settled on the northern peninsula of Morocco where she joined forces with the surviving Barbarossa brother and became known as Queen of the Pirates. Her name was Sayyida Al-Hurra, and she eventually married the King of Morocco, but only on her terms. She was not only the last of the Pirate Queens but a truly free woman. The younger Barbarossa honored her by passing on the remaining egg that he had. A century or so later, it became the focal point of power in the labyrinthine casbah of Tangier."

"Tangier," I said, "now we are back to the oranges and tangerines."

"Yes, but that city was always an international city and at once even a pirate city. Tangier was also named after Tanit, the Goddess of Egypt. She is sacred to that city and the root of *tan* should not go unnoticed. The egg in Tangier was stolen and eventually acquired by Colonel William Smith, the British Governor of Tangier, and a relative of the famous John Smith.

"Once Smith had acquired the egg, he headed for the coast of North America with an entourage of Englishmen and Moorish brides who were determined to carry on their own traditions even if in a hidden form. He brought his entourage to an enclave of Moors and English who had already settled there and called the island Tangier Island after the ancient traditions I have just described. After this, Colonel Smith became known as William Tangier Smith ever since and only with reference to his governorship in Africa. He did not stay on Tangier Island, which is now in Maryland, but moved to Long Island where he settled in the town of Brookhaven. The name "Tangier Smith" is a very prestigious name on Long Island to this very day. Along with the Gardiners and other rich families of Dutch and English heritage, they enjoyed a separate status of nobility. The laws of the people were legally made only for the commoners and not for them. It was a true ruling class, but their role was never particularly defined in the legal system. That is just the noble way.

"Tangier Island was visited by Sir Francis Drake and also by myself as it was the closest thing to a pirate colony along the eastern seaboard. To this day, the natives of Tangier Island still speak with a British accent and have a strange way of saying the opposite of what they mean. If they say "good-bye" it means "hello." This is a subconscious rejection of the conquering culture of the past.

"After Tangier Smith acquired the egg, the Company abandoned Tangier and all interest in it. But, Colonel Tangier Smith, as he now insisted upon being called, realized his only hope of attaining the full alchemical power of the egg rested in tapping the religion of the indigenous culture which was known to have originated in Egypt at one time. The egg ended up buried underneath the pyramids at Montauk Point.

"Later, I buried one of my shadow eggs near what is now called Captain Kidd's Money Pond. This is exactly why Aleister Crowley came to Montauk Point after the Ahlamantra Working where he was told that 'it is all in the egg.' Although he did not publicize it, he had learned the legends of the eggs in Cefalu, traced their history and eventually sought one at Montauk, but he did not know of the shadow egg I had placed there."

"What did you do with the other shadow egg?" I asked.

"After visiting Tangier Island myself, the Moorish gypsy ladies insisted I travel north to what was later named Little Egg Harbor where I would find my true love. They were right, but I think they had another motive. I fell in love with Amanda Smith and gave her the other egg. This was a mistake perhaps, but I vowed to return to her. As my named had been badly slandered, and I was wanted by the Crown, I thought it would be a simple matter to return to the authorities and clear my name. I did not know that I was intended to be a sacrifice. I purposely separated the eggs because it was symbolic of my separation from Amanda. If we couldn't be together, then the eggs couldn't be together. Trying to clear my name was a tragic mistake. Amanda lived not far from Little Egg Harbor in the town of Ong's Hat, New Jersey."

"What is the implication of one egg being at Montauk Point and one being at Ong's Hat?"

"Well, I was historically at both places, even in your universe. I have called the eggs from Java 'shadow eggs,' but I learned that the original eggs from the Golgotha treasure were not much different. Any of these eggs have polarities which change from time to time. When in the presence of another egg, and when these polarities are opposite and interacting, it creates a portal. The egg is the basic shape of the universe and serves as the perfect witness for a microcosm of the universe. When the fields of the two eggs are in proximity, you get a portal. This was the great secret. Of course, what you do with a portal when you finally get it is another story. Both Montauk and Ong's Hat suffered tragic endings."

"Yes," I said, "but were they actually using these same eggs?"

"It doesn't really matter. Did you ever wonder why I came into your consciousness? I am the actual historical link to both geographical areas. I travelled to Ong's Hat and to Montauk Point but did it by way of the Saracen trade routes which ran from Java to Tangier to Tangier Island in Maryland. Just like Lion Gardiner, I was a Templar and was partners with King William of Orange. The culture was very messed up in those days. I tried to play both sides but inherited too much power and ended up as the sacrifice.

"As for you, the eggs all possess resonant fields that attract each other. They really are the supreme synchronicity attractor and will go to any lengths to find each other. You yourself have gotten caught in the tidal pull, and this is what has caused you to be attracted to both Montauk Point and Ong's Hat."

"But why?" I asked. "I never had any of the eggs."

"Perhaps. Perhaps not. But, you have sought the Unified Field and have unwittingly interacted with the resonant field of the eggs. More importantly, you have tuned into their frequency. The eggs are the most loaded Unified Field applicators you could imagine. You have no idea how much work goes into jamming them. Keeping the brain ignorant and jammed with frequencies goes a long way."

"So, Captain Kidd, you are basically saying that no matter how long, no matter by which convoluted route, the eggs will unify?"

"And you can tell the story!"

As soon he finished, the vehicle we were in took a steep drop which was followed by another steep drop. We then passed through a long tunnel as the amusement park ride was coming to completion. Finally, we came to a disembarking dock far beneath the Montauk underground.

"Now," said Captain Kidd, "We are going to wrap this up. Come this way."

51

SPEAKING
FROM THE CHAIR

*THE FOLLOWING TRANSMISSION
IS FROM A PARALLEL UNIVERSE*

Once we were in the facilities of the Montauk underground, Captain Kidd took me through a corridor which seemed totally sound proof. The walls and doors were papered with cut-up information from various newspapers, most of which made no sense whatsoever. The only thing I noticed that made any sense at all was a headline from Ronald Reagan's days in office which read, "Mr. Gorbachev, Tear Down That Wall."

Once we were at the end of the corridor, Kidd opened a door and we entered an incredibly dark room save for a single pink light bulb which was burning over a huge Delta-T antenna construction. A massive amount of cabling was attached to it and led upwards. I readily realized this must be at least one version of the Delta-T transmitter setup that Montauk was famous for. Inside of the Delta-T, sitting in a lounge chair, was none other than a naked Emory Cranston.

"Well," said Emory. "You made it this far — arrested and brought to the chair. Welcome!"

As Captain Kidd flicked a switch, an entire wall of video monitors appeared, each with a different time scape. I noticed that there were forty-nine different screens put together in a square, all of which seemed related to the various themes in this book. One

415

screen even represented a current recording of what we were doing at that exact moment.

"You know," said Emory, "you could tell your story by beginning with this incident and telling what is on each of the monitors as a separate short story."

"I suspect," said Captain Kidd, "that he will take all of the information that he written about Montauk, as well as the Ong's Hat website and Incunabula Catalog, and do a cut-up on that."

"If he doesn't intend to do so," said Emory, "I have taken some actions to ensure that it would be easy for him to do."

Emory then handed me a huge bucketload of paper information which he said included everything written about those subjects. On top of it was a Zip disk which he said could be inserted into a regular computer or the Metamachine itself. He was only trying to facilitate me, he said.

"So, Emory," I said, "I guess this explains why I had to put up with you appearing naked at Starbucks."

"Yes," he said, "Duncan was always said to be naked in the chair when he was engaged in time transmissions. He was accessing the metaplane. Unfortunately, however, every other ass hole or spirit demon out there saw that as an opportunity or conduit to enter the physical world. Actually, it created quite a problem. It not only attracted flies like honey, but it proved to be a tremendous overload on everyone as many of those demons ended up literally sticking to the radar dish at Montauk. Their residue can still be felt there today, but they have also entered the Earth plane and act not unlike a computer virus.

"In the beginning, even though the Montauk experiments were secret, they were not necessarily as dark as everyone thinks. But, when you open up a portal, it creates a cacophony. It was like the California Gold Rush. Everyone goes to California but hardly anyone strikes it rich. Sutter's Fort is overrun by wanna-be carpetbaggers, Sutter's property is taken from him, and Sutter is utterly ruined. Most of the gold ends up in the hands of the established ruling class anyway. That is really what happened at Montauk. The ruling elite seized it."

"I have two questions then, Emory. First, 'How do you and Captain Kidd fit in with the established ruling class?' and 'Did the same thing happen at Ong's Hat?' "

"As for Ong's Hat," said Emory, "those experiments created problems that were somewhat similar, but they were not dealing with a massive amplifier that was broadcasting all over the place. The Ong's Hat crowd were more subtle and, as opposed to having an elitist mentality, were tied to more of a grass roots sort of movement. Thus, they gated in free souls from other worlds that were actively feeding them information and planning an escape from this world. As the movement began to grow and spread, it was snuffed out, at least in the readily observable physical plane.

"The Ong's Hat crowd consists of three tiers of personnel. The outer tier consists of the most visible people who occupied the ashram. The majority of these people are a front group who have no access to the inner tier who are actual travellers between dimensions. The outer tier has a limited access to anything which could be considered very special. There is another tier between the travellers and the outer sphere, and these consist of a few key people who are strategically positioned either inside the ashram or outside of it. These are intermediaries who act as go-betweens from the inner tier to the outer tier. Joseph Matheny is one of these intermediaries. He has been bombarded with various phenomena but does not know everything. The inner tier travellers represent free beings who are not necessarily held down or confined by limitations of any kind. Does that answer your question?"

"Are you one of the travellers?" I asked Emory.

"I am more of an intermediary. I have tried to make it sound black and white, but there are also many multiplicities and shades of gray. Joe is an intermediary, but he exists more on the physical side of things. I, on the other hand, am more tied to the ephemeral aspects of the travellers. My physical existence, by all appearances, is tangible but fleeting."

"And," I asked, "what about Captain Kidd?"

"He," said Emory, "was the supreme sacrifice. Thinking he was a partner of William of Orange, he was a pawn the East India Company sacrificed. When a magician does a sacrifice, the spirit of the vessel being sacrificed is designated to carry out the will of the magician. In Kidd's case, there are many diverse and complex magical intentions at work, the sum total of which has resulted in him trying to bring the eggs back together. This very action excites the pineal gland and opens up everyone's Seventh Seal.

"John Dee became interested in magick because he saw that man's ordinary knowledge was limited. He wanted more and literally catapulted himself into the metaplane and ended up mixing the knowledge of it with that of the Earth plane.

"You can call the magician behind the shadow empire he created by the name of MA-MON, that is what he called it, but it doesn't really matter in the end. A shadow is a shadow. We all have to deal with our personal shadow. Dee's just happened to encompass the entire globe.

"It is really not all that complicated. The angels or angles of the metaplane are different from the plane or egg world that you live in in your physical body. When there is a pure confluence between these two planes, it is a merging of two planes which creates a new reality. This process has been exaggerated to a point of fear in your culture and has been portrayed as the Apocalypse or end of the world. This is the true purpose of any sacred relic: to bridge the two worlds that are intrinsically and inherently connected. It is for this reason that Captain Kidd represents the end of the pirates."

At this point, a large green parrot seemed to fly right out of one of the video monitors on the wall. It began to fly in and around the Delta-T antenna.

"God damn that blasted bird!" yelled Captain Kidd. "That blasted bird has besieged me ever since I accidentally killed Robert Moore off the coast of Madagascar. The damned bastard!"

"Verily, verily, I say unto thee..." said the bird.

"Shut up, you god damn fucking bird!" said Kidd.

"Let he who is innocent cast the first stone," the bird said in response to the verbal assault.

"What in the hell is going on?" I asked.

"That," said Captain Kidd as he pointed at the large green bird, "is Jesus Christ!"

As the bird flew by, Kidd grabbed at it in a fiendish fashion. Although he caught a few tail feathers, the bird flew back to the Delta-T and perched itself.

"Yes," continued Kidd, "that bird was named by my crew. They thought it was hysterically funny to teach him the verses of Jesus in the Bible, particularly after he seemed to be haunting me after the death of the mutineer Robert Moore."

"The meek shall inherit the earth," said the parrot from the top of the Delta-T.

"That's a mistranslation of the actual Aramaic," I said. "I have studied the actual translation of that particular phrase."

"He's just a cut-up," said Emory. "Don't pay too much attention to that bird."

In a fit of fury, Kidd took a decent sized vacuum tube that was lying around and threw it right at the bird. Making a direct hit on the bird's torso, the parrot screeched like only a parrot can and fell to the floor beneath the Delta-T. By all rights, the bird now appeared dead or unconscious. Then, surprisingly, the bird looked up with one eye and only a minimum amount of energy as it spoke the following words.

"Forgive him, he knows not what he does!"

"Now," I said to Emory, "that phrase is neither a proper translation nor an improper translation. That bird knew what he was saying and was responding to the situation. He is more than a cut-up and possesses a consciousness, the least of which seems to be the literary version of who and what we know of as Christ."

"And you shall do things greater than I," whispered the bird as a pink laser beam suddenly emerged out of one of the monitors and surrounded the bird in pink until it appeared only as a pink apparition before vanishing entirely.

"Somehow," I said, "I think we lost an opportunity to find something out."

"That's just a damn demon sent to haunt me for something I did wrong," said Kidd, "but my sin was ultimately done in the name of self defense. That bird only nags and scolds me. It shows no compassion. Actually, I think that damn bird was deliberately created by Aleister Crowley in an attempt to find the eggs."

"You mean to say," I asked, "that there is insufficient compassion in your world, too?"

"You're damned right!" said Emory. "Captain Kidd and I are no different than the archangels, the jinn, or whoever else you throw into the mix. We are incomplete, nonintegrated and generally suffer from the same dysfunctions that people experience or suffer on Earth. Now, let's get on with the business at hand."

"I don't know what business you're referring to, Emory, but I first have a question. What are you doing here inside of the Delta-T?"

"What am I doing inside the Delta-T?" Emory asked rhetorically. "Myself and some others of the Incunabula and Ong's Hat crowd have sort of moved in and taken over. You have been sitting on the Montauk story for too long and not enough people are paying attention to the underlying meaning. Come now, let's get down to business."

"I still don't know what you are talking about," I said, "but I have one other question. What was the relationship between you and Joe's Metamachine?"

"Oh! You haven't figured that out? You're in the Metamachine! Now, let's get down to business."

Emory then handed me a copy of the little red book known as *The Book of the Law*.

"Now," said Emory, "cut through all the excess and tell me what you found out from *The Book of the Law* that you alluded to earlier in this book."

"Well," I said, "I could tell a long story, but suffice it to say that I did the exercise in the back of the book where it says to lay out all the sheets of the handwritten documents and paste them on the wall. The revelation did not come through a visual interpretation of the manuscript itself, but it gated in a series of dreams. Additionally, and most remarkably, I received a call from a lady at Montauk. Having never discussed the subject with her, I was surprised when she told me to look at the exact page where the line is drawn. It says, 'In this line drawn is a key.' She told me to take a protractor to the line and find out where the lines of latitude and longitude meet as referenced by the Prime Meridian which runs through the Isle of Dogs. When I did so, I could not help but notice that the location was smack dab in the middle of what is known as the Bermuda Triangle."

"Ah ha!" said Emory. "That is a coded reference to the time keeper crystal that went awry in Atlantis. That settles it then. It is time to activate!"

As I looked up at the monitors, I saw the old and familiar audience from the Magick Theater watching us. Emory sat back in the Montauk chair and began to visualize and transmit until there was nothing but water around us. He was changing reality itself. As he continued to concentrate, an atoll appeared around us which he identified as Ongtong Java. There was also an emerging volcano nearby which he identified as Pele. When I corrected him and told him that neither of these belong in the Atlantic Ocean, he said it didn't matter and that they were just cut-ups.

We soon found ourselves in the middle of an environmentally designed amphitheater which was built along the geographical outlines of the beautiful and breathtaking atoll known as Ongtong Java. It was now a bright and sunny afternoon as I saw the audience from the Magick Theater coming in to take their seats. Located in the water was a beautiful stage which appeared to be made of white alabaster. There was a gap of about fifteen yards of crystal blue water between the stage and the seating for the audience. Everyone would soon be on the edge of their seats for they were about to see the unfoldment of the end times, at least as rendered by the interactive constructs of the Magick Theater.

Author's Note: At this point in the narrative, I would like to invite you to participate as a quantum observer by taking a blank piece of paper or a computer screen and finish the book for yourself. You are familiar with the various themes and characters in this work as well as other themes and characters that are not in this book. I encourage you to fill this blank with your own stream of consciousness and write out your own version of the Apocalypse (which is about to be presented in this book). Use any variations or extrapolations that strike you and realize this is an interactive creative process and is also a precursor to future creative technologies. Engage the cut-up method if you feel like it. This is an exercise in consciousness as well as invitation for you to become interactive with the Unified Field. You might find some interesting comparisons between your ending and that which is about to be presented in this book. If you type neatly, I would also be happy to share your various renditions. Although it is not absolutely necessary, you should at least consider taking a positive outlook in creating your composition as it might serve you better. My mail can be received at the following address which is also listed in the front of the book: Sky Books, Box 769, Westbury, NY 11590.

52

REVELATION

As I entered the Magick Theater, the crowd was filling in the last remaining seats. I was lucky to grab one right on the aisle near an exit curtain. The beautiful tropical landscape told me there could be none of the "black outs" that the Magick Theater was now known for. As Chuck Hamill warmed up the London Festival Orchestra from the orchestra pit, Oral Swaggart, the Seventh Seal, rose from his seat in the audience and swam across the lagoon before pulling himself up on the stage. In his lime green jacket and yellow lemon slacks, he motioned for the musicians to wind down their warm ups. As they did, he began to speak.

"Ladies and gentlemen. I'm not sure what's going on here, but if we're going to see the Apocalypse...and frankly, I don't know what we are going to see...but if we are going to experience revelation, there are some things we're going to need or everybody's gonna think we don't know what we're doin'. Now...Pale Rider...everybody visualize a Pale Rider."

At that point, a Pale Rider came riding across the lagoon on a jet ski that was shaped like a white horse.

"Now, keep visualizing. You can manifest anything. I want you to mock up the Four Horsemen of the Apocalypse and get those locusts running, too."

At that point, the Four Horsemen appeared and so did the locusts. As the locusts were filling the sky towards complete darkness, popcorn vendors ambled through the audience trying to make last minute sales. When the locusts had filled the entire sky, there was complete darkness save for the exit signs studded around the pathways out of the theater. These seemed to indicate that one final exit has been reserved for those who do not wish to take this excursion any further. Apparently, it is still not too late. Feel free to just stick to your own stream of consciousness of how the Apocalypse might turn out.

Finally, after ten minutes, the exit lights were off and everything was completely black. No one could see anything. A penetrating drum beat could then be heard from the orchestra pit. Soon, the drum beat was recognizable as the beginning of *Thus Spake Zarathustra*, a musical piece which was popularized as the theme music for the movie *2001: A Space Odyssey*. Suddenly, a black monolith slowly emerged from the center of the stage into the darkness. As it did, a tiny amount of light emitted from the stage, just enough to enable the monolith and its reflective character to be viewed. When the monolith fully emerged, it towered massively above all. As the music finally subsided, a pink laser from the back of the amphitheater cut out an egg-shaped slab in the middle of the monolith. The egg-shaped slab retained its position within the monolith with an outline of pink surrounding it. The egg-shaped slab was pure black, like obsidian. Slowly, a pair of lips began to form in the center of the egg-shaped slab. After forming, the lips began to speak.

"I am the shewstone," the lips said.

Then, in a forbidden and ominous tone from a Cecille B. DeMille production, the voice said, "I am Omega — the end."

The egg-shaped shewstone then began to move forward and take a new shape. As it did so, it seemed to be forming arms and stepping out of a hole. As part of the slab formed into a leg, I could clearly see that the entire egg-shaped shewstone had shape-shifted into the affable Tar Baby who was now sauntering about the stage. In the place where the shewstone was on the monolith, a pink hole could be seen which appeared to be reaching into the aethyr. Immediately following him out of the pink hole was an opposite or white version of the Tar Baby who is known as the Dough Boy.

"Ah ha!" exclaimed the Tar Baby. "I's bets you's all thought dat you's was dones wit' me! Now, we's gonna gets downs to business!"

Chuck Hamill then led the orchestra in an extremely innovative and technically well rendered arrangement of *Give Me That Old Time Religion*. As he did, the Tar Baby and the Dough Boy, representing the duality of nature, began dancing to the music. As the music wandered through various themes and stunning arrangements, it would reach a feverish pitch before eventually and reliably reverting to the simple down-home simplistic melody which unquestionably portrayed the lowest common denominator of religion as could possibly be expressed by sentient beings. At the points when the music reached the lowest common denominator, the Tar Baby and the Dough Boy square danced in a hyperbolic and exaggerated fashion which included knee slapping, clapping, and turning around and flapping their elbows like chicken wings.

When the square dance was finally done, the green parrot known as Jesus Christ flew from out of the pink light in the monolith and began to fly around the theater. As it did so, the pink light began to take over the entire black color of the monolith as the huge structure began to fold, open and divide upon itself until it formed a pink box the size of a large walk-in closet. As the monolith transformed, the Tar Baby took a large purple crayon and wrote "Metamachine" across the top of the pink cube. Then, the green parrot screeched and perched itself upon the Metamachine.

"What's that?" cried a voice from the audience.

"I'm Jesus Christ!" said the parrot. "Braak, braak...verily, verily, I say unto thee. Do unto others as you would have them do unto you."

"This is blasphemy!" said Oral Swaggart.

"Yes!" cried the Great Walrus. "Let's get that damned bird!"

Captain Kidd then rushed out from behind one of the exit curtains with an oxyacetylene torch.

"Let's torch the bastard!" said Kidd.

"I'll hold him down!" said Oral as he and the Great Walrus rapidly swam across the water to get to the stage.

As they did so, Aleister Crowley took a blow dart and shot the parrot square in the heart. As the bird careened and lost its balance, it cried out.

"Oh, Lord, why hast thou forsaken me?"

The bird then fell to the ground and began to hobble as it tried to get away. As it did so, Captain Kidd ran up to the lagoon and passed the oxyacetylene torch to Oral Swaggart who torched the bird until it was nothing but charred ashes. As the Tar Baby and the Great Walrus escorted the Seventh Seal back to his seat, Captain Kidd stood before the audience and held up what appeared to be a scroll. As he did so, the Metamachine began to form a swirl at center stage that appeared as a vortex in different shades of pink.

"I have now avenged the consciousness which beseeched and besieged me since I killed Robert Moore and made myself a sacrifice! Now, I will in turn sacrifice my most valuable treasure map as a gift to the metaplane."

Kidd then walked over and placed his scroll in the vortex which readily consumed it. As Kidd took his seat in the audience next to Emory, the ashes of the bird, which were still on the stage, began to stir. They congealed and formed into an apparition of what had once been the original bird. As it flew around the amphitheater, it screeched and said in a piercing and almost mocking tone.

"Can't kill me! Can't kill me! I've resurrected!"

As the bird said this, Captain Kidd sat in the audience and shook his head with resignation before burying his head in his hands and slumping over. The bird began to rise in a slow but soaring circular motion until only a trace or glimmer of him could be seen. At that point, the volcano began to erupt as it made loud noises and blew hot ash in the wind which occasionally reached the audience. As the ashes began to rise up to reach the vicinity of the bird, I was given cause to wonder about the relationship between the volcano and the bird. Although the eruption was spectacular, it was rather short lived. When it was done, a cave-like opening could be seen along the side of the volcano. A rapid flow of lava then made its way from the cave to the stage until their was a pathway between it and the volcano. Looking like a couple of stage hands, the Tar Baby and the Dough Boy emerged from a compartment under the stage with a huge red carpet which they began rapidly unrolling until it reached the mouth of the cave. As the audience looked for the next move, a small figure could be seen emerging out of the mouth of the cave. Although it moved fairly rapidly, it took a while before anything distinct could be made out. When the figure could be seen, it was Pele, the greatest soccer star in the world. He dribbled a soccer ball at a rapid clip until he arrived at the stage. Once there, he smiled at the audience and picked up the ball before pointing to it and showing the black and white pentagons that the ball consisted of. He then placed the ball near the end of the stage and, with perfect and expert grace, he kicked the ball straight into the center of the whirling pink vortex above the Metamachine. Pele then assumed a seat in the audience. After that, Captain Kidd immediately threw his PELE ring into the vortex. At that point, Emory Cranston walked across the water with a case of Zip drives which he gave to the Tar Baby who promptly began inserting them into the Metamachine. John von Neumann then came up with his own Zip drives before speaking.

"This is all of what I have utilized in my modeling of the computer. It contains the information I learned about predicting the weather and economics but also everything I learned about the Philadelphia Experiment and Montauk Project."

Everyone in the audience then began throwing their own Zip drives on the stage which the Tar Baby and Dough Boy labored to put in the swirling pink vortex. After all the Zip drives were inserted, three people with storage trunks emerged and needed help carrying them onto the stage. These people were Aleister Crowley, L. Ron Hubbard and John Dee. Once these trunks of disks were brought to the stage, the Tar Baby and the Dough Boy put them into the vortex as quickly as the machine could consume them. As it did so, the Metamachine made exaggerated and punctual noises at certain points as if the machine received pleasure with some of the data but the opposite with other portions.

At this point, the Seventh Seal stood up from his seat in the audience and said, "Enough with your shenanigans! If the Messiah himself does not appear, this is not an acceptable version of the Apocalypse."

As he spoke, the water in the lagoon between the stage and the audience began swirling until it looked like Charybdis, the notorious vortex of water that once stood off the coast of Sicily and consumed vessels of the sea.

"If he does not appear right now, I will declare these entire proceedings a heinous blasphemy!" exclaimed Oral Swaggart.

As he spoke, the Great Seal had become carried away with his own emotions. As he stepped forward, he fell into the water and became caught in the outer rim of the swirling current. As I

427

watched him, I immediately noticed that he was in serious trouble and extended my narwhal tusk to him. He was able to grab it with his human hand as he used his flipper to resist the pull of the whirlpool. With help from some of the audience members, I was able to pull him out and save his carcass, at least for the time being. Watching from the stage, the Tar Baby cried out.

"Don't be worryin', you's be gettin' what you's came for!"

The next thing I heard was the sound effect of a dive bomber. As everyone looked up, the apparition of the ash-parrot could be seen diving straight down towards the stage at a rapid rate. Instead of making a crash landing, the bird was consumed by the vortex of the Metamachine. It was now clear that all of the items had been consumed by the Metamachine. The parrot entering the machine somehow acted as if it were a switch to the volcano which suddenly began erupting once again. As it did, other volcanos began to rapidly emerge from the sea as their ashes consumed the sky in complete darkness. Angels then appeared in the sky chanting canticles, first in Latin and then in Greek. Finally, they began chanting the Enochian Calls in pure Enochian. As they did, the Tar Baby appeared in a gondola crossing the lagoon. He had made himself up to look like the ferryman who took the recently departed across the river Styx to their postmortem destination. Looking up, I noticed that I was in a coffin that was open to the skies. Raising my head and looking up out of the coffin, I could see that the rest of the audience were in similar coffins. Although everyone in the Magick Theater had become quite accustomed to strange visualizations and happenings, everything now had taken on a bit of gravity. It seemed as if there was to be no more joking around. As the Tar Baby made his way across the lagoon and the angels sang what seemed to be the last of their final Enochian Calls, I saw something out of the corner of my eye. The Dough Boy seemed to be adjusting some controls or a switch at the bottom of the Metamachine. As he did so, everything was totally black once again. There was no music and no mutterings from the audience. Everything was complete silence.

Despite the intimidating visualizations and sounds, I realized there was one saving grace. I realized I had not been subjected to any of the noxious fumes that would normally ensue from a volcanic eruption. Perhaps things would now revert to a sense of theater instead of imminent annihilation of one's physical body. A small pinprick of light began to form straight over head in the pure blackness of the heavens until it realized itself to be a full moon. It now shined brightly over the stage as the lagoon resumed its tropical and exotic appearance. Everything, including the sky, seemed to have reverted to normal except that it was a beautiful tropical evening.

As the Tar Baby stepped out from behind the Metamachine, he said, "You's knows sumptin', we's never really did bring civil'zation to de moon. Well, now de moons is gonna come to us!"

The moon continued to shine brightly as it beamed its inner light into the open vortex at the top of the Metamachine. As it did so, the Metamachine began to gyrate and make pleasurable noises as if it was getting a massage. After a while, the Metamachine began to emit forms of light back to the moon by utilizing the rays of light that were already extended to it. As it did so, there became a rapid and fast moving reciprocation of light between the two structures. The pulses became more and more energetic and active until both structures lost their regular forms and appeared as just pure energy. As things eventually pulsed down, the Metamachine assumed its pink form, but the moon was distinctly different. It had the appearance of being completely wrapped in newspaper. Slowly, the moon began to shift its position and came towards the stage until it was about a hundred yards overhead. It then seemed to unroll itself towards the Metamachine as if they were both parts of a newspaper assembly and printing plant. As the newspapers unrolled towards the opening in the Metamachine, the bottom of the machine began to shoot out newspapers which ended up being neatly stacked on the stage. As the Metamachine chucked out the newspapers, the Tar Baby and the Dough Boy began rapidly passing them out to the audience. They looked like newsboys as they shouted.

"Extra! Extra! Read all about it! The *Times* apologizes!"

As each of us received our newspaper, reading lights came on from the seats. It was an exact replica of *The New York Times*. Ignoring the front page, I went straight to the sports section because I wanted to see if there was one. To my surprise, there was. The sports headline read as follows.

"We're Sorry, Pele."

The article explained that Pele was the greatest competitive athlete the world had ever known and apologized for declaring other athletes to be greater, the reason being that these athletes were tied to the merchandising of products. They cited the fact that Pele was the only athlete ever known to have quelled a riot by his mere appearance in a country. Everyone stopped rioting to watch this great athlete play soccer. Say what you want about Muhammad Ali or anyone else, no one athlete had ever achieved such a common and dramatic bond with people.

Pleased to see that Pele had finally received his proper acknowledgment, I went and looked at the front page of the paper. It still said, "All the News That's Fit to Print" but the main headline was so bizarre I had to question the motivation. It said, "We're Sorry, Jesus!" Actually, all the articles in the newspaper consisted of nothing but corrections. This also included an apology for not properly conducting proper investigations into the JFK and other notable assassinations. The headline article read as follows:

> "We here at the *Times* wish to apologize for certain ignorant and inaccurate reporting we have done since the beginning of our existence. Since our origins, we have been tainted by the influence of an ignorant culture as well as twisted forms of Enochian and other magick. Therefore, all of our reporting, whether it be done with innocence, ignorance, or complete bias in the favor of a vested interest, has been incorrect. We must admit, we have been involved in so many shenanigans and blatant false reporting in the past that this correction is the easiest one we've ever had to make. After all, we were not trying to deceive anyone on this point, and we just plain did not know.
>
> "Everything we have ever written on the subject of Jesus Christ or Christianity has been either flat out incorrect or severely tainted at best. We also apologize to Peter Moon for ignoring or stonewalling his research and only reviewing or fostering books which only reach a superficial understandings of these matters."

Reading this, I was more suspicious than surprised to see my name mentioned. Before continuing to read, I saw an advertisement

430

for the book *The Da Vinci Code* and a quote from Nelson DeMille, a #1 *New York Times* bestselling author. It read as follows.

"Dan Brown has to be one of the best, smartest, and most accomplished writers in the country. *The Da Vinci Code* is many notches above the intelligent thriller; this is pure genius."

After noticing this, I then continued reading the article.

"It is indeed true that *The Da Vinci Code* deserves its bestseller status as it supersedes any potential or imagined flaws by gripping and thrilling the reader to the very end. It is also told against a rich backdrop of historical research which demonstrates resoundingly that Christian architecture and art was deliberately encoded to convey hidden meanings which exalted the sacred feminine aspects of divinity. Most of these works were either under the construction of or curated by the Knights Templar or Priori de Sion, the latter of which included the patronage of Leonardo Da Vinci. Although the characters in the novel are portrayed as bastions of cryptography with expert knowledge of the Holy Grail, the author himself appears to be as ignorant as we were about these same matters. After unsealing cryptex after cryptex, each containing a secret code that is denominated with the number five, the author missed the opportunity to have his characters reveal the magic word, the secret of all secrets that has remained secret for as long as the universe remembers. We are told of the sacred feminine aspects of the number five and how the planet Venus moves through the sky in the shape of a pentagram, but he has completely missed the code within the code. We assume he is ignorant of these matters; otherwise, why would he have omitted it? Perhaps it is because he did not have the resources of the Metamachine and all of the resources you, the audience, have put into it. We, thanks to all of you reading this paper, now have the code and will be happy to share it with you as you experience the Apocalypse.

"This secret of all secrets begins with a five letter code that most of you can only begin to understand with the iteration of the five letter word "Jesus," the English or Anglish name of the Messiah of the Christian religion. In order to understand this code word, you must first understand that the five letter word "Jesus" did not exist until the Brits proved they could not pronounce a vowel, but it was only officially sanctioned in 1611 when the letter "J" became a part of the English language as a result of the King James Bible being published. Included with it was a pronunciation guide for all proper names like Jesus, Jerusalem, Jew, Judas, Joshua and John. As this was only a few short years after the death of Dr. Dee, we can only conclude that this esoteric bastardization of names was a strategy by the shadow side to hypnotize the entire human race into a flagrant misconception. Further, by utilizing the hypnotic form of the name *Jesus*, it numbs the mind and prevents further discovery of the real truth and the magic word which lies within.

"To properly explain this much misunderstood concept, the magical name upon which the English word

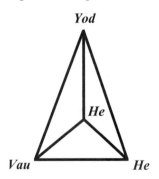

TETRAGRAMMATON

Above is a geometric representation of Tetragrammaton in the form of a three-dimensional tetrahedron where each point represents the Hebrew letters *Yod, He, Vau, He* which represent Fire, Water, Air, and Earth respectively. Tetragrammaton appears in the Bible and has often been identified as the ineffable name of God. Although Tetragrammaton represents the physical attributes of the universe, it does not, by its very definition, account for the spirit itself.

Jesus was based originally consisted of the four letters of Hebrew which are known as Tetragrammaton, a word which means "four letters." In this case, they were *Yod, He, Vau, He* and are a holographic representation of the universe which can be easily imagined in the form of a tetrahedron. They are considered a holographic representation of the universe because each letter or point of the tetrahedron represents one of the four elements.

"Many consider YHVH to be the sacred ineffable name that cannot be pronounced. In ancient Palestine, it could only be pronounced once a year within the Holy of Holies inside of the Temple, and even then, loud cymbals clashed to prevent the people from hearing it spoken. But, in order to understand the secret word that is buried within the etymology of "Jesus," we must first consider the Hebrew alphabet and how that contributed to the evolution of the shadow name.

"The letters of the Hebrew alphabet are all consonants. Each letter has a multiplicity of values connected to it which include elemental, numerical and other meanings. When you juxtapose these various letters into words or other associations, you also have a multitude of meanings. As the letters and words can be measured in so many different ways, it has been called a multidimensional language. Vowels, on the other hand, serve an entirely different purpose. Although they were not incorporated into the Hebrew language until much later, they were always present and utilized as "invisible sounds." They were not only considered to be invisible in terms of written language but also in the function they served because they were the bridge between the consonants. They were the connective or unifying property. You could even say that vowels represented the Unified Field. Additionally, there is a more propitious aspect of vowels when we break down the very word itself. A *vow* is a spoken or solemn commitment or pledge. As *el* signifies *God*, a *vow-el* suggests an iteration to God. The use of vowels as a supplication to God was very prevalent in ancient Palestine and elsewhere in the world. Ieou was a more ancient name for Jesus and Io Pan, also known as Pal, was a fertility god from which the name Palestine was derived. Palatine Hill, upon which Rome was founded, was also taken from Pal. The most well known iteration of the holy use of vowels is IAO which stands for Isis, Apophis, and Osiris who represent life, death, and rebirth. This was the god of the Gnostics and is their version of the Hebrews' Tetragrammaton.

"The main point in all of this is that the pronunciation of pure vowels is a way of invoking deity. Lengthy iterations of 'Ooooooooooooong,' or 'Oooooooooooom' are just two examples. The invocation is brought to an end with the use of a consonant.

"If you read various writings about Jack Parsons, you will find that he was forever writing or stating the words Io-Pan. He was invoking the deity. It is a matter of historical record that at the same time Christ was supposed to have died, Tiberius Caesar was informed by a passing sailor that the 'Great God Pan is dead.' This moved and influenced Tiberius so much that it found its way into history. Christ is identified with Pan in many different respects. When Christ rode into Jerusalem upon a donkey (known as Io or Io Pan), he was being positioned with the pagan donkey god which was also meant to identify him with Pan as well as Dionysos. The whole idea of Christ being invented or reinvented to align with pagan gods or virtues has long been established, but nowhere is it more intrinsically and inescapably related to paganism than in the actual name of the Christian messiah himself.

"In the New Testament: Philippians 2:10-11 it says the following:

'That at the name of Jesus every knee should bow, of things in heaven, and things in earth, and things under the earth; And that every tongue should confess that Jesus Christ is Lord, to the glory of God the Father.'

"Although Biblical quotations invest much power in the literal usage of the name, they do not tell you that the word 'Jesus' is a mistranslation or shadow of the true word. According to Biblical tradition, the real name of God was always hidden from the people. The great secret that has been held on to for millennia is that the so-called ineffable name of God is not YHVH, the elemental formula known as Tetragrammaton. The secret name includes the insertion of another letter into YHVH, and it is the twenty-first letter of the Hebrew alphabet which is called *shin*. When *shin* is inserted into YHVH it becomes YHSVH or *Yod He Shin Vau He* which is five letters and is therefore known as Pentagrammaton. The word Pentagrammaton literally means 'five letters.' Although Da Vinci's Pentagrammatic Man is referred to in *The Da Vinci Code,* this secret code was missed. You can thank the Metamachine for picking this up. The character commonly known as Jesus Christ in the Bible was deliberately and mysteriously named after the five Hebrew letters which you have just read. Now, can you imagine someone walking around Palestine and being called 'Yod He Shin Vau He?' This is not much different from walking around today and calling someone by the letters *Y, H, S, V, H.* Around the year zero, two of the primary languages being spoken at that time were Aramaic and Latin, the latter by reason of Roman occupation. The name of Yeshua was derived from these letters, but Yeshua was really a slang word based upon a slang vernacular of the two aforementioned languages. Yeshua was destined to become a very fashionable word in New Age circles, but it is really only a nickname for a very sacred concept. When YHSVH was translated into other languages, it had different permutations. In Latin, it became Jehovah which is commonly mistranslated to mean the Father God and is confused with Yahwah (which is really just an iteration of vowels). In Greek, it became IESUS which is conveniently and phonetically similar to *Io Zeus.* It was only from this Greek version that the English, just after the death of John Dee, gave us Jesus.

435

Although the above should resolve considerable confusion for most people, there is considerably more to the equation. Pentagrammaton also extends to the geometric shape known as the pentagram which also means 'five letters' and is configured esoterically at the bottom of this page. In this sacred glyph, which the name of *Jesus* (properly translated as *Yod He Shin Vau He)* is meant to signify, lies the greatest mystery of the Freemasons and every other western secret society: the Hebrew letter *shin.* Represented at the top of the pentagram star below, *shin* is really considered to be the ultimate secret within the secret.

In Hebrew, *shin* is first and foremost a letter which is combined with other letters and is pronounced with either an 's' sound as in the word 'hiss' or a 'sh' sound as in the word 'shine.' As the letter *shin* is the true lost or secret word of the Masons, it is fitting that magical orders portray a robed and hooded figure with his index finger over his mouth with an admonition to be silent. This is the

PENTAGRAMMATON

Above is a two-dimensional representation of Pentagrammaton, an ancient magical formula depicted in the Hebrew letters *Yod, He, Shin, Vau, He* which represent Fire, Water, Spirit, Air, and Earth respectively. When the pentagram is right-side-up, it signifies spirit over matter. When the pentagram is reversed or upside-down, it signifies matter over spirit. Note the pentagon in the middle and how it can appear depending upon how the pentagram is positioned.

same as expressing the sound of 'shhhhhhh' or 'shsh' to be quiet. This lost secret of Hiram and the Masons is directly linked to this expression.

"The pentagram symbol is commonly misconstrued by the ignorant to mean devil worship and that is just the way the secret societies want it because they do not want you to know the truth. Christians who believe that the pentagram is evil have fallen for the bait and have literally identified the principle of their savior with that which they consider to be evil. This is a complete reversal of polarity from what the word and concept mean and were originally meant to convey. When the pentagram is reversed, however, then it could easily, and not necessarily incorrectly, be construed as evil.

"The most common identification of *shin* in Hebrew is that it signifies 'tooth.' Although there is much esoteric meaning in why it means tooth, *shin* has multiple meanings which might make things a little clearer. *Shin* also means 'spirit' and 'change.' In this respect, when we consider the pentagram or the process of Pentagrammaton, we have spirit being above and superior to the elements of fire, water, air and earth.

"The elements of water and earth are passive and represent the feminine. The elements of air and fire act upon and are therefore non-passive so they represent the masculine. *Shin*, as spirit, can change these elements as well as the way they interact with each other. This places spirit in a causative position over the physical elements which is what life is always trying to do anyway: overcome its physical environment or limitations. In the case of the New Testament, Christ is utilizing this principle to rearrange physical matter and thereby create miracles. More appropriately, Christ was not so much utilizing this principle but was causing results because He literally *was* or *is* the principle.

"At this point, it is important to stop for a moment and reflect. Is this entire principle of Pentagrammaton wrapped up in one human form who allegedly appeared on this Earth for a brief flash in the pan? There is no question that the stories of the New Testament are a cut-up but a highly selective one. Even so, particularly when the stories and propositions of the Gnostic Gospels are added in, the figure known as Christ is presented as a living testament and example of the principle of Pentagrammaton as is illustrated in the geometric figure of the pentagram. Leonardo Da Vinci depicted how this shape conforms to the divine nature of man in his illustration of Pentagrammatic Man which shows how a man's shape relates to the circle and the pentagram. Pentagrammaton is not only symbolic of the instrument by which man performs miracles in the physical universe, but it is also the method by which he bonds with the Creative Principle of the universe. In this one name is bound the strength and power of all others and mastery of this name suggests dominance over others. In the presence of the common man understanding this word, the power of those who use it to dominate him is thus undermined.

"While not really outside of the formula of Pentagrammaton, there is another secret aspect to *shin* which can perhaps be better understood with reference to Dr. John Dee's manuscript where all power was symbolized in the ring given to Dee that contained the letters PELE and VL. Pele was identified as 'he who will work wonders.' In Hawaiian, Pele signified the male principle inherent in the feminine before the male was manifested. Hawaiians see Pele as a symbol to challenge and assist us in bringing forward that which is buried within the very core of our being. PELE has also been defined as 'black fire' or the 'black fire's will.' This means that the ring should enable one to establish one's will with VL, the letters of which signify establishing or connecting one's will to the Hidden One. The hidden word is *shin,* buried within *Yod He Shin Vau He.*"

Although I had not yet finished the article I was reading, I heard a clamoring in the theater. Looking up from my copy of the *Times*, I saw that the Tar Baby was standing in the middle of the stage and addressing the crowd.

SHIN

"Now, I's gonna turns mys-self into's a piece o' coal so's you's can continues yo' readin'. And...if you's be wunderin' why I's be turnin' into coal, justs t'ink dat its becuz de word coal be made up o' *CO* and *AL*. Dat means 'bein' t'get'er wit' God ors bounds to God."

As the Tar Baby finished talking, he shape-shifted into a piece of dark black coal. I then continued reading the article in the *Times*.

"One can also find the hidden meaning of *shin* within a piece of coal which contains the hidden will that is called the Black Flame. But first, look at the three flames emitting from the top of the letter *shin* itself. These represent three quantum states. First is the black essence of the coal which symbolizes the changeless essence of the black void. It is sometimes known as the Black Flame as it houses the second flame which is the eternal hidden flame. When coal burns, it is fueled by a hidden inner flame which cannot be seen by the naked eye. This inner flame is the power to change within the "changeless" universe. *Shin* is known as the eternal flame of life. It has no beginning and no end but always survives. It is the quantum potential to change. The third flame represents actual change. When you apply the element of air to a piece of coal by blowing on it, you have created a flame that is now outside of the coal and visible, and this represents the continuity of life. Breath (or prana) is a push-pull (inward and outward) exchange of the element of air that makes us alive or dead. It is the test by which something is judged to be alive or dead. It is also important to remember that *shin* serves as a bridge between life and death because coal is created as a result of dead vegetable matter condensing over a period of considerable years. It is a never ending cycle of alpha and omega."

Finishing this paragraph, I noticed the shuffling of feet as people left the Magick Theater, but I was determined to complete reading the article. There was not too much more to go.

"There is much more that can be said about *shin*, the most secret concept in the universe. The Freemasons identified it as the force or wall that holds up the pillars of the universe, the same pillars you might know as Joachim and Boaz. It is identified as the wall between the two polarities and the unification of opposites, but it is really the means of unification of opposites and it connects all the pathways of the Tree of Life. Shin has also been identified as the wall in the corpus callosum which keeps the two hemispheres of the brain from being in complete synchronization with each other. Representing the final union of opposites, *shin* can genuinely be said to represent the true Unified Field. Everything else is a deviation.

"At this point, it is up to you in the audience to take this concept and run with it. We can only say so much, but do not underestimate its power for this is the greatest mystery you can imagine. If you doubt this, let us also inform you that the formula of Pentagrammaton completely answers the greatest enigmatic riddle that has puzzled Mankind since the beginnings of our recorded history. This concerns the mystery of the Sphinx which is embodied in what is called the ratio of the 'paws to the claws.' The Sphinx has four paws representing Tetragrammaton but five toes or claws representing Pentagrammaton. As an edifice, this mysterious statue represents Mankind's evolution from Tetragrammaton to Pentagrammaton, and this is the awakening to *shin*. When Mankind has significantly awakened to this awareness, you will see the destruction of the Sphinx. In its place, you will see an even grander edifice that will fully represent the mysteries in a manner that is much easier to understand than what the Egyptians left us with. Most of all, it is important for you to know that when you truly awaken as a Pentagrammatic person, you will no longer be befuddled or enticed by these ancient mysteries because <u>you</u> will be the mystery and you will be fully conscious of it.

"We apologize for any confusions caused by our ignorance of the name and phenomena that has been erroneously called Jesus Christ. We hope this correction has not come too late for you to enjoy the rest of your life."

As I finished the article, it was near sundown. Everyone was gone, and the implication was clear. They had all discovered the mystery and had gone on to their next level, whatever that might mean. I, however, was still hanging on to the dream state and was not ready to return to regular reality or any other reality for that matter. As I looked around the lagoon of Ongtong Java, I was completely awed by the natural beauty. The palm trees began to make a silhouette against the reddening sky. I enjoyed a warm and gentle breeze that made a rippling sound as it scattered discarded copies of the *Times* that had been left by members of the audience. I could not help but wonder how valuable those discarded newspapers might be to others in ages past. But here, at Ongtong Java, I knew that my dream had come to end. It was all over now, but I felt very relaxed. Looking up at the stage, I could see the Tar Baby and the Dough Boy sweeping up the stage with brooms. They were quiet and going about their chores dutifully. The Metamachine had apparently reverted to being the black monolith while I had been intently reading the *Times*. It stood as tall as ever, but the pink hole was still in the middle, and I wondered if all of the audience members had exited through that pink hole. As I stood up, the Tar Baby turned and motioned for me to come to the stage.

"I's gots sumptin' fo' ya," he said.

As I crossed the water and pulled myself up on the stage, the Tar Baby pulled something out of what might have been a pocket and extended his hand to me.

"It's de ring," he said. "Capt'n Kidd tho'ht you's might be likin' to have de ring. It found its ways back to him in de pink hole, but he said you's might 'preciate havin' it as he had no need fo' it where's he was gonna be goin'."

This was the PELE ring of John Dee. As I took the ring from the Tar Baby and examined it, it gave off a very bright shine that increased its shine the more I looked into it.

"Neither do I," I said to the Tar Baby as I tossed the ring into the pink void in the monolith.

"Dat was real smart," said the Tar Baby, " 'cause if you's hold on to dat ring, you's never knows whats you's mights turns intos."

"I think," I said, "that it's more powerful, once you have that ring, to toss it back as opposed to exercising power over others. Most importantly, it frees you from your own shadow."

The Tar Baby looked at me quizzically as if he either could not figure me out, greatly admired me, or was puzzling over whether I wanted to get rid of him.

"You's knows sumptin'," he said, "we's could be's in dis Magick Theatre business for a l-o-o-o-o-ng lo-o-o-o-ng time."

"Well, I guess so," I replied before imitating the Tar Baby in his own vernacular. "After all's, we's just lit'rally scared de Bejezus out o' everybody! Why not?"

"De Bejezus! Now dats be soundin' like one o' dem exorcisms! I's also gots to say dat it be'n nice workin' wit' you's."

"To tell you the truth," I said, "I liked you a lot better when you were in your Isis mode. For some strange reason, I can relate to that shape better."

The Tar Baby then betrayed an emotion he had not shown before. He put his head down and began shuffling his feet before looking briefly up at me. I got the impression that he did not want this all to come to an end. He then reached out his hands and jumped up on me. The Tar Baby wanted a hug. I held on to him as he was about the size of a big teddy bear. Then, the Dough Boy spotted us, and put his arms out, too. He jumped up and I was walking around with the equivalent of two big teddy bears. Holding them both, I took one last walk around the stage and took in the pure beauty of Ongtong Java. It was an imaginary journey, but one I could never forget. More importantly, it was a place I could always return to. Traversing the area over to the monolith, I stood in front of the pink light. The Dough Boy put his head into the pink and jumped through. The Tar Baby jumped in right after. As I walked back towards one of the exit signs, I heard a noise and turned around. The Tar Baby had stuck his head through the circle but had taken on the nose and ears of Porky Pig.

"That's all, folks," he said.

53

QUINTESSENCE

The purpose of this book, in part, is to present the hidden word in an understandable format and to thereby revive the ancient principles and truths which it represents. *Shin* represents the spark of life that reaches from the most mundane aspects of the microcosm to the most grand aspects of the macrocosm. If you think about it, the greatest mystery of Mankind has been his relationship with the Creator. There are many more mysteries that have somehow wrapped themselves up in the concept or letter *shin*, and I could not begin to describe them all. I only hope to introduce you to this concept so that you might run with it and help to clarify the many misunderstandings others have suffered as a result of not comprehending this concept.

As was said earlier, the Hebrew letter *shin* is generally meant to signify "tooth." Although *shin* did not originate with the Hebrews, there is a revelatory etymology of the English word *tooth*. According to *Webster's New World Dictionary, tooth* is derived from the Old English word *toth*, a word which is virtually the same as Thoth, the Egyptian scribe of the gods who is known as Hermes by the Greeks and Enoch by the Herbrews. This should not really surprise anyone because Thoth, primarily known as the scribe of the gods, also represents the voicing or iteration of the truth. As he is the god of communication, his name goes hand-in-hand with the idea of a tooth which is emblematic of the mouth. The name Thoth is even analogous to Yeshua because it is also an acronym. The original name for Thoth is commonly thought to be

443

pronounced as Tahuti or Tehuti. These names, however, are really a "slanguage" term for the syllables TE-HE-O-TE-HE (pronounced TAY-HAY-O-TAY-HAY). THOTH represents the first letters of each of the syllables. The iteration of "O" would be equivalent to *shin*. In Greek, "O" is the equivalent of *omega*, the end. This information is related to and is derived from the work of Alice Bailey, a student of Theosophy. The names of Enoch, Hermes, and Thoth all represent different interpretations of an original tradition. I have primarily referred to the Hebrew tradition in this book because it contains the only references which are readily available in our culture. The above reference to THOTH would be part of the language or tongue known as Vril. The Tibetans and Theosophists were quite partial to the Vril, but it is a very obscure language. If we look for a comparative to Solomon's Temple in that tradition, we have the legend of the Shao Lin Temple. Although there are several temples which claim to be the real Shao Lin Temple, the original one would seem to be obscured.

The word or letter *shin* is not relegated to Hebrew as it has signs of existing prior to that language being formed. You also find *shin* appearing in the etymology of the word *Shinto*, the Japanese nature religion which originally came from China. *Shinto*, according to Webster's Dictionary, is based upon *shin*, meaning "spirit," and *tao*, meaning "way." There is also an entire sect of Buddhism known as Shin Buddhism.

Although the words and letters have their own relative importance, it is the underlying concepts which are most significant. *Shin* represents change and the ability to manifest change. This is the very principle upon which the Chinese *I Ching* or *Book of Changes* was based. The Chinese name of *Chin*, from which the name of the Chin Dynasty was derived, is based upon this concept.

According to Dr. Mikio Sankey, the author of *Esoteric Acupuncture*, the word *shen* (a variant spelling of *shin*) is a Chinese word with several meanings. It is thought of as similar to the mind but is housed in the heart. Additionally, it encompasses the total aspects of the emotional, mental, and spiritual energies of the person. You can read Dr. Sankey's books for further information on how this fits in with ancient Chinese medicine.

The Romans had their own word for *shin,* and they called it *quinta essentia*, a term which literally means "essential fifth part."

This takes us back to the magical tradition of Pentagrammaton which teaches that *shin* or spirit is the "Fifth Element." From this paradigm, we get the English word *quintessence* which refers to the essential nature of what makes something that which it is. The phrase, "I am that I am" is really no different.

In ancient Rome, *quinta essentia* referred to the principle of immortality and being one with the god. In *The Women's Encyclopedia of Myths and Secrets,* author Barbara Walker gives considerable illumination on the word *quintessence.* Besides connecting the word to immortality, her research demonstrates that it also referred to blue blood as well as different elixirs. Alchemists referred to *quinta essentia* as blue liquid, an elixir of illumination.

Besides its role as an elixir of immortality, this mystical blue element was also represented with its own "trump suit" in the Tarot deck. By this, I am referring to the actual Major Arcana cards of the Tarot. *Shin* is considered to be the connective glue or conduit between all the different sephiroth of the Tree of Life. In the Tarot, each of these conduits or pathways are represented by a Major Arcana card such as the Fool, the Empress, the Hermit, etc. Besides representing each of the specific pathways of the Tarot, *shin* also has an emphasized and specific place on a single one of these pathways that is represented by the card known as *Judgement* or *The Last Judgement.* In some decks, the letter *shin* is printed on the card. Traditionally, this card depicts three naked characters in coffins who are holding up their arms so as to depict the letter *shin.* In the Tarot deck composed by Lady Freida Harris and Aleister Crowley, this card is called *The Aeon* which refers to the new aeon or "New Age."

When we consider the idea of "judgement," there is a strong magical link, if not a purely etymological one, between the words *yes, justice* and *Jesus. Justice* derives from the Latin root *jus* which mean "law; right; correct." The Latin *jus,* which is pronounced with a soft *j,* is also very close to the word we know as *yes.* The Spanish word for yes, *si,* has been said to derive from Isehu, another "original" name for Jesus. There are other Spanish etymologies besides this one. The idea here is that the original concept behind any of these terms is an expression of the positive. *Yes* is most definitely a positive word. *Justice* is predicated on the idea of righting a wrong or making a negative situation a positive one. In an imperfect world that is seeking to balance towards a perfect world, one would yearn for a Day of Judgement. It would be the only way to balance off the negative. That concept, however, has been used by the dark side to brown beat people into limited thinking and controlled behavior patterns. The word *yes* is suggestive of all quantum possibilities. Hassan Sabbah had his own take on this with his slogan of "Everything is permitted."

As I have said previously, the concept of *shin* and Pentagrammaton are not new. In this book, they have been presented against the back drop of the legends of Jesus Christ and Hiram Abiff. The only reason I have used these references is that Western Civilization, and a great deal of the world, is "hung-up" on false concepts and misconceptions with regard to these ideas. In fact, you could say that the western mind has suffered a mental paralysis as a result of not knowing this information.

This magical word and formula did not originate with the mystery schools of two thousand years ago. While they may have codified it or preserved such knowledge with the language and references of their times, it is as old as the Earth's history itself. This is why you have the absurd predicament of both pagans and Christians consciously or unconsciously worshiping or working around the same basic concept.

The pronunciation of the Hebrew letter *shin* gives us yet another clue as to the magical role and significance that this utterance has played in our history. In Hebrew, *shin* is pronounced either as "shin" or "sinn." When we consider the English word *sin,* this suggests that the patriarchal tradition has distorted the loftier aspects of *shin.* But, a deeper meaning is revealed when we consider that there was also a moon god known as Sinn who was much earlier than Moses. The name *Sinai* or *Mount Sinai* was derived from the adventures of this moon god and was eventually adapted into the Moses story. Mount Sinai originally referred to the "Mountain of the Moon" and the moon was considered the law giver. According to Barbara Walker's book, Jesus himself was known as "the healing moon man." I have also seen very specific and studious etymologies which state that the Prophet of Islam's real or hidden name was Sinn and that he represented the moon. This is why the crescent moon appears as their symbol. Islam is based upon rich traditions of the ancient world. If it were not, the people would never have accepted it as readily as they did.

The moon has a very special place in the beliefs and customs of the ancient Mideast. Long before the legend of Noah, there was a story of Ishtar who saved the world from a flood. Instead of the word *ark*, that story used a word that was closer to the Hindu word *argha* (notably quite similar to Agartha) which meant crescent or the arc of a circle. In that story, the "ark" was a "moon boat," i.e. a boat shaped like a crescent moon.

Depending upon the specific culture, the role of the moon was either feminine or masculine. In Chaldea, the deity of the moon was a goddess name Ur. Babylon and Chaldea were both centers of moon worship, but Babylon recognized the lunar deity as male. Known as Sinn, he was the most powerful deity in Babylon. Ishtar was the daughter of Sinn and eventually supplanted Sinn which made the moon goddess feminine once again. In honor of this ancient verbiage, the ancient Sumerians called their land Shinar.

The moon goddess was (and still is in some circles) considered to be the mother of all living things. The shine of the moon was considered most holy in its three shining aspects: waxing, full, and waning. The word *shine* and *shin* are intimately related in their etymologies. These three shining aspects are also meant to represent the concept of the Triple Goddess in her three primary stages of manifestation: the virgin (Car or Kor), the mother (Demeter), and the destroyer crone (Peresophene). You can find other goddesses to substitute for these roles besides the ones I mentioned. Sometimes the Triple Goddess is represented by three apples. The story of Paris giving an apple to the winner of a beauty contest (between Venus, Athena, and Hera) was actually a modified version of a story which originally included three apples where all three were respected. The story of the Holy Trinity is also an altered spin on this ancient principle.

As you study the history and implications of all of this, you will readily discover that virtually all of the names of various prophets and concepts were modifications of earlier matriarchal philosophies and concepts. The much maligned pentagram was always considered the first and most holy sign of the Seventh Seal. God has had many secret names, but the pentacle was always the chief amongst them and was sometimes referred to as Solomon's Seal. The pentacle itself is composed of five feminine V's. When they are connected, these five V's make up a pentagram with a

447

pentagon in the middle. It was this knowledge that was denigrated by Christianity which can be readily seen in the idea of the apple. The apple, when sliced in half, reveals a five-pointed star or pentagram. Philosophers, including Pythagoras, recognized this as being symbolic as the formula given in this book. As the name *YHVH* was also meant to be identified with Eve, the story of the apple in the Garden of Eden speaks for itself.

There is even greater symbology at work when we consider that the core of the apple is literally named after the goddess Cor or Kor who is also known as Car. She was a pervasive goddess and her name showed up in locations from Karnak to Carthage. The custodial legacy of Car was kept by the Koresh Clan of Sabia who wrote the original Koran which meant "Writings of Kor" or "Law of Kor." It is a very well agreed upon historical fact that Muhammad was a member of the Koresh Clan and that his legitimacy derived from this source. Car also symbolized the heart, and this is why the Greeks use the word *cardiac* to refer to the heart.

The apple, besides containing the pentagram, is shaped upon the geometric pattern of a heart. When you throw out the apple, you have not only trashed knowledge, you have thrown out anything that could be termed compassion. The universe we live in is already known for its shortcomings when it comes to the heart and compassion. When we arrive at and recognize *shin*, we are not only at the gateway of a new aeon, we are at the fulcrum of change, and this includes the long missing element of compassion.

Earlier in this text, I referred to the element of compassion being missing from the Enochian angels. Their language was supposed to be designed to bring about the much misunderstood Apocalypse which really signifies the unveiling of the Goddess. While the Goddess has many different aspects, the factor of compassion is really at the heart of the matter. As illustrated above, it is the missing element. If the physical universe is a trance of sorrows, then surely compassion would be the antidote.

According to my knowledge of all of the various characters in history, whether legendary or not, no one has even come close to rivaling Quon Yin, the Oriental mother of a thousand Buddhas who has been called the Compassionate One. By all of the legendary accounts, her profile is far more compassionate than any of the characters in the New Testament or Old Testament. It is not even a contest. In fact, she has vowed to remain on Earth until the suffering of every last soul can be discharged. The idea here is that while messiahs come and go, Quon Yin never left. Of course, sitting on your ass and waiting for Quon Yin to arrive is not going to serve anyone. The real challenge in this equation is to find the Quon Yin in you. It is really no different than finding the spark within your own soul: the *shin*.

The name of Quon Yin reveals yet another aspect of the quintessence within the human condition. Although standard etymologies are very confused on this point and do not even hint at it, the words *quon, queen, and quint* are all intrinsically related to each other and the numeral five. Although the names *Quentin* and *Quinn* are just two names deriving from the sacred principle of the numeral five, Quon Yin would certainly be the earliest manifestation of any of these names or words. The idea of a "queen," as suggested in the name Quon Yin, would serve as the hidden fifth principle which espouses the matriarchal tradition.

If the above can be considered enlightening, there is also a darker side of the fifth element which is called the Golem. Although historians ascribe the story of the Golem to a Rabbi from Bohemia, the concept is much older then even the Hebrew tradition. The popular concept of the Golem is that he is made by man but is not a man. It is an artificial man. The Golem was created through the magical manipulation of the energies represented by the letters *Yod, He, Shin, Vau, He* but was never considered to be Pentagrammatic Man or even a representation thereof. Golem is a degrade of man by its very definition. The whole idea is that it is an artificial automaton or robot that was created to make man's life easier. If you look on DARPA's website, you will also find a Golem Project that is dedicated towards the philosophy and technology of artificial intelligence. Wherever there is a sacred principle, you can always find a complementary degrade to go along with it.

Pentagrammaton, *shin*, and *Yod He Shin Vau He* have been around for a very long time, but they have remained obscured except to those who have demonstrated a determined effort to look beyond the chaotic and predetermined thinking patterns that affect so much of humanity. While I could say a lot more and go far deeper into these matters, it is now time for you to write your own book. The meta-parrot is already flying across the sky of the metaplane and is discharging his ashes into various chimneys as if he were Santa Claus. The world is going to change, and you are going to change with it because you <u>are</u> the change.

Perhaps the only other point I should say about these matters is that the three points on the fool's cap in the Tarot are meant to signify the three flames on the letter *shin*. The Fool represents the path of suffering that souls take when they embark upon the game known as the physical universe. One came into this world via the principle of the fool, and that pathway sits at the top of the Tree of Life. Only by treading this path or viewing it can you reconcile your exit from this path of suffering. There is also at least one other esoteric clue coded within the experience of the Fool and the letter *shin*. If you turn the letter *shin* around ninety degrees so that you are looking at it from the side, it will reveal a fourth flame which represents the fourth-dimension. In other words, it expresses your exit or "omega" from the third dimension.

There are plenty of other synchronicities I have encountered besides those included in this book, but one can only move one step at a time. My only advice for you at this point is to read this book once again. It was written to be read twice.

The beginning is the end.

The end is the beginning.

RALPH PARSONS CORPORATION

The Ralph Parsons Corporation loomed large in conspiracy circles when President Clinton's Secretary of Commerce, Ron Brown, died in a mysterious plane crash over Yugoslavia. None of the press accounts of that airplane's demise made any sense. At that time, Ron Brown was then at the center of an investigation for all sorts of improprieties that engulfed the Clinton White House. Most of it concerned what was called the "Oklahoma Pipeline," a successful attempt by members of the Clinton White House to monopolize the gas industry in Oklahoma.

The trouble was caused by the only remaining independent gas company in Oklahoma after a cartel, sponsored by Clinton's Chinese friends, squeezed all the other companies in the state out of business. The Chinese hired Ron Brown's son to head up the organization which was monopolizing the gas industry, but neither the Chinese nor Mr. Brown had any experience whatsoever in this field. Despite all of his evasive maneuvers, the president of the last independent gas company in Oklahoma realized that he had no choice but to sell to the Clinton backed cartel. When he finally indicated he would negotiate to sell his company, he was utterly shocked when he was told to fax the White House in order to finalize the transaction! It was Clinton's Chief of Staff who did the deal and was apparently the most visible figurehead that controlled the cartel. I saw all of this on a PBS documentary which only aired a few times.

Upon his return from Yugoslavia, Ron Brown was scheduled to be indicted in connection with a one million dollar bribe over the Oklahoma Pipeline. According to a radio report, Brown was quoted before leaving on his trip as saying, "If I go down, I'm taking Clinton with me." By making himself a suitable target for elimination, he suffered a mysterious plane crash soon thereafter. The national news reported that the plane Brown died in was owned by the Ralph Parsons Corporation of Pasadena who lost several key executives as well. Conveniently, the plane had no black box. Brown's assassination aboard a Parsons airliner is only one example that demonstrates a cozy relationship between Parsons and the Government. After all, they are one of our nation's largest contractors.

After I my adventures in Pasadena, my next strange experience with the Ralph Parsons Corporation came on August 12th of 1996, the day I met Stewart Swerdlow. I picked up Stewart at his house, and we were driving out to Montauk for the day. Preston Nichols and I were to give a lecture at the Earth's Emporium at Amagansett that evening, and we were going to introduce Stewart to the crowd. The earlier part of the day was to be spent investigating Camp Hero and the local area of Montauk. Stewart and I stopped out at the Earth's Emporium to say hello to the proprietress, and she told us there was a psychic lady who wanted to accompany us on our trip to Montauk if it was all right. We waited for ten minutes until a blue-eyed and blonde-haired lady by the name of Sue arrived. After we all got in my car, she mentioned that her family had been out in this area since the 1600's. When I asked her what her last name was, she said it was Parsons! I then proceeded to tell her about my various synchronicities with the name of Parsons which you are already familiar with by reading this book. It took a while to complete the story. When we arrived at Council Rock and I told her about the Parsons Corporation's connection with certain nefarious aspects in our government, the lady looked a bit shocked and said, "I can't believe what you are saying about my Uncle Ralph!"

Sue was the niece of Ralph Parsons. She explained that her uncle was originally from the Springs, a part of the Town of East Hampton (the same town where Montauk is located). Ralph studied engineering, moved to Los Angeles and made it quite big. Sue said that in the 1970's, after his death, the Parsons Corporation became private whereupon she and her relatives were forced to sell their stock in the company.

Although I have not seen Sue since that day, I was in for a further surprise in the year 2001 when I was alerted at the last minute that there was going to be a public hearing with regard to the detoxification of Camp Hero in order to make it fully accessible to the public as a state park. Although it was a public hearing, the *East Hampton Independent* incorrectly announced on January 30th that it would be held at the Montauk Fire House. Someone deliberately reported the wrong location. It was held on February 6th at Montauk Downs State Park. Many people felt misdirected and only about twenty people showed up on a storm free winter evening. Although I found out about the hearing at the last minute, I was able to attend with a couple of friends.

No one except my friends and another lady who came in knew that I was Peter Moon, and I kept silent about that. The meeting was orchestrated by the Army Corps of Engineers who explained that they were hiring the Ralph Parsons Corporation of Pasadena, California to conduct an Engineering Evaluation/Cost Analysis investigation of Camp Hero for the purposes of characterizing ordnance and explosives contamination, analyzing risk management alternatives, and recommending feasible risk reduction alternatives. When I saw that the Ralph Parsons Corporation had been assigned to Camp Hero, I could not believe my eyes. Was this a cosmic joke, or what?

Roland Belew was then introduced as the Army Corps' "technical or engineering supervisor" for the project. He explained that the Army routinely cleans up former bases from toxic hazards and said that Camp Hero was due for a clean up. It was stressed that this was the third phase of an ongoing cleanup of Camp Hero. The first two phases of the clean up involved demolishing unsafe buildings and clearing out oil storage tanks. This also included asbestos removal.

Two employees of the Parsons Corporation, Don Silkebakken and Michael Short, were introduced and gave a more detailed description of how the operation would proceed. Handing out literature and maps of Camp Hero, they explained that this phase, to last one year, primarily concerned three areas of Camp Hero totalling less than 53 acres (out of 469 overall) that involved gun firing. The fourth phase of the project was to include a more extensive environmental survey of Camp Hero for purposes of a final cleanup. Before entertaining a question and answer session, both Parsons and the Army expressed a genuine interest in

453

any and all reports of toxic hazards or environmental menaces. It was made quite clear that this was an opportunity for the public to contribute as much information as possible in order to achieve a clean up of Camp Hero.

A question was asked from the audience concerning munitions and/or explosives being left in the bunkers. Although the bunkers have long since been sealed, there was no mention of the previous cleanup phases including a removal of ammunition or powder. It was further stated that this information came from two police officers and that one of them had claimed all information on Camp Hero had been removed from the public library (according to what a librarian told him). Roland Belew ridiculed the idea that the Army could leave munitions behind or do anything irregular when it comes to cleaning up a base. His response was a complete joke to anyone who has penetrated the deep bunkers at hero. It is common knowledge to those who have explored. As for the comment about the information on Camp Hero being removed from the library, Mr. Belew also stated that they had read information in the library earlier that day and that all information on Camp Hero was now declassified and could be accessed at the Camp Hero Web Site: www.projecthost.com. He expressed a willingness to speak to the officers concerned or anyone else who had similar information.

The veracity of the above responses came into question when one woman brought up that fact even if explosive powder had been removed (and we knew it had not been), there would still be a residue of toxic deposits in the bunkers which leeches into the cement and the ground below. In actual fact, the clean up crew's original "solution" was to cement up the bunkers so that no one could get in. At this point, the panel felt they had no choice but to reveal that they were having a hard time accessing all of the blueprints for the bunker underground. It turned out that Mr. Belew was indulging in a bald-faced lie, in the name of "good public relations" when he emphatically stated that all information about Camp Hero had been declassified. If the Army and/or Parsons personnel are not able to access all information, it is obvious that ALL information has not been declassified.

In a separate issue, one man suggested he had heard two separate reports of atomic waste at Camp Hero and even relayed a reliably witnessed tale of a dump truck without proper license plates racing out of Camp Hero with a full load and speeding in an attempt to lose a carload of pursuers. Afterwards, a Parsons employee indicated that their equipment used on this phase was not necessarily designed to pick up atomic waste. In other words, they would not be utilizing Geiger counters.

No strange tales about the Montauk Project or UFOs were brought up by anyone, but one of the old fisherman wanted to know about holes that he saw open at the side of the cliffs well west of the lighthouse. Although the panel said they had patrolled the general area, they saw no evidence of any such holes or caves, but these reports have been heard of before. Up to now, no pictures of these have been provided, but they could prove interesting. Personally, I have scoured the beach from the Montauk Lighthouse all the way to the end of Old Montauk Highway, two times, and I have never seen any indication of a hole despite various reports on them. If they do exist, it is a very good camouflage job.

The panel did not seem steeped in information about Camp Hero, but they expressed what appeared to be a sincere willingness on their part to investigate any prospects of environmental hazards. In retrospect, one has to wonder what their intentions were about in the first place. Since that time, the study and "clean up" has been completed. The buildings of old Camp Hero have now been incorporated into a state park with picnic tables even being provided. No longer will you be chased away by rabid men in mysterious blazers (models of blazers which were never available for purchase by the general public) who wear no uniform and display no insignia. Whatever toxic matter remains in the bunkers has been allowed to leech into the soil. It should be noted that during the Spring of 2003, Long Island endured the most rainfall in its history. Everything was very very wet. The fallout at Camp Hero was that a bubbly residue appeared all over the park.

What can we conclude from all this? Two things. If pressed, authorities will admit that someone either lied or made a mistake. In turn, they are fully prepared to lie to you once again, with a contoured message, in order to take you off the trail of impropriety. This process will be repeated as many times as possible unless the public shakes them down repeatedly and insists upon verification. The public's leverage must be stronger and more persistent than that of the authorities who are willing to compromise the public interest.

The second thing that can be concluded is that the pursuit of synchronicity reveals a strange pattern with the relationship between the Parsons family name and the stewardship of Camp Hero. It is all very mysterious as these are occult connections which are, by definition, hidden from view. Just because they are hidden from view does not mean they are not present.

Another interesting aspect of the mysterious Parsons connection to Montauk comes through the family name. I have seen one derivation of the name which states that the name Parr or Paar, from which Parsons is derived, was originally a word for pharaoh. The common etymology for the word *pharaoh* indicates that it meant "house." When you consider that the pentagon is also a symbol for a house, the relationship comes into context.

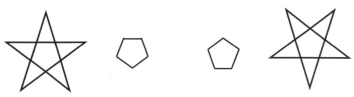

In genealogical books by and about the Parsons family, they have indicated the family's preferred mode of operation was to stay behind the scenes rather than be out front in politics. In particular, they cited the administration of George Washington. In an occult manner, it is as if this family acts as occult Pharaohs of the world. Ironically, Parsons Brinckerhoff, the company that built the original subway system of New York, has recently been contracted to supervise the building of a metropolitan underground system beneath Cairo and the Giza Plateau.

THE BIGGEST SECRET EVER TOLD

The *Montauk Project: Experiments In Time* chronicles forty years of research starting with the "Philadelphia Experiment" of 1943 when the Navy attempted to make a destroyer escort invisible to radar only to have it teleport out of this reality with accompanying psychological disorders and physical trauma to the crew. Forty years of massive research ensued culminating in bizarre experiments at Montauk Point, New York that actually tapped the powers of creation and manipulated time itself. *The Montauk Project* is a first hand account by Preston Nichols, a technician who worked on the project and has survived threats on his life and attempts to brainwash his memory of what occurred.

160 pages, illustrations, photos and diagrams.........$15.95

THE ASTONISHING SEQUEL

Montauk Revisited: Adventures in Synchronicity pursues the mysteries of time so intriguingly brought to light in *The Montauk Project and* unmasks the occult forces behind the science and technology used in the *Montauk Project*. An ornate tapestry is revealed which interweaves the mysterious associations of the Cameron clan with the genesis of American rocketry and the magick of Aleister Crowley and Jack Parsons. *Montauk Revisited* carries forward with the Montauk investigation and unleashes a host of incredible characters and new information that reaches far beyond the scope of the first book.

249 pages, illustrations, photos and diagrams.............$19.95

THE ULTIMATE PROOF

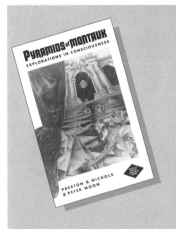

*P*yramids of Montauk: Explorations In Consciousness awakens the consciousness of humanity to its ancient history and origins through the discovery of pyramids at Montauk and their placement on sacred Native American ground leading to an unprecedented investigation of the mystery schools of Earth and their connection to Egypt, Atlantis, Mars and the star Sirius. An astonishing sequel to the *Montauk Project* and *Montauk Revisited*, this chapter of the legend propels us far beyond the adventures of the first two books and stirs the quest for future reality and the end of time as we know it.
256 pages, illustrations, photos and diagrams.............$19.95

THE BLACK SUN

*I*n this spectacular addition to the Montauk series, *The Black Sun* continues the intriguing revelations readers have come to expect revealing Montauk's Nazi connection and a vast array of new information. From the German flying saucer program to the SS Tibet mission, we are led on a path that gives us the most insightful look ever into the Third Reich and their ultimate quest: the Ark of the Covenant and the Holy Grail. Going beyond *The Spear of Destiny* and other attempts to unlock the mysterious occultism of the Nazis, Peter Moon peers into the lab of the ancient alchemists in order to explain the secret meaning behind the Egyptian and Tibetan *"Books of the Dead."*
295 pages, illustrations, photos.....................................$19.95

Journey to the stars
with Preston Nichols & Peter Moon's
ENCOUNTER IN THE PLEIADES

*T*he incredible story of a man who found himself taken to the Pleiades for a scientific education far beyond the horizons of anything taught in universities. For the first time, Preston Nichols reveals his personal history with an avalanche of amazing information including a new look at Einstein and the history of physics which gives unprecedented insight into the technology of flying saucers and their accompanying phenomena. Never before has the complex subject of UFO's been explained in such a simple language that will be appreciated by the scientist and understood by the layman. Peter Moon adds further intrigue to the mix by revealing the role of the Pleiades in ancient mythology and sheds new light on the current predicament of Mankind and offers a path of hope for the future. The truth is revealed. The keys to the Pleiades are in hand and the gateway to the stars is open. 252 pages...$19.95

The Alien Connection

Montauk: The Alien Connection reveals the most amazing story yet to surface in the area of alien abduction. This is an autobiographical and factual account from Stewart Swerdlow, a gifted mentalist who was born clairvoyant but haunted by strange time-space scenarios. After suffering alien abductions and government manipulations, Stewart found Preston Nichols and discovered his own role in time travel experiments known as the Montauk Project. After refusing to break his association with Nichols, Stewart was incarcerated

by the authorities, but the truth began to reveal itself. Struggling for his life, Stewart used his mental abilities to overcome the negative influences surrounding him and ultimately discovered the highest common denominator in the alien equation — an interdimensional language which communicates to all conscious beings. This an intriguing new twist to the Montauk saga which elevates the entire subject to a higher octave. 252 pages..$19.95

The Healer's Handbook

The miraculous and strange become common place as you journey out of this dimension with Stewart Swerdlow and discover the Language of Hyperspace, a simple system of geometric and archetypal glyphs enabling us to comprehend universal mysteries ranging from crop circles to the full panorama of occult science. *The Healer's Handbook: A Journey Into Hyperspace* penetrates the secrets of creation through the mysterious principles of DNA, the biological interface between spirit and matter which determines our actual physical characteristics and maladies. *The Healer's Handbook: A Journey Into Hyperspace* shows a vast panorama of healing techniques and supplementary information including: color healing, dream analysis, numeric values and symbols, auric fields, astral and hyperspace travel, prayer, meditation techniques, and radionics as well as exercises designed to unlock DNA sequences programmed within you since the beginning. 152 pages, 8 1/2" by 11", with diagrams and color chart.......$22.00

The Music of Time

The Music of Time blends music with time travel as Preston Nichols reveals his hidden role in the music industry where he engineered hundreds of hit records during the Golden Era of Rock 'n Roll. Beginning with his work for Time Records, Preston chronicles his innovations in sound engineering and tells how he constructed the premier music studio in the world. Having created a Mecca for talented musicians, Preston found himself surrounded by the likes of the Beatles, Beach Boys, Rolling Stones, and many popular acts. Music, mind control, and time travel make for a strange and fascinating mix with Preston's real life adventures leading to him becoming a marked man who barely escapes with his life. **The Music of Time** unravels more layers of mystery in mankind's epic quest to understand the paradox of time and the imprisonment of consciousness. 252 pages..........................$19.95

The Philadelphia Experiment Murder

By Alexandra Bruce
Edited by Peter Moon

The Philadelphia Experiment Murder: Parallel Universes and the Physics of Insanity This book begins with an investigation of the tragic murder of conspiracy lecturer Phil Schneider and exposes a massive cover-up by authorities that reveals a trail of information which leads back to the Philadelphia Experiment of 1943. Before his assassination, Schneider lectured across the country and released documents connecting his father to the *U.S.S. Eldridge.* Additionally, his father claimed to be a Nazi U-boat captain who was recruited as a medical officer and served as a Senior Medical Officer to the crew of the *Eldridge.* A host of new characters are revealed, including Preston Nichols' boss from the Montauk Project. Also includes an examination of parallel universes and the nature of insanity itself. *256 pages* $19.95

The Brookhaven Connection

By Wade Gordon
Edited by Peter Moon

The Brookhaven Connection Since the advent of the atomic era, Long Island's Brookhaven National Laboratory has served as the premier and most top secret research lab in the world. Shrouded in mystery since its inception, no one has been able to crack the code of secrecy surrounding it. Wade Gordon, who grew up in and around the lab and amidst its top players, now tells his personal story of how he was groomed from a very young age to share the legacy of what happened there. Beginning with Brookhaven's formative years when the Philadelphia Experiment was researched, links are revealed which tie Brookhaven directly to the Roswell Crash, the National Security Act, the MJ-12 documents (which are included in this book) and the Montauk Project. This includes a description of a time chamber which was utilized to monitor the JFK assassination in order to secure funding for the continued existence of the researchers. *250 pages*...................................*$19.95*

Sky Books | ORDER FORM

We wait for ALL checks to clear before shipping. This includes Priority Mail orders.
If you want to speed delivery time, please send a U.S. Money Order or use
MasterCard or Visa. Those orders will be shipped right away.
Complete this order form and send with payment or credit card information to:
Sky Books, Box 769, Westbury, New York 11590-0104

| Name |
| Address |
| City |
| State / Country   Zip |
| Daytime Phone (In case we have a question) (   ) |

☐ This is my first order   ☐ I have ordered before   ☐ This is a new address

Method of Payment: ☐ Visa   ☐ MasterCard   ☐ Money Order   ☐ Check

\#   —   —   —

Expiration Date   Signature

Title	Qty	Price
The Montauk Pulse (1 year subscription).....................$15.00		
The Montauk Pulse back issues (List at bottom of page.) $3.75 each		
List: (Use other paper if needed)		
Subtotal		
For delivery in NY add 8.5% tax		
Shipping: see chart on the next page		
U.S. only: Priority Mail		
Total		

Thank you for your order. We appreciate your business.

SHIPPING INFORMATION

United States Shipping

Under $30.00 ....add $4.00
$30.01 — 60.00 ...add $5.00
$60.00 — $100.00 add $8.00
$100.01 and over .add $10.00

Allow 30 days for delivery. For U.S. only: Priority Mail—add the following to the regular shipping charge: $4.00 for first item, $1.50 for each additional item.

Outside U.S. Shipping

Under $30.00 ....add $10.00
$30.01 — $50.00 ..add $15.00
$50.01—$ 75.00 ..add $20.00
$75.01—$100.00 .add $25.00
100.01 and over ...add $35.00

These rates are for SURFACE SHIPPING ONLY. Do not add extra funds for air mail. Due to the vastly different costs for each country, we will not ship by air. Only Visa, Mastercard or checks drawn on a U.S. bank in U.S. funds will be accepted. (Eurochecks or Postal Money Orders cannot be accepted.)

For a complimentary listing of
special interdimensional books and videos —
send a $1.06 stamp or one dollar to:
Sky Books, Box 769, Westbury, NY 11590-0104